Enterprise JavaBeans 2.1

STEFAN DENNINGER and INGO PETERS with ROB CASTANEDA
translated by David Kramer

Enterprise JavaBeans 2.1
Copyright ©2003 by Stefan Denninger and Ingo Peters with Rob Castaneda

ISBN (pbk): 1-59059- 088-0

Printed and bound in the United States of America 12345678910

Translator, Editor, Compositor: David Kramer

Technical Reviewer: Mary Schladenhauffen

Editorial Directors: Dan Appleman, Gary Cornell, Simon Hayes, Martin Streicher, Karen Watterson, John Zukowski

Managing and Production Editor: Grace Wong

Proofreader: Lori Bring

Cover Designer: Kurt Krames

Manufacturing Manager: Tom Debolski

Distributed to the book trade in the United States by Springer-Verlag New York, Inc.,175 Fifth Avenue, New York, NY, 10010 and outside the United States by Springer-Verlag GmbH & Co. KG, Tiergartenstr. 17, 69112 Heidelberg, Germany

In the United States, phone 1-800-SPRINGER, email orders@springer-ny.com, or visit http://www.springer-ny.com

Outside the United States, fax +49 6221 345229 email orders@springer.de, or visit http://www.springer.de,

For information on translations, please contact Apress directly at 2560 Ninth Street, Suite 219, Berkeley, CA 94710. Phone 510-549-5930, fax: 510-549-5939, email info@apress.com, or visit http://www.apress.com.

The information in this book is distributed on an "as is" basis, without warranty. Although every precaution has been taken in the preparation of this work, neither the author nor Apress shall have any liability to any person or entity with respect to any loss or damage caused or alleged to be caused directly or indirectly by the information contained in this work.

The source code for this book is available to readers at http://www.apress.com in the Downloads section.

Contents at a Glance

Contents

About the Authors

Stefan Denninger

Stefan Denninger completed his university education in February 1996 with
a degree in business management. He has worked as a software engineer
for Kromberg & Schubert in Abensberg, Germany, IXOS Software in Munich,
Germany, and eCircle Solutions in Munich. He currently works for ConSol GmbH
in Munich as a senior software consultant.

Ingo Peters

Ingo Peters currently works with the HypoVereinsbank, a group of European
banks managing Internet portals and applications. As a project manager, he
has guided many different applications and Internet portals using Enterprise
JavaBeans to success. He started programming with Enterprise JavaBeans in 1998.

Rob Castaneda

Rob Castaneda is Principal Architect at CustomWare Asia Pacific, where
he provides architecture consulting and training in EJB/J2EE/XML-based
applications and integration servers to clients throughout Asia and America.
Rob's multinational background, combined with his strong real-world business
experience, enables him to see through the specifications to create realistic
solutions to major business problems. He has also contributed to and technically
edited various leading EJB and J2EE books.

Acknowledgments

Working on this book has been a great pleasure for all of the authors. Long discussions about local interfaces and dependent objects have resulted in several chapters being rewritten and then rewritten again, and changes in the specification have led to many interesting discussions and insights.

Without the active support of colleagues and friends, work on this book would not have been nearly so interesting, nor so productive. Stefan Denninger and Ingo Peters would like particularly to thank Stefan Schulze and Alexander Greisle, whose constructive and highly competent feedback have significantly improved the quality of this book. They would also like to thank the readers of the first German edition, whose support and feedback made the second edition possible. Finally, they wish to thank their editor, Martin Asbach, of Addison-Wesley, for his great care and friendly collaboration in bringing this book into the world, to the staff of Apress for making the English translation possible, and for their amiable and uncomplicated collaboration.

Rob Castaneda would like to thank John Zukowski, Grace Wong, and the team at Apress, as well as colleagues at CustomWare Asia Pacific, including Ian Daniel, Nathan Lee, and Scott Babbage, as well as his wife, Aimee Castaneda. Without the support of the these individuals, this work would not have been achievable.

Preface

ENTERPRISE JAVABEANS (EJB) IS THE standard component architecture for the creation of distributed business applications in the programming language Java. EJB offers all mechanisms necessary for the creation of applications for enterprise-wide deployment and for the control of critical business processes. Application developers can profit from distribution of processes, transaction security, pooling of network connections, synchronous and asynchronous notification, multithreading, object persistence, and platform independence. With EJB, programming remains relatively simple.

In March 1998 the first specification of Enterprise JavaBeans was published by Sun Microsystems. In relatively short order there followed in December 1999 the consolidated version 1.1. In the meantime, the component architecture has accounted for considerable change in the market for application servers, so that today, the large majority of application servers support EJB. EJB has also established itself in the growing market for finished application components. Today, there exists a large market for everything from specialized solutions to specific problems to complete application frameworks.

In August 2001 version 2.0 was released. The new version offers considerable extensions and improvements, which are considered in this book, now in its second edition. The first edition has been greatly revised in order to take account of the following developments:

- The new message-driven beans (EJB 2.0) offer completely new ways to achieve asynchronous communication and parallel processing of business logic. This is made possible by the integration of the Java Message Service (JMS) into tht EJB architecture.

- Local interfaces (EJB 2.0) enable optimization of process-internal communication among Enterprise Beans and between local clients and Enterprise Beans.

- The persistence manager has been introduced (EJB 2.0). With relationships between entity beans it is now possible to model complex data structures. The associated query language EJB QL makes it possible to work efficiently with these structures.

- A new chapter (Chapter 8) deals with security issues of EJB.

- The chapter on practical applications (Chapter 9) has been greatly expanded.

- All the examples have been reworked, with emphasis on ease of execution.

Today, one may safely state that Enterprise JavaBeans has brought the success of the programming language Java to the server, particularly in the areas of portals and integration of older applications, where EJB has become a widely used solution strategy. However, information technology is on the verge of yet new changes. The trend today is in the direction of freely combinable application components from a variety of producers that are connected via web services. EJB 2.0 offers answers to these growing requirements. Particularly the new developments in the areas of marketplaces, private stock exchanges, e-procurement, and electronic funds transfer can profit from using EJB as the base architecture.

This book is directed to the reader who wishes to learn more about Enterprise JavaBeans. It discusses the fundamental concepts underlying the EJB architecture. Building on this foundation, it explains the technical details and concrete programming of Enterprise Beans. Many examples are used to clarify and expand on the concepts introduced. The source code for all the examples in this book is available at http://www.apress.com in the "Downloads" section. A knowledge of the Java programming language and a basic understanding of distributed programming are prerequisites for reading this book.

#### CHAPTER 1

Introduction

A Hypothetical Scenario

Imagine that you are an application programmer working for a midsize firm in the automobile industry that maintains numerous offices in a number of European countries. Your firm is pursuing the strategy of developing its own business applications in house. At first glance such a strategy may seem rather odd. But extreme competition and increasing cost pressures now demand a high level of flexibility and stability from the development team, and your division leader has guaranteed that the software systems developed will have these characteristics, and this is the justification for management's decision to support in-house development.

Up to now each office has installed and maintained its own software system, since the development teams in each branch have been working independently of one another.

First the Bad News

One fine day, you are summoned to your division leader's office. He informs you that big events are about to occur in the data processing division of the company. To accommodate increasing international growth and to promote efficiency, all the software in the entire company is to be unified, standardized, and streamlined into a single distributed system. The development teams will remain at the individual offices, but beginning at once they are all to report to a newly appointed division leader, under whose direction they are to work together to achieve the stated goals. Existing software at the individual branch offices is to be replaced piece by piece by the newly developed replacement packages. Isolated systems in various parts of the company (such as personnel management and accounting) are to be integrated into the new system. Thus you, a specialist in accounting and supply systems, are affected by the new developments.

The Task

Your job is to develop a prototype for this new system, which after an evaluation phase is to be further developed into a stable building block of the new system.

Your piece of the action is to be a rudimentary accounting system. Other offices are to develop compatible inventory and annual accounts modules, and they together with your accounting module are to be presented to company management. A number of users from the various divisions must be able to use the system simultaneously. Since your company is planning on introducing telecommuting, the system must also be usable from outside the company, over the Internet, for example. In order to avoid bottlenecks during critical periods (such as the end of a quarter or year) the system must be able to operate under heavy usage. Furthermore, anticipated growth in the number of employees must also be taken into account.

The Solution

A superficial reading of the above text could easily lead one to the conclusion that the task as set out should give little trouble to an application developer who is an expert in business applications. But if one reads more closely, a rather more complex picture begins to present itself (see Figure 1-1). The crux of the problem is in the new set of circumstances that confront our application specialist. These altered circumstances bring problems that will complicate the development of a prototype of a rudimentary accounting system. Let us examine the situation more closely in terms of the following observations.

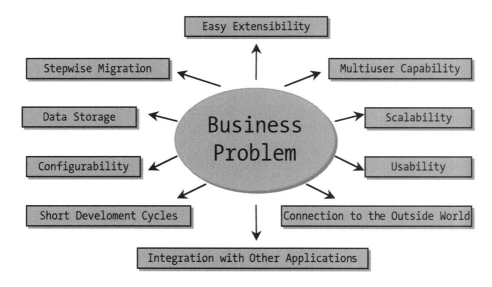

Figure 1-1. Solution of a business problem.

Multiple-User Capability

The accounting system, which until now has been conceived as an isolated solution, must now be integrated into a larger system and enable a number of users to work simultaneously. For this the system must satisfy the following requirements:

- multiprocess capability (multithreading),
- transactions,
- user control,
- security mechanisms,
- networking capability.

A further consideration is the necessity of ensuring that the requirements listed above are standardized and consistent among all modules of the system. This is a very important requirement to consider. It is often overlooked because it does not directly map to any user requirements, and it becomes a critical factor in working with remote development teams.

Scalability

To accommodate an increase in the number of employees the system must be scalable. If the previously available resources become overtaxed, then it must be possible to expand the software to include additional resources. This goal results in a distribution of the applications among several servers usually located within a cluster. The system should then (possibly after a reconfiguration) make use of the new resources and thus offer improved performance without the occurrence of bottlenecks. It is important that the reconfiguration and redeployment of an application be flexible and not require major source code modifications and recompilation. Rigid designs that require that source code modifications be made in reconfiguring and redeploying the system reduce the system's flexibility and increase the burden on the system administrator.

Availability

In general, but most importantly at critical junctures such as end of quarter or year end, the system must offer a high degree of availability. If a computer becomes unavailable, then another computer must be able to take over the requisite functions without a great deal of effort (or perhaps none at all) in reconfiguring the system. This requires that the system be capable of transferring functional units from one computer to another.

Connection with the Outside World

Since the company hopes to work with greater cooperation among its associated parts and also plans on introducing telecommuting, the system must offer an interface to the outside world (for example, through a defined port through the corporate firewall). The result is not only an increase in security requirements, but also in the requirements on the system architecture in general, since the structure of Internet applications is fundamentally different from that of traditional applications.

Integration with Other Applications and Rapid Extensibility

In the ideal case the method of integration is such that various applications that have been developed as a collection of building blocks can be assembled into a complete system. Each application should itself be constructed of building blocks and have the capacity to make itself available to other applications in a limited way by means of clearly defined interfaces. The system can be extended through the provision of additional building blocks. This means that the basic structure of the system supports a suitable degree of granularity.

Short Development Cycles

In the software development process the requirement of efficiency places one fundamental goal in the foreground: shortening the development cycle and thereby reducing development costs. The challenge for the development team is to reduce development costs, while maintaining (or even improving!) the quality and robustness of the system. This is achieved, as a rule, through increasing the granularity. Legacy applications can also be added into the system by the creation of building blocks that wrapper existing functionality. A large and unwieldy project is subdivided into many small, easily managed projects, each of which constitutes a building block. The totality of all the building blocks is the system. Each building block can be defined, built, and tested as an individual piece of functionality to ensure quality. Thus this building-block approach contributes not only to integrability and extensibility, but to the shortening of the development cycle as well. It also helps to provide for remote development, since building blocks can be designed and then developed at remote offices and integrated once completed for end-to-end testing.

Configurability

If applications that are developed in one location are to be usable at another (just think of differences in national laws, languages, notation, and on and on), then there must be a high degree of configurability, so that the applications can be adapted without the necessity of being recompiled. As a further alternative one might imagine (thinking again of the building-block approach) replacing building blocks that cannot be implemented at a particular location by location-optimized building blocks.

Stepwise Migration and Data Storage

Rome, as has often been observed, was not built in a day (and it is still under construction!), and neither can a system redesign and reconfiguration take place overnight. Therefore, the step-by-step changeover to a new system is an important topic. It should be simple to create interfaces to existing systems, a requirement that results in something even more important: In the ideal case it should make no difference to a particular application where data is stored. It can be located in a database belonging to the new system, in a database belonging to an old system, or indeed in an external database that does not belong to the system at all.

Summary

The number of considerations that are required in order to produce the solution to our problem can easily exceed the capabilities of a normally endowed application developer. However, today a number of software companies offer solutions to developers that provide ways of overcoming the problems inherent in a project such as the one that we have described, and a great deal of the thought and design required to handle the issues listed above have been collected into a number of industry standard platforms. This book discusses one of these platforms in great detail: Enterprise JavaBeans (or EJB for short). So wake up and smell the coffee, and let's get started.

So Now What?

In Chapter 2 we discuss the fundamentals of Enterprise JavaBeans and place them in the context of the technologies for software development. In Chapter 3 we devote our attention to the fundamental architecture of Enterprise JavaBeans as well as the roles that the development team can play during the development, deployment, and management stages of the system. The different varieties of components (known as beans), namely, *entity, session,* and *message-driven* beans, are discussed in Chapters 4, 5, and 6. Building on this we go on in Chapter 7 to discuss the topic of *transactions,* while Chapter 8 is devoted to *security.* In each of these chapters extensive examples are introduced to clarify the discussion. In Chapter 9 we discuss several aspects of the practical application of the principles discussed (again with extensive examples). Finally, in Chapter 10, we discuss web services and the integration of Enterprise JavaBeans to other platforms that exist within common enterprises.

After you have read this book you should have a firm grasp of the capabilities of the Enterprise JavaBeans platform. Furthermore, you should be in a position to translate the knowledge you have gained from theory into practice.

CHAPTER 2

Fundamentals

Enterprise JavaBeans is an architecture (Framework) for component-oriented distributed applications. *Enterprise Beans* are components of distributed, transaction-oriented business applications.

—Sun Microsystems, 2001

Enterprise

The programming language Java is known primarily for two features: its platform independence and its ability to beautify web pages by means of *applets*. However, Java has many capabilities to offer above and beyond the decoration of web pages. Java is a full-fledged object-oriented programming language that is increasingly being used for the development of enterprise-critical applications. As Figure 2-1 shows, Enterprise JavaBeans is a building block in the product and interface catalog of Sun Microsystems for the development of enterprise applications.

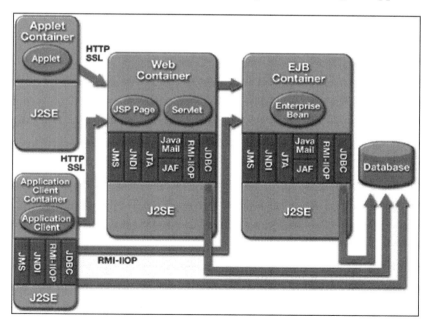

Figure 2-1. The place of Enterprise JavaBeans in Sun's enterprise concept [J2EE-APM, 2000.]

In the figure, J2EE stands for *Java 2 Platform, Enterprise Edition,* JSP for *JavaServer Pages,* and EJB for *Enterprise JavaBeans.*

Enterprise JavaBeans is not a product, but merely a specification. Any individual who feels the calling may bring to market an implementation of the Enterprise JavaBeans specification.

That Enterprise JavaBeans involves a client–server architecture should be no cause for wonderment (Sun has positioned Enterprise JavaBeans in the domain of server-side applications logic. *Three-tiered architecture* is currently the one favored by most system architects (the trend is in the direction of *multitiered,* or *multilayered,* architectures).

Three-tiered systems are distinguished in that the actual program logic (in relation to enterprise applications often called "business logic") is located in the middle layer (on an application server); see Figure 2-2.

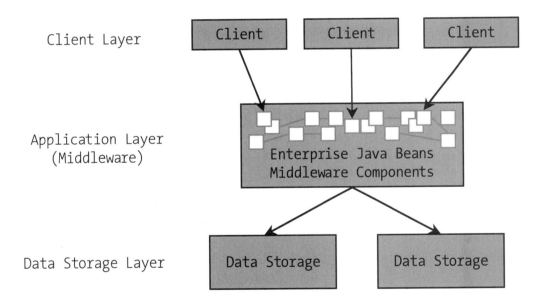

Client Layer

Application Layer
(Middleware)

Data Storage Layer

Figure 2-2. Three-tiered architecture.

The bundling of the application logic on its own server in a layer between the clients and the database offers the following advantages over traditional two-tiered systems:

- The client programs become significantly smaller (and therefore are often called "thin clients") and thus require fewer resources of the client computer.

- The database is transparent to the client developer. The middle layer (application layer) is completely abstracted from access to the data and concerns itself with data stability (which simplifies considerably the development of client programs).

- Applications are more easily scalable, since a division of tasks can already take place on the application layer (for example, in the case of server overload a client query can be passed to another server).

- A particular application logic is programmed only once and made available to all clients centrally in the middle layer, and so the system is easy to maintain and extend. If there is a change in the application logic, then only a central component is affected and not a large number of individual client applications.

If we were to attempt to classify existing system architectures in order to locate Enterprise JavaBeans, then we might end up with a picture like that shown in Figure 2-3.

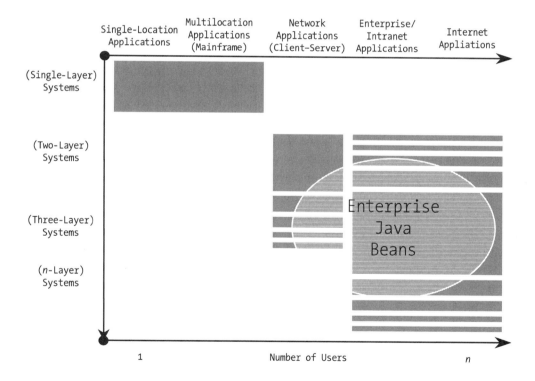

Figure 2-3. Classification of Enterprise JavaBeans in a system portfolio.

Enterprise JavaBeans is at its best in the domain of enterprise, intranet, and Internet applications, which are built primarily on a three-tiered, or even n-tiered, architecture and are developed in an object-oriented language (in this case Java).

One speaks of a multitiered architecture (also called n-tiered) if in addition to the client, application, and database layers there are additional layers for increasing the level of abstraction or to improve scalability, or else when several three-tiered systems are arranged in a cascade.

Since the word "enterprise" appears explicitly in the name, one feels compelled to ask what the Enterprise JavaBeans specification provides to assist developers in meeting the demands of business today. To answer this question we must first consider on what criteria a decision for or against a given technology should be based.

Economic Viability

Economic viability refers to the domains of development, acquisition, maintenance, and adaptation. Economic viability in development exists when the technology actively supports a shortening of the development cycle. An increase in productivity thus leads to reduced costs, which can then be passed along (this is what economic viability in acquisition means to nondevelopers). Economic viability in maintenance is the result of stability, which results in lower servicing requirements. Economic viability as it relates to further development and adapation is offered by a technology that enables a system to be extended or adapted without great expense and risk.

Security

The question of security must be examined with extreme care. In relationship to an investment, such security exists if the technology promises a certain minimum life span and is assured of long-term support. Security also refers to security against breakdown, that is, to availability. Its purpose is to avoid costs due to failure in parts of the system or to system breakdowns. Security means as well the capability of a technology to protect sensitve data from prying eyes and to protect the system from unwelcome intruders.

Requirements

The deployment of a particular technology is justified only at the point where there is a requirement for the capabilities that it offers. An enterprise will not institute a technology or product merely on account of its current popularity without experiencing a genuine need.

In the following chapters this book will lay out in detail how the Enterprise JavaBeans specification attempts to deal with the requirements of modern enterprises for a stable system.

Java

Enterprise JavaBeans is designed to help the programming language Java make the jump from the client platform to the server platform. To be sure, it is possible to develop a server without Enterprise JavaBeans. However, Java offers in its standard libraries extensive support for network communication as well as support for threads. With Enterprise JavaBeans it is possible even for "ordinary" programmers, that is, those who are not server specialists, to expand the functionality of an application server or to develop server-side logic.

How can Java contribute to making Enterprise JavaBeans into a successful concept for the development of enterprise-critical applications?

Object Orientation

Java is an object-oriented programming language, and thus it offers the developer the advantages of object-oriented techniques. Java is also well equipped for the next step, namely, in the direction of component-oriented software development, for which object-oriented technologies are the best starting point (more on this in the section "Beans."

Platform Independence

Many enterprises find themselves confronted with the problem of a heterogeneous hardware and software landscape that can lead to almost insuperable difficulties. Many software systems are available only for specific platforms. Java source code is translated by the Java compiler not into machine code, but into machine-neutral byte code, which is then interpreted by a Java run-time environment. Therefore, applications that are developed in "pure" Java can run on all platforms for which a Java run-time environment is available. The run-time environment is platform-dependent and provides the Java program an implementation of abstract interfaces for system-dependent operations (for example, for access to file systems, access to network interfaces, and the display of graphical interfaces). Java applications offer an enterprise increased security and continuity through their platform independence.

Dynamics

As an interpreted language Java provides the capability of loading byte code either from the local file system or over a network into the address space of a process and from this to generate objects at run time (that is, program segments can be reloaded at run time, even over a network). Thus the stony path of rigid, inflexible systems is smoothed into dynamic run-time systems with a high degree of adaptability, and a contribution as well to greater flexibility and continuity. Java classes can be examined at run time (reflection). Methods can be called dynamically, attributes recognized and modified, and so on. With increasing support for Java in database systems (Oracle, for example), groupware systems (such as Lotus Notes), web servers (via Servlet API and JavaServer Pages), and browsers there are numerous possible combinations for system development. Even the linkage with other platform-independent technologies such as XML offers interesting perspectives. Thus in version 1.1 of the EJB specification XML replaces serialized classes as deployment descriptors (more details on deployment descriptors in Chapter 3).

Stability

The Java programming language is relatively easy to learn (compared, for example, to C++) and less subject to programming errors to the extent that certain language features (such as pointers to variables and functions) are absent, in favor of a consistent object orientation. Since it is platform-independent, to the extent to which the system in question has been developed in pure Java, no porting is necessary. Thus the possibility of porting errors does not arise. Since Java is an interpreted language, serious run-time errors (such as access to invalid object references, null pointers) do not lead to uncontrolled system crashes. The program is terminated in a controlled manner by the run-time environment. Thus critical errors can be located and fixed more rapidly.

Security

Java supports security through the features of the language. Thus direct access to memory by means of pointers is forbidden, stack overflow and exceeding array bounds are trapped and reported as an error in the form of an exception, and so on. Java also supports the *sandbox concept*, which has application primarily to applets.

On the other hand, security is supported under Java by means of program interfaces and implementations that belong to the standard range of run-time and development environments (currently version 1.3). With an implementation of a Java SecurityManager customized to individual requirements it is possible to keep track of, for example, critical operations of objects (such as reading and writing of files, opening of network connections) and prohibit them as necessary. Java offers management of private and public keys as well as program interfaces for encryption. There is also the possibility of signing Java archive files (JAR files) for preventing the manipulation of byte code by a third party. An excellent and thorough treatment of the topic of security in relationship to Java is given in [16].

Performance

The advantages that Java gains from the properties of an interpreted language must be paid for with performance limitations. Although much has been done to improve Java's performance (for example, by just-in-time compilation), execution speed remains a critical point (in complex client applications as well as in server applications). Through continual improvement in hardware and the Java run-time environment this problem has perhaps become less severe. However, until Java reaches the execution speed of a compiled language, there will remain the necessity of developmental work in the area of virtual machines.

Beans

When speaking about Sun Microsystems and components, the talk is always about beans. The currently most popular component of Java is most likely JavaBeans. Before we go into the difference between JavaBeans and Enterprise JavaBeans, we need to dive briefly into the world of componentware, without wishing to get involved in a full-blown discussion of the component paradigm. There are numerous books about components that show the variety of ways that this topic can be addressed. Here, however, we shall merely take a glance at the topic (which plays an important role with respect to Enterprise JavaBeans) in order to increase our understanding a bit.

In order to avoid misunderstandings we should mention explicitly that the intention of this book is not to give the reader instructions in how to develop good components. This book describes the component architecture of Enterprise JavaBeans, their practical application, and the requirements that components must fulfill if they are to be deployed in an EJB server.

Software Components

We would like to offer a definition of software components, cited in [6] as well as in [17], that represents a relatively neutral middle ground between the very broad and the very narrow:

> A component is a piece of software that is small enough to create and maintain in one piece and big enough to offer useful and practical functionality and to justify its separate maintenance; it is equipped with standardized interfaces that allows it to cooperate with other components.

First, we simplify the view of a component by imagining it as a sort of Lego building block. The inner workings of the building block remain hidden from view. Nonetheless, one can see that it has connectors that allow it to be attached to other building blocks. A combination of suitable building blocks results in a structure that serves a particular purpose (a house, a garage, a road). Software components are also building blocks in that one cannot necessarily see inside (see Figure 2-4). Each component offers an encapsulated partial functionality (in analogy to Lego building blocks, such as the frame for a window, a stone as part of a wall, or a slab for the foundation of a house), while hiding its implementation. Its functionality can be deduced only from the public interface, which in addition to allowing it to be used, also permits linkage to other components. As with Lego building blocks, with software components the crucial property is reusability. A component that can be used in only one application scenario is not a genuine component.

A component is distinguished from traditional objects or classes in a number of ways (see also [6]):

- Components must be able to be used in a variety of application scenarios and thereby be highly reusable. Traditional objects, on the other hand, are developed as a rule for a particular scenario. Furthermore, in fulfilling their appointed tasks traditional objects frequently make use of other objects and through this involvement make reusability more difficult.

- As a rule, objects are not big enough to deal with a complete task from beginning to end. They serve more for structuring and mapping to models.

- The development cost of a component is considerably greater than that of a traditional object, since with a component one must take into consideration both reusability in a variety of applications and the ability of the component to be integrated into a system.

- A component can be used only in a particular way that has been defined by the public interface. Objects can, by the process of derivation, be altered (almost) at will.

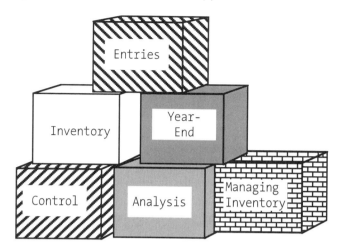

Components of a Business Application

Figure 2-4. Example of components in a commercial enterprise.

- Objects also offer the concept of the interface, which as a rule, however, is narrowly coupled to the underlying system technology and thus limits interoperability.

Undoubtedly, the close relationship between objects and components is clear. The object-oriented approach and techniques thus seem to offer the best basis for the development of components and component-oriented software.

A fundamental concept of the component paradigm is that of the *interface*. The interface of a component is a sort of contract whose conditions the components are obligated to fulfill. It is an interaction point with the components, documenting their features and capacities. A component can have several interfaces. Each interface represents a service provided by the component (for a detailed discussion of interfaces see, for example, [33]). Chapter 3 will show in detail how this aspect of components is transplanted into Enterprise JavaBeans.

An advantage of component-oriented software development is (as mentioned previously) in the reusability of code. A further advantage is the possibility, with the aid of completed components, of rapidly developing application prototypes (for an extensive treatment of this see [9]). The early availability of a prototype means that in the early stage of development one is already able to confront design choices; (pilot) customers or (pilot) users can be brought into the development process at an earlier stage, and so on. The reuse of code in the form of (mature) software components can lead to a shortening of development cycles and savings in development costs.

Component Architecture

As mentioned above, Enterprise JavaBeans is a component architecture. The domains of application and variety of forms of a component architecture can be quite diverse. Enterprise JavaBeans represents a quite particular variant: a component architecture for distributed, server-side, and transaction-oriented components. Thus Enterprise Beans are components that provide services to many clients on a single server. Without a framework that embeds the components into a sort of run-time environment and provides them necessary services, each component that is to be made available over a network would have to have its own server. This would make the development of such components much more difficult and if several components were deployed on one computer would result in an unnecessary strain on its resources. Even the reusability of a component could thereby become endangered, since servers must frequently be matched to the underlying platform. A component architecture such as Enterprise JavaBeans makes possible the deployment of components for distributed applications without the components themselves being significantly affected (see Figure 2-5).

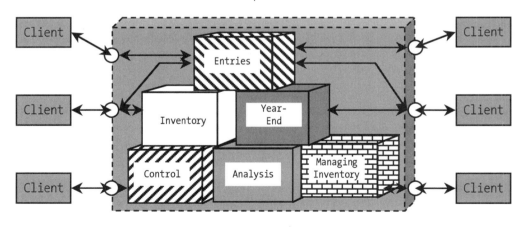

Figure 2-5. Example of component architecture.

Griffel [6] gives a list of requirements that a component architecture must fulfill:

- Independence of the environment: Components should be deployable without reference to programming language, operating system, network technology, etc.

- Locational transparency: For the user of components it should make no difference whether the component offers its services in the user's local address space or in the address space of another, remote, computer. The requisite mechanisms for the transparent use of local or remote components should be made available via the component architecture.

- Separation of interface and implementation: The specification of a component should be completely independent of its implementation.

- Self-descriptive interfaces: To achieve a loose coupling of components at run time, a component should be capable of giving information about its capabilities and entry points.

- Immediate problem-free usability (Plug & Play): A component should be usable on any platform without having to be adapted in any way (which implies a binary independence of the component code).

- Capacity for integration and composition: In combination with other components, a component should be able to contribute to the creation of new, usable components.

However, Enterprise JavaBeans is not only a component architecture. The specification defines a system-technically oriented *component model* (for the notion of a component model, see, for example, [6]). This makes possible the implementation of various types of Enterprise Beans. It defines protocols for the management of components, for cooperation and communication of the components among themselves, and for the their use by a client.

JavaBeans Versus Enterprise JavaBeans

> A JavaBean is a reusable software component that can be manipulated visually in a builder tool.
> —Sun Microsystems, 1997

JavaBeans is a component model for Java produced by Sun Microsystems. A JavaBean is essentially a Java class that follows the rules laid down in the JavaBeans specification. The most important attributes of a bean are its public interface, the possibility of its being analyzed based on its composition, its adaptability to individual requirements, and its capacity for persistence (via object serialization). The public interface consists of the properties of a bean, the methods that it allows others to use, and the events that it receives or executes. A bean can be a visible (a button, for example) or an invisible component (for instance, a network service). Listing 2-1 demonstrates a valid JavaBean:

Listing 2-1. Example of a JavaBean.

```
public class AValidBean implements AEventListener {
    private int aProperty;
    private Vector beanListeners;
    public AValidBean()
    {
        aProperty = -1;
        beanListeners = new Vector();
    }
    public void setAProperty(int value)
    {
        aProperty = value;
    }
    public int getAProperty()
    {
        return aProperty;
    }
    public void addBEventListener(BEventListener listener)
    {
        beanListeners.addElement(listener);
    }
    public void removeBEventListener(BEventListener listener)
    {
        beanListener.remove(listener);
    }
    private void fireBEvent() {
        BEventListener l;
        for(int i = 0; I < beanListener.size(); i++) {
            l = (BEventListener)beanListener.elementAt(i);
            l.notify(new BEvent(this));
        }
    }
}
```

```
    //Implementation of AEventListener Interface
    public void notify(AEvent event)
    {
        //processing the event
    }
}
```

This bean class is not derived from any class. It does not implement any standard interface, and is nevertheless a valid JavaBean (only visible JavaBeans must be derived from `java.awt.Component`). It simply follows the naming conventions established in the specification. It has the property aProperty, which can be manipulated and read by the methods setAProperty and getAProperty. Since it implements the interface AEventListener, it can react to the event AEvent. It triggers the event BEvent, for which other beans can register via addBEventListener and unregister via removeBEventListener. By exchanging events beans can pair with one another dynamically, since they can register and unregister for particular events at run time. This coupling over events is also a loose coupling, since the bean is abstracted from the actual type by means of the corresponding Listener interfaces.

With the naming convention ⟨type⟩ get⟨property⟩, void⟨property⟩(⟨type⟩), implements ⟨EventType⟩Listener, void add ⟨EventType⟩Listener(), and void remove⟨eventTypeListener⟩(), etc., a builder tool can, for example, analyze (introspection) the bean with the help of the Java Reflection API with respect to its properties and the possibility of binding it to events. The tool can place the user in a position to manipulate the bean visually. Thus the JavaBeans specification concentrates essentially on the description of the program interface for:

- recognizing and using properties of JavaBeans,

- adaptation of JavaBeans to particular circumstances,

- registering for events and sending then between individual JavaBeans,

- the persistence of JavaBeans components.

The Enterprise JavaBean specification, on the other hand, focuses on distributed computing and business transactions. JavaBean objects do not have a distributed character. The EJB specification describes a service framework for server-side components. Enterprise Beans are never visible server components. One may search in vain through the EJB specification for a discussion of properties and events of an Enterprise Bean, since it describes primarily the programming interface and the properties of the framework.

Of course, servers can be developed based on traditional JavaBeans. Then, however, the framework itself, which offers the components the relevant server utilities and sees to the distribution, would have to be developed. One could, however, imagine a combination of invisible JavaBeans and Enterprise Beans in which an Enterprise Bean provides a certain interface in the EJB server and delegates calls to JavaBeans (for example, by the triggering of JavaBean events).

One should not attempt to seek out too many similarities between the two models, since in spite of a superficial similarity in name, the two models are quite different in emphasis. However, JavaBeans and Enterprise Beans are not to be seen as opposing concepts, but rather as complementary.

The different viewpoints suggested by the words *Enterprise, Java,* and *Beans* will be made more concrete in the remaining chapters of this book. In Chapter 3, "Architecture of Enterprise JavaBeans," we shall investigate the extent to which the EJB specification corresponds to the viewpoint discussed in this chapter.

CHAPTER 3

The Architecture of
Enterprise JavaBeans

IN CHAPTER 2 WE INDICATED that Enterprise JavaBeans (EJB) is a component of the Java-2 platform, Enterprise Edition (for details see [26]). In this model EJB takes over the part of the server-side application logic that is available in the form of components: the Enterprise Beans. This chapter introduces the architecture of Enterprise JavaBeans. Figure 3-1 shows *Enterprise Beans* (in their incarnations as *entity*, *message-driven*, and *session* beans) as the central elements.

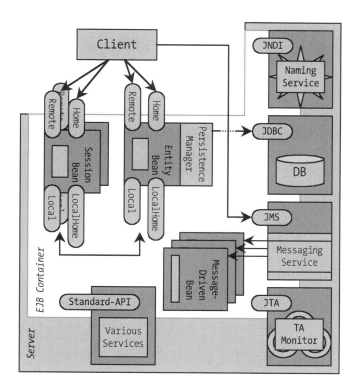

Figure 3-1. Overview of the EJB architecture.

They contain the application logic used by the *client* programs. Enterprise Beans reside in an *EJB container*, which makes a run-time environment available to them (so that, for example, they can be addressed by client programs via the *home* and *remote* interfaces and have the possibility of communication among one another via the *local home* and *local* interfaces, so that life-cycle management can be provided). The EJB container is linked to *services* via the standard programming interface, services that are available to the bean (for example, access to databases via JDBC, access to a transaction service via JTA, and access to a message service via JMS). The EJB container is installed (possibly in addition to other containers) in an *application server*.

We shall now go into the details of the individual components of the architecture and their interrelationships.

The Server

The server is the fundamental component of the EJB architecture. Here we are deliberately not speaking of an *EJB server*. Actually, it should be called a *J2EE server*. Sun Microsystems' strategy in relationship to enterprise applications in the framework of the J2EE platform involves Enterprise JavaBeans to a considerably greater extent in the full portfolio of Java-based programming interfaces and products than was the case in version 1.0 of the Enterprise JavaBeans specification.

The specification of Enterprise JavaBeans in version 2.1 does not define any sort of requirement on the server (just as in versions 1.0 and 1.1). The reason for this is presumably their stronger integration into the Java 2 platform, Enterprise Edition (see Figure 3-2).

A J2EE-conforming server is a run-time environment for various containers (of which one or more can be EJB containers). Each container, in turn, makes a run-time environment available for a particular type of component. Creators of Java application servers tend more and more to support the J2EE platform. There is scarcely a producer who offers a pure EJB server. Many suppliers of databases, transaction monitors, or CORBA ORBs have meanwhile begun to support Enterprise JavaBeans.

In the environment of the J2EE platform (and thus indirectly in the EJB architecture) the server component has the responsibility of providing basic functionality. This, includes, for example:

- Thread and process management (so that several containers can offer their services to the server in parallel);

- Support of clustering and load sharing (that is, the ability to run several servers cooperatively and to distribute client requests according to the load on each server to obtain the best-possible response times);

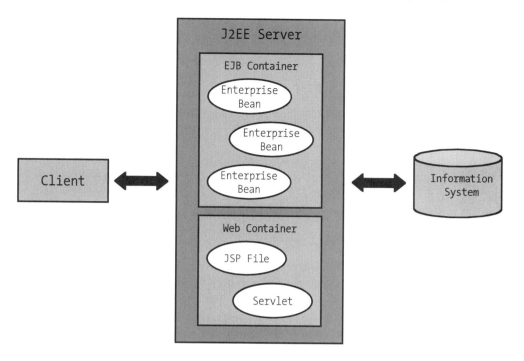

Figure 3-2. EJB in the context of Java2, Enterprise Edition.

- Security against breakdown (fail-safe);

- A naming and directory service (for locating components);

- Access to and pooling of operating system resources (for example, network sockets for the operation of a web container).

The interface between the server and containers is highly dependent on the producer. Neither the specification of Enterprise JavaBeans nor that of the Java 2 platform, Enterprise Edition, defines the protocol for this. The specification of Enterprise JavaBeans in version 2.1 assumes that the producer of the server and that of the container are one and the same.

The EJB Container

The EJB container is a run-time environment for Enterprise Bean components. Just as an EJB container is assigned to the server as a run-time environment and service provider, a bean is dependent on its EJB container, which provides it a run-time environment and services. Such services are provided to the bean via standard programming interfaces. The specification in version 2.1 obliges the EJB container to provide *at least* the following programming interfaces:

- The API (Application Programming Interface) of the Java 2 platform, Standard Edition, in version 1.4;

- The API of the specification of Enterprise JavaBeans 2.1;

- The API of JNDI 1.2 (Java Naming and Directory Interface);

- The UserTransaction API from JTA 1.0.1 (Java Transaction API);

- The API of the JDBC 2.0 extension (Java Database Connectivity);

- The API of JMS 1.1 (Java Message Service);

- The API of Java Mail 1.3 (for sending e-mail);

- The API of JAXP 1.1, 1.2 (Java XML Parser);

- The API of JAXR and JAX-RPC 1.0 (Java XML Remote Procedure Calls);

- The API of Java Connectors 1.5;

- The API of Java Web Services 1.0.

A provider of a Java application server may offer additional services via the standard interface. Some producers offer, for example, a generic service interface particular to the producer by means of which specially developed services (such as a logging service or user management) can be offered. If an Enterprise Bean uses such proprietary services, then it cannot simply be placed in any available container.

The EJB container provides Enterprise Beans a run-time environment, and also offers the Enterprise Beans particular services at run-time, via the above-mentioned (static) programming interfaces. We now would like to examine the most important aspects of both domains (that of the run-time environment as well as that of provided services).

Control of the Life Cycle of a Bean (Run-Time Environment)

The EJB container is responsible for the life cycle of a bean. The EJB container generates bean instances (for example, when a client requests one), deploys them in various states via callback methods, and manages them in pools in case they will not be needed until a later time. The bean instances are also deleted by the EJB container. The states and respective methods that lead to a state transition depend on the type of bean. They are discussed in detail in Chapter 4, "Session Beans"; Chapter 5, "Entity Beans"; and Chapter 6, "Message-Driven Beans."

Instance Pooling (Run-Time Environment); Activation and Passivation

A system that supports mission-critical applications must be capable of dealing with great demands. It must be capable of serving a large number of concurrent clients without them having to put up with long response times. The greater the number of clients, the greater generally the number of objects generated in the server.

In order to keep the number of bean instances from growing without bound and to prevent bean instances from continually being created and then destroyed, an EJB container maintains a certain number of bean instances in a pool. As long as a bean is in the pool, it is in a Pooled state and is to a certain extent deactivated. On demand (as a rule, as a result of a client request) the first available bean instance of the requisite type is taken from the pool. It is reactivated and placed in a Ready state.

Such instance pooling is common practice in database applications. This practice has also proved itself in the management of thread objects (such as in server development). With pooling, fewer bean instances than the number of client connections are needed, as a rule. By avoiding permanent object generation and destruction, system performance is enhanced. Instance pooling is closely connected with the life-cycle management of a bean. Finally, we note that the specification does not obligate an EJB container to support instance pooling.

A further possibility for the EJB container to save system resources is to make Enterprise Bean instances that are currently not needed (for example, from object serialization) persistent and to remove them from memory (*passivation*). Upon demand these instances can again be deserialized and made available in memory (*activation*). Such a temporary storage of bean instances (those, for example, for which a certain time period has expired) on secondary media can reduce the burden on system memory resources. This behavior is similar to that of an operating system page file.

Whether bean instances can be pooled, activated, or passivated depends on their type. In the description of bean types in what follows we shall make the necessary distinctions.

Distribution (Run-Time Environment)

The EJB container ensures that Enterprise Beans can be used by client programs, which as a rule are not running in the same process. The client does not know on what server the Enterprise Bean that it is currently using is located. Even when an Enterprise Bean uses another Enterprise Bean, it is a client. The place where the Enterprise Bean exists is transparent to the client. The use of an Enterprise

Bean on another computer is not essentially different for the client from the use of objects that are located in the same address space.

For distributed communication between the various parties, Java Remote Method Invocation (Java RMI) is used. To achieve interoperability among application servers supplied by different manufacturers the EJB specification prescribes support for the communications protocol of the CORBA specification, IIOP, for an EJB container that conforms to specifications. Distributed communication thus takes place over the protocol RMI-IIOP (RMI over IIOP). In no case does the developer of an Enterprise Bean have to worry about the bean being able to be accessed from outside. This is the sole task of the EJB container.

This book assumes that the reader is already familiar with the techniques of remote method invocation (or else see [13] and [4] for information on RMI). In particular, the reader should understand the notions of *stub* and *skeleton*.

Since version 2.0 of the Enterprise JavaBeans specification the client has had the ability to communicate with an Enterprise Bean via the *Local* interface. In many applications it is necessary that Enterprise Beans, all of which are installed in the same EJB container (aggregation of components), communicate with one another. In version 1.1 of the EJB specification this means a remote call to a component located in the same address space. The overhead of the RMI protocol is unnecessary, and it leads to a degradation of performance. The advantage of using local interfaces is that RMI is thereby completely ignored. Local interfaces can then be sensibly used only if client and Enterprise Bean are located in the same address space of a Java virtual machine. The location of the Enterprise Bean is thus no longer transparent to the client. Transparency of location applies only to EJB components that are called over the remote interface. Furthermore, the semantics of a method call to a component are altered when a local interface is used. With calls to the local interface, parameters are passed via *call by reference*, while calls to the remote interface use *call by value*.

The various chapters on various types of beans will deal extensively with the difference between the remote and local interfaces and will delve deeply into the viewpoint of the client with respect to an Enterprise Bean.

Naming and Directory Service (Service)

If a client wishes to find a bean, it is directed to a naming interface. A naming service offers the possibility of associating references to removed objects under a particular name, which may be assigned arbitrarily, at a definite place (binding). It also offers the possibility of looking up the object bound to the naming service under that name (lookup). This is similar to the white pages, whereby one looks up an object by name.

A directory service is more powerful than a naming service. It supports not only binding of references to a name, it can also manage distributed objects and other resources (such as printers, files, application servers) in hierarchical structures, and it offers wide-ranging possibilities for administration. With a directory service a client can be provided with additional descriptive information about a reference to a remote object. This is similar to the yellow pages, whereby one looks up an object by its attributes.

The interface over which the naming and directory services are accessed is JNDI (Java Naming and Directory Interface). The bean, too, can receive information via the naming and directory service. The EJB container provides the bean instance information, for example, that was established at the time of installation of the component (so-called environment entries). In this way it is possible to influence the behavior of Enterprise Beans by external parameterization. The bean also has the possibility of accessing particular resources, such as database connections or a message service, via the naming and directory services.

Persistence (Service)

The EJB container provides the beans, via the naming and directory services, the possibility of accessing database connections. Beans can thereby themselves ensure that their state is made persistent. However, the specification of Enterprise JavaBeans provides for a mechanism by which the state of certain Enterprise Bean types can be made persistent automatically. (We shall return to this mechanism in Chapter 5, "Entity Beans.")

As a rule, in the case of automatic storage of the state of Enterprise Beans by the EJB container the data are made persistent in a database. One can imagine other EJB containers that provide persistence mechanisms that place the data in other storage systems (for example, in the file system or electronic archives). There is also the possibility of developing EJB containers that make use of the interfaces of other application systems in order to read or write data from or to that location. Thus, for example, the data in an old main-frame system can be bound by means of special EJB containers to component-oriented systems (the container then acts to a certain extent as a wrapper for the old systems).

However, what is really at issue is that in the case of automatic persistence of an Enterprise Bean, the bean couldn't care less where the data are stored. The EJB container takes on the task of ensuring that the data are stored and remain in a consistent state. Thus a particular bean can be installed in various EJB containers that support varying storage systems as persistence medium. For the Enterprise Bean the persistence remains transparent. It doesn't know where its data are stored or where the data come from that the EJB container uses to initialize it.

Transactions (Service and Run-Time Environment)

Transactions are a proven technique for simplifying the development of distributed applications. Among other things, transactions support the applications developer in dealing with error situations that can occur from simultaneous access to particular data by multiple users.

A developer who uses transactions splits up the actions to be executed into atomic units (transactions). The transaction monitor (the EJB container) ensures that the individual actions of a transaction are all executed successfully. If an action fails, the successful actions thus far executed are canceled.

The support of transactions is a fundamental part of the specification of Enterprise JavaBeans. In distributed systems in which several users work simultaneously on many separate actions with the same data (which may be distributed among several back-end systems), a transaction service on the level of the application server is unavoidable. It is the task of the EJB container to ensure that the necessary protocols (for example, the two-phase commit protocol between a transaction monitor and a database system, context propagation, and a distributed two-phase commit) for handling transactions are available. The specification of Enterprise JavaBeans supports flat transactions; that is, transactions cannot be nested.

The developer of an Enterprise Bean can choose how he or she wishes to use transactions. On the one hand, transactions can be used explicitly, by communicating over JTA directly with the transaction service of the EJB container. Alternatively, the developer can opt for declarative (or implicit) transactions. In this case, at the time of installation of an Enterprise Bean in the EJB container it is specified what methods should run within which transactions. The EJB container intervenes when these methods are called, and it ensures that they are called within the appropriate transaction context.

In the case of declarative transactions the bean developer does not need to be concerned with manipulating the transactions. During installation in EJB container $\mathcal{A}$, a bean can be installed with a completely different transactional behavior from that during installation in EJB container $\mathcal{B}$. The bean itself remains untouched in each case, since in every case the container remains responsible for guaranteeing the desired transactional behavior. Much more detail on transactions in the EJB context is to be found in Chapter 7, "Transactions."

Message (Service)

With version 2.0 of the specification of Enterprise JavaBeans the EJB container is obligated to integrate a message service via JMS-API (Java Message Service). With the definition of a new bean type—the message-driven bean—the message service is integrated into the EJB container in a significant way. The development of applications based on Enterprise JavaBeans thus gains two additional dimensions: asynchronicity and parallel processing.

Basically, a message system enables the asynchronous exchange of messages among two or more clients. In contrast to the case of a client–server system, here the architecture of a message system is designed around a loose coupling of equal partners. Each client of the message system can send and receive messages asynchronously. The sender of a message remains largely anonymous, and the same holds for the recipient. Message systems are also known under the name *message-oriented middleware* (MOM).

In addition to the use of message-driven beans, the message service can, of course, also be used for asynchronous message exchange between any two parties. Enterprise Beans, like clients, can also send messages. Through the use of messaging, processes can, for example, decouple from each other or even create interfaces to other systems, making it an excellent component for enterprise integration.

Chapter 6 offers a fuller discussion of Java Message Service message-driven beans.

Security (Run-Time Environment)

The specification obligates the EJB container to provide Enterprise JavaBeans an infrastructure for security management as a part of the run-time environment. It is the task of the system administrator and of the installer of the Enterprise Beans to establish security policy. Once again, the EJB container is responsible for the implementation of this security policy. The goal here is (as with container-managed automatic persistence and declarative transactions) to make the security mechanisms transparent to the Enterprise JavaBeans, so that they can be deployed in as many systems as possible.

If the security strategy were implemented in the bean, it would be problematic to employ the same bean under both more- and less-strict security requirements. On the other hand, it makes much more sense to place the security mechanisms in the run-time environment of the components. They are thereby reusable to a great extent, and the security policy can be adapted from the outside as the situation warrants. The specification of Enterprise JavaBeans specifically mentions that it is preferable that no logic relating to security be present in the code of a bean.

It is possible to define *user roles*. In every Enterprise Bean particular *permissions* can be assigned to a particular role. The assignment takes place, as with the establishment of the user roles, at one of the following times:

- The time of bean installation;

- The time at which several beans are combined into an *aggregate*.

Permissions are focused essentially on whether the user is permitted to call particular methods of an Enterprise Bean. At run time the EJB container determines whether a client call to a bean method should be allowed to be executed. To this end it compares the role of the client with the permissions of the respective Enterprise Bean method.

As a rule, in addition to the security mechanisms that we have described, an EJB container offers the following security attributes:

- Authentication of the user by a user ID and password;

- Secure communication (for example, via the use of secure socket layers).

Chapter 8 contains a more detailed discussion of security in relation to Enterprise JavaBeans.

Finally, we note that the EJB container is the central instance in the component model of Enterprise JavaBeans. It provides the Enterprise Beans (the components) a convenient run-time environment at a very high level of abstraction and makes a variety of services available by way of standard interfaces.

The Persistence Manager

The persistence manager is the building block in the architecture of Enterprise JavaBeans that enables the automatic persistence of particular components. It was introduced with version 2.0 of the EJB specification to achieve a better separation of the physical data storage from the object model. The goal was to improve the portability of persistent EJB components to application servers of other manufacturers. Moreover, improvements were introduced for the mapping of a persistent component onto the storage medium, as well as the possibility of constructing declarative relations between persistent components and an abstract query language. In version 1.1 one was often forced, in the situation of automatic container-governed persistence, to rely on the use of proprietary tools (object-relational "OR" mapping tools) or the use of proprietary extensions of the EJB container, with the result that the portability of the components was greatly compromised.

As always, persistence is managed by the EJB container; that is, it determines *when* the data of a component are loaded or stored. The EJB container also determines whether in the case of an action's failure a successfully executed saving operation should be undone (transaction). The persistence manager, on the other hand, is responsible for *where* and *how* the persistent data are stored. It takes over communication with the storage medium (for example, a database). The mapping of the persistent data of an Enterprise Bean onto the storage medium (for example, the mapping onto one or more database tables) is determined at the installation of a component. The persistence manager plays no role when the Enterprise Bean itself looks after persistence or when the components possess no persistent data.

In most cases a database is used for storing data. In spite of the ANSI SQL standard the databases of different producers are not one hundred percent compatible with one another. For example, they use different key words in the syntax of their query languages. It is usual that particular database functions that distinguish one database from those of other producers are usable only with proprietary extensions of the standard query language SQL. The persistence manager is supposed to catch these difficulties as well. Depending on the implemented database, a specialized persistence manager can be used that is able to deal with the peculiarities of the database system.

A further responsibility of the persistence manager is the formulation of search queries. With knowledge of the mapping of the data and of the peculiarities of the storage medium in use it can translate abstract search queries into concrete search queries. For the formulation of abstract search queries for finding EJB components the specification of Enterprise JavaBeans offers a query language called EJB-QL (Enterprise JavaBeans Query Language). EJB-QL was introduced in version 2.0 of the EJB specification and is further enhanced in version 2.1.

The persistence manager and the query language EJB-QL are dealt with extensively in Chapter 5.

Enterprise Beans

Enterprise Beans are the server-side components used in the component architecture of Enterprise JavaBeans. They implement the application logic on which the client programs rely. The functionality of the server and the EJB container ensures only that beans can be used. Enterprise Beans are installed in an EJB container, which offers them an environment at run time in which they can exist. Enterprise Beans rely implicitly or explicitly on the services that the EJB container offers:

Implicitly in the case of

- container-managed persistence (CMP);
- declarative transactions;
- security.

Explicitly in the case of

- The use of explicit transactions;
- bean-managed persistence (BMP);
- the sending of asynchronous messages.

Types of Enterprise Beans

There are three different forms of Enterprise Beans, which differ more or less sharply one from the other: entity beans, message-driven beans, and session beans. Table 3-1 describes the basic differences among these three types of Enterprise Beans.

Table 3-1. Defining characteristics distinguishing session, message-driven, and entity Beans (see [25]).

	Session Bean	Message-Driven Bean	Entity Bean
Task of the bean	Represents a server-side service that executes tasks for a client.	Represents server-side enterprise logic for the processing of asynchronous messages.	Represents an enterprise object whose data are located in permanent storage.
Access to the bean	A session bean is a private resource for the client, available to the client exclusively.	A message-driven bean is not directly accessible to the client. Communication is effected exclusively via sending messages over a particular channel of the message service.	An entity bean is a central resource; the bean instance is used simultaneously by several clients, and its data are available to all clients.
Persistence of the bean	Not persistent. When the bound client or server is terminated, the bean is no longer accessible.	Not persistent. When the server is terminated, the bean is no longer accessible. The messages that have not yet been delivered to the bean are persistent as required. (More on this in Chapter 6.)	Persistent. When bound clients or server is terminated, the state of the entity bean is located in a persistent storage medium. The bean can be recreated at a later time.

Session beans model ordinary processes or events. For example, this could be the entering of a new customer in an enterprise resource planning system (ERP), the execution of a booking in a booking system, or setting a production plan based on open orders. Session beans can be viewed as an extension of the client's arm toward the server. This point of view is supported by the fact that a session bean is a private resource of a particular client.

Entity beans, on the other hand, represent objects in the real world that are associated with particular data, such as a customer, a booking account, or a product. An instance of a particular entity bean type can be used simultaneously by several clients. Session beans usually operate on data represented by entity beans.

Message-driven beans are recipients of asynchronous messages. A message service acts as a mediator between the sender of a message and the message-driven bean. Entity and session beans are addressed via the *remote* or *local* interface. Calls to entity or session beans are synchronous; that is, the execution of the client is blocked until the method of the Enterprise Bean has been processed. After the method call has returned, the client can continue its processing. Message-driven beans can be addressed by the client only (indirectly) by sending a message over a particular channel of the message service. A particular type of message-driven bean receives all messages that are sent over a particular channel of the message service. Communication over a message service is asynchronous. That is, the execution of the client can proceed directly after a message is sent. It does not remain blocked until the message has been delivered and processed. The container can deploy several instances of a particular message-driven bean type for the processing of messages. Thus in this case parallel processing is possible. Message-driven beans have no state between the processing of several messages. Furthermore, they have no identity vis-à-vis the client. In a certain sense the are similar to *stateless* session beans (see the following paragraph). For the processing of a message, message-driven beans can use session or entity beans as well as all services that the container offers.

There is another distinction to be made with regard to session beans, namely, whether a session bean is *stateless* or *stateful*. Stateless session beans do not store any data from one method call to the next. The methods of a stateless session bean operate only with the data that are passed to it as parameters. Stateless session beans of the same type all possess the same identity. Since they have no state, there is neither the necessity nor the possibility of distinguishing one from the other.

Stateful session beans, on the other hand, store data over many method calls. Calls by methods to stateful session beans can change the state of the bean. The state is lost when the client is no longer using the bean or when the server is taken down. Stateful session beans of the same type have differing identities at run time. The EJB container must be able to distinguish them, since they have differing states for their clients.

A session bean receives its identity from the EJB container. In contrast to entity beans, the identity of a session bean is not externally visible. Since clients always work with a session bean that for them is an exclusive instance, there is no need for such visibility.

Entity beans can be distinguished by whether they themselves are responsible for making their data persistent or whether the EJB container takes over this task. In the first case one speaks of *bean-managed persistence*, while in the second the talk is of *container-managed persistence*.

Entity beans of the same type have differing identities at run time. An entity bean of a particular type is identified at run time by its primary key, which is allocated by the EJB container. It is thereby bound to particular data, which it represents in its activation phase. The identity of an entity bean is outwardly visible.

The bean types play a role in resource management of the EJB container. With entity beans, message-driven beans, and stateless session beans the container can instigate pooling, while with stateful session beans it can instigate passivation and activation (serialization and deserialization onto a secondary storage medium).

The interface between an entity bean and the EJB container is called the *context* (`javax.ejb.EJBContext`). This interface is again specialized for the three bean types (to `javax.ejb.EntityContext`, `javax.ejb.MessageDrivenContext`, and `javax.ejb.SessionContext`). The bean can communicate with the container using the context that is passed by the EJB container to the bean. The context remains bound to a bean during its entire life span. By means of the context the EJB container manages the identity of an Enterprise Bean. With a change in the context the EJB container can change the identity of a bean.

Chapters 4, 5, and 6 provide an extensive discussion of the technical details of session, message-driven, and entity beans. The second section of Chapter 9 deals with the differing semantics of the various bean types.

Components of an Enterprise Bean

An Enterprise Bean possesses the following components:

- The remote interface and the (remote) home interface *or* the local and local home interface (for entity and session beans);

- The bean class (for entity, message-driven, and session beans);

- The primary key or primary key class (for entity beans);

- The deployment descriptor (for entity, message-driven, and session beans).

One speaks of the remote client view when an Enterprise Bean is addressable over the remote interface. If an Enterprise Bean uses the local interface, one speaks of the local client view. Basically, an Enterprise Bean can support both the local and remote client views. However, the specification advises that one choose one of the two cases.

Let us describe the individual components of a bean by way of an example. We would like to develop an entity bean that represents a bank account. The components should make it possible to ascertain the account number, a description of the account, and the current balance of the account. Furthermore, the balance of the account should be capable of being raised or lowered by an arbitrary amount. The bank-account bean should be able to be addressed by the remote client, that is, from a client that is located outside the address space of the bank-account bean.

This chapter concentrates on the representation of the special features determined by the architecture. In this example we shall not go into the special features of a particular bean type (that will be done extensively in Chapters 4, 5, and 6). Since an entity bean exhibits all the components mentioned above, it is best suited for this introductory example. Moreover, we shall not use the local interface in this example. Since EJB is a distributed component architecture, the use of the remote interface is standard. The use of the local interface is analogous to that of the remote interface, and it will be dealt with in Chapters 4 and 5.

Remote Interface

The remote interface defines those methods that are not offered externally by a bean. The methods of the remote interface thus reflect the functionality that is expected or demanded by the components. The remote interface must be derived from javax.ejb.EJBObject, which in turn is derived from java.rmi.Remote. All methods of the remote interface must declare the exception java.rmi.RemoteException. See Listing 3-1.

Listing 3-1. Remote interface of BankAccount.

```
package ejb.bankaccount;

import java.rmi.RemoteException;
import javax.ejb.EJBObject;

public interface BankAccount extends EJBObject
{
  //ascertain account number
  public String getAccNumber()
    throws RemoteException;
  //ascertain account description
  public String getAccDescription()
    throws RemoteException;
  //ascertain account balance
  public float getBalance()
    throws RemoteException;
  //increase account balance
  public void increaseBalance(float amount)
    throws RemoteException;
  //reduce account balance
  public void decreaseBalance(float amount)
    throws RemoteException;
}
```

Home Interface

The home interface must be derived from `javax.ejb.EJBHome` (in this interface is to be found the method for deleting a bean; it does not need to be separately declared). `EJBHome`, for its part, is likewise derived from `javax.rmi.Remote`. In the home interface as well all methods declare the triggering of an exception of type `java.rmi.RemoteExeption`. As in the case of the remote interface, everything points to the distributed character and the embedding in the EJB framework. See Listing 3-2.

Listing 3-2. The home interface of BankAccount.

```
package ejb.bankaccount;

import java.rmi.RemoteException;
import javax.ejb.CreateException;
import javax.ejb.EJBHome;
import javax.ejb.FinderException;

public interface BankAccountHome extends EJBHome
{

  //generate an account
  public BankAccount create(String accNo,
                                    String accDescription,
                                    float initialBalance)
    throws CreateException, RemoteException;

  //find a particular account
  public BankAccount findByPrimaryKey(String accPK)
    throws FinderException, RemoteException;

}
```

Bean Classes

Bean classes implement the methods that have been declared in the home and remote interfaces (with the exception of the `findByPrimaryKey` method), without actually implementing these two interfaces. The signatures of the methods of the remote and home interfaces must agree with the corresponding methods in the bean class. The bean class must implement an interface that depends on its type, and indeed, it must be `javax.ejb.EntityBean`, `javax.ejb.MessageDrivenBean`, or `javax.ejb.SessionBean`. The bean implements neither its home nor its remote interface. Only in the case of an entity bean with container-managed automatic persistence is the class *abstract*. The classes of session, message-driven, and entity beans, which manage their own persistence, are *concrete* classes. See Listing 3-3.

Listing 3-3. Bean class of BankAccount.

```
package ejb.bankaccount;
import javax.ejb.CreateException;
import javax.ejb.EntityBean;
import javax.ejb.EntityContext;
import javax.ejb.RemoveException;
public abstract class BankAccountBean implements EntityBean {
  private EntityContext theContext;
  public BankAccountBean() {
  }
  //the create method of the home interface
  public String ejbCreate(String accNo,
                              String accDescription,
                              float initialBalance)
    throws CreateException
  {
    setAccountNumber(accNo);
    setAccountDescription(accDescription);
    setAccountBalance(initialBalance);
    return null;
  }
  public void ejbPostCreate(String accNo,
                              String accDescription,
                              float initialBalance)
    throws CreateException
  {
  }
  //abstract getter/setter methods
  public abstract String getAccountNumber();
  public abstract void setAccountNumber(String acn);

  public abstract String getAccountDescription();
  public abstract void setAccountDescription(String acd);
  public abstract float getAccountBalance();
  public abstract void setAccountBalance(float acb);
```

```
    //the methods of the remote interface
    public String getAccNumber() {
      return getAccountNumber();
    }
    public String getAccDescription() {
      return getAccountDescription();
    }
    public float getBalance() {
      return getAccountBalance();
    }
    public void increaseBalance(float amount) {
      float acb = getAccountBalance();
      acb += amount;
      setAccountBalance(acb);
    }
    public void decreaseBalance(float amount) {
      float acb = getAccountBalance();
      acb -= amount;
      setAccountBalance(acb);
    }

    //the methods of the javax.ejb.EntityBean interface
    public void setEntityContext(EntityContext ctx) {
      theContext = ctx;
    }

    public void unsetEntityContext() {
      theContext = null;
    }

    public void ejbRemove()
      throws RemoveException
    {
    }

    public void ejbActivate() {
    }

    public void ejbPassivate() {
    }

    public void ejbLoad() {
    }

    public void ejbStore() {
    }
}
```

Primary Key (Primary Key Class)

The primary key is relevant only for entity beans. Its purpose is to identify an entity of a particular type uniquely. As in the case of the primary key of a database table, it contains those attributes that are necessary for unique identification. With the primary key a particular entity can be found, which then is associated by the EJB container with an entity bean instance of the correct type. With the primary key the identity of an entity bean is externally visible. The primary key class is irrelevant for session and message-driven beans, since their identity is never externally visible. The specification distinguishes two types of primary keys:

- primary keys that refer to a field of the entity bean class;

- primary keys that refer to several fields of the entity bean class.

A primary key that refers to only a single field of the entity bean class can be represented by a standard Java class (for example, java.lang.String, java.lang.Integer). In our example the class java.lang.String is the primary key class, since the unique identification of an account is possible via its (alphanumeric) account number.

A primary key that refers to several fields of the entity bean class is represented, as a rule, by a class specially developed for that purpose. Such a class must be a public class, and it must have a public constructor without arguments. The fields of the primary key class that represent the primary key of the entity bean must address those of the entity bean class by name. Furthermore, these fields must also be public. The class must be RMI-IIOP compatible (serializable), and it must implement the methods equals( ) and hashCode( ). Listing 3-4 shows an example of such a primary key class for an account bean that requires for its unique identification the number of the client as well as the account number (client-capable system).

Listing 3-4. Example of a primary key class for multipart keys.

```
package ejb.custom;
public class CustomAccountPK implements java.io.Serializable
{
  public String clientNumber;
  public String accountNumber;
  public CustomAccountPK() {
  }
  public int hashCode() {
    return clientNumber.hashCode() ^
      accountNumber.hashCode();
  }
```

```
      public boolean equals(Object obj) {
        if(!(obj instanceof CustomAccountPK)) {
          return false;
        }
        CustomAccountPK pk = (CustomAccountPK)obj;
        return (clientNumber.equals(pk.clientNumber)
          && accountNumber.equals(pk.accountNumber));
      }
      public String toString() {
        return clientNumber + ":" + accountNumber;
      }
    }
```

The Deployment Descriptor

The deployment descriptor is a file in XML format (details on XML can be found in [3]) that describes one or more beans or how several beans can be collected into an aggregate. All such information that is not to be found in the code of a bean is placed in the deployment descriptor. Essentially, this is declarative information. This information is of particular importance for those collecting several Enterprise Beans into an application or installing Enterprise Beans in one EJB container. The EJB container is informed via the deployment descriptor how it is to handle the component(s) at run time.

The deployment descriptor contains information on the structure of an Enterprise Bean and its external dependencies (for example, to other beans or to particular resources such as connections to a database). Furthermore, it contains information about how the components should behave at run time or how they can be combined with other components into more complex building blocks. We shall illustrate this for our example bean by showing in Listing 3-5 a suitable complete deployment descriptor (for a full description of the deployment descriptor see [21]).

Listing 3-5. Deployment descriptor of BankAccount.

```
<?xml version="1.0" ?>
<ejb-jar version="2.1" xmlns="http://java.sun.com/xml/ns/j2ee"
xmlns:xsi="http://www.w3.org/2001/XMLSchema-instance"
xsi:schemaLocation="http://java.sun.com/xml/ns/j2ee
http://java.sun.com/xml/ns/j2ee/ejb-jar_2_1.xsd">
  <description>
    This deployment descriptor contains information on
    the entity bean BankAccount.
  </description>
```

```xml
<enterprise-beans>
  <entity>
    <!-- Name of the Enterprise Bean -->
    <ejb-name>BankAccount</ejb-name>
    <!-- class of the Home Interface -->
    <home>ejb.bankaccount.BankAccountHome</home>
    <!-- class of the Remote Interface -->
    <remote>ejb.bankaccount.BankAccount</remote>
    <!-- class of the Enterprise Bean -->
    <ejb-class>ejb.bankaccount.BankAccountBean</ejb-class>
    <!-- type of persistence -->
    <persistence-type>Container</persistence-type>
    <!-- class of the primary key -->
    <prim-key-class>java.lang.String</prim-key-class>
    <!-- specifies whether the implementation of the
     Enterprise Bean is reentrant -->
    <reentrant>False</reentrant>
    <!-- the EJB version for which this Enterprise
     Bean was developed -->
    <cmp-version>2.x</cmp-version>
    <!-- Name of the persistence mechanism -->
    <abstract-schema-name>AccountBean
    </abstract-schema-name>
    <!-- list of the persistent attributes
     of the Enterprise Bean -->
    <cmp-field>
      <description>account number</description>
      <field-name>accountNumber</field-name>
    </cmp-field>
    <cmp-field>
      <description>account description</description>
      <field-name>accountDescription</field-name>
    </cmp-field>
    <cmp-field>
      <description>account balance</description>
      <field-name>accountBalance</field-name>
    </cmp-field>
    <!-- primary key field -->
    <primkey-field>accountNumber</primkey-field>
  </entity>
</enterprise-beans>
<assembly-descriptor>
  <!-- Definition of the user role 'Banker'-->
  <security-role>
```

```
      <description> the role of the banker
      </description>
      <role-name>Banker</role-name>
    </security-role>
    <!-- Definition of access rights at the method level-->
    <method-permission>
      <role-name>banker</role-name>
      <method>
        <ejb-name>BankAccount</ejb-name>
        <method-name>*</method-name>
      </method>
    </method-permission>
    <!-- Definition of transactional behavior
      per method of the Enterprise Bean -->
    <container-transaction>
      <method>
        <ejb-name>BankAccount</ejb-name>
        <method-name>increaseBalance</method-name>
      </method>
      <trans-attribute>Required</trans-attribute>
    </container-transaction>
    <container-transaction>
      <method>
        <ejb-name>BankAccount</ejb-name>
        <method-name>decreaseBalance</method-name>
      </method>
      <trans-attribute>Required</trans-attribute>
    </container-transaction>
  </assembly-descriptor>
</ejb-jar>
```

Since our example deals with an entity bean with container-managed persistence, instructions for the persistence manager must also be provided. It must know which fields of the bean are to be mapped to which columns in which table or tables. Moreover, it requires instructions about the database in which the data are to be stored. The specification does not specify what form these instructions are to take. It prescribes only that the creator must provide tools by means of which such instructions can be supplied. It is thus clear that these tools will be different depending on the creator, as also will be the format in which the instructions are provided. In the simplest case these instructions can be given in a file in XML format. Listing 3-6 shows an imaginary example. Later in this chapter we shall call these instructions the *persistence descriptor*.

Listing 3-6. Example of mapping instructions for the persistence manager.

```
<abstract-schema>
 <name>AccountBean</name>
 <data-source>
  <name>test-db</name>
  <type>oracle</type>
 </data-source>
 <table-name>account</table-name>
 <field-mapping>
  <bean-field>accountNumber</bean-field>
  <column>acno</column>
 </field-mapping>
 <field-mapping>
  <bean-field>accountDescription</bean-field>
  <column>acdesc</column>
 </field-mapping>
 <field-mapping>
  <bean-field>accountBalance</bean-field>
  <column>acbal</column>
 </field-mapping>
</abstract-schema>
```

If all components are present, then according to bean type, the home and remote interfaces, the bean class(es), the primary key class(es), and the deployment descriptor (which can contain a description of several Enterprise Bean components) are packed in JAR format into a file. The acronym JAR stands for "Java archive" and corresponds to the popular ZIP format. The components of an Enterprise Bean are then complete and are packed as component(s) in a jar file (further details on packing a component in a jar file can be found in [21]). Table 3-2 shows once more which components are relevant to which bean type.

Table 3-2. Overview of the components of various bean types.

	Entity		Session	Message-Driven
	Container Managed	Bean Managed		
Remote, local interface	X	X	X	
Local & remote home interface	X	X	X	
Concrete bean class		X	X	X
Abstract bean class	X			
Deployment descriptor	X	X	X	X
Persistence descriptor	X			

How Everything Works Together

Let us assume that the component BankAccount is not included in an aggregate, but is installed directly in an EJB container, in order to be used by client programs. The installation takes place with the help of the relevant tools. The specification obligates the creator of an EJB container and the persistence manager to provide these tools. It is left to the creator to determine what these tools look like and how they are to be used. As a rule, they support the capturing of all relevant data for the installation of a component via a graphical user interface. However, of primary importance is the result of the tool-supported installation procedure. It provides the missing links in the EJB architecture: the implementation of the home and remote interfaces (respectively the local home and local interfaces) of the Enterprise Bean and in the case of a container-managed entity bean the implementation of the concrete bean class. Figure 3-3 shows these relationships.

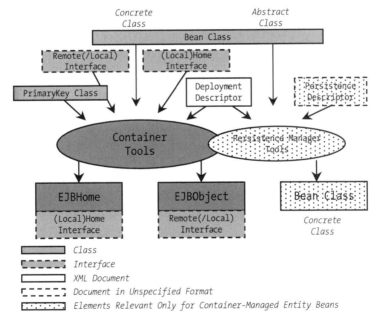

Figure 3-3. Generation of the missing architectural components.

As we have already mentioned, an Enterprise Bean uses either local or remote interfaces. The implementation class of the home or local home interface is usually called EJBHome, while that of the local or remote interface is denoted by EJBHome, while the remote interface is usually known as EJBObject. The classes EJBHome and EJBObject are generated from the components of a bean by the tools of the container's creator.

If we are dealing with an entity bean with container-managed persistence, then it is the job of the persistence manager to generate a concrete class. This is derived from the abstract bean class and represents the necessary code for persistence. For this generation, the additionally created instructions regarding the database and table(s) from the persistence descriptor as well as the persistence fields of the components are employed (see in this respect the example in Listing 3-6).

The EJBHome object serves at run time as a sort of object factory, and the EJBObject as a sort of functional wrapper for the Enterprise Bean in question. (See Figure 3-4.) They are the extension of the run-time environment of the EJB container for particular bean types.

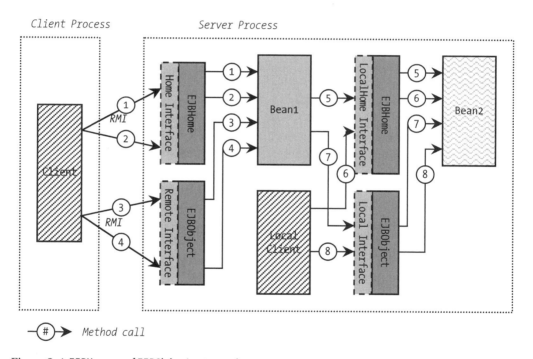

Figure 3-4. EJBHome *and* EJBObject *at run time.*

If the Enterprise Bean uses remote interfaces, then they are both remote objects in the sense of Java RMI. If the Enterprise Bean uses local interfaces, then they are traditional Java objects. In both cases the client calls upon the methods of the EJBHome and EJBObject, never directly those of the bean instance. EJBHome and EJBObject delegate the respective method calls (after or before particular container-related routines) to the bean instance.

With this indirection the EJB container is able to bring its implementation of the declarative instructions into the deployment descriptor. The content of the deployment descriptor influences considerably the generated code of the EJBHome and EJBObject classes.

The EJBHome class contains the code for the generation, location, and deletion of bean instances. Often, code is generated for resource management into the EJBHome class. The EJBObject class implements the transaction behavior, security checking, and, as needed, the logic for container-managed persistence. The implementation of these classes depends to a great extent on the creator. The specification makes no compulsory prescriptions for the creator with respect to the implementation of EJBHome and EJBObject.

No instance other than the EJBHome and EJBObject objects can cooperate with the bean instance. It is completely protected by the container classes. Communication between beans also always takes place by way of the container classes EJBHome and EJBObject.

From this state of affairs we obtain answers to questions that may have been left unanswered in the previous section. The home and remote interfaces do not need to be implemented, since the implementation classes are generated by the container tools. (The same holds in the case where a local home interface and local interface are used.) The Enterprise Bean is not a remote object, since it is never to be addressed externally. It should be able to be addressed via EJBHome and EJBObject. The EJB container would otherwise have no possibility of intervention to keep up with its tasks. Therefore, the interfaces javax.ejb.EJBHome and javax.ejb.EJBObject (the basic interfaces of the home and remote interfaces) are also derived from java.rmi.Remote.

It is even clear why the signatures of the bean methods and the methods in the home and remote interfaces must agree. The interfaces are implemented by EJBHome and EJBObject classes. They delegate the calls to the interface methods to the corresponding methods of the bean class. The code necessary for this is generated. If the signatures in the methods declared in the interfaces do not agree with the corresponding bean methods or if these methods don't even exist in the bean class, then a complaint will be registered in the generation of EJBHome and EJBObject by the container tools, or else the result will be a run-time error.

Finally, EJBHome and EJBObject ensure that in the case of session beans each client is able to work with an instance exclusive to it, while in the case of entity beans several clients can share the same instance.

The Client's Viewpoint

If a client now wishes to use the bank account bean installed in the EJB container, it must first locate the bean. For this it uses the naming and directory service. This is addressed via the JNDI interface. (See Figure 3-5.)

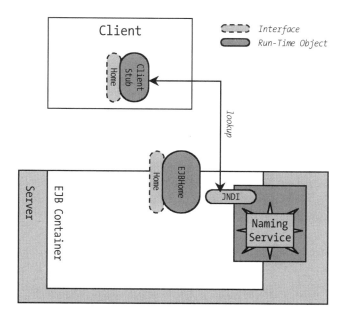

Figure 3-5. Finding an Enterprise Bean via JNDI.

Like the Enterprise Bean, the client uses the naming and directory service of the EJB container or of the server in which the bean is installed. The EJB container is responsible for making the Enterprise Bean accessible under a particular name via the naming and directory service. In many cases the name of the bean in the deployment descriptor is used for this purpose. The field of the deployment descriptor in which the name of the Enterprise Bean is entered is called `ejb-name` (and occurs in our `BankAccount` example). We now assume that the EJB container uses this name for the publication of the bean's name via the naming service (JNDI). Listing 3-7 shows how a client finds the bank account bean.

Listing 3-7. Finding the home interface using JNDI.

```
//depending on the creator of the container or server the appropriate settings
//in the environment should be made in order to generate the correct context.
final String BANK_ACCOUNT = "java:comp/env/ejb/BankAccount";
//generation of the context for access to the naming service
InitialContext ctx = new InitialContext();
//location of the bean BankAccount
Object o = ctx.lookup(BANK_ACCOUNT);
//type transformation; details on this in Section 4
BankAccountHome bh = (BankAccountHome)
 PortableRemoteObject.narrow(o,BankAccountHome.class);
```

Using the naming and directory service the EJB container provides the Enterprise Bean with an instance of the client stub of the implementation class of the home interface (EJBHome).

Using the methods of the home interface (and those of the interface javax.ejb.EJBHome) the client can govern the life cycle of the bean. For example, it can generate a new account with the following code fragment:

```
BankAccount ba = bh.create("0815", "sample account", 0.0);
```

The EJBHome object generates a new bean instance (or takes one from the pool), generates a new data set in the database, and generates an EJBObject instance (see Figure 3-6).

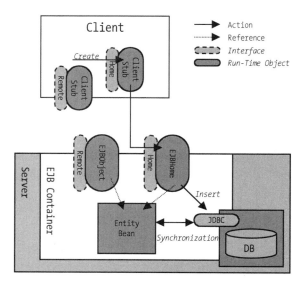

Figure 3-6. Generating a new bean via the home interface.

From the parameters of the create method a primary key object is generated, which is associated with the bean instance (via the context of the bean). In this way the bean instance acquires its identity. As a result of this operation the client is provided with the stub of the EJBObject instance. The stub represents the client with respect to the remote interface of the bean.

From this point on the client can use the functionality of the bean by calling the methods of the remote interface. For example, it can increase the bank balance by one hundred units:

```
ba.increaseBalance(100.0);
```

The call to the method increaseBalance(float) on the client stub passes to the EJBObject instance on the server. From there it is again delegated to the bean instance, which finally has the consequence of changing the data with the assistance of the transaction monitor (for this method it was specified in the deployment descriptor that it must take place in a transaction). (See Figure 3-7.)

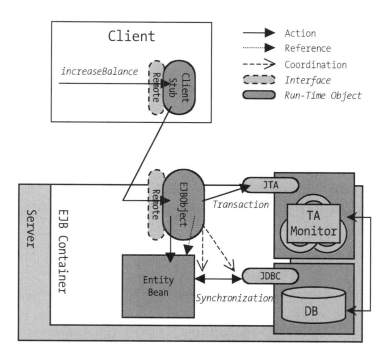

Figure 3-7. Invoking a method via the remote interface.

For the client there is no big difference between using an Enterprise Bean and a traditional Java object located in the same process, although it communicates with a transaction-protected component on a remote computer. What begins with a one-line instruction in the code of the client can trigger very complex actions on the server.

From the client's point of view the way that an Enterprise Bean is used via the local interface is analogous to the use of an Enterprise Bean via the remote interface. Similar analogies hold in the processing of the `EJBHome` and `EJBObject` classes.

The information presented in this section applies primarily to session and entity beans. Message-driven beans differ from the other two types (as already mentioned) in that they cannot be addressed directly by a client. They can be addressed only indirectly via the asynchronous sending of a message. A message-driven bean is less complex than a session or entity bean and is also easier for the container to manipulate, since the message service takes over a large part of the work. Chapter 6 discusses this issue in detail and makes clear the differences between this type and the other two types of bean.

What an Enterprise Bean May Not Do

The specification of Enterprise JavaBeans is very restrictive for the developer of an Enterprise Bean as it relates to the use of certain interfaces. The most important restrictions will be presented in this section. What is most interesting is the question of the reason for such prohibitions. We shall investigate this question after we briefly introduce the most important restrictions (the complete list of restrictions can be found in [21]):

- An Enterprise Bean may not use static variables. Static constants, on the other hand, are permitted.

- An Enterprise Bean may not use a thread synchronization mechanism.

- An Enterprise Bean may not use the functionality of the AWT (Abstract Windowing Toolkit) to produce output via a graphic user interface or to read input from the keyboard.

- An Enterprise Bean may not use any classes from `java.io` to access files or directories in a file system.

- An Enterprise Bean may not listen in on a network socket; it may not accept a connection to a network socket; and it may not use a socket for multicast.

- An Enterprise Bean may not attempt to use introspection or reflection to access information from classes and instances that are supposed to remain secret according to the Java security policy.

- An Enterprise Bean may not generate a class loader; it may not use a class loader; it may not change the context of a class loader; it may not set a security manager; it may not generate a security manager; it may not stop the Java virtual machine; and it may not change the standard input the standard output, or the standard error.

- An Enterprise Bean may not use an object of the class `Policy`, `Security`, `Provider`, `Signer`, or `Identity` from the `java.security` package or attempt to change their values.

- An Enterprise Bean may not set a socket factory that is used by the classes `ServerSocket` and `Socket`. The same holds for the stream handler factory of the `URL` class.

- An Enterprise Bean may not use threads. It may neither start nor stop them.

- An Enterprise Bean may not directly read or write file descriptors.

- An Enterprise Bean may not load a native library.

- An Enterprise Bean may never pass `this` as an argument in a call to a method or `this` as the return value of a method call.

To "program" an Enterprise Bean means to develop server-side logic at a relatively high level of abstraction. The specification of Enterprise JavaBeans describes a component architecture for distributed applications. Through the component model the specification seeks to establish a clear distribution of labor among various tasks. The server and the EJB container are responsible for system-specific functionality. The bean uses this infrastructure as its run-time environment and thus need not concern itself with system-specific functionality. The task of the bean is to concentrate on the logic for enterprise-related processes. In order to be able to carry out this task, it should use the services made available to it by the EJB container, and no others. These restrictions imposed by the specification of Enterprise Beans should serve to ward off conflicts between the EJB container and the Enterprise Beans.

EJB Assignment of Roles

The specification of Enterprise JavaBeans splits the responsibilities for development into various roles. The idea is to achieve a certain level of abstraction in the EJB model in order to encourage diversification through the allocation of concrete tasks to various expert groups and thereby achieve a synergistic effect. To put it another way, everyone should develop what he or she can best develop. Figure 3-8 provides an overview of the various roles and their interaction.

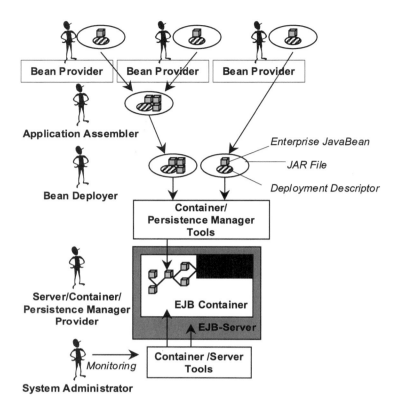

Figure 3-8. EJB assignment of roles.

Server Provider

The server provider is responsible for the provision of basic server functions. It must ensure that a stable run-time environment is available to various containers (e.g., above all, EJB containers). This includes—as already mentioned in the previous chapter—the network connection, thread and process management, sizing (clustering), and resource management.

Container Provider

The container provider sits on top of the interfaces of the server provider and offers the components (Enterprise Beans) a convenient run-time environment. The implementation of a container provider must be in accordance with the conditions set forth in this chapter. It must ensure that accesses to an Enterprise Bean take place solely via the container, and the same holds for the Enterprise Bean's communication with its environment. Primarily, the container provider provides for persistence of components, mechanisms for dealing with transaction-oriented processes, security features, resource pooling, and support for making available versions of components (this last feature is not more precisely defined in the specification). For beans to be installed in a container, the container provider must make available tools that enable the bean deployer (see below) to generate the necessary interface code (EJBHome and EJBObject). The container provider must make tools available to the system administrator for monitoring the container and the beans.

Persistence Manager Provider

The persistence manager provider must provide tools with which the code needed for the persistence of a container-managed entity bean can be generated. The tools are used when an Enterprise Bean is installed in a particular container. The persistence manager provider is typically a specialist in the area of databases. It is therefore necessary that the following conditions hold:

- The state of an entity bean is stored with container-managed persistence in the database.

- The referential integrity of the entity bean is ensured with respect to other entity beans to which it is related.

Since the EJB container governs the persistence of an entity bean (that is, it determines, for example, when the state should be saved), an interface between container and persistence manager is necessary. The specification leaves it to the container and persistence manager providers to define such an interface.

Bean Provider

The role of the bean provider belongs to those developers who implement the actual business logic. They package their application knowledge into components that make this knowledge reusable. Building on the products of the server and container providers, the bean developer is freed from the development of basic server tasks (such as multithreading, network connection, transactions). Therefore, such a developer can devote his or her complete energy to the task at hand. In addition to the component, the bean provider provides the deployment descriptor, which contains information about the component itself, as well as about its external dependencies (e.g., on what services from the server the component depends). The deployment descriptor (an extensive example was presented in Listing 3-5) provides all information that the bean deployer (to be discussed shortly) requires for installing the component in a server.

The application assembler (see the next heading) also needs this information in order to assemble applications or modules of an application from various components. The result of the work of a bean provider is a file in JAR (Java Archive) format that contains the bean class(es) and the interfaces of the bean(s) as well as the deployment descriptor.

Application Assembler

Finally, the application assembler is responsible for linking the functionalities of the beans installed in the container to applications. To this can belong the development of client applications and the associated control of information exchange with the Enterprise Beans. The application assembler can, however, also assemble several (smaller) components provided by bean providers into a new (larger) component. The application assembler can enlarge this conglomerate with its own Enterprise Beans, whose task consists, for example, in the coupling of other Enterprise Beans. The resulting "supercomponents" already represent an aspect of a concrete application.

The application assembler documents its work, just like the bean provider in the deployment descriptor. Thereby the bean deployer (see the next section) understands how to install the components so that from the individual building blocks a complete application results. Additionally, the application assembler can provide instructions and information for the bean deployer in regard to the user interface or dependencies on non-EJB components in the deployment descriptor.

Bean Deployer

To install the components selected for a particular business problem in a container is the task of the bean deployer. To this belongs, above all, the provision of the tools of the container and persistence manager providers as well as the correct parameterization of the components to be installed. This operation assumes an extensive knowledge of the application and system contexts as well as of the internal system linkages. In particular, the deployer must resolve the external dependencies defined in the deployment descriptor (for example, by ensuring the existence of required services or related Enterprise Beans) and take into account the instructions of the application assembler contained in the deployment descriptor.

System Administrator

The system administrator monitors the EJB server with the assistance of the tools provided by the producer and takes care of the operation of the required infrastructure (e.g., for an operational network) of an EJB server.

The EJB assignment of roles represents an ideal scenario, and the translation of the EJB specification into practice will show whether it can be maintained in this form. Thus today servers and containers are offered in a single product. The Java-2 platform, Enterprise Edition (J2EE), already provides a variety of containers (at least an EJB container and a web container) for an application server. In the meantime, the specification of Enterprise JavaBeans assumes that server and container are always offered by the same producer and cannot be exchanged for others. The same holds for the persistence manager. As long as the specification defines no protocol between EJB containers and persistence managers, both will be offered in a single product.

This role-playing is supremely adapted (in theory) to component-oriented software, at least from the point of view that one is dealing with a number of individuals. Thus a container provider (a container is, after all, a type of component) does not know during development what beans will later be put into this container. Nor does a bean provider know at the time of development to what purpose those components will later be used. The provider merely packs a well-rounded functionality into a component with the goal of optimal reusability. If the correct components have been installed and parameterized by the bean deployer, then it is simple for the application assembler to link the functionality that is offered to applications or to create modules out of available components. The work of the application assembler is, moreover, not bound temporally to the work of the bean deployer. The application assembler can use, via the deployer, already installed components, or can transmit "supercomponents" that have assembled to the deployer for installation.

The roles of the server and container providers are intended for system specialists, who provide a stable basis. For an application developer (such as described in the introductory chapter, "Motivation") there are a variety of approaches. One could slip into the role of the bean provider by encapsulating one's knowledge into beans and then installing them in a purchased application server that offers an EJB container. Or instead, one could leaf through the catalog of a software manufacturer and look for components that offer a solution to one's problem(s). One's task would then be limited to installing the purchased beans on the server and correctly parameterizing them (corresponding to the role of the bean deployer).

In the next step our developer (or a colleague) could write an application using the installed beans that takes over the interaction between the user and the communication with the components (application assembler, limited to the development of the client scenario).

In any case, one thing is clear to the application developer (above all in the role of the bean provider): He or she can concentrate fully on the solution to his or her problems. Technical problems such as the implementation of a stable, efficient, and scalable server are taken over by the server and container providers.

In the rest of this book we shall for the most part restrict our attention to the roles of the bean provider, the bean deployer, and the application assembler.

Points of View

Once the architecture and the significant features and concepts of the specification of the Enterprise JavaBeans are known, we would like, in conclusion, to clarify various perspectives on the architecture.

EJB from the Point of View of Application Development

It is interesting to consider Enterprise JavaBeans from the point of view of application development. For this we should return to the scenario of Chapter 1. The application developer described there could use Enterprise JavaBeans as a basis for the prototype to be developed. He or she could use a J2EE-compatible server including an EJB container from any supplier and develop the prototype in the form of Enterprise Beans. We would like to consider whether the secondary problems that arise from the business problem can be neutralized using Enterprise JavaBeans as the basis technology. We wish to investigate whether the application developer can concentrate completely on the problems of the application domain. To this end we recall a figure from Chapter 1 (see Figure 3-9).

There is certainly the requirement of *reusability* due to the client–server-oriented architecture. There is also the necessity for security characteristics of the transaction service of Enterprise JavaBeans in order to ensure a smooth multiuser operation.

The characteristic of scalability means that applications that are realized as Enterprise Beans or as aggregates of beans can be partitioned among several servers. For example, the servers can use the same database as back-end system. Thus the burden of client queries, depending on the application, is divided among several servers, while the database is centrally located. Through locational transparency of Enterprise Beans with a remote interface (which is ensured by a central naming and directory service) the following are possible:

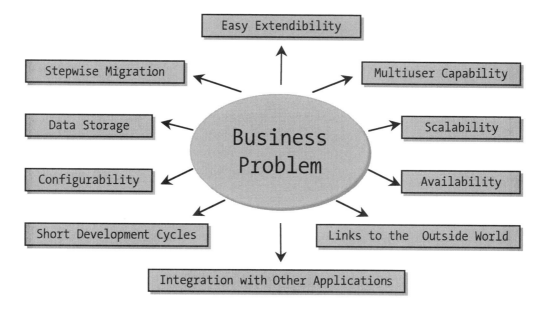

Figure 3-9. Secondary issues in a business problem.

- Distribute individual applications of an application system among several servers.

- Store individual beans from one server on another server.

- Set up additional servers and store beans or aggregates of beans there.

Moreover, many application servers offer mechanisms for the allocation of tasks. In this regard a cluster of application servers (independent of the application that the client uses) concerns itself with the optimal servicing of the client's queries. However, this feature is provider-dependent and not required by the architecture of Enterprise JavaBeans.

The subject of availability becomes significant in regard to the locational transparency of Enterprise Bean components, which is ensured by the central naming and directory service. If an application server goes out of service, the beans installed there are installed on another server. The information necessary for the installation is already contained in the deployment descriptor of the Enterprise Beans, and they can generally be transported unaltered. A change in the configuration in the naming and directory service allows them to be placed at the service of clients on another server without the configuration of the client having to be changed.

Since Enterprise JavaBeans are ever more tightly bound in the context of the Java 2 platform, Enterprise Edition, the *connection with the outside world* is not a critical topic. With the support of a web container (see Figure 3-2), at least the basic technological and architectural prerequisites are given to create a connection with the outside world. In Chapter 9 we shall devote ourselves to this topic in somewhat greater detail.

Once all the uses of an application system have been realized based on Enterprise JavaBeans, then the potential for integration of the applications among one another is very high. The exchange of data within the application is simple in this case (even more so if a central database is used). Enterprise JavaBeans can also be used to integrate applications belonging to various systems. Using a message service, which the EJB container has had to integrate since version 2.0, it is even possible to achieve dynamic coupling of applications and systems. A message service makes a number of communication channels available over which n-to-n communication with dynamically changing partners is possible.

Through the use of specialized EJB containers, which use an application system other than a database system as persistence system, these systems can be integrated into EJB-based systems. Under certain conditions one can also envision employing Enterprise Beans as wrappers and interfaces to simple systems (to the extent to which that is possible within the limits of programming restrictions).

Applications are constructed from a number of Enterprise Beans, each of which encapsulates a particular functionality. This granularity, as established by the component paradigm, makes it possible for the development of an application system to be structured from a variety of viewpoints. Each component can be a partial project. It is easier to manage each subproject than to keep track of the entire project all at one time.

The interfaces to the outside world are defined for each component (and thus for each subproject). This results in a trend toward shortening the development cycle. Not least, the architecture of Enterprise JavaBeans plays an active role, since the application developer (i.e., the bean developer) is freed from the development of system-technical functionality. The presence of a unified platform allows this system-technical functionality to be reused, and the bean developer can concentrate fully on the solution of the application-related problems.

The configurability of an EJB-based system is given primarily via the deployment descriptor. This makes it possible for beans, at the time of installation in a server, to adapt themselves to a variety of situations. The run-time behavior of an Enterprise Bean can also be influenced by the settings in the deployment descriptor. Using the bean environment, parameters can be set that the bean can evaluate at run time.

An EJB-based system can also be configured via the exchange of bean classes. In fact, the new bean classes offer the same interface; that is, they use the same home and remote interfaces as the old bean classes, but they offer a different implementation. To the client the beans with altered implementation appear under the same names in the JNDI as before. For the client the exchange of implementations plays no role, in that the old agreement (the promised functionality of the interface) is preserved.

In the case of container-managed persistence, Enterprise JavaBeans offer the concept of transparent, automatic data storage. The Enterprise Bean leaves data storage to the EJB container and the persistence manager. It need not concern itself with the technical aspects of data storage. Such a bean can be used without difficulty in other EJB containers.

Through the deployment of specialized EJB containers (as can be seen in Figure 3-10) it is possible to achieve a stepwise migration from the old system. The state of the data and the systems can be reused. For the bean the EJB container is not only a run-time environment and service provider but also the interface to the old system (which to the bean is essentially transparent). After the complete takeover of the data (for example, into a relational database system) the beans already developed can be reused through installation in another EJB container.

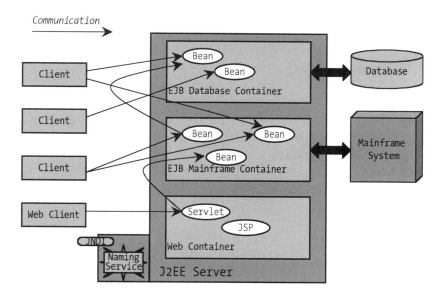

Figure 3-10. An Enterprise JavaBean scenario.

It is possible to extend the functionality of an EJB-based system without difficulty by installing new Enterprise Beans. Under certain conditions new beans can make use of the functionality of already existing beans.

From the viewpoint of the application developer as described in the scenario of Chapter 1 all the secondary problems that arise can be neutralized by the use of Enterprise JavaBeans. EJB was the correct approach to the solution of the problem.

EJB from the Point of View of the Component Paradigm

An additional point of view from which Enterprise JavaBeans can be considered is that of the component paradigm. In the preceding chapters some basic points about this were presented. Two questions then arise:

- Are Enterprise Beans genuine components?

- Do Enterprise JavaBeans fulfill the requirements of the component architecture?

To elucidate these questions we must measure the properties of Enterprise Beans and the EJB architecture against the requirements presented in Chapter 2.

In view of the definition presented in Chapter 2, Enterprise Beans are genuine components. The fundamental characteristic of the standardized interface is given in the form of the home and remote interfaces or the local home and local interfaces. The interface is standardized by the guidelines of the component model of the Enterprise JavaBeans specification. The interface represents a sort of contract to which an Enterprise Bean is compelled to adhere. This interface is independent of the implementation. A bean can be developed and maintained as a single unit. Whether this represents a self-contained functionality depends on the developer. This characteristic of a component cannot be compelled by the specification, but it should serve as a guideline to the developer of an Enterprise Bean.

In order to determine whether the architecture of the Enterprise JavaBeans does justice to the requirements of the component paradigm, we would like to evaluate the various characteristics that we presented in Chapter 2:

- *Independence of the environment*: Enterprise JavaBeans are based completely on the programming language Java. Enterprise Beans can be deployed only in a Java environment. However, via CORBA they can be used in conjunction with other environments. The specification of version 2.1 designates RMI-IIOP as communications protocol, which should ensure compatibility with CORBA.

- *Locational transparency*: The location of a component with a remote interface is fully transparent, since the Enterprise Beans can be located via the naming and directory service as well as RMI, and also can be addressed on remote computers. The specification also requires a producer to include a naming and directory service in the system environment and emphasizes the distributed nature of Enterprise Beans. Locational transparency is not a characteristic of Enterprise Beans with a local interface.

- *Separation of the interface and implementation:* This property is provided to Enterprise JavaBeans through the concept of the home and remote, respectively local home and local remote, interfaces.

- *Self-descriptive interfaces:* In the case of Enterprise JavaBeans it is possible to obtain information about the remote interface(s) of a component. The home object uses the method getEJBMetaData( ) to return an object of type javax.ejb.EJBMetaData (for relevant details see [21]). This object provides, among other things, information about the home and remote interfaces of an Enterprise Bean. Using the Java reflection API (see [4]) it is possible to investigate the interfaces at run time and to program dynamic calls to Enterprise Bean methods. The combination of naming and directory services (JNDI), the metadata interface (javax.ejb.EJBMetaData), and the Java reflection API offers possibilities comparable to those of the interface repository of CORBA (cf. [17]). It is the task of the EJB container to generate for an Enterprise Bean a corresponding implementation class for the metadata interface from the specifications of the deployment descriptor.

- *Problem-free immediate usability (Plug & Play):* At the time of installation of an Enterprise Bean the implementation classes for the home and remote interfaces must be generated and compiled. By means of these an Enterprise Bean component becomes usable (without it having to be altered in the process) by the EJB container of a particular producer. All information that is necessary for the installation process is contained in the bean class itself and in the deployment descriptor (which is a part of the component). The binary independence of the component code of an Enterprise Bean exists to the extent that the components comply with the binary standard defined by the Java programming language. This results is problem-free usability of an Enterprise Bean component in every EJB container.

- *Ability of integration and composition:* This issue is accommodated by a certain role in the EJB process model, the application assembler. The composition of Enterprise Beans into an aggregate is specifically provided for.

Enterprise JavaBeans can be considered a component architecture. It will be interesting to see what extensions and improvements are offered in future versions.

EJB from the Enterprise Point of View

A final point of view is that of Enterprise JavaBeans from the point of view of the Enterprise. In Chapter 2 we defined criteria that a basic technology should satisfy from this viewpoint: economic viability, security, and meeting the enterprise's requirements. It is difficult to give an objective evaluation of a technology according to such global criteria. Nonetheless, we may certainly conclude that Enterprise JavaBeans, on grounds of economic viability as defined in Chapter 2, are certainly of interest to an enterprise, particularly for those businesses that engage in application development (whether internally or for external customers).

In the sections above we have already seen the advantages of such a technology. In the development of enterprise-related logic in Enterprise Beans the developer is freed totally from having to deal with technical system issues. The technological basis has been developed by specialists in this field and conforms to a (quasi) standard. Thus development can be focused directly on the problems of the particular enterprise. The component-oriented point of view enables a greater granularity and thereby makes development more transparent and more easily kept under control. The EJB technology offers all the prerequisites for allowing the application systems to grow with the enterprise (with respect both to greater functionality and to growth in the number of employees).

With respect to security the enterprise is supported not only by the security mechanisms of the specification and the programming language Java. Since Enterprise JavaBeans defines a standard in a certain sense that is already supported by a number of producers, there are relatively few dependencies on a particular application server vendor. It would, however, be desirable to achieve an official standardization of Enterprise JavaBeans through the work of a standardization committee. Nevertheless, an investment in this technology could pay off over a long period of time.

The specification defines many conditions that ensure the fail-safe operation of EJB-based systems. An example is the stringent restrictions on the development of beans. Among other things, this should help to avoid unstable conditions in the system. Another example is the separation of system functionality and enterprise-specific functionality. It benefits reliability and security that the system functionality has been developed by a specialist. A wide deployment of the system among many customers by a responsible developer should lead more rapidly to a higher quality than what could be obtained by in-house development.

As for the needs of enterprises, the EJB specification is directed precisely at those enterprises that develop their own applications or act as a service provider for other enterprises. As a rule, the developers in such enterprises are specialists in particular application areas, but not in the domain of system development. The result is often applications that deal with the technical problems, but cause dissatisfaction through shortcomings in the technological foundations. With the model of Enterprise JavaBeans it is precisely this issue that is dealt with. The demand for a stable basic architecture that offers a convenient component model that can be embedded in the application logic should exist in many areas and in many enterprises. Precisely because applications deployed in businesses are becoming ever more complex, there is ever increasing demand for stable, secure, and flexible basic architectures.

CHAPTER 4
Session Beans

Introduction

A session bean is a business object, since it typically implements a business process. In practice, the functionality of a session bean can constitute, for example, setting up a balance sheet in a bookkeeping system, executing transfer of funds in banking software, or managing a materials supply depot.

Logically, a session bean is viewed as the server-side extension of the client program. A client has exclusive access via the EJB container to a particular instance of a session bean and can use its functionality. The notion of "client" extends also to other beans on a server and client programs on a client computer. For the implementation of its functionality a session bean can use other enterprise beans as well as the services that the EJB container and J2EE Application server provide. (See Figure 4-1.)

When a client uses a session bean, it can execute various actions that lead to changes of state, that is, to changes in the data of enterprise beans. One distinguishes persistent and transient changes of state:

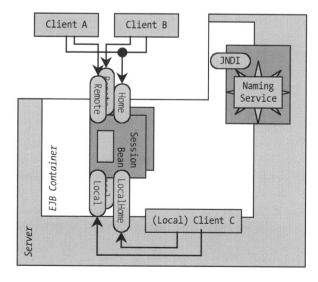

Figure 4-1. Overview of a session bean.

- A persistent change of state remains over multiple sessions of the client. Altered data, for example, can be stored in a database. Session beans themselves do not have a persistent state, but use entity beans for the storage of persistent data (see Chapter 5, on entity beans) or, for example, access a database directly via JDBC.

- A transient change of state lasts only for the duration of a session. The transient state thereby describes the state of the session of the conversation between client and server. Therefore, one speaks here also of a *conversational state*. The transient state is stored partly by the client and partly by the session bean. Therefore, the session bean can also be viewed as a logical extension of the client.

There are two types of session beans: *stateless* session beans and *stateful* session beans. In contrast to the stateful session beans, the stateless session beans do not have a conversational state. This means that no application method of a stateless session bean alters the state of a bean instance.

One must always keep the two types separate, since the EJB container treats them differently in managing bean instances. This affects the programming of methods for state management. These methods are called by the EJB container at run time to inform the bean instance about a state change. In the section on the life cycle of a session bean instance we shall go into the precise differences.

Methods of session beans can be executed in a transaction. This depends on whether the session bean uses explicit transactions or whether the EJB container is instructed by the configuration to guarantee a particular transactional behavior. A transaction guarantees that the corresponding method either is successfully executed or is made completely revocable. Thus there are no inconsistent states in the case of an error. Since the subject of transactions is rather complex, it will be dealt with in detail in Chapter 7.

Concepts

Conversational State

A session bean offers services to its client in the form of methods. As a rule, the client calls a number of methods to achieve its goal. A call to a method can access an available service by writing, for example by changing the data in a database. The altered data are available to all clients and influence the results of subsequent method calls for various beans.

A method call can also itself change the state of the session bean instance itself (that is, its instance variables). The session bean instance is then stateful. The state of a session bean instance can be influenced only by method calls to the corresponding instance.

This state of an instance of a stateful session bean is called the conversational state (Figure 4-2). The EJB specification defines the conversational state as the state of all attributes of a session bean instance including the transitive hull of all objects that are reachable via Java references by the session bean instance. The conversational state is thus constructed out of all attributes and applied resources of the session bean. In practice, the conversational state consists, for example, of attribute values, open resource connections, database connections, references to other beans, and similar resources.

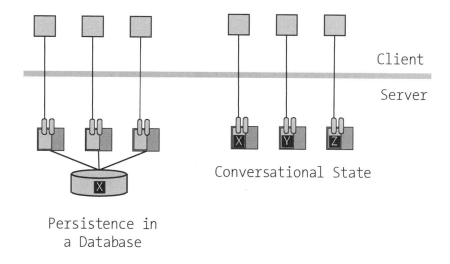

Figure 4-2. Conversational state.

The conversational state remains only for the duration of a session of a client and is exclusively at this client's disposal. For this reason the session bean is understood to be a logical server-side extension of the client.

When a session bean instance stores its state for precisely one client, then each client requires its own bean instance. In order to prevent the unlimited growth of stateful session beans on the server, the EJB container employs a strategy of periodic decommissioning of instances from active storage. This decommissioning is called *passivation*, while a restoration is called *activation*.

During passivation the EJB container writes the state of a stateful session bean to a secondary storage medium (for example, to the hard drive). For this the serialization of Java objects is commonly used, which is part of the language definition of Java itself. This mechanism transforms Java objects into a byte stream, which, for example, can simply be written to a file. The opposite mechanism is called *deserialization* and is used during activation. Here the byte stream is retransformed into Java objects.

With the aid of these mechanisms (which, moreover, can be used only with session beans with a conversational state) the EJB container can work with a limited number of session bean instances in order to conserve available resources. If more bean instances are necessary, then instances that are not immediately needed can be stored. If a stored instance is again needed, then first another bean instance must be removed from active memory. Then the required bean is fetched into active memory. Here the EJB container uses a classical cache procedure. One strategy is to remove the bean instance that has gone unused the longest (LRU = least recently used). The maximum number of bean instances with which the EJB container can work is generally a configurable number.

Yet there is a problem with this mechanism: Not all Java objects can be simply serialized. For example, a socket or database connection cannot be simply written to the hard drive. The Java language definition requires all Java classes whose objects are to be serializable to implement the interface java.io.Serializable. Logically, in the Java class library the only classes that implement the interface are those whose objects are serializable. The EJB specification defines more precisely the conditions that objects of the conversational state of a session bean must satisfy:

- Serializable object;

- Reference to NULL;

- Reference to a remote interface;

- Reference to a home interface;

- Reference to a local interface;

- Reference to a local home interface;

- Reference to the SessionContext;

- Reference to the JNDI naming service of the bean environment;

- Reference to the interface; UserTransaction;

- Reference to a resource factory (to be discused later).

A session bean instance is always notified before its passivation to a secondary storage medium via a call to the method ejbPassivate. The session bean instance must then establish the above-named conditions. This means, for example, that resources and database connections must be closed. To avoid problems in serialization, all references to additional resources must be declared *transient*. If the session bean instance is again brought into active memory, then it will be notified via a call to the method ejbActivate. Then, for example, it can reestablish its resources and database connections and reset all variables.

Stateless and Stateful Session Beans

Session beans can have their own conversational state or be stateless (Figure 4-3). Based on these properties we distinguish two types of session beans:

- Stateless session beans;

- Stateful session beans.

Whenever a stateful session bean is newly generated, its state must be initialized. For this purpose it offers several `create` methods, to which the necessary data are passed as parameters by the client. A stateless session bean does not need to initialize a state. Therefore, it always has only one `create` method without parameters. For each session bean class there is a definition in the deployment descriptor telling which type it belongs to and the methods it offers.

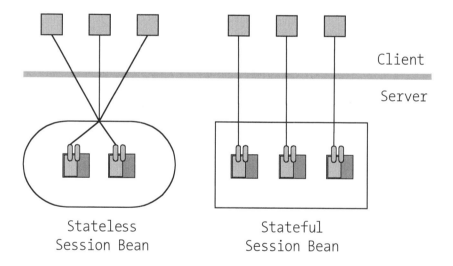

Figure 4-3. Stateful and stateless session beans.

This distinction between the two types helps the EJB container in the management of bean instances. In order to minimize resource requirements and maintain high performance, the EJB container employs management strategies that avoid as far as possible the generation and destruction of Java objects.

An instance of a stateless session bean can be used by the EJB container for another client after each method call. Since these possess no conversational state, the sequential method calls of a client can also be processed by various instances. An instance of a stateless session bean is thus available exclusively for a given client only for the duration of the method call. The EJB container divides the method calls into a pool with a fixed number of bean instances. The number of required bean instances is thus much smaller than the number of parallel client sessions.

In the case of stateful session beans the EJB container has another problem to solve. In order for the conversational state to remain and be available exclusively to a client during a session, each client requires its own session bean instance. Thus each instance of a stateful session bean is always available to only a single client for the duration of a session.

In order to keep the number of bean instances under control even in the case of a very large number of parallel clients, a particular strategy is employed. During activation or passivation a session bean can be removed from active memory and be reloaded at a later time (compare the implementations in the preceding section).

The crucial difference is that activation and passivation are necessary only for stateful session beans. This difference was of great enough significance for the division in the EJB concept into two classes of session beans.

The EJB container can thus work significantly more efficiently with stateless session beans than with stateful session beans. The serialization and deserialization of Java objects is a relatively expensive operation; that is, it requires a great deal of CPU time. Therefore, the implementation of stateless session beans pays off particularly well when there are many parallel clients to serve. A comparison with web servers may be useful here: One of the reasons for the success of the worldwide web is that a web server can work with static web pages in stateless mode and thereby serve many parallel clients.

Due to their higher demand on resources, stateful session beans are sometimes called *heavyweight beans*, while stateless session beans are known as *lightweight beans*.

Stateless session beans are nevertheless suitable for particular applications. Table 4-1 summarizes the differences between stateless and stateful session beans.

Table 4-1. Comparison of stateless and stateful session beans.

Stateless Session Beans	Stateful Session Beans
Have no conversational state	Have a conversational state
Are lightweight	Are heavyweight
Are not activated and passivated	Are activated and passivated
Instance is available to a client for the duration of method calls	Instance is available to a client for the duration of multiple method calls

Session Beans from the Client's Point of View

In dealing with EJB it is important to note the two different points of view: the client's view and the container's view. The client's view is concerned with what functionality is provided and how to interact with beans, while the container's view is more concerned with how the functionality is provided to the client in the most efficient manner.

The client has a very simple view of session beans. The EJB container conceals the mechanisms for managing bean instances from the client. How the client uses a session bean depends greatly on whether the client is located in the same Java process as the session bean.

Local vs. Remote Client View

The *remote client view* is the viewpoint of the client toward a session bean that is located in a different Java process from that of the client itself. The remote client view is the standard case of the client's view of a session bean. The local client view has existed only since version 2.0 of the EJB specification. The remote client view is used by, for example, client applications installed on client computers that use Enterprise Beans of an application server over a network. The remote client view is also used by enterprise beans that in fulfilling their mission use other enterprise beans that are installed on another, remote, application server.

Using the method `create` of the home object (compare in this regard Chapter 3) the client can create new session beans of a particular class. The session bean is available exclusively to that client until it deletes it via a call to the method `remove` on the remote object. As long as the session bean exists the client can call its methods via the remote object. The parameters and return values of the methods that the client calls via the remote object are passed under the call by value paradigm (as a copy). These semantics of a method call are determined by Java RMI, which is the basis of the remote-client-view.

The *local client view* is the viewpoint of the client toward a session bean that is located in the same process as the client itself. This could involve, for example, enterprise beans that in carrying out their mission use other enterprise beans that are installed on the same application server. Another example is that of server-side JMS clients or servlets that perform their services in the same Java process (that is, in the same application server) as the respective session bean.

With the method `create` of the local home object (see in this regard Chapter 3) the client can create new session beans of a particular class. The session bean is available exclusively to that client until it deletes it via a call to the method `remove` on the local object. As long as the session bean exists the client can call its methods via the local object. The parameters and return values of the methods that the client calls via the remote object are passed under the call by reference paradigm. The semantics of a method call are determined by the programming language Java. From the point of view of the client this is the crucial difference from the remote client view.

The bean developer determines whether a session bean is to be used with the local or remote client view. Based on the specification an enterprise bean should support either the local or remote client view. Theoretically, it would be possible for an enterprise bean to support both the local and remote client views. A particular client programs a particular session bean in each case either with respect to the local or remote interface of the session bean. If the client is not located in the same Java process as the enterprise bean, it must use the remote client view. If in this case the session bean offers only a local client view, the client cannot use the session bean. If the client is located in the same Java process as the session bean, then it will use the local client view (provided that the session bean offers it), since run-time efficiency is significantly greater than with the remote client view (there is no RMI overhead). If the session bean supports only the remote client view and the client is located in the same process as the session bean, then the client can nevertheless use the bean.

Stateless and Stateful Session Beans

The client need make no distinction in using stateful or stateless session beans. The client may not even know whether it is dealing with a stateless or stateful session bean.

The client must distinguish four states. These result from the fact that the client does not work directly with the bean instance. The client works with proxy objects of the EJB container (local home and local object or home and remote object) that delegate the respective calls to the actual bean instance:

1. *Nonexistent*: The client has no reference to the remote or local object. From its perspective there thus exists no session bean instance on the server.

2. *Existent and referenced*: The client possesses a valid reference to the remote or local object and can thereby access the session bean instance indirectly.

3. *Nonexistent, but referenced*: This state is important for error handling. After the client has deleted the session bean instance with *remove*, the remote or local object no longer represents a valid reference. If the client nonetheless calls a method on the remote or local object, an exception is triggered, since the EJB container has no available bean instance for this call. The EJB container also deletes bean instances that have not been used for a long time (Timeout) or those for which a system error has occurred. The client then comes into this state automatically.

4. *Existent, but not referenced*: The client deletes its reference to the home or local home object without first executing the method remove. After a certain period of time the EJB container deletes the bean instance (Timeout).

Life Cycle of a Session Bean Instance

As already mentioned, a session bean instance assumes various states during its lifetime. Transitions from one state to another are initiated by the client (e.g., with create and remove method calls) and the EJB container (via the management of its resources). The state transitions are managed exclusively by the EJB container (by calling Callback methods).

In order for the EJB container to be able to manage the state transition of a session bean instance, the bean class must implement the interface javax.ejb.SessionBean. The interface represents a sort of contract between the EJB container and the session bean. The EJB container is under obligation to notify the session bean instance about an impending state transition by a call to the relevant methods in the interface. The bean instance must ensure that its state is compatible with the following state.

The life cycles of stateless and stateful session beans are not the same, and they will be presented in detail later. On the other hand, whether a session bean supports the remote or local client view is immaterial as regards the life cycle. A detailed understanding of the life cycle of a session bean instance is a prerequisite for developing them.

Stateless Session Beans

An instance of a stateless session bean knows only two different states.

- *Nonexistent*: The instance does not exist.

- *Pooled Ready*: The instance exists and is available for method calls.

Figure 4-4 shows the life cycle of a stateless session bean. The figure distinguishes the cases of whether the EJB container or the client effects a state transition.

The EJB container manages the bean instances. If it requires an instance, then it first generates an instance of the corresponding bean class. Then it calls the method setSessionContext and thereby informs the instance of its session context. The session context enables the instance to access its environment (identity and role of the client, transaction context) and also to access the EJB container.

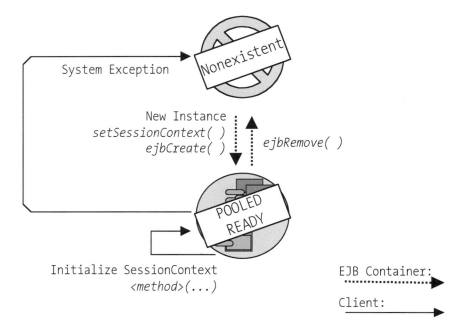

Figure 4-4. Life cycle of a stateless session bean instance.

Then the EJB container calls the method `ejbCreate`, after which the bean instance is in the state `Pooled Ready`. It is kept in readiness by the EJB container in a pool with other instances of its bean class.

The method `ejbCreate` corresponds to the method `create` in the home or local home interface, with which the client can obtain for itself a new instance. A client's call can nonetheless be seen as completely independent of a call of the EJB container. If the client calls `create` for a stateless session bean, it obtains as a result a local or remote object (depending on which client view it uses) that is only a reference to the bean class and not to a concrete bean instance.

For each client call of an application method an arbitrary bean instance is taken from the pool. For the bean instance to be able to execute the method, the correct environment for it must first be created (for example, by the initialization of the session context, the transaction context and the identity of the client are announced to it). Now the EJB container can proceed with the client call to the bean instance. After the method has been executed, the instance is returned to the pool.

By this mechanism it is ensured that a bean instance always executes only one client method call at a time. The EJB container serializes all calls for the bean instance or uses multiple separate instances to handle the requests. The implementation of a bean thus does not have to concern itself with accesses via parallel threads.

An error can occur in the execution of a method. Declared exceptions of the method are simply passed along to the client, and the instance is again taken into the pool. However, if an exception of type `java.lang.RuntimeException` is triggered, which does not have to be declared, then the EJB container experiences a system error. This exception is also passed to the client. The bean instance, however, is not taken up again into the pool, but is removed and discarded.

The EJB container can limit the number of bean instances in the pool. To do this it first calls the method `ejbRemove` on the bean instance to inform the instance of the impending deletion, and then discards the instance. At a later time the garbage collection utility will delete the instance. All commonly used EJB implementations provide the functionality of finely controlling the number of bean instances contained within a pool.

Stateful Session Beans

The life cycle of stateful session beans is more complex than that of stateless session beans. Four states are distinguished:

- *Nonexistent*: The session bean instance does not exist.

- *Ready*: The session bean instance exists and was allocated to a client. It is available for method calls or can be passivated by the EJB container in this state.

- *Ready in TA*: The session bean instance is engaged in a transaction and is waiting for a client method call (see Chapter 7, *Transactions*). The EJB container is not allowed to passivate instances engaged in transactions.

- *Passivated*: The session bean instance was removed temporarily from active memory, but it is still allocated to a client. When the client wishes to execute a method, the EJB container must first reactivate the instance.

Figure 4-5 shows the life cycle of a stateful session bean. A distinction is made as to whether the EJB container or the client is responsible for a state transition.

In contrast to the stateless session beans, the EJB specification does not provide a pool for stateful session beans. The life-cycle of a stateful session bean is tightly coupled to its client.

Whenever the client calls a `create` method on the (local) home object to obtain a new session bean, the EJB container makes available exclusively to the client a new bean instance. The EJB container first generates an instance of the relevant bean class and informs it of the session context. Then the client method call is relayed to the corresponding bean instance `ejbCreate` method. Using parameters this method initializes the state of the bean instance. Then the bean instance is in the state Ready.

If at a later time the client no longer needs the session bean and calls the method remove on the remote or local object, the bean instance is removed from the EJB container. The EJB container calls the method ejbRemove in order to inform it about the impending removal. Then the situation will be as if the bean instance no longer existed, even though the garbage collector will delete the bean instance only at a later point in time.

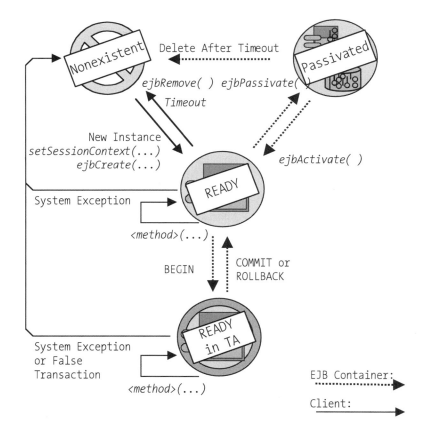

Figure 4-5. Life cycle of a stateful session bean instance.

An individual bean instance is required for each concurrent client that uses a stateful session bean. An EJB container must nevertheless limit the number of bean instances in active memory. Using passivation and activation it has the ability to remove bean instances temporarily from active memory. Before a bean is passivated, the EJB container calls the method ejbPassivate to inform the bean of its impending change of state. Upon activation the bean instance is first reloaded into active memory and then informed of the fact by the method `ejbActivate`.

After the client has obtained a session bean, it can access the bean instance via the remote or local object. The method calls are relayed by the EJB container to the bean instance. All client method calls are serialized by the EJB container. If a `RuntimeException` occurs in a method, then, as with stateless session beans, the bean instance is discarded by the EJB container.

A method can be executed in a transaction. Normally, the EJB container institutes a separate transaction for each method call and terminates it after the method executes (this depends on the configuration of the bean). It is also possible, however not usually recommended, to combine several method calls in a single transaction. This case is covered in the state `Ready in TA`. For technical reasons the EJB container is not able to passivate a bean instance if it is contained in a transaction. In order for the bean to be passivated, the transaction must time out. Transactions are covered in detail in Chapter 7.

The EJB container must also handle the case in which the connection to the client is broken. Here a simple heuristic is employed. If the client has not executed a method call within a certain period of time (`Timeout`), then the session is considered terminated. The EJB container deletes the bean instance, depending on the state, with `ejbRemove` or by deletion of the serialized bean instance.

Programming

Overview

Figure 4-6 provides a complete overview of the classes and interfaces for the case of the remote client view. To the right is the session bean class, and to the left are the interfaces that are also available to the client and are implemented via the home or remote object of the EJB container (see also Chapter 3). The methods in the figure whose names are struck through cannot be sensibly implemented with session beans. They are conceived for entity beans.

The session bean class implements the interface `javax.ejb.SessionBean`. The bean developer implements this class, which realizes the functionality of the session bean. There is no actual constructor and no `finalize` method in the bean class. If a constructor is defined, it must be declared `public`, and it is not permitted to have any parameters (default constructor) Constructors are generally not used in implementing EJB components.

The home and remote objects belong to the container classes and are generated (cf. Chapter 3). The bean developer defines the associated home and remote interfaces. The bean's home interface inherits from the interface `javax.ejb.EJBHome`, while the remote interface inherits from `javax.ejb.EJBObject`.

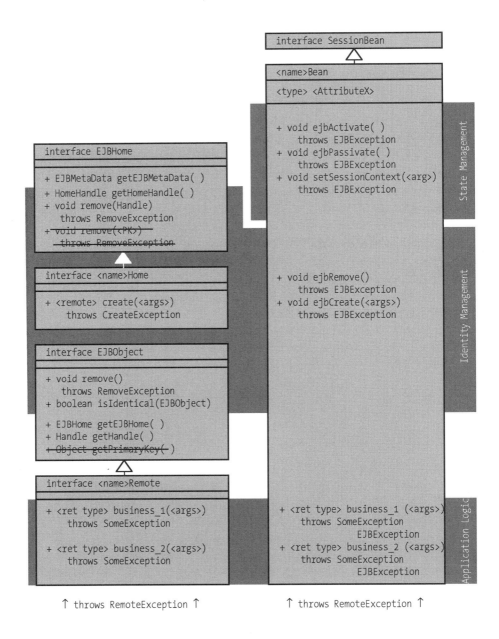

Figure 4-6. Interfaces of a session bean with remote client view.

Figure 4-7 provides a complete overview of the classes and interfaces for the case of the local client view. To the right is the session bean class, and to the left are the interfaces used by the client and implemented via the local home and local objects of the EJB container (see also Chapter 3). The struck-through methods in the figure cannot be used sensibly with session beans. They are conceived for entity beans. In the case of the local client view the session bean class is identical to that of the remote client view.

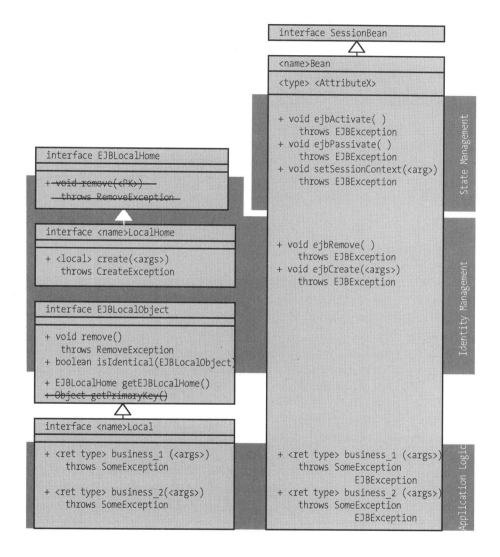

Figure 4-7. Interfaces of a session bean with local client view.

The local home and local objects belong to the container classes and are generated (cf. Chapter 3). The bean developer defines the associated local home and local interfaces. The bean's local home interface inherits from the interface javax.ejb.EJBLocalHome. The local interface inherits from the interface javax.ejb.EJBLocalObject.

A session bean could implement the remote as well as the local client view. However, according to the specification an enterprise bean should implement either the local *or* the remote client view; not both.

All the methods of the bean class as well as the home and remote interfaces can be divided into three groups:

- state management;

- identity management;

- application logic.

The following subsections describe the individual methods in these groups. In addition, the session context and the interfaces that the client program uses will be introduced. Those interested in a more rapid plunge into the subject may skip the following descriptions on a first reading. The program examples for session beans give the reader a rapid entry into practical programming.

State Management

In Figures 4-6 and 4-7 the methods for state management are listed first. These methods are called by the EJB container to notify the bean instance of a state transition. These methods implement the logic that prepares the bean instance for the new state.

Both the actions of the client and the internal processes of the EJB container can trigger the state transition that leads to these method calls. The client, however, does not obtain direct access to these methods.

void setSessionContext(*SessionContext ctx*)

The method setSessionContext is called by the EJB container after the creation of the bean instance. The EJB container transfers to the session bean its SessionContext. The implementation of this method has the task of storing the SessionContext. Further initialization steps should normally not be taken here. The passed object of the class SessionContext defines the environment of the bean instance (see also the later section on session context).

void ejbPassivate( )

The method ejbPassivate is called by the EJB container before it passivates a stateful session bean instance. Stateless session beans do not need this method and leave the implementation empty, since these methods are invoked by the EJB container only for stateful session beans.

The method is used to bring the bean instance into a state suitable for passivation. The additional resources that were used by the bean instance must be released. For example, network or database connections must be closed. All references and additional resources (other enterprise beans, network connections, database connections, etc.) should be declared transient by the developer. If this has not occurred, these references must be initialized to null. The preceding section, on the conversational state, gives the precise conditions that a bean must satisfy for passivation.

Note that the method ejbPassivate is not executed in a transaction. The EJB container ensures that no bean instance within a transaction is passivated. Thus at the time of passivation the conversational state of the bean instance receives no data that need to be protected with a transaction. The passivation must thereby also be possible without transactions.

If an error occurs in this method that prevents the passivation of the bean instance, then the exception javax.ejb.EJBException should be triggered (with EJB 1.0 the exception java.rmi.RemoteException is still used). The EJB container considers this exception a system error and destroys the bean instance.

void ejbActivate( )

The method ejbActivate is the complement of ejbPassivate. The EJB container calls this method after it has reloaded a passivated bean instance into active memory.

This method is used to reserve additional resources that were released during passivation. For example, network or database connections can be reopened.

As with ejbPassivate, with ejbActivate no transaction is available. Error handling is analogous to that of ejbPassivate.

Identity Management

The methods for identity management constitute the second group in the figures. They enable the generation and deletion of session bean identities. These methods are again located in the local home, local, home, and remote home interfaces and are available to the client even before it has a bean instance.

void ejbCreate(...)

The client obtains a bean instance through a create call in the home or local home interface. Stateful session beans can offer several create methods, which are distinguished by their signatures. Stateless sessions beans have only one create method, without parameters. After the EJB container has generated a new bean instance, it calls its ejbCreate method. In the case of stateful session beans it relays the client's create call to the bean's ejbCreate method with the appropriate signature.

The bean developer defines the create methods in the home and local home interfaces and implements the ejbCreate methods in the bean class. The signatures of the methods in the bean class and in the home and local home interfaces must be identical. The implementation of the ejbCreate methods has the task of initializing the bean instance. A stateful session bean instance initializes the conversational state using parameters.

The methods are not part of the interface javax.ejb.SessionBean, since the signatures differ for each bean class. Each method is announced to the EJB container in the deployment descriptor.

void ejbRemove()

The client gives the order to delete a session bean identity by a call to the method remove in the remote or local interface. If it is working with a Handle (see the later subsection on the client), it can also use the method remove(Handle) in the home interface (remote client view only). The method remove(Object) in the home interface is reserved for entity beans and cannot be used by session beans.

In the case of stateful session beans a client call by the EJB container is relayed to the method ejbRemove of the relevant bean instance. In the case of stateless session beans the EJB container is not directly ordered by the client to call the method ejbRemove.

The method remove is defined in javax.ejb.EJBObject and javax.ejb.EJBLocalObject; the bean developer implements ejbRemove in the bean class. The implementation of ejbRemove releases reserved resources. After a call to the method the bean instance is deleted.

The method `ejbRemove` can be called by the EJB container with a transaction. The associated transaction attribute in the deployment descriptor defines the behavior of the EJB container (see Chapter 7 on transactions).

Application Logic

The third group in the figure is that of the methods for the application logic, which are also found in the remote and local interfaces. These methods are implemented in the bean class by the bean developer. The definition in the bean class has the same signature as the definition in the remote or local interface.

The EJB container controls all calls to the methods of a bean. It relays the client calls to the relevant methods of the bean class. The client never accesses the bean instance directly. The transaction attributes in the deployment descriptor define the transaction context in which the methods are executed.

In these methods the bean developer implements the actual logic of the session bean. In contrast, all previously discussed methods fulfill only management tasks.

If an irremediable error occurs in the application logic, a `java.ejb.EJBException` must be triggered. The EJB container considers this a system error and destroys the bean instance.

The Session Context

Every session bean instance has an object of the class `javax.ejb.SessionContext` that is made available to it by the EJB container in the method `setSessionContext`. The session context defines the environment of the bean instance. The session bean instance uses the transmitted session context for its entire lifetime. The EJB container can change the session context of a bean instance and thereby allocate to it an altered environment. If, for example, various clients use an instance of a stateless session bean one after the other, the EJB container sets the identity of the client in the session context before each method call.

The session context enables the bean instance to access the home object, the identity of the client, and the active transaction. In what follows the most important methods from the interface `SessionContext` will be presented. A complete description can be obtained in the EJB specification (see [21]).

EJBHome getEJBHome( )

The method `getEJBHome` enables the bean instance to access its own home interface. The data type of the return value must be converted into the special home interface of the bean class. This method triggers an exception of type java.lang.IllegalStateException if the session bean has no home interface (but instead a local home interface).

EJBLocalHome getEJBLocalHome( )

The method getEJBLocalHome enables the bean instance to access its own local home interface. The data type of the return value must be converted to the special local home interface of the bean class. This method triggers an exception of type java.lang.IllegalStateException if the session bean has no local home interface (but instead a home interface).

void setRollbackOnly( )

The method setRollbackOnly serves to control transactions (see Chapter 7). A bean instance uses this method in the case of an error to ensure that the active transaction is terminated with a rollback.

boolean getRollbackOnly( )

The method getRollbackOnly is the "read" complement to the method setRollbackOnly. With getRollbackOnly it can be checked whether it is still possible to terminate the active transaction with Commit.

UserTransaction getUserTransaction( )

Normally, the EJB container takes control over transactions. The method getUserTransaction requires a bean instance only if it wishes to take over the transaction control itself. The return value of the method is an object of the class transaction.UserTransaction, which enables access to the transaction context (see Chapter 7).

Principal getCallerPrincipal( )

The method getCallerPrincipal permits a bean instance to determine which user has announced itself to the client. The return value is an object of the class java.security.Principal (see Chapter 8).

```
boolean isCallerInRole(java.lang.String roleName)
```

With this method a check is made as to whether the announced user has a particular role in the security concept. The possible roles are defined in the deployment descriptor (see Chapter 8).

The Client

Naming Service as Object Store

A naming service manages name–value pairs in a namespace. Each name in the namespace is unique and identifies a particular value. The EJB concept uses the naming service for management of the home object and other resources. The home objects is stored as a value and entered under the name of the bean in the naming service (this holds for the local and remote client views). Each client can thereby request the bean's home object from the naming service if it knows the name of the bean. It then receives indirect access to the bean via the home object.

For access by Java to the naming service, JNDI (Java Naming and Directory Interface) is available. The interface was defined by Sun Microsystems and has belonged to the Java development kit (JDK) since JDK version 1.2.

In practice, a separate naming service, addressed via JNDI, is integrated into many application servers. The use of an external naming service can nonetheless also be a good idea. JNDI supports the following protocols:

- RMI Registry (Java Remote Method Invocation);

- LDAP (Lightweight Directory Access Protocol);

- COS (CORBA Services Naming Service).

To obtain access to JNDI, the class `javax.naming.InitialContext` is used. This class implements the interface `javax.naming.Context`. Every instance of this class has a preinitialized namespace, which is initialized with data from two sources:

- In the constructor a hash table object can be passed. Its name–value pairs are transferred into the namespace of `InitialContext`.

- The file `jndi.properties` in the class path likewise contains name–value pairs. These are also taken in.

Certain name–value pairs from the hash table object that is passed in the constructor are not simply taken into the namespace, but serve for the initialization of JNDI. The interface `Context` defines the needed constants that define the names that are used:

- INITIAL_CONTEXT_FACTORY: The name of a class must always be stored under this name, which serves as a factory (cf. design pattern factory in [5]) for a name service. The value required here must be provided by every creator of an EJB container or naming service.

- PROVIDER_URL: Here a URL is defined for the naming service. The URL is a string that contains the network name of the server and the port that is used. The creator of the naming service must provide precise information on the form of this URL.

- SECURITY_PRINCIPAL: Here the user name for the naming service is defined. Depending on the configuration of the naming service it can also be possible to work without user names.

- SECURITY_CREDENTIALS: Here the associated password to the declared user name is defined.

The following import instructions are necessary in our case for us to be able to use JNDI:

```
import javax.naming.Context;
import javax.naming.InitialContext;
```

Listing 4-1 shows a method that a client program could use for the initialization of InitialContext. The boldface strings in the listing should be replaced by the appropriate values, depending on the server used.

Listing 4-1. getInitialContext: *Initialization for JNDI access.*

```
final static String ctxUser = "CtxUser";
final static String ctxPassword = "CtxPassword";
final static String ctxFactory = "CtxFactory";
final static String ctxUrl = "CtxURL";
/**
 * Fetches and initializes InitialContext.
 * The method uses the
 * following variables:
 * ctxUser, ctxPassword,
 * ctxFactory, ctxUrl
 *
 *@return Context - InitialContext Object
 *@exception javax.naming.NamingException
 */
static public Context getInitialContext()
  throws javax.naming.NamingException
```

```
{
  Hashtable p = new Hashtable();

  p.put(
    Context.INITIAL_CONTEXT_FACTORY,
    ctxFactory);
  p.put(
    Context.PROVIDER_URL,
    ctxUrl);
//This part is optional
  p.put(
    Context.SECURITY_PRINCIPAL,
    ctxUser);
    p.put(
      Context.SECURITY_CREDENTIALS,
      ctxPassword);
  //This part is optional

    return new InitialContext(p);
}
```

Access to a Session Bean

With the aid of the naming service a client obtains access to the home or local home interface. With a call to the method lookup on a Context object it passes the bean's unique JNDI name as parameter and receives as return value the implementation of the home or local home interface. The JNDI name of an enterprise bean is set at deployment, and the allocation of the JNDI name is creator-specific.

The return value of the method lookup has the data type Object. In the case of the local client view the return value can be converted with type casting into the type of the local home interface. With the remote client view this cannot easily be done. Since version 1.1 of the EJB specification introduced support for RMI-IIOP, an extra level of conversion and casting of remote objects has been required for complete compatibility between all systems.

For the proper conversion of data types there is the method narrow of the class javax.rmi.PortableRemoteObject. This class has belonged to the standard language since Java version 1.3. For older versions of Java one can fall back on the RMI-IIOP mapping. The process for data type conversion of the home interface is always the same, and this conversion is demonstrated in Listing 4-2. After the home interface is recognized, the client can create a new bean, and it receives as return value the bean's remote interface. The client can work with the bean via the remote interface almost as if it were a local object and were not being executed on the server. After the bean has been used, it must be deleted (remove).

Listing 4-2. Client access to a session bean (remote client view).

```
  ...
javax.naming.Context ctx;
String beanName = "BeanName";
HomeInterfaceClass home = null;
RemoteInterfaceClass bean = null;
try {
  ctx = getInitialContext();
  home = (HomeInterfaceClass)
    javax.rmi.PortableRemoteObject.narrow(
    ctx.lookup(beanName),
    HomeInterfaceClass.class);
  bean = home.create(...);
  ...
  bean.remove();
}
catch(javax.ejb.CreateException e){
  System.out.println(
    "Bean generation error");
}
catch(javax.ejb.RemoveException e){
  System.out.println(
    "Bean removal error");
}
catch(javax.naming.NamingException e) {
  System.out.println(
    "Name service reports an error");
}
catch(RemoteException e) {
  System.out.println(
    "Problem with the network connection");
}
...
```

Listing 4-3 demonstrates the use of a session bean with the local client view.

Listing 4-3. Client access to a session bean (local client view).

```
  ...
javax.naming.Context ctx;
String beanName = "LocalBeanName";
LocalHomeInterfaceClass home = null;
```

```
LocalBeanInterfaceClass bean = null;
try {
  ctx = getInitialContext();
  home = (LocalHomeInterfaceClass)
              ctx.lookup(beanName);
  bean = home.create(...);
  ...
  bean.remove ();
}
catch(javax.ejb.CreateException e){
  System.out.println(
    "Bean generation error");
}
catch(javax.ejb.RemoveException e){
  System.out.println(
    "Bean removal error");
}
catch(javax.naming.NamingException e) {
  System.out.println(
    "Name service reports an error");
}
...
```

The Identity of a Session Bean

The client uses the identity of session beans only to determine whether two references are to point to the same or different bean instances. The uses of stateless and stateful session beans are different here, and they will be described in what follows.

Every stateful session bean has its own identity, which is an ID that the EJB container uses for internal management of instances. The ID itself is not accessible by the client. For comparing session beans the EJB container makes available to the client an implementation of the method isIdentical, which is defined in the interface javax.ejb.EJBObject or javax.ejb.EJBLocalObject as follows:

```
public abstract boolean isIdentical (EJBObject obj);
```

or

```
public abstract boolean isIdentical (EJBLocalObject obj);
```

Listing 4-4 demonstrates the use of the method for stateful session beans in the case that the session bean has a remote interface. The use of the method isIdentical for local interfaces is similar.

Listing 4-4. Comparison of identities of stateful session beans.

```
// Fetch the HomeObject using JNDI
StatefulBeanHome homeObject = ...;

// generate two
// stateful session beans
StatefulBean sfb1 = homeObject.create(...);
StatefulBean sfb2 = homeObject.create(...);

// comparison of identities
if (sfb1.isIdentical(sfb1)) {
// This comparison yields "true".
}
if (sfb1.isIdentical(sfb2)) {
// This comparison yields "false".
}
```

In contrast to stateful beans, individual instances of a stateless session bean are not distinguished by a conversational state. The EJB container views all instances of a stateless session bean that have the same home or local home interface as equivalent, since they are interchangeable. Therefore, all instances of a stateless session bean class have a common identity. Listing 4-5 clarifies this relationship for the case that the session bean has a remote interface. Here, too, the application in the case of local interface is similar.

Listing 4-5. Comparison of identities of stateless session beans.

```
//Fetch the HomeObject using JNDI
StatelessBeanHome homeObject = ...;

// Create two stateless session beans
StatelessBean slb1 = homeObject.create(...);
StatelessBean slb2 = homeObject.create(...);

// Compare identities
if (slb1.isIdentical(slb1)) {
// This comparison yields "true".
}
if (slb1.isIdentical(slb2)) {
// This comparison yields "true".
}
```

Handles

Handles are of relevance only in the case of the remote client view. They are deployed when a reference to the home or remote interface is necessary that can also be used externally to the client process. Handles can be sent or stored beyond the lifetime of the client. A handle can be understood as a serializable reference to a remote or home object. The existence of a handle object does not, however, influence the life cycle of the bean instance. When the bean instance is deleted (under the control of the client or after a timeout) the handle object becomes invalid.

To create a handle every remote interface possesses a method getHandle, which returns a handle object to the remote interface of this bean instance (see Listing 4-6). The corresponding method in the case of a home object is getHomeHandle. Handle objects have for their part a method getEJBObject, whose return value is the bound remote object of the bean.

Listing 4-6. Use of a remote handle.

```
...
try{
  javax.ejb.Handle handle;

  // get Handle
  Handle handle = remote.getHandle();

// get Remote-Object with handle
  RemoteClass remote = (RemoteClass)
    javax.rmi.PortableRemoteObject.narrow(
    handle.getEJBObject(),
    RemoteClass.class);
}catch(RemoteException e){
  // cannot get handle
}
...
```

However, the EJB container cannot take into account the existence of a handle in managing the bean instances. After a configured time interval has elapsed (timeout) every session bean is deleted by the EJB container. The attempt to access a deleted instance leads to a RemoteException.

The Bean's Environment

A bean is always executed in a defined environment. All bean instances of a class that have the same home or local home interface have the same environment. The environment of a bean consists of the following components:

- Environment variables for configuration values;

- References to other bean classes;

- Resources of the EJB container;

- Administered objects.

The bean developer determines what properties the environment of the bean will have. He determines which configuration parameters the bean will have, with what other beans it will work, and what EJB container resources it will use. On this basis the application assembler and the deployer define the concrete run-time environment. They determine the values for the configuration, select the bean classes for the references, and configure the available services.

At run time the EJB container provides the bean instance with its environment in a naming service. Among the defined names the bean instance finds the individual components of its environment. The process is comparable with the client's access to JNDI. The EJB container provides the bean with the suitable InitialContext, so that it can access its own environment.

The Enterprise Edition of Java, version 2 (J2EE) suggests a convention for naming the various services in the naming service. The following names should be used, since version 1.1, by EJB-conforming servers:

- java:comp/env/ — Environment variables;

- java:comp/env/ejb — References to other bean classes;

- java:comp/env/jdbc — Access to JDBC databases;

- java:comp/env/jms — Access to Java messaging service topics and queues;

- java:comp/env/mail — Access to JavaMail resources;

- java:comp/env/url — Access to web servers and related services.

Environment Variables

The bean developer can provide for a later configuration of a bean. To this end environment variables (description, name of the variable, data type) are defined, to which the application assembler or deployer must assign values (value). Only certain simple data types are allowed: String, Integer, Boolean,

Double, Byte, Short, Long, Float. The data type must be completely specified in the deployment descriptor (see Listing 4-7).

Listing 4-7. Schematic deployment descriptor with the definition of an environment variable.

```
...
<enterprise-beans>
  <session>
    ...
    <env-entry>
      <description>
        description
      </description>
      <env-entry-name>
        name
      </env-entry-name>
      <env-entry-type>
        data type
      </env-entry-type>
      <env-entry-value>
        value
      </env-entry-value>
      ...
    </env-entry>
  </session>
</enterprise-beans>
...
```

At run time a bean instance can access its environment variables via JNDI (see Listing 4-8). The variable can be found under its name in the path `java:comp/env/` (see Listing 4-8).

Listing 4-8. Schematic of selected environment variables.

```
javax.naming.Context beanCtx =
  new javax.naming.InitialContext();
data type something = (data type)
  beanCtx.lookup("java:comp/env/name");
```

References

A bean has the option of using other beans. With EJB version 1.1 the management of these dependencies was improved, and EJB version 2.0 further strengthened the use of this new concept. The bean developer addresses other beans only with a logical name. He defines all references to other beans in the deployment descriptor (description, reference name, bean type: session or entity).

Only later does the application assembler define which bean will actually be used. For this he extends the definition in the deployment descriptor. He names the referenced bean (ejb-link). Here the name of the bean in the deployment descriptor (as in ejb-name) is used. If a bean in another deployment descriptor is referred to, then here is given the path and name of this deployment descriptor, followed by the # symbol and the name of the bean (as in ejb-name). Alas, we must state here that the procedure that we have described is not followed with the same degree of punctiliousness by all producers of EJB containers, and sometimes proprietary interfaces must be used.

Listing 4-9 shows the definitions in the deployment descriptor of the bean provider and application assembler for a reference to a bean with remote interface. Listing 4-10 shows analogously the definitions for a reference to a bean with local interface.

Listing 4-9. Schematic deployment descriptor with reference to another bean (remote interface).

```
...
<enterprise-beans>
  <session>
    ...
    <ejb-ref>
      <description>
        description
      </description>
      <ejb-ref-name>
        ejb/reference name
      </ejb-ref-name>
      <ejb-ref-type>
        session or entity
      </ejb-ref-type>
      <home>
        HomeInterface
      </home>
      <remote>
```

```
            RemoteInterface
        </remote>
        <ejb-link>
            name of the referenced bean
        </ejb-link>
      </ejb-ref>
      ...
    </session>
  </enterprise-beans>
...
```

Listing 4-10. Schematic deployment descriptor with reference to another bean (local interface).

```
...
<enterprise-beans>
  <session>
      ...
    <ejb-local-ref>
      <description>
          description
      </description>
      <ejb-ref-name>
          ejb/reference name
      </ejb-ref-name>
      <ejb-ref-type>
          session or entity
      </ejb-ref-type>
      <local-home>
          LocalHomeInterface
      </local-home>
      <local>
          LocalInterface
      </local>
      <ejb-link>
          name of the referenced bean
      </ejb-link>
    </ejb-local-ref>
      ...
  </session>
</enterprise-beans>
...
```

At run time the bean instance can access the referenced beans via JNDI. The referenced bean's home or local home interface can be found under its logical name in the path `java:comp/env/ejb`. Listing 4-11 clarifies this relationship using a reference to a bean with remote interface. The modus operandi with a reference to a bean with local interface is analogous; in such a case use of the method `narrow` can be avoided.

Listing 4-11. Schematic use of reference to another bean.

```
...
javax.naming.Context beanCtx =
  new javax.naming.InitialContext();
Object temp = beanCtx.lookup(
  "java:comp/env/ejb/reference name");
HomeInterface home = (HomeInterface)
  javax.rmi.PortableRemoteObject.narrow(
  temp, HomeInterface.class);
...
```

Resources

The EJB container offers access to various resources as services. For each resource it provides a *resource factory*, with the help of which the bean obtains access to the service. To clarify the mechanisms we shall explain the use of a JDBC database.

A bean has the ability to address a database directly. So that a bean can be used in a variety of applications, since version 1.1 a flexible configuration has been provided for. The bean developer defines only one logical name for the database in the deployment descriptor (*name, description, security strategy: application* or *container*). Moreover, the developer can specify (via the optional element `res-sharing-scope`) whether connections to the database from this resource can be shared with other enterprise beans.

The deployer uses tools of the EJB container to determine later the actual database, which is allocated in the reference in Listing 4-12.

Listing 4-12. Schematic deployment descriptor with reference to a JDBC database.

```
...
<enterprise-beans>
  <session>
    ...
    <resource-ref>
      <description>
```

```
      description
    </description>
    <res-ref-name>
      jdbc/reference name
    </res-ref-name>
    <res-type>
      javax.sql.DataSource
    </res-type>
    <res-auth>
      Application or Container
    </res-auth>
    <res-sharing-scope>
      Shareable or Unshareable
    </res-sharing-scope>
  </resource-ref>
    ...
  </session>
</enterprise-beans>
...
```

If the application server also manages additional resources with JNDI, then additionally, only the logical name must be mapped to the correct JNDI name. Listing 4-13 shows what an application server might look like in this configuration language.

Listing 4-13. Mapping the logical name to the JNDI name of the resource.

```
<reference-descriptor>
  <resource-description>
    <res-ref-name>
      jdbc/reference name
    </res-ref-name>
    <jndi-name>
      JNDI name: Database
    </jndi-name>
  </resource-description>
</reference-descriptor>
```

At run time the bean can obtain access to the referenced JDBC database via JNDI. The resource factory can be found under its defined logical name in the path java:comp/env/jdbc. The name definition in the deployment descriptor is relative to java:com/env, the environment of the bean. The resource factory is an object of the class javax.sql.DataSource. This class must be present on every

EJB-conforming server that supports version 1.1 or 2.0/2.1. It is also a part of J2EE or available with the optional extension to JDBC 2.0. See Listing 4-14.

Listing 4-14. Schematic use of a reference to a JDBC database.

```
javax.naming.Context beanCtx =
  new javax.naming.InitialContext();
javax.sql.DataSource ds =
  (javax.sql.DataSource)
  beanCtx.lookup(
  "java:comp/env/jdbc/reference name");
java.sql.Connection con =
  ds.getConnection();
```

Administered Objects

Since version 2.0 there has been the possibility of entering *administered objects* in the deployment descriptor. Administered objects are such items as JMS topics or JMS queues. If an enterprise bean uses JMS (Java Message Service) for a purpose such as sending information about the topic *event topic*, then it needs access to a topic factory and to the topic being addressed. The topic factory is a resource factory, and the topic is an *administered object.* Listing 4-15 shows how such an entry is to be made in the deployment descriptor. Chapter 6 deals extensively with this set of topics in relation to the Java message service and explains the meaning of the terms *topic* and *topic factory* and how these things are used.

Listing 4-15. Use of a reference to administered objects.

```
...
<enterprise-beans>
  <session>
    ...
    <resource-ref>
      <description>
        description
      </description>
      <res-ref-name>
        jdbc/TopicFactory
      </res-ref-name>
      <res-type>
```

```
        javax.jms.TopicConnectionFactory
      </res-type>
      <res-auth>
        Container
      </res-auth>
    </resource-ref>
    <resource-env-ref>
      <resource-env-ref-name>
        jms/Event Topic
      </resource-env-ref-name>
      <resource-env-ref-type>
        javax.jms.Topic
      </resource-env-ref-type>
    </resource-env-ref>
  </session>
  ...
</enterprise-beans>
...
```

Examples

This section should give the reader easy access to programming session beans. We shall present two simple examples. The first demonstrates the implementation of a stateless session bean. The second presents a stateful session bean.

Both examples use JDBC (Java database connectivity) for access to a database. JDBC is not the main focus of this book. In the following examples the program code for database access is presented only in brief. For a rapid introduction to JDBC we recommend the tutorial from Sun Microsystems [22].

The following examples should also run under EJB 1.1 without any changes. To run them under EJB 1.0, certain changes will be necessary:

- In the bean class, instead of java.ejb.EJBException, java.rmi.RemoteException should be used to announce a system error.

- EJB 1.0 does not understand the concept of resource factory reference. Therefore, the database connection must be opened directly using the correct database driver.

- The deployment descriptor of EJB 1.0 consists of serialized objects and not of XML. Changes to account for this are necessary.

Stateless Session Beans

Overview

We are going to develop a simple session bean step by step. As our example we have chosen to perform a conversion between the euro and other currencies. The symbolic name of the bean is EuroExchangeSL (the "SL" in the name stands for "stateless," which seems appropriate for a transnational currency).

The bean offers a service on the server that performs the calculation with the aid of a conversion table. The table of exchange rates resides in a database. For buying and selling currencies two different exchange rates are used. The bean itself will not possess a conversational state. With each query it accesses the exchange table in the database.

First, we will define the home and remote interfaces. We will not present an additional implementation for the local interface, since the differences in programming are very slight. At the relevant points we will explain the differences. Next, we shall prepare the database and implement the bean class itself. Then we shall see to the deployment descriptor. Finally, we develop a simple client to test the bean.

Interfaces

To establish the bean's functionality we first define the interfaces that will be available to the client. Often, the program code for the home and remote interfaces with extensive commenting represents a sufficient specification of the bean.

The home and remote interfaces will be used on the client computer, and almost all the method calls will be relayed over the network to the server. Therefore, every method in these interfaces can trigger a RemoteException. The appearance of this exception signals the client that there is a network problem or a system error on the server.

The home interface inherits from the interface javax.ejb.EJBHome. In addition to the inherited methods, session beans define only create methods. In the case of stateless session beans there always exists only one create method without parameters. Every create method declares javax.ejb.CreateException in addition to java.rmi.RemoteException (Listing 4-16).

Listing 4-16. The home interface of the stateless session bean EuroExchangeSL.

```
package ejb.exchangeSL;
import java.rmi.RemoteException;
import javax.ejb.CreateException;
import javax.ejb.EJBHome;
public interface EuroExchangeHome extends EJBHome {
    public EuroExchange create()
        throws RemoteException, CreateException;
}
```

If the session bean were to use a local interface, then EuroExchangeHome (see Listing 4-16) would inherit from EJBLocalHome instead of from EJBHome. Since communication with the session bean would take place in the same Java process, it would also be the case that the exception RemoteException would not be declared in any method.

The remote interface (see Listing 4-17) defines the methods of the application logic that the client can access. Our bean has two methods for converting currencies. The method changeFromEuro converts euros into other currencies, while the method changeToEuro converts in the other direction.

There is also a method setExchangeRate, with whose help new exchange rates can be brought into the table. To keep our example simple, we will not implement a full-fledged management system for exchange rates. This method should merely provide a simple way to test the bean.

Listing 4-17. Remote interface of the stateless session bean EuroExchangeSL.

```
package ejb.exchangeSL;
import java.rmi.RemoteException;
import javax.ejb.EJBObject;
public interface EuroExchange extends EJBObject {
    public float changeFromEuro(String currency, float amount)
        throws RemoteException;
    public float changeToEuro(String currency, float amount)
        throws RemoteException;
    public void setExchangeRate(String currency, float euro, float foreignCurr)
        throws RemoteException;
}
```

If the session bean were to use a local interface, then EuroExchange would inherit from EJBLocalObject instead of from EJBObject. Since communication with the session bean would take place in the same Java process, the exception RemoteException would not be declared in any method.

The Database

Our example accesses a database using JDBC. The database contains the table with exchange rates. The table is simply kept there and is generated, for example, with the SQL commands of Listing 4-18.

Listing 4-18. SQL commands for the exchange rate table.

```
CREATE TABLE EURO_EXCHANGE
(CURRENCY CHAR(10) NOT NULL,
 EURO REAL ,
 FOREIGNCURR REAL )
ALTER TABLE EURO_EXCHANGE ADD CONSTRAINT
 EURO_PRIM PRIMARY KEY (CURRENCY)
```

The Enterprise Bean

For the implementation of the bean class we use interfaces, classes, and exceptions from EJB. Therefore, we shall import parts of the ejb package. The use of the naming service requires the naming package. In accessing the database JDBC is used, for which the importation of parts of the sql package is required. In addition, we use the class DataSource from the package javax.sql as resource factory for database connections. The following list shows the necessary import instructions for implementing the bean class:

```
import java.sql.Connection;
import java.sql.PreparedStatement;
import java.sql.ResultSet;
import java.sql.SQLException;
import javax.ejb.CreateException;
import javax.ejb.EJBException;
import javax.ejb.SessionBean;
import javax.ejb.SessionContext;
import javax.naming.Context;
import javax.naming.InitialContext;
import javax.naming.NamingException;
import javax.sql.DataSource;
```

Since we are writing a session bean, our bean class implements the interface `javax.ejb.SessionBean`. Every method from the interface must be implemented in the bean class. All bean classes must be `public` and may not define a `finalize` method. The name of the bean class does not have to correspond to the name under which it appears in the naming service.

A state of the session bean is kept in instance variables, which are initialized upon the generation of an instance. This is a purely technical state, which does not relay the state of a client session, as is possible in the case of stateful session beans (see Listing 4-19). The context of the bean is placed in `beanCtx`, and in `dataSource` an object of the class `javax.sql.DataSource`, which relates to a resource factory for database connections to a particular database. The name of this resource factory is stored in the constant `dbRef`.

Listing 4-19. Class definition for `EuroExchangeBean`.

```
public class EuroExchangeBean implements SessionBean {
    public static final String dbRef = "java:comp/env/jdbc/EuroDB";
    private SessionContext beanCtx = null;
    private DataSource dataSource = null;
    ...
}
```

First we look at the creation of a bean instance. The EJB container calls the method `ejbCreate` for each new bean instance. In the case of a stateless session bean the method `ejbCreate` has the task of initializing the bean instance. The bean instance reserves resources for itself that are necessary for its work. We mention once again that a stateless bean instance has no conversational state and can be used in turn by various clients. The initialization of a stateless session bean is therefore restricted to resources shared by all clients.

In our example (see Listing 4-20) the initial context of the naming service is created. Then the resource factory for the required database is read from the naming service, which is retained for the entire lifetime of the bean.

Listing 4-20. `EuroExchangeBean.ejbCreate()`.

```
...
    public void ejbCreate()
        throws CreateException
    {
        try {
            Context c = new InitialContext();
```

```
            this.dataSource = (DataSource)c.lookup(dbRef);
        } catch(NamingException ex) {
            String msg = "Cannot get Resource-Factory:"
                            + ex.getMessage();
            throw new CreateException(msg);
        }
    }
...
```

The counterpart to the method `ejbCreate` is the method `ejbRemove` (see Listing 4-21). The EJB container calls this method to let it know of its impending destruction. In this method it must be ensured that all resources that the bean instance uses are released. In our example the reference to the resource factory that was created in the method `ejbCreate` is released.

Listing 4-21. `EuroExchangeBean.ejbRemove()`.

```
...
    public void ejbRemove() {
        this.dataSource = null;
    }
...
```

The simple example that we are presenting here does not use the session context that it receives from the EJB container. To support later extensions, however, the session context will be stored in the method `setSessionContext` (see Listing 4-22). The methods `ejbActivate` and `ejbPassivate` must be implemented to be in line with the interface `Session-Bean`. However, the implementation remains empty, since stateless session beans are neither activated nor passivated.

Listing 4-22. Methods for state management.

```
...
    public void ejbPassivate() {}
    public void ejbActivate() {}
    public void setSessionContext(SessionContext ctx) {
        this.beanCtx = ctx;
    }
...
```

The implementation of the application methods is now comparatively easy. Through the interplay of ejbCreate and ejbRemove the application methods are freed from responsibility for the naming service and DataSource.

The method changeFromEuro has the task of converting an amount in euros to another currency. To begin, a database connection must be established using the resource factory DataSource. Then a Statement for the execution of database accesses is created. The result is returned in ResultSet. At the end of the method, Connection, Statement, and ResultSet are closed in the finally block.

The amount and chosen currency are passed as parameters. The method reads the required exchange rate from the database and then calculates the value, which it returns. If an error occurs, an EJBException is triggered. The EJB container relays this as a RemoteException. If the bean were to use a local interface, then the EJB container would itself relay the EJBException. Listing 4-23 shows the implementation. The method changeToEuro works analogously and is therefore not displayed.

Listing 4-23. EuroExchangeBean.changeFromEuro(...).

```
...
    public float changeFromEuro(String currency, float amount) {
        if(currency == null) {
            throw new EJBException("illegal argument: currency");
        }
        final String query =
          "SELECT FOREIGNCURR FROM EURO_EXCHANGE WHERE CURRENCY=?";
        Connection con = null;
        PreparedStatement st = null;
        ResultSet rs = null;
        try {
            con = this.dataSource.getConnection();
            st = con.prepareStatement(query);
            st.setString(1, currency);
            rs = st.executeQuery();
            if(!rs.next()) {
                throw new EJBException("no such currency:" + currency);
            }
            return amount * rs.getFloat(1);
        } catch(SQLException ex) {
            ex.printStackTrace();
            throw new EJBException("db-error:" + ex.getMessage());
```

```
        } finally {
            try { rs.close(); } catch(Exception ex) {}
            try { st.close(); } catch(Exception ex) {}
            try { con.close(); } catch(Exception ex) {}
        }
    }
...
```

With setExchangeRate only a simple test of our example is possible. The method can be used to write exchange rates into the database. In case of error, again an EJBException is triggered. Listing 4-24 shows the implementation.

Listing 4-24. EuroExchangeBean.setExchangeRate(...).

```
...
    public void setExchangeRate(String currency,
                                float euro,
                                float foreignCurr)
    {
        if(currency == null) {
            throw new EJBException("illegal argument: currency");
        }
        final String delQuery =
            "DELETE FROM EURO_EXCHANGE WHERE CURRENCY=?";
        final String insQuery =
            "INSERT INTO EURO_EXCHANGE" +
            "(CURRENCY, EURO, FOREIGNCURR) VALUES(?, ?, ?)";
        Connection con = null;
        PreparedStatement del = null;
        PreparedStatement ins = null;
        boolean success = false;
        try {
            con = this.dataSource.getConnection();
            con.setAutoCommit(false);
            del = con.prepareStatement(delQuery);
            del.setString(1, currency);
            del.executeUpdate();
            ins = con.prepareStatement(insQuery);
            ins.setString(1, currency);
            ins.setFloat(2, euro);
            ins.setFloat(3, foreignCurr);
            ins.executeUpdate();
            success = true;
```

```
        } catch(SQLException ex) {
            ex.printStackTrace();
            throw new EJBException("db-error:" + ex.getMessage());
        } finally {
            if(success) {
                try { con.commit(); } catch(Exception ex) {}
            } else {
                try { con.rollback(); } catch(Exception ex) {}
            }
            try { del.close(); } catch(Exception ex) {}
            try { ins.close(); } catch(Exception ex) {}
            try { con.setAutoCommit(true); } catch(Exception ex) {}
            try { con.close(); } catch(Exception ex) {}
        }
    }
}
```

This completes the implementation of the bean class. All methods for identity management, state management, and application logic have been implemented.

Deployment

In order for the bean to be used by a client, it must be installed in the EJB container (Deployment). To this end information about the bean is collected in the deployment descriptor in XML syntax (see Listing 4-25). The bean developer, the application assembler, and the deployer are responsible for this. Most developers of application servers offer tools that simplify the creation of such deployment descriptors through the use of graphical interfaces. Nonetheless, it is common practice to create deployment descriptors "by hand" (with a text editor).

Listing 4-25. Deployment descriptor for the session bean EuroExchangeSL.

```xml
<?xml version="1.0" ?>
<ejb-jar version="2.1" xmlns="http://java.sun.com/xml/ns/j2ee"
xmlns:xsi="http://www.w3.org/2001/XMLSchema-instance"
xsi:schemaLocation="http://java.sun.com/xml/ns/j2ee
http://java.sun.com/xml/ns/j2ee/ejb-jar_2_1.xsd">
  <description>
    This deployment descriptor contains information
    about session bean exchange.
  </description>
  <enterprise-beans>
    <session>
```

```
            <ejb-name>Exchange</ejb-name>
            <home>ejb.exchangeSL.EuroExchangeHome</home>
            <remote>ejb.exchangeSL.EuroExchange</remote>
            <ejb-class>ejb.exchangeSL.EuroExchangeBean</ejb-class>
            <session-type>Stateless</session-type>
            <transaction-type>Bean</transaction-type>
            <resource-ref>
               <description> Euro-database </description>
               <res-ref-name>jdbc/EuroDB</res-ref-name>
               <res-type>javax.sql.DataSource</res-type>
               <res-auth>Container</res-auth>
            </resource-ref>
         </session>
      </enterprise-beans>

      <assembly-descriptor>
      </assembly-descriptor>

</ejb-jar>
```

In the deployment descriptor the bean developer needs to provide only information that the EJB container cannot itself provide through the examination of the classes (Introspection). First he establishes that the subject is a session bean (session), and gives the bean a unique name (ejb-name). When the deployer installs the bean later in the EJB container, this name is frequently used to register the bean with the naming service.

Then he declares the names of the required classes and interfaces. He defines the home interface (home) and the remote interface (remote) as well as the implementation class of the bean (ejb-class). Were the bean to use local interfaces, then instead of home, the element local-home would be used, and instead of remote, local, to declare the classes for the local home and local interfaces.

The EJB container requires information as to whether a stateful or stateless session bean is involved (session-type: Stateful/Stateless). In our simple example the bean takes over the transaction control (transaction-type) itself.

Moreover, the bean developer must define the reference to the requisite database (resource-ref). He defines a logical name (res-ref-name) relative to the environment of the bean (java:comp/env) and sets the data type of the resource factory (res-type) and determines that the EJB container should set the security strategy (res-auth). In addition, he describes in a comment the task of this reference (description) in order to make the job of the deployer possible.

The task of the bean provider is now complete. He has prepared all necessary information about the bean. The application assembler could define the access rights and determine the interplay with other beans. For our simple example these definitions are not absolutely necessary.

As a rule, further information is necessary for deployment, which varies from application server to application server. Thus, for example, it must be determined under what name the bean is to appear in JNDI. The resource reference must be mapped to an existing database, which contains the required tables. In many cases it is necessary to inform the EJB container about parameters for the run-time environment, for example, the size of the instance pool, cache size, or timeout values. The nature and extent of such additional specifications vary, as we have said, from product to product, as also the way in which these specifications must be made. Listing 4-26 presents an imaginary example of how additional specifications for deployment of the EuroExchange bean can be made.

Listing 4-26. Definitions for the deployment of an EJB container.

```
<bean>
  <ejb-name>Exchange</ejb-name>
  <stateless-session-descriptor>
    <max-pool-size>100</max-pool-size>
  </stateless-session-descriptor>
  <resource-reference-description>
    <res-ref-name>jdbc/EuroDB</res-ref-name>
    <jndi-name>jdbc/Oracle_Test_DB</jndi-name>
  </resource-reference-description>
  <jndi-name>
    ExchangeSL
  </jndi-name>
<bean>
```

The Client

For the session bean EuroExchangeSL a simple client will be developed (see Listing 4-27). It defines the exchange rate for the U.S. dollar, according to which it will convert dollars into euros and vice versa. Our client requires access to the naming service javax.naming and must be able to cope with network errors (javax.rmi.RemoteException). Furthermore, the client requires the bean interfaces with which it wants to work. We have collected these interfaces in the package ejb.exchangeSL. The bean's JNDI name is ExchangeSL. This name was associated with the bean via the additional deployment instructions in Listing 4-26.

Listing 4-27. Client program for the session bean EuroExchangeSL.

```
package ejb.exchangeSL.client;

import ejb.exchangeSL.EuroExchange;
import ejb.exchangeSL.EuroExchangeHome;

import java.rmi.RemoteException;

import javax.ejb.CreateException;
import javax.ejb.RemoveException;
import javax.naming.Context;
import javax.naming.InitialContext;
import javax.naming.NamingException;
import javax.rmi.PortableRemoteObject;

public class Client {

    private EuroExchange exchange;

    public Client() { }

    public void init()
        throws NamingException, RemoteException, CreateException
    {
        java.util.Properties p = new java.util.Properties();
        p.put(Context.INITIAL_CONTEXT_FACTORY,
            "JNDI-PROVIDER-CLASS");
        p.put(Context.PROVIDER_URL, "JNDI-URL");
        Context ctx = new InitialContext(p);

        Object o = ctx.lookup("ExchangeSL");
        EuroExchangeHome home =
            (EuroExchangeHome)PortableRemoteObject.narrow(o,
                            EuroExchangeHome.class);
        this.exchange = home.create();
    }

    public void run() {
        try {
            this.exchange.setExchangeRate("US-Dollar", 2f, 0.5f);
        } catch(RemoteException ex) {
            ex.printStackTrace();
            return;
        }
        System.out.println("Changing 100 US-Dollars to Euro");
        float amount = 0f;
```

```
        try {
            amount = this.exchange.changeToEuro("US-Dollar", 100);
        } catch(RemoteException ex) {
            ex.printStackTrace();
            return;
        }
        System.out.println("Result: " + amount);

        System.out.println("Changing " + amount +
                            " Euro to US-Dollars");
        float n_amount = 0f;
        try {
            n_amount =
                this.exchange.changeFromEuro("US-Dollar", amount);
        } catch(RemoteException ex) {
            ex.printStackTrace();
            return;
        }
        System.out.println("Result: " + n_amount);
    }
    public void cleanUp() {
        try {
            this.exchange.remove();
        } catch(RemoteException ex) {
            ex.printStackTrace();
        } catch(RemoveException ex) {
            ex.printStackTrace();
        }
    }
    public static void main(String[] args) {
        Client c = new Client();
        try {
            c.init();
        } catch(Exception ex) {
            ex.printStackTrace();
            return;
        }
        c.run();
        c.cleanUp();
    }
}
```

Were the bean to use local interfaces instead of remote ones, not much would change in the client programming. The client would then have to use `PortableRemoteObject.narrow` only if the naming service were not going to run in the process of the application server. As a rule, the naming service of the application server is used. If the client uses local interfaces, it must be located in the same process as the enterprise bean, that is, in the process of the application server. In this case it could use type casting to convert the return value of the method `lookup` directly into the desired type. Moreover, in the case of local interfaces the declaration of `java.rmi.RemoteException` does not apply. As we have already mentioned, the main difference in the use of local interfaces has less to do with programming than with run-time behavior. On the one hand, RMI overhead is avoided, since the client is located in the same process, while on the other hand, the calling parameters and return values are passed not as call by value but as call by reference (with the exception of Java's primitive data types, which are always passed as call by value).

Entity Beans

Introduction

An entity bean is an object that represents persistent data. In most cases the data are stored in a database. An entity bean, however, is more than a simple device for storing data. Rather, an entity bean may be thought of as an enterprise object with its own functionality. It allows a number of clients simultaneous access to transaction-secure data. A graphical overview of entity beans is given in Figure 5-1.

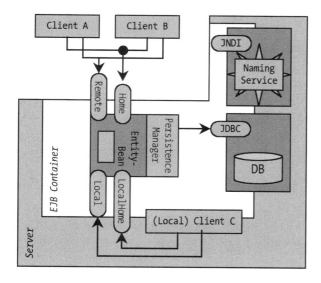

Figure 5-1. Overview of entity beans.

Entity beans have been given an ever greater significance in the course of the development of the Enterprise JavaBeans specification. While entity beans were still defined in version 1.0 as an optional component, in version 1.1 they became a necessity for every EJB container. Version 2.0 changed the definition of entity beans in a number of particulars and extended their functionality considerably. To ensure the compatibility of version 2.0 with earlier versions, both types of entity beans (1.1 and 2.0) are part of specification 2.0 and must be supported by EJB containers. Version 2.1 added some extra enhancements to specification 2.0. The overall structure between 2.0 and 2.1 is largely the same with some extra functions available to be used in EJB-QL (described within this chapter). Throughout this chapter any reference to capabilities of version 2.0 entity beans can also be applied to version 2.1 entity beans. Any differences will be clearly distinguished.

An application works with entity beans when it stores information over several program runs, and so the state of the object is not lost if the server is stopped and later restarted. An entity bean exists until a client explicitly deletes it. In contrast, session beans, about which we have spoken earlier, are not persistent. Therefore, the state of a session bean is always lost when the client or server are terminated.

Since entity beans enable several clients to access the same data in parallel, they are seen as a central resource. Every client of an entity bean works almost as if it had exclusive access to the bean. The EJB container avoids the usual problems that result from parallel access through partial serialization of accesses and by the implementation of transactions (see also Chapter 7).

Entity beans are distinguished from session beans by this parallel access by several clients. With stateful session beans, every client uses a separate bean instance. The state of a session bean is thus always available exclusively to a single client. If clients access the same data set in parallel, they all use the same entity bean. The state of an entity bean that represents a particular data set is available to all clients.

An entity bean defines methods, attributes, relationships, and a primary key. As with session beans, the methods realize the functionality of the bean and thereby determine its behavior. The attributes hold the data and thus determine the state of an entity bean. Relations define dependencies among entity beans. One or more attributes of an entity bean are collected into a primary key, which makes it possible to identify each instance of the class uniquely. The home object (which we met in Chapter 3 as the EJBHome object) and the value of the primary key together determine the identity of the entity bean. They identify a particular bean that models an object, for example, a customer or an item of stored merchandise.

The modeling of complex structured data by relationships among entity beans in conjunction with the local client view has been satisfactorily supported by the EJB container only since version 2.0 of the specification. Previously, the mapping of complex data structures had to be programmed by hand or with proprietary tools. Another alternative was the use of so-called OR mapping tools from third-party producers. However, when OR mapping tools were implemented an Enterprise Bean became no longer easily portable.

The persistence mechanism of the EJB container has the job of writing the state of an entity bean to a database or another storage system. When the bean is needed again, the persistence mechanism reads out the persistent data and places an entity bean instance in active memory. In this way every entity bean can always be identified with its home object and primary key.

With the use of a persistence manager (container-managed persistence) the task of implementation is simplified. The bean provider can also implement the persistence mechanism in the entity bean (bean-managed persistence) to gain flexibility.

An EJB container offers one or more persistence managers. Each persistence manager implements a particular persistence mechanism that stores the persistent data using a particular methodology. In the case of container-managed persistence the query language EJB-QL enables access to persistent data independently of the methodology used.

Concepts

Entity Bean Types

We will consider three types of entity beans. In presenting the concept of entity beans we will compare all three types. The following types of entity beans should be distinguished:

- *Container-Managed Persistence 2.0/2.1.* These are entity beans with container-managed persistence as defined in the Enterprise JavaBeans 2.0 and 2.1 specifications.

- *Container-Managed Persistence 1.1.* These are entity beans with container-managed persistence as defined in the Enterprise JavaBeans 1.1 specification. For backward compatibility these are also a part of the Enterprise JavaBeans 2.0 and 2.1 specifications.

- *Bean-Managed Persistence.* These are entity beans that do not use the persistence manager but implement the persistence mechanism themselves. They were defined in version 1.1 of the Enterprise JavaBeans specification and were taken into version 2.0 largely unaltered.

The following considerations compare these three types of beans. In the parallel descriptions of container-managed persistence 1.1 and 2.0 the advantages of the new architecture will be pointed out. We will employ examples to highlight the development aspects of the different concepts.

Attributes and Dependent Objects

The persistent state of an entity bean is stored in its attributes. During development the storage process must be given careful consideration. A significant difference among the three entity bean types is in how the persistent attributes are handled.

Bean-Managed Persistence

If the bean developer takes responsibility for persistent storage in attributes, then it is also his or her responsibility to determine how attributes are dealt with. In a later section we will present programming examples.

Container-Managed Persistence 1.1

Version 1.1 of the Enterprise JavaBeans specification provides for the persistent attributes to be defined as attributes of the bean class and given in the deployment descriptor. The attributes can have the following data types:

- Primitive data types of the programming language Java (for example, int, float, long);

- Serializable data types of the programming language Java.

The attributes are defined as public, so that the EJB container has access to them. It is the responsibility of the EJB container to synchronize the persistent attributes of the bean with the underlying database.

Container-Managed Persistence 2.0/2.1

With version 2.0 of the Enterprise JavaBeans specification the manipulation of persistent attributes changed fundamentally. The bean developer works with an abstract bean class. Instead of attributes in the form of member variables of the bean class, he or she defines abstract access methods for reading and writing of attributes (so-called getter/setter methods). During deployment the EJB container generates a derived class that implements all the abstract methods. The concrete implementation is a component of the persistence mechanism.

The attributes are permitted to have the following data types:

- Primitive data types of the programming language Java (for example, int, float, long);

- Serializable data types of the programming language Java.

Serializable data types are all classes that implement the interface `java.io.Serializable`. This includes above all the classes `java.lang.String` and `java.util.Date`. Frequently, instead of Java's primitive data types, the relevant wrapper classes of the primitive data types (such as `java.lang.Integer`, `java.lang.Float`, `java.lang.Long`) are used. As a rule, these data types can be mapped without problems to the data types of databases. In the case of individual data types (custom classes that use the `Serializable` interface) that are declared as a persistent attribute of an entity bean, this is not possible without further ado. These can often be processed only as binary data (so-called BLOBs = Binary Large Objects) by the databases in which they are stored as persistent data. Attributes of this type are called *dependent value classes*. The use of such individual data types as persistent attributes of an entity bean is rather the exception. The mapping of complex and searchable data structures is accomplished via the use of several entity bean classes whose dependencies are defined by relationships.

Persistent Relationships

A persistent relationship (container-managed relationship) makes it possible to navigate from one instance to a related instance; this is relevant only to entity beans with container-managed persistence 2.0. As an example let us consider two entity bean classes for a project management scenario: project bean and employee bean. A relationship is the correct means to model which workers work on which projects. Given the project (instance of a project bean), all associated employees (instances of the employee bean) can be found using the relationship. The tracking of relationships from one object to a related object is called *navigation*.

A database is used for storing relationships (for example, a foreign key relationship in a relational database), and thus relationships are searchable using database methods.

Relationships can exist only between entity beans defined in the same deployment descriptor, where the relationship is formally described. Furthermore, relationships between entity beans are possible only in the local client view (for details on the local client view see Chapter 4, "Local vs. Remote Client View"). The EJB container takes care of generating instances during navigation across relationships. Furthermore, the EJB container sees to it that the relationships between instances of entity beans are made persistent.

From the developer of an entity bean's points of view a relationship is represented as a pair of abstract methods: one `get<relationshipname>` method and one `set<relationshipname>`. The abstract get method allows navigation via a relationship. The `set` permits the association of a relationship to a specific instance. As with the abstract methods for storing attributes, during deployment, concrete implementations of the abstract methods for handling relationships are generated by the tools of the EJB container.

For every relationship a *cardinality* is defined. This represents the numerical type of the relationship between related instances. These are the possible cardinalities:

- $1 : 1$. An instance of class $\mathcal{A}$ joined to one or no instances of class $\mathcal{B}$;

- $1 : n$. One instance of class $\mathcal{A}$ is joined to an arbitrary number of instances of class $\mathcal{B}$.

- $n : m$. One instance of class $\mathcal{A}$ is joined to an arbitrary number of instances of $\mathcal{B}$, and the elements of class $\mathcal{B}$ are joined to an arbitrary number of instances of class $\mathcal{A}$.

Relationships can be navigable in one or both directions. If the relationship is navigable in both directions, then each partner in the relationship recognizes the linked instances. One speaks in this case of a bidirectional relationship. If the relationship is navigable in only one direction, then only one partner in the relationship has access to the linked instances. The other partner has no information about the relationship. In this case one speaks of a unidirectional relationship.

A relationship also offers the possibility to define an existence dependency. When one instance is deleted it is possible to delete instances linked by a relationship. This modus operandi is called *cascading deletion.*

Primary Key

Every entity bean class requires a primary key, which makes it possible to identify all entity bean identities uniquely. A client uses the primary key to search for entity beans. The EJB container uses the primary key as unique identifier to be able to locate each entity bean identity.

The primary key can come from one or more persistent attributes of the entity bean. It must be seen to that each instance of an entity bean class possesses a different combination of values among the attributes of the primary key.

The customer number in a mail-order company is an example of a primary key with a single attribute. It is unique for each customer. In contrast to this, the registration number of an automobile is not sufficient to serve as a primary key for the set of all registered motor vehicles. In addition there is a number that is increased each time the same registration number is issued. Taken together, the registration number and the increasing number are unique and serve as an example of a primary key that consists of several attributes.

The attributes that constitute the components of the primary key (see Figure 5-2) are collected by the bean developer into a class of their own. In this primary key class the attributes have the same name and data type as in the Enterprise Bean class. The EJB container is notified of the primary key class in the deployment descriptor. The client also uses the primary key to search for particular entity beans.

An exception is the case of primary keys that consist of a single attribute. In order to simplify programming one may here do without a special primary key class. Instead, a standard Java class can be used, corresponding to the type of the primary key. Examples are java.lang.String, java.lang.Integer, java.lang.Long. The primary key attribute is given in the deployment descriptor.

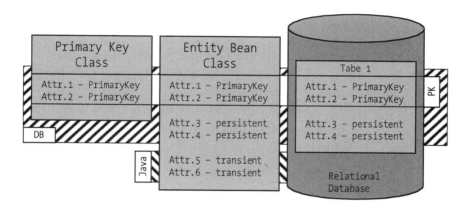

Figure 5-2. Overview of the attributes of an entity bean.

Bean Instance and Bean Identity

In working with entity beans it is very important to separate the viewpoint of the developer of the client program from that of the developer of the bean. It is particularly important that the terms *bean instance* and *bean identity* be understood.

The home object and the value of the primary key together constitute the entity bean identity. Such an identity could, for example, represent customer number 123 (see Figure 5-3). An object of an entity bean class in active memory is called an *entity bean instance*. In the case of an entity bean identity in a database without an entity bean instance in active memory one speaks of a *passivated bean*.

From the client's point of view the picture is simple: There exist entity bean objects each with an entity bean identity. The bean object offers the client the remote or local interface for access. For managing the bean object the client has available the (local) home interface of the bean class. If the client wishes to work with an entity bean identity, it obtains a reference to the associated bean object via the (local) home interface. In general, the (local) home interface enables the client to create, delete, and find bean objects. The client view is thereby limited precisely to those aspects of the bean that are relevant.

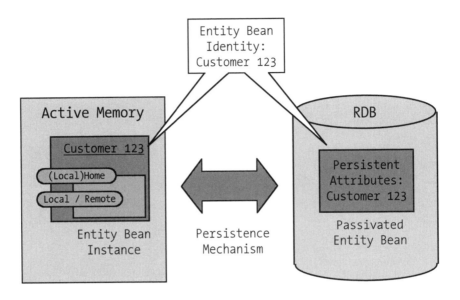

Figure 5-3. Entity bean identity in the customer example.

The bean developer requires another viewpoint. He implements the application logic in the bean class. In addition, he writes a (local) home and a remote or local interface for this bean class that publish the functionality of the bean. The methods of this interface are implemented partially by the developer of the bean in the bean class and are partially provided by the EJB container.

When the client works with a bean object, the associated functionality of a bean instance is provided. However, there is an important difference between the viewpoint of the developer of the client program toward the bean object and that of the bean developer toward the bean instance. The bean object always has the same bean identity, while the bean instance can change the bean identity during its life cycle. This fact must, of course, be taken into account by the developer of the entity bean. The following section treats this topic in detail.

Persistence

A typical business application manages very large data sets. In implementing Enterprise JavaBeans these data are normally stored in entity beans. The large number of resulting entity beans cannot remain continuously in active memory, but must be stored somewhere with large storage capacity. As a rule, a database is implemented for this that stores the data on a hard drive and offers mechanisms for data security (such as tape backup).

In order to make an entity bean persistent, all persistent attributes must be stored. If an instance is needed again, then the instance can be recreated in its original state with the saved attributes. By *persistence mechanism* is understood the process of storing and recreating this state.

In reference to the persistence of entity beans the following two types of persistence are distinguished:

- *Bean-Managed Persistence*: An entity bean can itself see to the storage of its attributes.

- *Container-Managed Persistence*: The responsibility for the persistent storage of attributes of an entity bean is transferred to the persistence manager of the EJB container.

In the first case it is the task of the bean developer to implement the methods that enable the EJB container to manage the entity beans. With these methods the developer can freely select the strategy by which the attributes are written, loaded, and searched. The possibility of realizing the persistence mechanism in the bean itself gives the bean developer great flexibility. He need not restrict himself to the persistence mechanism of the EJB container and can use application-specific methods.

In the second case the developer of the entity bean is completely freed from programming the access methods. The persistence manager sees to it that the persistent attributes of the entity bean are stored.

The EJB specification defines that the EJB container stores the persistent data by a process that is comparable with Java's serialization. Within the framework of this definition, however, the most diverse imaginable processes are possible. In managing large data sets, as a rule a database is implemented. In addition to the popular relational databases (RDB) one might also consider the deployment of object-oriented databases (OODB) and other persistence systems.

In an existing infrastructure it can be necessary to use the storage mechanisms of existing applications. This is of particular interest in using an existing database in mainframe applications. The advantage of this is that all data of the existing application as well as those of new EJB applications are available. This makes possible a soft migration of legacy systems, avoiding the complete substitution of a particular system by a particular time.

The EJB container has one or more persistence managers, which are responsible for generating the necessary access methods. A persistence manager determines the type of implemented persistence system and the mapping of persistent data to this system. As a rule, the EJB container makes precisely one persistence manager available, which supports storage in relational databases. If there are several persistence managers, then at the time of deployment the persistence mechanism is determined by the choice of persistence manager.

For generating the access methods the persistence manager requires precise information about the entity bean. Therefore, it analyzes the entity bean class, the dependent classes (if any), and the deployment descriptor at deployment time. Depending on the chosen persistence mechanism, additional data may be needed, such as tables and column names for the attributes of an entity bean in a database. The deployment procedure must be repeated for the installation of the bean in another EJB container.

The implementation cost can be minimized by the use of container-managed persistence. In this case the bean relies on the infrastructure of the EJB container and has itself no access to the database. Therefore, the bean remains portable and can be used without additional expenditure with other databases or other EJB containers.

Storage in Relational Databases

With entity beans the EJB architecture uses an object-oriented structure for all data storage. Therefore, it is logical to consider storage in object-oriented databases. However, relational databases are more established in the marketplace and are in wider use in both new and existing applications. For these reasons Enterprise JavaBeans is used mostly with relational databases. The persistence mechanism must thus map an object-oriented data structure onto a relational structure (*object-relational mapping*). See Figure 5-4.

The mapping of object-oriented data structures to the tables of a relational database is a complex topic. However, entity beans do not work with inheritance, since component inheritance is not covered by the EJB specification. As a result, the required procedure is relatively simple.

A bean class that possesses only simple attributes can be mapped to individual database tables (called a *relation*). Each simple persistent attribute of the class thereby obtains an individual column (called an *attribute*). Each of the instances of the bean is written in a row (called a *tuple*). In this way the attributes of the primary key are contained in particular columns of the database table. The primary key of the entity bean is also used as primary key of the associated database table. Thus in addition to the required searchability one has ensured more efficient access to particular entity bean identities.

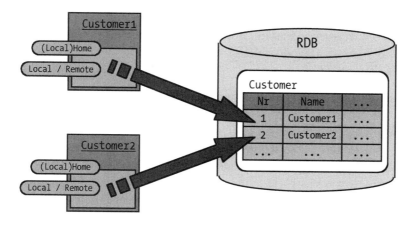

Figure 5-4. Object-relational mapping of entity beans.

For modeling complex structures the simple data types that can be mapped to a column in a database no longer suffice. Here one may use dependent value classes or several entity bean classes in association with container-managed relationships. In mapping objects to a relational database the difference between the two methods becomes clear:

- *Objects of dependent value classes* are serialized and stored in a database column for binary data (BLOB). The database is unable to interpret the stored binary format. Therefore, these columns cannot be searched. In addition, these columns cannot be used for foreign key relations to other tables.

- *In the case of several entity beans that are associated via container-managed relationships* each entity bean is stored in its own table. The tables are related via the attributes of the entity beans. The attributes of the entity beans are searchable, and one may navigate via the relationships.

If one chooses modeling with several entity beans and container-managed relationships for the mapping of complex data structures (which is possible only for the container-managed persistence of version 2.0/2.1), then for the mapping of relationships to the database one must choose between two procedures, depending on the cardinality of the entity bean relationship:

- *Simple foreign key relationship:* This method is suitable only for the cardinalities $1 : 1$ and $1 : n$. The table with cardinality n (either table in the $1 : 1$ case) contains in addition the attributes of the primary key of the other table.

- *Relationship table:* For the cardinality $n : m$ an additional table is introduced. The attributes of the relationship table are the totality of the primary key attributes of both tables that are linked by the relationship. Each row of the relationship table associates one row of one table with a row of the other table.

The possible navigational directions have no effect on the modeling. In Figure 5-5 we see a comparison between the two methods using the project management example introduced earlier. If an employee is able to work on only one project, then there is a $1 : n$ relationship between the entity Project and the entity Employee. The relationship between the two entities is stored using the foreign key (column Project-ID) in the entity Employee, which refers to the associated project. If an employee can work on several projects, then we are dealing with an $n : m$ relationship between the entity Project and the entity Employee. The relationship between the two entities is stored in this case using the table ProjectEmployee (a *relationship table*). This table is not modeled as an entity bean. It is used by the EJB container merely for the storage of relationships between the two entities Project and Employee.

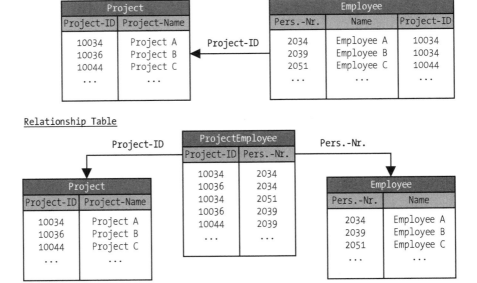

Figure 5-5. Foreign key versus relationship table.

The persistence mechanism is implemented by the persistence manager. In order to carry out this task, precise information is needed about which attribute of the entity bean is to be stored in which database table and in which column.

The same holds for relationships. The persistence manager must know the attributes by which the entity beans stand in relationship to one another, the cardinality of the relationship, and how the relationship is to be stored (via a foreign key relationship or a relationship table). This information is provided by the deployer. Moreover, the organization of the database must be defined in the database. Here one consults a database expert, who defines the optimal scheme with the correct indexes, taking into consideration the effects on performance and memory requirements.

Life Cycle of a Bean Instance

An understanding of the life cycle of an entity bean instance is a prerequisite for developing one. Figure 5-6 shows the various states and state transitions of an entity bean. A distinction is made in the state transitions as to whether the EJB container or the client triggers the state transition.

The EJB specification distinguishes three states of an entity bean instance. To clarify the issues in programming we subdivide the state Ready into three substates:

- *Nonexistent*: The instance does not exist.

- *Pooled*: The instance exists, but it has not yet been assigned a bean identity. The instance is used to execute client accesses to the home interface, since this does not relate to a particular bean identity.

- We divide the state *Ready* into three substates:

    1. *Ready-Async*: The attribute values are possibly not in conformity with the current database contents. Either the attributes have not yet been installed, or the database content has changed on account of a parallel access.
    2. *Ready-Sync*: The attribute values are current.
    3. *Ready-Update*: The bean attributes have been changed by the client. Usually, the bean has been involved in a transaction. The new values have not yet been written, or have been written only partially, to the database.

For every entity bean class the EJB container has a pool in which it manages the instances. The pool represents a performance optimization, which above all is achieved by the use of automated memory management (garbage collection). The EJB container avoids the continual generation and deletion of Java objects, using the instances in the pool one after the other for various bean identities. Since one instance can possess only one bean identity at a given time, the pool must contain at least as many instances as there are distinct bean identities that are to be used in parallel.

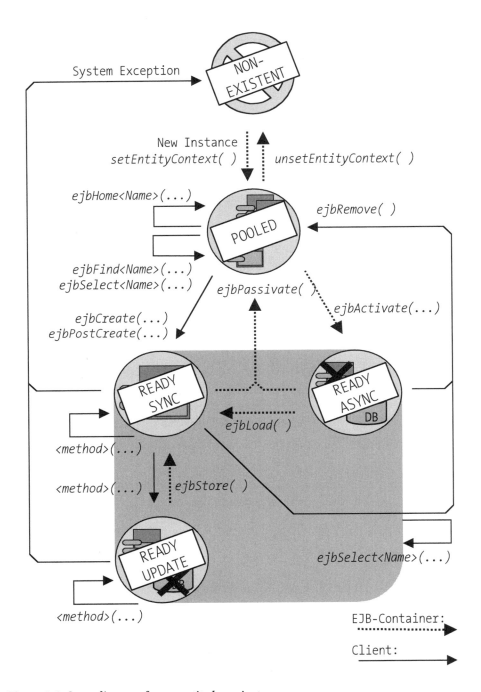

Figure 5-6. State diagram for an entity bean instance.

If the EJB container requires a new instance in the pool, then it generates an instance of the bean class and installs it using setEntityContext. The instance does not yet possess a bean identity. If at some other time the EJB container wishes to reduce the number of bean instances in the pool, then it calls the method unsetEntityContext and then decommissions the instance.

Suppose now that the client is looking for a bean object with the findByPrimaryKey method of the home interface. The EJB container relays the call to an arbitrary bean instance. This is possible because the bean instance does not need a bean identity for the execution of the method.

The corresponding method with the same parameters was implemented in the entity bean class either by the been developer (bean-managed persistence) or provided by the EJB container (container-managed persistence).

As a result, the client obtains the remote or local interface of the found bean object (if the search has more than one result, then a *collection* or *enumeration* is used for the return of several remote or local objects). The EJB container must prepare the corresponding bean instance for the method calls. For this it activates an arbitrary bean instance and informs it of the bean identity in the form of the primary key. Then it calls the method ejbActivate. The bean instance is now in the state Ready-Async.

When the client calls a bean method, the EJB container must see to it that the bean instance has the current attribute value. To this end, the persistence mechanism of the EJB container synchronizes the bean instance with the persistence medium (container-managed persistence). Then the method ejbLoad is called to inform the bean about the synchronization that has been achieved. If the persistence mechanism is inherent to the bean (bean-managed persistence), then the synchronization is implemented in the method ejbLoad by the bean provider. After the call to ejbLoad the bean instance is in the state Ready-Sync. All read operations of the client are executed in this state.

If the client executes a write access to the entity bean and changes its attribute values, then the bean instance is temporarily not in sync with the database. The bean instance is now in the state Ready-Update. The EJB container carries out the synchronization at a given time. The persistence mechanism of the EJB container takes over writing the attributes to the database (container-managed persistence). Then the method ejbStore is called to inform the bean instance about the synchronization that has just been accomplished. If the persistence mechanism is provided for within the bean itself (bean-managed persistence), then the synchronization is implemented within the method ejbStore by the bean provider. After a call to ejbStore the bean instance is again in the state Ready-Sync. All write accesses are normally protected by transactions (configured via the deployment descriptor), so that differences between the attribute values and the database contents present no danger to the consistency of the state of the data (see Chapter 7 for details on transactions).

All bean instances that are not currently being used by a client and that are not involved in a transaction can be reused by the EJB container for other bean identities. With a call to the method ejbPassivate the EJB container notifies the bean instance that its state is changing to Pooled. If the old bean identity is needed by the client again, then the EJB container can use and activate an arbitrary bean instance for this purpose.

For the developer of entity beans this means that the bean instance might have to be initialized in the method ejbPassivate. Since under some circumstances a bean instance might languish a long time in the pool, at the time of passivation it should release all of the resources that it commands. Moreover, one should ensure that the bean can be reused for another bean identity.

The generation of a new bean identity functions similarly. The client calls the method create of the home interface. The EJB container relays this call to the corresponding method ejbCreate of a bean instance in the state Pooled. The method evaluates the parameters and sets the attribute values of the bean instance accordingly. Then the EJB container method ejbPostCreate is called with the same parameters. In contrast to ejbCreate, the bean identity in the bean context is available to the method ejbPostCreate. Thus this method can execute further initialization steps. In the case of container-managed persistence the EJB container takes care of the corresponding entry in the database. In the case of bean-managed persistence, the bean provider must program the storage of the new data record in the method ejbCreate of the bean class itself. After the execution of ejbCreate and ejbPostCreate the bean instance is in the state Ready-Sync.

The client has two ways of deleting a bean identity: with the method remove of the (local) home interface using the primary key and by means of a call to the method remove on the local or remote interface of the entity bean. In the first case the EJB container takes over the necessary intermediate steps. It activates a bean instance as required for the bean identity and calls ejbRemove. In the case of container-managed persistence the associated data are deleted by the EJB container (using the persistence manager) from the database. In the case of bean-managed persistence the bean provider must program the deletion of the data set in the method ejbRemove. Upon deletion of the data record in the database, the associated entity bean identity is deleted as well. The bean instance then goes into the state Pooled.

In the life cycle of an entity bean instance system errors can occur. For example, a network error can happen or the database may be unavailable. If a system error occurs in an entity bean instance, then the EJB container deletes this instance, and the instance is not placed again in the pool. For each succeeding access to the associated bean identity the EJB container must activate a new bean instance from the pool. For the bean developer this means that in the case of a system error the bean instance does not need to be initialized for the pool.

After this introduction, which is relevant to all types of entity beans, we shall proceed in the next section to discuss in detail the particular features of the individual entity bean types.

Entity Context

The entity context (interface javax.ejb.EntityContext) is, like the session context in the case of session beans, the interface between the EJB container and the entity bean instance. After it is generated, the entity context is associated with the bean instance via the callback method setEntityContext. The entity bean uses this context during its entire lifetime. The context of an entity bean is frequently changed by the EJB container during its life cycle. Whenever the entity bean changes from the state Pooled to the state Ready, the context of the entity bean changes as well. Through the context the entity bean learns from the EJB container what identity it represents at the moment, the identity of the client that is currently calling a business method, and information about the current transaction.

In the rest of this section we shall introduce the most important methods of the entity context.

EJBHome getEJBHome()

This method gives the bean instance access to its own home interface. The data type of the return value must be transformed (type casting) into the specific home interface of the bean class. The method triggers an exception of type java.lang.IllegalStateException if the entity bean does have a home interface (but rather a local home interface).

EJBLocalHome getEJBLocalHome()

This method gives the bean instance access to its own local home interface. The data type of the return value must be transformed into the specific local home interface of the bean class. The method triggers an exception of type java.lang.IllegalStateException if the entity bean does not have a local home interface (but instead a home interface).

Object getPrimaryKey()

This method gives the bean instance access to the primary key. The primary key reflects the identity that the entity bean currently represents. This method cannot be called in the method ejbCreate. If the method ejbCreate is called, a transition to the Ready state is not yet excluded. The primary key is available to the bean only in the method ejbPostCreate, not in ejbCreate. Later (after the bean has been created), it can obtain the primary key via getPrimaryKey in every method (except unsetEntityContext, of course).

void setRollbackOnly()

This method helps in running transactions (see also Chapter 7). An entity bean instance uses this method in the case of an error in order to ensure that an active transaction ends with a rollback. For example, an error can be a failure in saving persistent attributes of entity beans with bean-managed persistence.

boolean getRollbackOnly()

The method getRollbackOnly is the read counterpart to the method setRollbackOnly. One can check with getRollbackOnly whether it is still possible to terminate the active transaction with commit.

UserTransaction getUserTransaction()

Normally, the EJB container takes over control of transactions. The method getUserTransaction requires an entity bean instance only when it wishes to take over the transaction itself. The return value of the method is an object of the class javax.transaction.UserTransaction, which enables access to the transaction context (see Chapter 7).

Principal getCallerPrincipal()

This method enables an entity bean instance to determine the identity of the client. The return value is an object of the class java.security.Principal (see also Chapter 8).

boolean isCallerInRole(java.lang.String roleName)

With this method a check is made as to whether the declared user has a particular role in the security concept. The possible roles are defined in the deployment descriptor (see also Chapter 8).

Container Managed Persistence 2.0/2.1

Overview

Figure 5-7 provides a sweeping overview of the classes and interfaces of an entity bean with container-managed persistence since version 2.0, which supports the remote client view. On the right is the entity bean class, whose objects are managed by the EJB container at run time. On the left are the interfaces over which the client accesses the bean and that are implemented via the home or remote object of the EJB container.

In the figure all symbolic names that must be replaced during actual programming by the proper terms appear in pointy brackets (<abc>). A plus sign (+) denotes a *public* method. Abstract methods are written in a slant font.

The entity bean class implements the interface javax.ejb.EntityBean. In this entity bean class the bean provider implements the actual functionality of the bean. For each persistent attribute two abstract access methods (get and set) are defined.

The get method is for reading the attribute. It possesses no parameters, and its return value has the data type of the persistent attribute.

The set method is for writing the attribute. It has one parameter with the data type of the persistent attribute and no return value. The EJB container takes over implementation of this method at deployment.

In the upper left part of Figure 5-7 is the class for the bean's primary key. Since objects of this class must be transported between server and client over the network, this class must be serializable. It implements the interface java.io.Serializable. In the primary key class are defined the attributes that form the primary key of the associated entity bean class. For each (virtual) persistent attribute of the bean a *public* attribute is defined. The data type is the same as for the return value of the get method. If the primary key consists of only a single attribute, then its data type can be used as primary key class. In this case no special primary key class needs to be implemented.

Figure 5-8 provides a sweeping overview of the classes and interfaces of an entity bean with container-managed persistence since version 2.0, which supports the local client view. On the right is the entity bean class, and on the left are the interfaces that are used by the client and are implemented by the local home object or local object of the EJB container. The entity bean class of the local client view is identical to that of the remote client view. The differences between the two cases are manifested by the EJB container through the implementation of the relevant interfaces. The bean class and bean instance remain untouched. For the client of an entity bean the differences between local and remote client views are the same as for session beans. These differences have been discussed already, in Chapter 4.

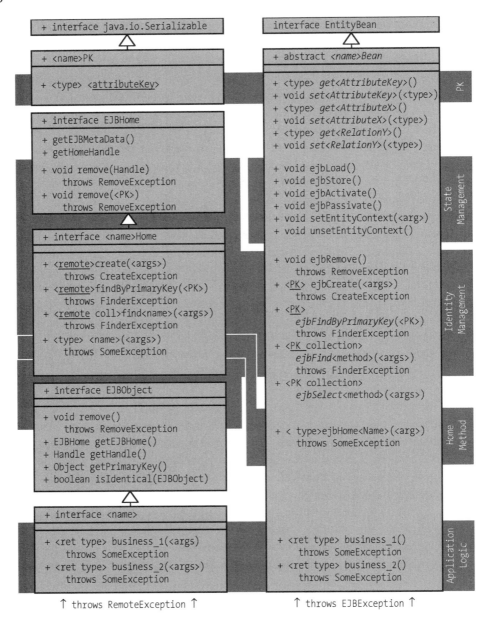

Figure 5-7. Remote interfaces and classes of the CMP entity bean (EJB 2.0).

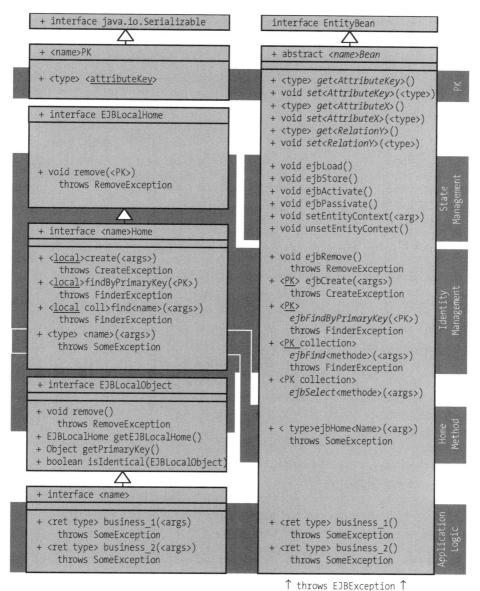

Figure 5-8. Local interfaces and classes of the CMP entity bean (EJB 2.0).

The primary key class should implement java.io.Serializable in the case of the local and remote client views, since objects of this class may be used only inside or outside of a single Java process. Every entity bean is specified in the deployment descriptor (see Listing 5-1) (entity). Here a unique name for the entity bean is defined (ejb-name). Moreover, the home interface (home), the remote interface (remote), the bean class (ejb-class), and the primary key class (prim-key-class) are completely specified. In the element a distinction is made as to whether one is dealing with an entity bean with container-managed persistence (Container) or with bean-managed persistence (Bean). Furthermore, it must be specified that the entity bean is using the persistence mechanism of version 2.x of the EJB specification (cmp-version). Finally, a name for the entity bean's persistence schema must be given (abstract-schema-name). This name will be used later by the deployer for mapping the data of the entity bean to the current persistence medium. Moreover, this name plays an important role in EJB-QL.

Listing 5-1. Schematic deployment descriptor for an entity bean.

```
<?xml version="1.0" ?>
<ejb-jar version="2.1" xmlns="http://java.sun.com/xml/ns/j2ee"
xmlns:xsi="http://www.w3.org/2001/XMLSchema-instance"
xsi:schemaLocation="http://java.sun.com/xml/ns/j2ee
http://java.sun.com/xml/ns/j2ee/ejb-jar_2_1.xsd">
  <enterprise-beans>
    <entity>
      <ejb-name>name of the bean</ejb-name>
      <home>home interface</home>
      <remote>remote interface</remote>
      <ejb-class>bean class</ejb-class>
      <persistence-type>container orbean</persistence-type>
      <prim-key-class>primary key class</prim-key-class>
      <reentrant>True or False</reentrant>
      <cmp-version>2.x</cmp-version>
      <abstract-schema-name>
          name of the persistence schema
      </abstract-schema-name>
      ...
  </enterprise-beans>
  ...
</ejb-jar>
```

Like a session bean, an entity bean can be configured externally via the bean environment. The entries for the bean environment are made in the deployment descriptor. Working with the bean environment was dealt with in Chapter 4, on session beans, and we shall not repeat that material here.

The following sections present programming with the necessary definitions in the deployment descriptor for aspects of entity bean with container-managed persistence 2.0/2.1. To this topic belong the persistent attributes of an entity bean, state management of the EJB container, the generation and deletion of an entity bean, search methods (finder and select methods), and the methods of the application logic.

Attributes

The names of all persistent attributes for which abstract `getter/setter` methods have been defined are declared in the deployment descriptor. Each name must begin with a lowercase letter. This is how during installation the tools of the EJB container identify the abstract methods responsible for storing the attributes. The declaration takes place within the `entity` section and is represented schematically in Listing 5-2.

Listing 5-2. Definition of an attribute of an entity bean in the deployment descriptor.

```
...
    <entity>
      ...
      <cmp-field>
        <description>description of the attribute1</description>
        <field-name>attributeName 1(e.g., surname)</field-name>
      </cmp-field>
      <cmp-field>
        <description>description of the attribute2</description>
        <field-name> attributeName 2 (e.g., given name)</field-name>
      </cmp-field>
      ...
    </entity>
...
```

For each persistent attribute abstract access or mutator methods (commonly known as *getter/setter* methods) are defined in the entity bean class. Their names begin with get (read access) and set (write access), followed by the name of the attribute with the beginning of each word an uppercase letter (Listing 5-3).

Listing 5-3. Access methods for an attribute of an entity bean.

```
...
public abstract void set<attributeName>(<type>)
public abstract <type> get<attributeName>();
...
```

A persistent attribute of an entity bean for which, for example, the abstract methods getMyAttribute and setMyAttribute were defined will be declared in the deployment descriptor of the entity bean under the element field-name with the value myAttribute.

The client does not have direct access to the getter/setter methods for reading and writing the persistent attributes of an entity bean. The entity bean must make available corresponding methods in the local or remote interface that permit indirectly the writing and reading of the persistent attributes, by delegating read and write access to the getter/setter methods. The attributes of the primary key may not be changed after the entity bean is generated, since that would jeopardize the integrity of the data.

State Management

At the top of Figures 5-7 and 5-8 are the methods for state management. In the case of container-managed persistence the EJB container calls these methods in order to inform the bean instance of state transitions. These include the methods for management of the context and for activation and passivation, which we already know about from our discussion of session beans. In addition, there are the methods ejbLoad and ejbStore, which belong to the persistence mechanism of the bean.

void setEntityContext(EntityContext ctx)

The method setEntiyContext is called by the EJB container when a bean instance is generated and changes into the state Pooled. It serves to initialize the bean. The EJB container gives the entity bean its context. This method should only save the context and not possess any business-logic-related functionality.

void unsetEntityContext()

This method is called by the EJB container when it no longer needs a bean instance and wishes to remove it from the pool. The call informs the bean instance that the associated context will be invalid.

void ejbActivate()

The EJB container calls this method to inform the entity bean instance that it has received a particular entity bean identity. The identity that it now possesses can be discovered using the entity context.

The bean instance changes into the state Ready-Async. In this state in the EntityContext the primary key can be queried with getPrimaryKey, and the remote and local interfaces with getEJBObject and getEJBLocalObject, respectively. However, the bean instance has not yet been synchronized with the database, and thus the values of the persistent attributes have not yet been set.

This method can be used to open a database connection or to reserve other resources. It is important to note that there are no transactions available to this method.

void ejbPassivate()

This method is the complement to ejbActivate. It is called by the EJB container when the bean instance is transformed from the state Ready to the state Pooled. Thereafter, the bean instance no longer possesses a bean identity. However, in this method the bean identity can still be used, since the state transition is not yet closed when this method is called.

This method is used to release resources that were reserved with ejbActivate or later in the state Ready.

void ejbLoad()

The method ejbLoad is called by the EJB container after the state of the bean instance has been synchronized with the database. This is necessary if the bean instance was not initialized or if the database contents have changed due to a parallel access. The EJB container can synchronize the bean at any time in the state with the persistence medium. This frequently occurs before a method of the application logic is called. The bean changes from the state Ready-Async into the state Ready-Sync.

The entity bean can use this method, for example, to recalculate transient attributes from persistent attributes (which the EJB container has just synchronized with the persistence medium).

void ejbStore()

When a client changes the state of an entity bean, the altered attribute values must be rewritten to the database. As a result, the bean instance changes from the state Ready-Update into the state Ready-Sync.

Generating and Deleting

The methods for generating and deleting entity bean identities are part of identity management and are displayed in the second group in Figures 5-7 and 5-8. These methods are to be found in the (local) home interface and are available to the client already before it knows about a bean instance.

<primKeyClass> ejbCreate(<args>)

For the generation of entity beans there are one or more methods, all called ejbCreate and all of which define the primary key class of the bean as return value. The methods are distinguished by their parameters and can be freely defined by the bean developer. These methods are not part of the entity bean interface, since the parameters and return types are different for each entity bean class.

The methods are available to the client and are therefore also declared in the entity bean's (local) home interface. The signatures of the methods in the bean class and in the (local) home interface are differentiated by their return values and their names. The methods in the (local) home interface have the bean's remote or home interface as return value and are called create. The methods of the bean class use the primary key as return value and have ejb as a prefix in their names. The EJB container manages the necessary conversion between the primary key as return value of the ejbCreate method of the entity bean and the remote or local object of the create method of the (local) home interface.

The bean developer has the task in this method of initializing all or a part of the persistent attributes with the aid of the passed parameters. The transaction context for the ejbCreate methods is set in the deployment descriptor.

void ejbPostCreate(<args>)

For each ejbCreate method the bean developer must define an ejbPostCreate method with the same parameter types and with no return value. The ejbPostCreate method is always executed by the EJB container after the corresponding ejbCreate method with the same transaction context.

Further initialization methods can be executed in these methods. In contrast to the ejbCreate methods, the bean identity is available to these methods. With the execution of ejbCreate and ejbPostCreate the bean instance changes from the state Pooled into the state Ready-Update.

void ejbRemove()

For managing bean identities we also have the methods for deleting beans. The client gives the order to delete an entity bean identity by a call to the method remove in the (local) home, remote, or local interface. The method ejbRemove on the bean instance is then called by the EJB container before the entity bean identity has been deleted. After deletion, the bean instance passes into the state Pooled. The method ejbPassivate is not called for this state transition.

In the case of container-managed persistence the bean developer does not have to implement deletion. The EJB container takes care of deleting the data. The method ejbRemove gives the bean developer the possibility of releasing additional resources before the entity bean is deleted.

The method ejbRemove can also be called by the EJB container with a transaction. Here, the associated transaction attribute in the deployment descriptor defines the behavior of the EJB container (see Chapter 7).

Search Methods

Finder Method

There are several search methods available. By definition, a bean can always be found by means of its primary key. Thus the associated method findByPrimaryKey must always exist. This search can have only a single entity bean as its target. In addition, there can be other search methods that search according to other criteria. By the naming convention, their names always begin with find, followed by a descriptive name for the search method. These methods can be defined for a single targetor a set of targets.

The search methods are declared in the (local) home interface, and the associated searches are defined in the deployment descriptor with EJB-QL (EJB Query Language). An implementation in the bean class is not required (or, to put it better, not possible) in the case of container-managed persistence.

Searches that are allowed only one target use the bean's remote or local interface directly as data type for the return value. If a search can have several targets, then java.util.Enumeration (Java 1.1) or java.util.Collection (Java 1.2) is used as data type for the return value. The method findByPrimaryKey possesses exactly one parameter, which is, in fact, the primary key. For the other search methods parameters can be declared arbitrarily.

Listing 5-4 shows an imaginary example of a home interface that defines the search methods findByPrimaryKey (must) and findByAttributeA (may). The latter method can return several targets and therefore uses java.util.Collection as return value. A search method always declares an exception of type javax.ejb.FinderException. If we are dealing with the remote client view, then in addition, the exception java.rmi.RemoteException is declared. An exception of type FinderException is then triggered if a system error occurs during the execution of the search method. With search methods that return exactly one element as target, an exception of type javax.ejb.ObjectNotFoundException is triggered if no suitable element was found. ObjectNotFoundException is derived from FinderException. With search methods that return several elements, an empty set is returned if no suitable element could be found.

Listing 5-4. Imaginary example of a home interface with find methods.

```
...
public interface SomeHome extends EJBHome
{
    ...
    public Some findByPrimaryKey(SomePK pk)
        throws FinderException, RemoteException;
    public Collection findByAttributeA(double attrValue)
        throws FinderException, RemoteException;
    ...
}
```

For every search method (other than the method findByPrimaryKey) there is defined in the deployment descriptor a search (query). The search query (ejb-ql) is associated with the particular search method via the element query-method. The name must agree with the name of the search method in the home interface. All parameters (method-params) are given in the order in which they appear in the method definition. For each parameter the data type (method-param) must be defined.

The definition of the search is formulated in EJB-QL, which will be discussed in detail later in this chapter. Listing 5-5 shows the definition of a search for the method findByAttributeA in anticipation of what is to come in this section.

Listing 5-5. EJB-QL for the method findByAttributeA

```
...
<enterprise-beans>
  <entity>
    ...
    <query>
      <query-method>
        <method-name>findByAttributeA</method-name>
        <method-params>
          <method-param>double</method-param>
        </method-params>
      </query-method>
      <ejb-ql>
        SELECT OBJECT(a) FROM SomeBean AS a WHERE a.attributeA = ?1
      </ejb-ql>
    </query>
  </entity>
</enterprise-beans>
...
```

The defined parameters of the search method can be used in the search. They are referred to by their position in the definition. Thus the first parameter is addressed as ?1, the second as ?2, and the *n*th as ?<*n*>.

Select Methods

Select methods are similar to finder methods, except that they are more complex and are used by a bean internally, for example, in business methods. They are not designed for client use and are not published in the (local), home, remote, and local interfaces. The select methods are declared in the bean class as abstract methods with the prefix ejbSelect, and the associated search is defined in the deployment descriptor with EJB-QL. At the time of installation in the EJB container, the tools of the EJB container take care of the generation of a concrete method that at run time can be used by the entity bean instance.

Select methods, like finder methods, can return one or several references to other entity beans. However, they can also return values of persistent attributes of entity beans. Select methods can declare arbitrary parameters. The parameters are used in the finder methods for limiting the set of search results.

Listing 5-6 shows an imaginary example of an entity bean that defines the select methods ejbSelectAllABeansByName and ejbSelectAllABeanNames. The former method is to return all entity beans of type ABean whose names correspond to the passed attribute. The latter method returns all names that are used by ABean instances. It thus returns a set of String objects, which are the values of the persistent attribute name of all the Enterprise Beans of type ABean.

Listing 5-6. Pseudocode for the bean class of a select method.

```
...
public abstract BBean implements EntityBean
{
  ...
  public abstract Collection ejbSelectAllABeansByName(String name)
    throws FinderException;

  public abstract Collection ejbSelectAllABeanNames()
    throws FinderException
  ...
}
```

Listing 5-7 shows the definition of a search for the select methods in the deployment descriptor using EJB-QL. As we have already mentioned, EJB-QL will be discussed in a later section of this chapter. This example is a foretaste of the use of EJB-QL.

Listing 5-7. EJB-QL for the bean's select methods.

```
...
<enterprise-beans>
  <entity>
    ...
    <query>
      <query-method>
        <method-name>ejbSelectAllABeansByName</method-name>
        <method-params>
          <method-param>java.lang.String</method-param>
        </method-params>
      </query-method>
```

```
    <ejb-ql>
      SELECT OBJECT(a) FROM ABean AS a WHERE a.name = ?1
    </ejb-ql>
  </query>
  <query>
    <query-method>
      <method-name> ejbSelectAllABeanNames</method-name>
      <method-params>
        <!-- This method has no parameters -->
      </method-params>
    </query-method>
    <ejb-ql>
      SELECT DISTINCT a.name FROM ABean AS a
    </ejb-ql>
  </query>
  </entity>
</enterprise-beans>
...
```

The select method `ejbSelectAllABeansByName` returns references to other entity beans. These can be entity beans that support the local or remote client view. If an entity bean has a remote and a local interface, then according to the standard, a reference to the local interface of the entity bean is returned. With the element `result-type-mapping` within the element `query` it can be expressly determined whether a reference to the local or remote interface of the entity bean is returned. Permissible values for the element `result-type-mapping` are `Local` for a reference to the bean's local interface, and `Remote` for a reference to the bean's remote interface.

With select methods one can search for all entity beans and their attributes that are defined within the same deployment descriptor as the entity bean that is defined by a particular select method. Select methods can be used in an entity bean in home methods, business methods, and in the methods `ejbLoad` and `ejbStore`.

A select method has no transactional context of its own. Whether it is executed in a transaction depends on the transactional context of the method that calls the select method (for transactions, see Chapter 7).

Application Logic and Home Methods

The last group of methods constitute the application logic. Here is where the actual functionality of the entity bean is implemented. Normally, these methods refer to a particular bean instance. In the application methods (business methods) the access methods for reading and writing of attributes and relationships are used. The business methods are implemented by the bean developer in the bean class and published in the remote or local interface. The definition in the bean class has the same signature as the definition in the remote or local interface (see Figures 5-7 and 5-8). The name of the method may not be a reserved method name (not get<name>, set<name>, or ejb<name>).

In exceptional cases, however, there is also application logic that does not refer to a specific instance. This can be realized as a so-called home method. Home methods are published in the (local) home interface and are available to the client, even if it has no available entity bean instance. Its name in the bean class always begins with ejbHome, followed by a name for the method. In the home interface the prefix is omitted (see also Figures 5-7 and 5-8). The name for the method may not be a reserved method name (not create<name> or find<name>).

In the implementation of a home method one needs to note that the object has no identity. The particular ejbHome method is called on an instance in the state Pooled. Therefore, no access methods other than the select methods may be called. Furthermore, the generation and deletion of bean instances is prohibited.

The application methods in the home and remote interfaces of the remote client view always define the RemoteException, while the methods in the bean class use EJBException to signal a system error. The exeception EJBException is transformed by the EJB container into a RemoteException. Application methods of the local home and local interfaces do not define any exception of type RemoteException. If an error occurs, then EJBException is relayed directly to the local client.

The EJB container controls all calls to the methods of a bean. It delegates the method calls on the (local) home, remote, or local interface to the corresponding methods of the entity bean instance. The client never directly accesses the bean instance. The EJB container uses its position as intermediary between client and bean instance for a variety of tasks. For example, the EJB container ensures that a method is executed with the correct transaction context. It evaluates the transaction attribute of the method in the deployment descriptor, compares this with the client's transaction context, and then carries out the necessary actions to comply with the method's transactional requirements (see Chapter 7). Other examples of tasks of the EJB container are access protection for beans (see Chapter 8) and error logging.

Example Counter

To clarify the fundamental aspects of an entity bean with container-managed persistence 2.0, which was dealt with in this section, we will now look at a simple example; an application with many remote clients must manage a variety of counters; the counters should be available to all clients and be centrally managed;

and each client must have the ability to change a particular counter. The counter may not be less than 0 nor greater than 100.

The entity bean Counter fulfills these requirements. It supports the remote client view. With it, it is possible to manage various counters on the application server that are accessible by all clients. Each client can read and change the state of a particular counter.

First the remote interface of the counter bean is defined, which represents the functionality with respect to remote clients (see Listing 5-8). It defines the method inc for increasing a particular counter, the method dec to decrease a particular counter, and the method getValue to return the current state of a particular counter.

Listing 5-8. Remote interface of the counter bean.

```
package ejb.counter;
import java.rmi.RemoteException;
import javax.ejb.EJBObject;
public interface Counter extends EJBObject {
    public void inc()
        throws RemoteException, CounterOverflowException;
    public void dec()
        throws RemoteException, CounterOverflowException;
    public int getValue()
        throws RemoteException;
}
```

In addition to the RemoteException, the methods inc and dec declare the exceptions CounterOverflowException (see Listing 5-9). It is triggered if the state of a counter overflows, that is, if the value after a decrement would be less than 0 or if the value after an increment would be over 100.

Listing 5-9. Exception CounterOverflowException.

```
package ejb.counter;
public class CounterOverflowException extends Exception {
    public CounterOverflowException() {
        super();
    }
    public CounterOverflowException(String message) {
        super(message);
    }
}
```

A further component of the counter bean is the home interface (Listing 5-10). It defines the method create, by which a new counter can be generated. The counter has an ID in the form of a string object. The counter can be uniquely identified with this ID and can be located using the method findByPrimaryKey. Moreover, the initial state of the counter is passed to the counter in the method create. Furthermore, the home interface defines a home method for the counter bean with the name getAllCounterIds. It returns the IDs of all existing counters in the form of string objects. This functionality is not coupled to a particular counter and is therefore implemented in the home method. A client has the ability to determine via the home method what counters exist. If it has an interest in a particular counter, then it can access that counter using its ID with the method findByPrimaryKey.

Listing 5-10. Home interface of the counter bean.

```
package ejb.counter;

import javax.ejb.CreateException;
import javax.ejb.EJBHome;
import javax.ejb.FinderException;
import java.rmi.RemoteException;

public interface CounterHome extends EJBHome {

    public Counter create(String counterId, int initCounterValue)
        throws CreateException, RemoteException;

    public Counter findByPrimaryKey(String counterId)
        throws FinderException, RemoteException;

    public java.util.Collection getAllCounterIds()
        throws RemoteException;

}
```

After the home and remote interfaces have been defined, the bean class is defined (see Listing 5-11). It is an abstract class that implements the interface javax.ejb.EntityBean. It defines the method ejbCreate, corresponding to the create method of the home interface (as well as the method ejbPostCreate prescribed by the specification). The counter bean has two persistent attributes, namely, counterId and counterValue. The attribute counterId serves as the primary key of the counter bean. For each attribute the abstract getter/setter methods are defined.

Listing 5-11. Bean class of the counter bean.

```java
package ejb.counter;

import javax.ejb.CreateException;
import javax.ejb.EntityBean;
import javax.ejb.EntityContext;
import javax.ejb.FinderException;

public abstract class CounterBean implements EntityBean {

    public final static int VALUE_MAX = 100;
    public final static int VALUE_MIN = 0;

    private transient EntityContext ctx;

    //The create method of the home interface
    public String ejbCreate(String counterId,
                            int initCounterValue)
        throws CreateException
    {
        if(counterId == null) {
            throw new CreateException("counterId is null!");
        }
        if(initCounterValue < VALUE_MIN ||
           initCounterValue > VALUE_MAX)
        {
            String s = "initCounterValue out of range: "
                    + initCounterValue;
            throw new CreateException(s);
        }
        this.setCounterId(counterId);
        this.setCounterValue(initCounterValue);
        return null;
    }

    public void ejbPostCreate(String counterId,
                              int initCounterValue)
    {}

    //Abstract getter/setter methods
    public abstract void setCounterId(String id);
    public abstract String getCounterId();
    public abstract void setCounterValue(int value);
    public abstract int getCounterValue();
```

```
//Abstract select methods
public abstract java.util.Collection ejbSelectAllCounterIds()
    throws FinderException;

//Methods of the remote interface
public void inc() throws CounterOverflowException {
    if(this.getCounterValue() < VALUE_MAX) {
        this.setCounterValue(this.getCounterValue() + 1);
    } else {
        String s = "Cannot increase above " + VALUE_MAX;
        throw new CounterOverflowException(s);
    }
}

public void dec() throws CounterOverflowException {
    if(this.getCounterValue() > VALUE_MIN) {
        this.setCounterValue(this.getCounterValue() - 1);
    } else {
        String s = "Cannot decrease below " + VALUE_MIN;
        throw new CounterOverflowException(s);
    }
}

public int getValue() {
    return this.getCounterValue();
}

//Methods of the entity bean interface
public void ejbActivate() {}

public void ejbPassivate() {}

public void setEntityContext(EntityContext ctx) {
    this.ctx = ctx;
}

public void unsetEntityContext() {
    this.ctx = null;
}

public void ejbLoad() {}

public void ejbStore() {}

public void ejbRemove() {}

// Home methods
public java.util.Collection ejbHomeGetAllCounterIds() {
    java.util.ArrayList al = new java.util.ArrayList();
    try {
```

```
            java.util.Collection col =
                this.ejbSelectAllCounterIds();
            java.util.Iterator it = col.iterator();
            while(it.hasNext()) {
                al.add(it.next());
            }
        } catch(FinderException ex) {
            ex.printStackTrace();
        }
        return al;
    }
}
```

In addition to the abstract methods for the persistent attributes, an abstract ejbSelect method is defined. It returns all counter IDs in the form of string objects and is used by the home method getAllCounterIds in carrying out its responsibilities. The home method getAllCounterIds of the home interface gets the prefix ejbHome in the bean class, as required by the specification.

The methods inc, dec, and getValue of the remote interface are also implemented in the bean class. The callback methods of the entity bean interface remain largely empty. In the case of container-managed persistence the EJB container takes over the lion's share of the work, so that for the bean class itself there is little to implement.

Finally, the deployment descriptor of the counter bean is defined (see Listing 5-12). Worthy of note is the element query, in which the method ejbSelectAllCounterIds is declaratively implemented using EJB-QL, which will be discussed later in this chapter. Moreover, in the assembly descriptor it is set that the methods inc and dec must be called in a transaction, again a foretaste of Chapter 7, in which transactions will be handled in detail.

Listing 5-12. Deployment descriptor of the counter bean.

```
<?xml version="1.0" ?>
<ejb-jar version="2.1" xmlns="http://java.sun.com/xml/ns/j2ee"
xmlns:xsi="http://www.w3.org/2001/XMLSchema-instance"
xsi:schemaLocation="http://java.sun.com/xml/ns/j2ee
http://java.sun.com/xml/ns/j2ee/ejb-jar_2_1.xsd">
  <enterprise-beans>
    <entity>
      <ejb-name>Counter</ejb-name>
      <home>ejb.counter.CounterHome</home>
      <remote>ejb.counter.Counter</remote>
```

```
            <ejb-class>ejb.counter.CounterBean</ejb-class>
            <persistence-type>Container</persistence-type>
            <prim-key-class>java.lang.String</prim-key-class>
            <reentrant>False</reentrant>
            <cmp-version>2.x</cmp-version>
            <abstract-schema-name>CounterBean</abstract-schema-name>
            <cmp-field>
              <description>The Id of the counter</description>
              <field-name>counterId</field-name>
            </cmp-field>
            <cmp-field>
              <description>The value of the counter</description>
              <field-name>counterValue</field-name>
            </cmp-field>
            <primkey-field>counterId</primkey-field>
            <query>
              <query-method>
                <method-name>ejbSelectAllCounterIds</method-name>
                <method-params>
                </method-params>
              </query-method>
              <ejb-ql>
                SELECT DISTINCT cb.counterId FROM CounterBean AS cb
              </ejb-ql>
            </query>
          </entity>
      </enterprise-beans>

      <assembly-descriptor>
        <container-transaction>
          <method>
            <ejb-name>Counter</ejb-name>
            <method-name>inc</method-name>
          </method>
          <method>
            <ejb-name>Counter</ejb-name>
            <method-name>dec</method-name>
          </method>
          <trans-attribute>Required</trans-attribute>
        </container-transaction>
      </assembly-descriptor>

  </ejb-jar>
```

With this the components of the entity bean counter are complete from the point of view of the bean developer. One task for deployment yet to be done is the mapping of the bean's persistent attributes to the database. These tasks are generally handled by the deployer. How these instructions are to be made depends on the application server. Listing 5-13 shows an imaginary example of how such instructions might be given.

Listing 5-13. Imaginary database mapping for the counter bean.

```
<database-mapping>
    <bean-mapping>
        <ejb-name>Counter</ejb-name>
        <data-source-name>postgres</data-source-name>
        <table-name>counter</table-name>
        <field-map>
            <cmp-field>counterId</cmp-field>
            <dbms-column>id</dbms-column>
        </field-map>
        <field-map>
            <cmp-field>counterValue</cmp-field>
            <dbms-column>value</dbms-column>
        </field-map>
    </bean-mapping>
</database-mapping>
```

The attributes of the entity bean counter are stored in a table with the name counter. The bean attribute counterId is stored in the column id, the attribute counterValue in the column value. The persistence manager should use the preconfigured JDBC data source with the JNDI name postgres for the connection. Listing 5-14 shows the SQL statement for the generation of the table counter.

Listing 5-14. SQL statement for generating the table counter.

```
CREATE TABLE COUNTER (
  ID VARCHAR(128) NOT NULL UNIQUE,
  VALUE INTEGER NOT NULL
)
```

To conclude, Listing 5-15 shows how an imaginary client might use the counter bean.

Listing 5-15. Imaginary example of a client of the counter bean.

```
...
  InitialContext ctx = new InitialContext();
  Object o = ctx.lookup("Counter");
  CounterHome counterHome =
    (CounterHome)PortableRemoteObject.narrow(o, CounterHome.class);
  Counter counter = counterHome.create("carsInGarage", 0);

  ...
  try {
      counter.inc();
  } catch(CounterOverflowException ex) {
      throw new IllegalStateException("garage is full");
  }

  ...
  try {
      counter.dec();
  } catch(CounterOverflowException ex) {
      this.garageIsEmpty = true;
  }
...
```

Relations Among Entity Beans (EJB 2.0/2.1)

Persistent relationships managed by the EJB container (container-managed relationships) among entity beans are one of the important innovations of version 2.0 of the EJB specification. They make possible the mapping of complex data structures through the use of several related entity beans with container-managed persistence.

Relationships are directed; that is, there is a source object and one or more target objects. Unidirectional relationships are relationships in which only one part of the relationship is active. Navigation is then possible in only one direction. Bidirectional relationships are those in which both parties know about the relationship, and navigation can take place in either direction.

Entity beans that stand in relationship to one another must be defined in the same deployment descriptor. Such related entity beans are dependent on one another. Only when they are defined in the same deployment descriptor can the EJB container ensure at run time that the linked entity beans are available.

If the linked entity beans were defined in different deployment descriptors, then they could be installed on different application servers. Thus the EJB container could no longer guarantee the availability of the linked entity beans at run time. The other application server might no longer be operational, or the linked entity beans might have been deinstalled.

Entity beans that belong to the navigable part of a relationship must support the local client view. Otherwise, a reference cannot be made to them via a relationship. Since entity beans that are related must be defined in the same deployment descriptor, at run time they will be found in the same application server process. The use of the local client view ensures optimal performance in navigation across relationships due to the lack of network overhead. Moreover, the management of relationships for the EJB container becomes significantly simpler through use of the local client view and the consequent call-by-reference semantics.

From the point of view of the developer, a relationship between two entity bean types in the sense of this section consists of three components:

The first component consists of the abstract relationship methods in the entity bean class. A relationship to another entity bean receives a name similar to that of a persistent attribute. Depending on the type of relationship (unidirectional or bidirectional) the bean class defines a pair of abstract methods: a method set<relationshipname> and a method get<relationshipname>. The set method serves to create or change a relationship to a particular instance or instances of the other bean type, while the get method supports navigation across the relationship.

The second component is the formal description of the relationship in the deployment descriptor. There it is defined which entity beans stand in relationship to which other beans over which attributes (that is, over which abstract relationship methods) the relationship is established, whether the relationship is uni- or bidirectional, and the cardinality of the relationship.

The third component is the mapping of the relationships to the persistence medium. In the course of this section we shall assume that a relational database is used as persistence medium. It must be determined how the relationship is to be stored, that is, whether a foreign key or a relation table will be used. Moreover, it must be determined over which entity bean attributes (that is, over which table columns) a relationship is defined. The description of the third component is the task of the deployer, and its form is not set by the specification. Descriptions of the mapping of relationships to the persistence medium differs according to the application server.

In the following sections we will discuss the fundamentals of the various types of relationships.

One-to-One Relationships

Unidirectional

An example of a one-to-one relationship is the relationship between an automobile and the customer who is currently renting that automobile in an application involving an auto rental agency. An automobile can be rented at a particular time to exactly one customer. A customer can use precisely one automobile at a given time. If there is no relationship between a particular automobile and a customer, then that automobile is not currently rented. Figure 5-9 offers a graphical representation of the situation. The figure shows a unidirectional relationship that is stored via a foreign key relationship. The table automobile contains the column customernr (foreign key), which creates the relationship to the particular customer in the table customer.

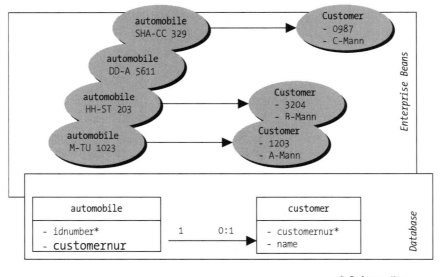

Figure 5-9. Example of a unidirectional one-to-one relationship.

For the case of a unidirectional relationship between an automobile bean and customer bean only the automobile bean defines the abstract relationship methods in the bean class (see Listing 5-16). The data type of the relationship is always the type of the local interface of the related entity bean.

Listing 5-16. Abstract relationship methods for an automobile bean.

```
...
    //Persistent attributes
    public abstract void setIDnumber(String id);
    public abstract String getIDnumber();
    //Persistent Relationshps
    public abstract void setCustomer(CustomerLocal customer);
    public abstract CustomerLocal getCustomer();
...
```

The direction of the relationship is from the automobile bean to the customer bean. Therefore, the customer bean must support the local client view, since it is reachable by the automobile bean using navigation. The automobile bean need not support the local client view in the case of a unidirectional relationship, since it is not reachable by navigation across the relationship. If there is no relationship to the customer bean, then a call to the method getCustomer returns the value null.

Listing 5-17 shows the formal description of the relationship in the deployment descriptor. The element ejb-relation involves the element ejb-relationship-name and always two elements ejb-relationship-role, one for each side of the relationship. Each side of the relationship receives a name via the element ejb-relationship-role-name. This name will have later meaning for the mapping to the database. For each part of the relationship the cardinality is given via the element multiplicity. The entity bean that will take part in the relationship is specified via relationship-role-source. The element cmr-field names the attribute of the bean over which the relationship is to be stored. If this field is missing on one of the two sides of the relationship, then we are automatically dealing with a unidirectional relationship; the direction depends on which side the element cmr-field is defined. The automobile bean has defined the methods setCustomer and getCustomer for the storage and navigation of the relationship. Thus the value for the element must be cmr-field-name customer, since otherwise, the EJB container would not be able to create the assignment to the relationship methods.

Listing 5-17. Formal description of the relationship Automobile–Customer *(unidirectional).*

```
...
  <enterprise-beans>
    <entity>
      <ejb-name>Automobile</ejb-name>
      ...
    </entity>
```

```
  <entity>
    <ejb-name>Customer</ejb-name>
    <local-home>CustomerLocalHome</local-home>
    <local>CustomerLocal</local>
    ...
  </entity>
  ...
</enterprise-beans>
...
<ejb-relation>
  <ejb-relation-name>Automobile-Customer</ejb-relation-name>
  <ejb-relationship-role>
    <ejb-relationship-role-name>
      automobile-has-customer
    </ejb-relationship-role-name>
    <multiplicity>One</multiplicity>
    <relationship-role-source>
      <ejb-name>Automobile</ejb-name>
    </relationship-role-source>
    <cmr-field>
      <cmr-field-name>customer</cmr-field-name>
    </cmr-field>
  </ejb-relationship-role>
  <ejb-relationship-role>
    <ejb-relationship-role-name>
      cutomer-uses-automoble
    </ejb-relationship-role-name>
    <multiplicity>One</multiplicity>
    <relationship-role-source>
      <ejb-name>Customer</ejb-name>
    </relationship-role-source>
  </ejb-relationship-role>
</ejb-relation>
...
```

The missing component is the description for how the relationship is to be mapped to the database. As we have already mentioned, its form is not determined by the specification. Every application server has its own format of how this mapping to the persistence medium is to be described. Listing 5-18 shows an imaginary example for the sake of clarifying the principle of this association.

Listing 5-18. Mapping of the Automobile–Customer *relationship to the database.*

```
<bean-mapping>
  <ejb-name>Automobile</ejb-name>
  <data-source-name>postgres</data-source-name>
  <table-name>automobile</table-name>
  <field-map>
    <cmp-field>IDnumber</cmp-field>
    <dbms-column>IDnumber</dbms-column>
  </field-map>
</bean-mapping>
<bean-mapping>
  <ejb-name>Customer</ejb-name>
  <data-source-name>postgres</data-source-name>
  <table-name>customer</table-name>
  <field-map>
    <cmp-field>customernr</cmp-field>
    <dbms-column>customernr</dbms-column>
  </field-map>
  <field-map>
    <cmp-field>name</cmp-field>
    <dbms-column>name</dbms-column>
  </field-map>
</bean-mapping>

...
<relation-mapping>
  <relation-name>Automible-Customer</relation-name>
    <relationship-role>
      <relationship-role-name>
        automobile-has-customer
      </relationship-role-name>
      <column-map>
        <foreign-key-column>customernr</foreign-key-column>
        <key-column>customernr</key-column>
      </column-map>
    </relationship-role>
</relation-mapping>
```

First the mapping of the entity beans Automobile and Customer to the database is described (bean-mapping). Then the mapping of the relationship is described. The EJB container knows from the deployment descriptor that the automobile and customer beans are participating in a relationship. Furthermore, it knows that it is dealing with a one-to-one relationship and that the relationship is unidirectional (from the automobile bean to the customer bean). From the description of the relationship (`relation-mapping`) it now also knows that the foreign key is stored in the table of the automobile bean. It is the part of the relationship with the name `automobile-has-customer` (whose `relationship-role-source` the automobile bean is) that is described and not the part `customer-uses-automobile`. The EJB container then maps the relationship via the column `customernr` of the table `automobile` (foreign key) to the column `customernr` of the table `customer`. With this information the tools of the EJB container and those of the persistence manager are able to generate the necessary code for managing the relationship and to handle the relationship correctly at run time.

Bidirectional

In order to extend the unidirectional relationship depicted in Figure 5-9 to a bidirectional relationship, the automobile bean must now support the local client view. Otherwise, it cannot be referred to by the customer bean. Like the automobile bean, the customer bean must define abstract relationship methods (see Listing 5-19).

Listing 5-19. Abstract relationship methods of the customer bean.

```
...
    //Persistent attributes
    public abstract void setCustomernr(String kn);
    public abstract String getCustomenr();
    public abstract void setName(String name);
    public abstract String getName();
    //Persistent relationships
    public abstract void setAutomobile(AutomobileLocal fl);
    public abstract AutomobileLocal getAutomobile();
...
```

If a relationship between the automobile and customer beans is created via the method `setCustomer` on the side of the automobile bean, then the relationship is also immediately visible by the customer bean. The same holds in the opposite direction. If a relationship is created between automobile and customer beans by a call to the method `setAutomobile`, then the relationship is also at once visible to the automobile bean. In the case of a bidirectional relationship it thus suffices to create the relationship on one of the two sides. It is then automatically navigable from the other side. If there is no relationship between two Enterprise Beans that are linked with cardinality one-to-one, then a call to the relevant `getter` methods returns the value `null`.

The bidirectionality of the relationship is declared in the deployment descriptor by the fact that now the element `cmr-field` is declared for both sides of the relationship (see Listing 5-20). Finally, the declaration in the deployment descriptor is the crucial factor for the relationship to be navigable in both directions.

Listing 5-20. Formal description of the relationship Automobile–Customer *(bidirectional).*

```
...
  <enterprise-beans>
    <entity>
      <ejb-name>Automobile</ejb-name>
      <local-home>AutomobileLocalHome</local-home>
      <local>AutomobileLocal</local>
      ...
    </entity>
    <entity>
      <ejb-name>Customer</ejb-name>
      <local-home>CustomerLocalHome</local-home>
      <local>CustomerLocal</local>
      ...
    </entity>
    ...
  </enterprise-beans>
...
  <ejb-relation>
    <ejb-relation-name>Automobile-Customer</ejb-relation-name>
    <ejb-relationship-role>
      <ejb-relationship-role-name>
        automobile-has-customer
      </ejb-relationship-role-name>
      <multiplicity>One</multiplicity>
      <relationship-role-source>
        <ejb-name>Automobile</ejb-name>
      </relationship-role-source>
      <cmr-field>
        <cmr-field-name>customer</cmr-field-name>
      </cmr-field>
    </ejb-relationship-role>
    <ejb-relationship-role>
      <ejb-relationship-role-name>
        customer-uses-automobile
```

```
      </ejb-relationship-role-name>
      <multiplicity>One</multiplicity>
      <relationship-role-source>
        <ejb-name>Customer</ejb-name>
      </relationship-role-source>
      <cmr-field>
        <cmr-field-name>automobile</cmr-field-name>
      </cmr-field>
    </ejb-relationship-role>
  </ejb-relation>
...
```

The description of the mapping to the database does not have to be changed. The EJB container already knows how the relationship is to be stored. The foreign key relation illustrated in Figure 5-9 enables navigation in both directions. It matters little for the programming whether the relationship is uni- or bidirectional. For the EJB container the navigation in one direction or the other of the relationship is merely a reflection of a database query.

One-to-n Relationships (One to Many)

Unidirectional Relationships

An example of a one-to-n relationship is the relationship between a department and its employees, as depicted in Figure 5-10. A number of employees work in one department. An employee is always associated with precisely one department (if an employee could be associated with several departments, then we would no longer be dealing with a a one-to-n relationship). In this case as well, the relationship is stored using a foreign key relation between the relevant tables. The table employee contains the column accountingnr (= foreign key), which creates the department in the table department. Alternatively, one could use a relation table. The use of a relation table will be discussed in the next section.

For the case of a unidirectional relationship between the department and employee beans only the department bean implements the abstract relationship methods in the bean class (see Listing 5-21). Since the department bean can have a relationship to several employee beans, the data type of the relationship is of type java.util.Collection or java.util.Set.

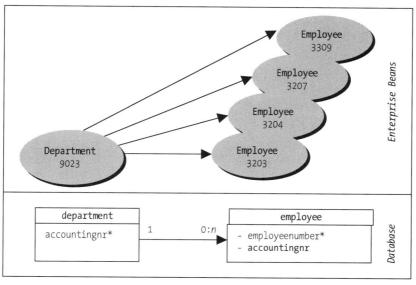

Figure 5-10. Example of a unidirectional one-to-n relationship.

Listing 5-21. Abstract relationship methods of the department bean.

```
...
    //Persistent attributes
    public abstract void setAccountingnr(String knr);
    public abstract String getAccountingnr();
    //Persistent relationships
    public abstract void setEmployee(Collection ma);
    public abstract Collection getEmployee();
...
```

The difference between java.util.Collection and java.util.Set is that a Collection is allowed to contain duplicate members, while a Set cannot. In our example is doesn't matter which class is used. An employee can in any case be associated with only one department. The accounting number of the employee in unique, since it is the primary key in the table. Therefore, the database ensures that there are no duplicates.

The employee bean must support the local client view, since it can then be referenced through navigation by the department bean. The department bean need not support the local client view, since the relationship is unidirectional, pointing from the department bean to the employee bean.

The description of the relationship in the deployment descriptor is distinguished from one-to-one relationships only in the cardinality (Listing 5-22). Furthermore, it must be specified by the element `cmr-field-type` whether `java.util.Collection` or `java.util.Set` will be used as the data container.

Listing 5-22. Formal description of the relationship Department–Employee *(unidirectional).*

```
...
  <enterprise-beans>
    <entity>
      <ejb-name>Department</ejb-name>
      ...
    </entity>
    <entity>
      <ejb-name>Employee</ejb-name>
      <local-home>EmployeeLocalHome</local-home>
      <local>EmployeeLocal</local>
      ...
    </entity>
    ...
  </enterprise-beans>
...
  <ejb-relation>
    <ejb-relation-name>Department-Employee</ejb-relation-name>
    <ejb-relationship-role>
      <ejb-relationship-role-name>
        department-has-employee
      </ejb-relationship-role-name>
      <multiplicity>One</multiplicity>
      <relationship-role-source>
        <ejb-name>Department</ejb-name>
      </relationship-role-source>
      <cmr-field>
        <cmr-field-name>employee</cmr-field-name>
        <cmr-field-type>java.util.Collection</cmr-field-type>
      </cmr-field>
    </ejb-relationship-role>
    <ejb-relationship-role>
      <ejb-relationship-role-name>
```

```
          employee-is-in-department
        </ejb-relationship-role-name>
        <multiplicity>Many</multiplicity>
        <relationship-role-source>
          <ejb-name>Employee</ejb-name>
        </relationship-role-source>
      </ejb-relationship-role>
    </ejb-relation>
...
```

The description of the mapping to the database (see Listing 5-23) is just about the same as that of one-to-one relationships. But be careful in describing the foreign key relation: One must describe the foreign key relation for the correct side of the relationship. In this case we are dealing with the side `employee-is-in-department`, since the `relationship-role-source` is the employee bean. It is mapped to the table `employee`, which contains the foreign key.

Listing 5-23. Mapping of the Department–Employee *relationship to the database.*

```
<bean-mapping>
  <ejb-name>Department</ejb-name>
  <data-source-name>postgres</data-source-name>
  <table-name>department</table-name>
  <field-map>
    <cmp-field>accountingnr</cmp-field>
    <dbms-column>accountingnr</dbms-column>
  </field-map>
</bean-mapping>
<bean-mapping>
  <ejb-name>Employee</ejb-name>
  <data-source-name>postgres</data-source-name>
  <table-name>employee</table-name>
  <field-map>
    <cmp-field>personnelnr</cmp-field>
    <dbms-column>personnelnr</dbms-column>
  </field-map>
</bean-mapping>
...
<relation-mapping>
  <relation-name>Department-Employee</relation-name>
    <relationship-role>
      <relationship-role-name>
        employee-is-in-department
      </relationship-role-name>
```

```
  <column-map>
    <foreign-key-column>accountingnr</foreign-key-column>
    <key-column>accountingnr</key-column>
  </column-map>
  </relationship-role>
</relation-mapping>
```

A feature of note for the bean developer in the use of a one-to-*n* relationship is the use of the cardinality *n* of the relationship, which is represented by the data type java.util.Collection or java.util.Set.

In contrast cardinality 1, the get method with the cardinality *n* never returns the value null. If no relationship exists between the bean instances, then the return value is a Collection or Set object containing no elements (thus is empty).

To set up relationships between the department and employee beans, the bean developer has two options: The variant shown in Listing 5-24 uses the method setEmployee of the department bean. It creates a relationship to employees A, B, and C. If the department bean already had a relationship to employees D and E, then that relationship would be deleted. The semantics of a set method are to overwrite existing values. This is also the case with relationships. The relationship to employees D and E would be overwritten by the relationship to A, B, and C. The relationship to employees D and E would no longer exist.

Listing 5-24. Setting relationships using the method setEmployee().

```
...
EmployeeLocalHome employeeHome = ...
DepartmentHome departmentHome = ...

Department department = departmentHome.findByPrimaryKey(...);

EmployeeLocal mA = employeeHome.create("A", ...);
EmployeeLocal mB = employeeHome.create("B", ...);
EmployeeLocal mC = employeeHome.create("C", ...);

java.util.ArrayList al = new java.util.ArrayList();
al.add(mA);
al.add(mB);
al.add(mC);

department.setEmployee(al);

...
```

Listing 5-25 shows how relationships to employees can be set up without overwriting existing relationships.

Listing 5-25. Adding relationships using the method Collection.add().

```
...
EmployeeLocalHome employeeHome = ...
DepartmentHome departmentHome = ...
Department department = departmentHome.findByPrimaryKey(...);
java.util.Collection col = department.getEmployee();
EmployeeLocal mA = employeeHome.create("A", ...);
EmployeeLocal mB = employeeHome.create("B", ...);
EmployeeLocal mC = employeeHome.create("C", ...);
col.add(mA);
col.add(mB);
col.add(mC);
...
```

The object that the method getEmployee of the department bean returns is an implementation of the interface java.util.Collection, which is supplied by the EJB container. With the Collection object the EJB container grants the bean developer access to the cardinality *n* of the relationship with the employee bean. Method calls on this Collection object are processed by the EJB container. Changes are relayed immediately to the database by the EJB container.

The bean developer must note that an employee bean can be linked to only one department bean. If employee H is in department B, then adding employee H to department C would have the effect of deleting the link to department B. This behavior is determined by the fact that the relationship has cardinality 1-to-*n*. If an employee can be related to two or more departments, then we are dealing with a cardinality of *n*-to-*m*.

Listing 5-26 shows how the bean developer can navigate over a relationship of cardinality *n* to a particular bean.

Listing 5-26. Navigation over the cardinality n to the department bean.

```
...
java.util.Collection col = department.getEmployee();
java.util.Iterator it = col.iterator();
while(it.hasNext()) {
    EmployeeLocal ma = (EmployeeLocal)it.next();
    if(ma.getName().equals(nameToSearchFor)) {
        ...
    }
    ...
}
...
```

The objects contained within the collection are always of the type of the local interface of the linked bean. Therefore, it is unnecessary to employ type narrowing via the method `narrow` of the class `javax.rmi.PortableRemoteObject`.

Listing 5-27 shows how the bean developer can delete a relationship to a bean of cardinality *n*.

Listing 5-27. Deleting a relationship to the department bean of cardinality n.

```
...
java.util.Collection col = department.getEmployee();
java.util.Iterator it = col.iterator();
while(it.hasNext()) {
    EmployeeLocal ma = (EmployeeLocal)it.next();
    if(ma.isFired()) {
        it.remove();
    }
}
...
```

The deletion of a relationship does not, of course, mean the deletion of the linked bean instance. Only the relationship between the two entity beans is deleted. The EJB container sets the value of the foreign key column to `null`.

Bidirectional Relationships

To transform a unidirectional one-to-*n* relationship into a bidirectional one-to-*n* requires the same steps as in the case of a one-to-one relationship. The department bean must also support the local client view, since otherwise, it cannot be referenced by the employee bean. Moreover, the employee bean must define abstract relationship methods (see Listing 5-28). Since the cardinality is declared to be 1 from the department bean side of things, the relationship methods are of type `DepartmentLocal`.

Listing 5-28. Abstract relationship methods of the employee bean.

```
...
    //Persistent attributes
    public abstract void setPersonnelnumber(String pn);
    public abstract String getPersonnelnumber();
    //Persistent relationships
    public abstract void setDepartment(DepartmentLocal al);
    public abstract DepartmentLocal getDepartment();
...
```

The abstract relationship methods of the employee bean must still be declared in the deployment descriptor (see Listing 5-29). It is only the declaration of the relationship methods in the deployment descriptor that makes the relationship bidirectional.

Listing 5-29. Formal description of the relationship Department–Employee *(bidirectional).*

```
...
  <enterprise-beans>
    <entity>
      <ejb-name>Department</ejb-name>
      <local-home>DepartmentLocalHome</local-home>
      <local>DepartmentLocal</local>
      ...
    </entity>
    <entity>
      <ejb-name>Employee</ejb-name>
      <local-home>EmployeeLocalHome</local-home>
      <local>EmployeeLocal</local>
      ...
    </entity>
    ...
  </enterprise-beans>
...
  <ejb-relation>
    <ejb-relation-name>Department-Employee</ejb-relation-name>
    <ejb-relationship-role>
      <ejb-relationship-role-name>
        department-has-employee
      </ejb-relationship-role-name>
      <multiplicity>One</multiplicity>
      <relationship-role-source>
        <ejb-name>Department</ejb-name>
      </relationship-role-source>
      <cmr-field>
        <cmr-field-name>employee</cmr-field-name>
        <cmr-field-type>java.util.Collection</cmr-field-type>
      </cmr-field>
    </ejb-relationship-role>
    <ejb-relationship-role>
      <ejb-relationship-role-name>
        employee-is-in-department
      </ejb-relationship-role-name>
```

```
        <multiplicity>Many</multiplicity>
        <relationship-role-source>
          <ejb-name>Employee</ejb-name>
        </relationship-role-source>
        <cmr-field>
          <cmr-field-name>department</cmr-field-name>
        </cmr-field>
      </ejb-relationship-role>
    </ejb-relation>
...
```

The description of the mapping to the database is (as with one-to-one relationships) identical to the unidirectional one-to-n relationship. At the database level the relationship is already navigable. Navigation in the other direction is merely the mirror-image formulation of a database query.

n-to-m Relationships (Many to Many)

Unidirectional Relationships

An example of an n-to-m relationship is that between a product and a product part. Figure 5-11 clarifies the situation. A product part can be used with several products. However, in this case, for storing the relationship a foreign key relation can no longer be used. A necessary condition for being able to use a foreign key relation is that uniqueness exist in at least one direction of the relationship. In the case of n-to-m relationships that is no longer the case. Therefore, for storing the relationship a relation table is used. It exists only for the purpose of storing relationships. It contains all fields of the primary key of the entities that are involved.

For the case of unidirectional n-to-m relationships only the product bean defines the abstract relationship methods in the bean class (see Listing 5-30). Since the product bean relationships can have several product part beans, the abstract relation methods are of type java.util.Collection and java.util.Set.

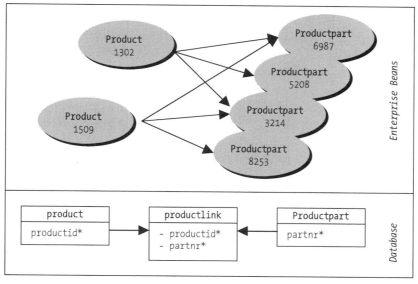

* Primary Key

Figure 5-11. Example of a unidirectional n-to-m relationship.

Listing 5-30. Abstract relationship methods of the product bean.

```
...
    //Persistent attributes
    public abstract void setProductId(String pid);
    public abstract String getProductId();


    //Persistent relationships
    public abstract void setOptionalpart(Collection zt);
    public abstract Collection getOptionalpart();
...
```

The differences between java.util.Collection and java.util.Set and their uses in setting up, adding, and deleting relationships was handled in the previous section. However, there exists a noteworthy difference in comparison with the one-to-n relationships that is based on the semantics of the n-to-m relationships.

For example, if product A has a relationship to product part X, and now product part X is placed in relationship to product D, then this has no effect on the relationship to product A. Both products, A and D, have a relationship to product part X. In a one-to-n relationship the relationship to product A would have been deleted by the relationship to product D.

Listing 5-31 shows the description of the unidirectional n-to-m relationship between the product bean and product part bean in the deployment descriptor. The product part bean must support the local client view, since it is referred to by the product bean via navigation. In the case of a unidirectional relationship the product bean need not support the local client view.

Listing 5-31. Formal description of the relationship Product–Optionalpart *(unidirectional).*

```
...
  <enterprise-beans>
    <entity>
      <ejb-name>Product</ejb-name>
      ...
    </entity>
    <entity>
      <ejb-name>Optionalpart</ejb-name>
      <local-home>OptionalpartLocalHome</local-home>
      <local>OptionalpartLocal</local>
      ...
    </entity>
    ...
  </enterprise-beans>
  ...
  <ejb-relation>
    <ejb-relation-name>Product-Optionalpart</ejb-relation-name>
    <ejb-relationship-role>
      <ejb-relationship-role-name>
        product-has-optionalpart
      </ejb-relationship-role-name>
      <multiplicity>Many</multiplicity>
      <relationship-role-source>
        <ejb-name>Product</ejb-name>
      </relationship-role-source>
      <cmr-field>
        <cmr-field-name>optionalpart</cmr-field-name>
        <cmr-field-type>java.util.Collection</cmr-field-type>
      </cmr-field>
```

```
  </ejb-relationship-role>
  <ejb-relationship-role>
    <ejb-relationship-role-name>
      optionalpart-is-in-product
    </ejb-relationship-role-name>
    <multiplicity>Many</multiplicity>
    <relationship-role-source>
      <ejb-name>Optionalpart</ejb-name>
    </relationship-role-source>
  </ejb-relationship-role>
 </ejb-relation>
...
```

Listing 5-32 shows an imaginary example of how the mapping of the relation to the database can be described. What is new in comparison to the previous examples is the necessity of using a relation table.

Listing 5-32. Mapping of the Product–Optionalpart *relationship to the database.*

```
<bean-mapping>
  <ejb-name>Product</ejb-name>
  <data-source-name>postgres</data-source-name>
  <table-name>product</table-name>
  <field-map>
    <cmp-field>productId</cmp-field>
    <dbms-column>productid</dbms-column>
  </field-map>
</bean-mapping>
<bean-mapping>
  <ejb-name>Optionalpart</ejb-name>
  <data-source-name>postgres</data-source-name>
  <table-name>optionalpart</table-name>
  <field-map>
    <cmp-field>partNumber</cmp-field>
    <dbms-column>partnr</dbms-column>
  </field-map>
</bean-mapping>
...
<relation-mapping>
  <relation-name>Product-Optionalpart</relation-name>
  <relation-table>productlink</relation-table>
    <relationship-role>
      <relationship-role-name>
```

```
        product-has-optionalpart
     </relationship-role-name>
     <column-map>
        <foreign-key-column>productid</foreign-key-column>
        <key-column>productid</key-column>
     </column-map>
   </relationship-role>
   <relationship-role>
     <relationship-role-name>
        optionalpart-is-in-product
     </relationship-role-name>
     <column-map>
        <foreign-key-column>partnr</foreign-key-column>
        <key-column>partnr</key-column>
     </column-map>
   </relationship-role>
</relation-mapping>
```

First the mapping of the persistent attributes of the entity beans is described in the relevant tables. The description of the relationship specifies that a relation table is being used and gives its name. Then the mapping must be described for both sides of the relationship in the relation table. The description for only one side of the relationship, as with the use of a foreign key, is insufficient, since both sides of the relationship have a foreign key relationship to the relation table.

Bidirectional Relationships

As was the case for one-to-one and one-to-n relationships, the extension of a unidirectional n-to-m relationship to a bidirectional n-to-m relationship is relatively easy. The product bean must also support the local client view, so that it can be referenced by the product part bean. The product part bean must declare abstract relationship methods (see Listing 5-33) to enable navigation in the opposite direction (from the product part bean to the product bean). Since a product part bean can be related to several products, the relationship is of type java.util.Collection (or java.util.Set).

Listing 5-33. Abstract relationship methods of the product part bean.

```
...
   //Persistent attributes
   public abstract void setPartNumber(String tn);
   public abstract String getPartNumber();
```

```
//Persistent relationships
public abstract void setProduct(Collection p);
public abstract Collection getProduct();
...
```

The next building block for the extension into a bidirectional *n*-to-*m* relationship is the declaration of the abstract relationship methods in the product part bean in the deployment descriptor (see Listing 5-34).

Listing 5-34. Formal description of the relationship Product–Optionalpart *(bidirectional).*

```
<enterprise-beans>
  <entity>
    <ejb-name>Product</ejb-name>
    <local-home>ProductLocalHome</local-home>
    <local>ProductLocal</local>
    ...
  </entity>
  <entity>
    <ejb-name>OptionalPart</ejb-name>
    <local-home>OptionalpartLocalHome</local-home>
    <local>OptionalpartLocal</local>
    ...
  </entity>
  ...
</enterprise-beans>
...
<ejb-relation>
  <ejb-relation-name>product-optionalpart</ejb-relation-name>
  <ejb-relationship-role>
    <ejb-relationship-role-name>
      product-has-optionalpart
    </ejb-relationship-role-name>
    <multiplicity>Many</multiplicity>
    <relationship-role-source>
      <ejb-name>Product</ejb-name>
    </relationship-role-source>
    <cmr-field>
      <cmr-field-name>optionalpart</cmr-field-name>
      <cmr-field-type>java.util.Collection</cmr-field-type>
    </cmr-field>
  </ejb-relationship-role>
```

```
  <ejb-relationship-role>
    <ejb-relationship-role-name>
      optionalpart-is-in-product
    </ejb-relationship-role-name>
    <multiplicity>Many</multiplicity>
    <relationship-role-source>
      <ejb-name>Optionalpart</ejb-name>
    </relationship-role-source>
    <cmr-field>
      <cmr-field-name>product</cmr-field-name>
      <cmr-field-type>java.util.Collection</cmr-field-type>
    </cmr-field>
  </ejb-relationship-role>
 </ejb-relation>
...
```

The description of the mapping to the database is (as with the other types of relationships) identical to the unidirectional n-to-m relationship. The use of a relation table enables navigation in both directions.

Cascading Delete

When a relationship between entity beans is deleted, the entity beans themselves remain untouched. That is, only the relationship between the entity beans is deleted, not the entity beans themselves. However, in many cases the relationship between two entity beans is such that the existence of the beans without the relationship makes little sense. An example of this is a bidirectional one-to-one relationship between the entity bean User and the entity bean Userprofile. The entity bean User stores data such as user name, encrypted password, or the user's access privileges. These data are a precondition for the user being able to operate within the system. The entity bean Userprofile stores data such as the full name of the user, the department in which he or she works, and a telephone number. These data constitute additional information that might be used, say, for analysis. If the user bean of a particular user is deleted (for example, if the employee leaves the company), the relationship to the user profile bean is also deleted by the EJB container. The user profile bean of this user is now a floating cadaver within the system if it has not been explicitly deleted. Without the user, the user profile can no longer be referenced.

For such cases one can notify the EJB container that when the entity bean is deleted, all entity beans related to it are to be deleted as well. This mechanism is called *cascading delete*. Listing 5-35 shows how one can notify the EJB container to execute a cascading delete.

Listing 5-35. Declaration of a cascading delete.

```
...
  <enterprise-beans>
    <entity>
      <ejb-name>User</ejb-name>
      ...
    </entity>
    <entity>
      <ejb-name>Userprofile</ejb-name>
      ...
    </entity>
    ...
  </enterprise-beans>
  ...
  <ejb-relation>
    <ejb-relation-name>User-Userprofile</ejb-relation-name>
    <ejb-relationship-role>
      <ejb-relationship-role-name>
        user-has-userprofile
      </ejb-relationship-role-name>
      <multiplicity>One</multiplicity>
      <relationship-role-source>
        <ejb-name>User</ejb-name>
      </relationship-role-source>
      <cmr-field>
        <cmr-field-name>profil</cmr-field-name>
      </cmr-field>
    </ejb-relationship-role>
    <ejb-relationship-role>
      <ejb-relationship-role-name>
        userprofile-belongs-to-user
      </ejb-relationship-role-name>
      <multiplicity>One</multiplicity>
      <cascade-delete/>
      <relationship-role-source>
        <ejb-name>Userprofile</ejb-name>
      </relationship-role-source>
      <cmr-field>
        <cmr-field-name>user</cmr-field-name>
      </cmr-field>
    </ejb-relationship-role>
  </ejb-relation>
...
```

If a particular user bean is deleted, then the (XML) element `cascade-delete` in Listing 5-35 has the effect that the linked user profile bean will automatically be deleted along with it by the EJB container. Cascading delete can proceed only from an entity bean whose cardinality is one. Otherwise, one could not be sure that the deleted entity bean didn't still have other relationships, and that could jeopardize the consistency of the stored data.

The instruction `cascade-delete` is a powerful tool, and it should be used with care. The user profile bean could, for example, have a relationship to another bean in which a `cascade-delete` is declared, which could have a relationship to another bean in which a `cascade-delete` is declared, which could, well, you get the idea. That is, cascading deletion of one entity bean could result in a virtual chain reaction being set off. In complex applications with many relationships it can be difficult to keep track of all the dependencies, which is necessary in using `cascade-delete` correctly.

To conclude this section on relationships among entity beans we would like to call the reader's attention to the explanations of relationships between entity beans in Sections 10.3.6 and 10.3.7 of the EJB specification (see [21]).

EJB-QL (EJB 2.0/2.1)

Introduced in version 2.0 and enhanced in 2.1 is the query language EJB-QL. EJB-QL CMP stands for *EJB Query Language for Container-Managed-Persistence Query Methods*. As the name suggests, this is an EJB-specific query language for formulating searches across entity beans with *container-managed persistence*. The syntax of EJB-QL is based largely on the syntax of the query language SQL92. Earlier sections on finder and select methods have already given a foretaste of EJB-QL.

Search queries formulated with EJB-QL can be implemented unchanged in various EJB containers and diverse persistence systems. For the formulation of finder methods in the case of container-managed persistence, many application servers have developed their own proprietary languages, since there was no independent query language defined in the specification before version 2.0. In porting an entity bean with container-managed persistence the search queries must then be modified to comply with the finder methods on the application server of the EJB container in question.

EJB-QL is not interpreted at run time, but is translated into another query language at the time of deployment by the EJB container. For example, if an entity bean with container-managed persistence is linked to a relational database at deployment, then the EJB container would translate the search query from EJB-QL into SQL. When the search query is called, the EJB container executes the corresponding SQL commands.

EJB-QL search queries are always related to a particular query space. The boundaries of such a query space are set by the deployment descriptor. In formulating a search query, which is always defined within the confines of a particular entity bean type, all entity beans with container-managed persistence defined in the same deployment descriptor can be accessed.

In practice, EJB-QL is implemented for the definition of the following methods:

- **Finder methods**
  Finder methods are defined in the home or local home interface of an entity bean with container-managed persistence. They are implemented by specifying an EJB-QL query in the deployment descriptor. If a finder method is defined in the home interface of an entity bean, then the type of the return value of the associated EJB-QL query must be of the type of the remote interface of the entity bean. If the finder method was defined in the local home interface of the entity bean, then the type of the return value of the associated search query must be of the type of the local interface of the entity bean.

- **Select methods**
  Select methods are declared as abstract methods in the bean class, and they provide access to the persistent state of other entity beans. They are implemented (like the finder methods) by specifying an EJB-QL query in the deployment descriptor. The type of the return value of such queries can be of the type of the remote or local interface or of a persistent attribute of an entity bean.

Listing 5-36 shows a segment from the deployment descriptor, in which the entity bean Person and the entity bean Address are defined. Both entity beans are in bidirectional relationship to each other. The Person bean defines the persistent attributes name (for the surname) and firstname, which together with the persistent relationship to the Address bean belong to the abstract persistence schema of the Person bean, to which the name PersonAPS is given via the element abstract-schema-name. The suffix APS stands for *abstract persistence schema*, and it is used here to avoid confusion between the bean name and the name of the abstract persistence schema (usually, one uses the same name for both elements). The Address bean defines the persistent attributes (foreign key for the relationship to the person bean), street, zip (for the postal code), and city. Together with the persistent relationship to the Person bean they belong to the abstract persistence schema of the Address bean, which is called AddressAPS. In the course of this section we shall always return to this deployment descriptor in our EJB-QL examples.

Listing 5-36. EJB-QL example for the entity bean Person.

```
...
<entity>
    <ejb-name>PersonBean</ejb-name>
    <local-home>PersonLocalHome</local-home>
    <local>PersonLocal</local>
    <ejb-class>PersonBean</ejb-class>
    <persistence-type>Container</persistence-type>
    <prim-key-class>java.lang.String</prim-key-class>
    <reentrant>False</reentrant>
    <cmp-version>2.x</cmp-version>
    <abstract-schema-name>PersonAPS</abstract-schema-name>
    <cmp-field>
        <field-name>name</field-name>
    </cmp-field>
    <cmp-field>
        <field-name>firstname</field-name>
    </cmp-field>
    <primkey-field>name</primkey-field>
</entity>
<entity>
    <ejb-name>AddressBean</ejb-name>
    <local-home>AddressLocalHome</local-home>
    <local>AddressLocal</local>
    <ejb-class>AddressBean</ejb-class>
    <persistence-type>Container</persistence-type>
    <prim-key-class>java.lang.String</prim-key-class>
    <reentrant>False</reentrant>
    <cmp-version>2.x</cmp-version>
    <abstract-schema-name>AddressAPS</abstract-schema-name>
    <cmp-field>
        <field-name>name</field-name>
    </cmp-field>
    <cmp-field>
        <field-name>street</field-name>
    </cmp-field>
    <cmp-field>
        <field-name>zip</field-name>
    </cmp-field>
    <cmp-field>
        <field-name>city</field-name>
    </cmp-field>
    <primkey-field>name</primkey-field>
```

```
</entity>
...
<ejb-relation>
    <ejb-relation-name>Person-Address</ejb-relation-name>
    <ejb-relationship-role>
        <ejb-relationship-role-name>
            person-has-address
        </ejb-relationship-role-name>
        <multiplicity>One</multiplicity>
        <relationship-role-source>
            <ejb-name>PersonBean</ejb-name>
        </relationship-role-source>
        <cmr-field>
            <cmr-field-name>address</cmr-field-name>
        </cmr-field>
    </ejb-relationship-role>
    <ejb-relationship-role>
        <ejb-relationship-role-name>
            address-belongs-to-person
        </ejb-relationship-role-name>
        <multiplicity>One</multiplicity>
        <relationship-role-source>
            <ejb-name>AddressBean</ejb-name>
        </relationship-role-source>
        <cmr-field>
            <cmr-field-name>person</cmr-field-name>
        </cmr-field>
    </ejb-relationship-role>
</ejb-relation>
...
```

Constructing the Search Query

All search queries are divided into four parts:

1. SELECT clause: This determines the type of the return value for the search query. This can be a reference to an entity bean or a persistent attribute of an entity bean.

2. FROM clause: This determines the domain of the instructions in the SELECT and optional WHERE clauses. Queries relate to the CMP 2.0 entity beans defined in the deployment descriptor or to their persistent attributes and relationships.

3. WHERE clause (optional): This serves to limit the result set.

4. `ORDER BY` clause (optional): This serves to order the result set. This was added in EJB 2.1 and does not exist in version 2.0 of the specification.

Listing 5-37 shows the simplest example of an EJB-QL query. It is assumed that the `Person` bean defines a finder method in its home interface with the name `findAllPersons`. The query defined via the element `ejb-ql` is associated with the method `findAllPersons` via the element `query-method`.

Listing 5-37. Simple EJB-QL query for `findAllPersons`.

```
...
<entity>
    <ejb-name>PersonBean</ejb-name>
    ...
    <query>
        <query-method>
            <method-name>findAllPersons</method-name>
        </query-method>
        <ejb-ql>
            SELECT OBJECT(p) FROM PersonAPS AS p
        </ejb-ql>
    </query>
</entity>
...
```

The query returns all objects that correspond to the abstract persistence schema `PersonAPS`, that is, all existing `Person` entity beans. The client that calls the `findAllPersons` method receives an object of type `java.util.Collection`, which contains the local references to the found `Person` beans.

The following points hold generally for search queries in EJB-QL:

- Queries always relate to the abstract persistence schema of one or more entity beans with container-managed persistence 2.0.

- To the abstract persistence schema of an entity bean belong the persistent attributes and the persistent relationships to other entity beans.

- EJB-QL queries are defined in the deployment descriptor, in fact, in the domain of a particular entity bean.

- EJB-QL queries are always associated with a particular finder or select method.

- In the search query the only entity beans that may be involved are those defined in the same deployment descriptor as the entity bean in whose domain the search query is defined.

Attribute Search

The result set of a query can be limited by using attributes of an entity bean (which are a component of the abstract persistence schema). Let us assume that the person bean defines the following finder method in its local home interface:

```
java.util.Collection findByFirstname(java.lang.String firstname)
    throws javax.ejb.FinderException;
```

The purpose of this method is to find persons that have a particular first name. Listing 5-38 shows the corresponding definition in the deployment descriptor.

Listing 5-38. EJB-QL query for findByFirstname.

```
...
<entity>
    <ejb-name>PersonBean</ejb-name>
    ...
    <abstract-schema-name>PersonAPS</abstract-schema-name>
    ...
    <cmp-field>
        <field-name>firstname</field-name>
    </cmp-field>
    ...
    <query>
        <query-method>
            <method-name>findByFirstname</method-name>
            <method-params>
                <method-param>java.lang.String</method-param>
            </method-params>
        </query-method>
        <ejb-ql>
            SELECT OBJECT(p) FROM PersonAPS AS p WHERE p.firstname=?1
        </ejb-ql>
    </query>
</entity>
...
```

With the WHERE clause the search result is restricted to all objects whose first name corresponds to the value of the first parameter (?1) of the method findByFirstname (in this case the parameter firstname). The types of the parameters must be set using the element method-params.

In addition to the restriction of the search results using attributes, the values of persistent attributes can also be returned. However, this is reserved for the select methods, since finder methods are permitted only to return references to entity beans. Finder methods are called by the client, not select methods.

We assume that the person bean defines a select method

```
public abstract Collection ejbSelectNamesInCity(String city)
    throws FinderException;
```

in order to determine which persons live in a particular city. The associated declaration in the deployment descriptor is shown in Listing 5-39.

Listing 5-39. EJB-QL query for ejbSelectNamesInCity.

```
...
<entity>
    <ejb-name>PersonBean</ejb-name>
    ...
    <query>
        <query-method>
            <method-name>ejbSelectNamesInCity</method-name>
            <method-params>
                <method-param>java.lang.String</method-param>
            </method-params>
        </query-method>
        <ejb-ql>
            SELECT p.name FROM AddressAPS AS p WHERE p.city=?1
        </ejb-ql>
    </query>
</entity>
<entity>
    <ejb-name>AddressBean</ejb-name>
    ...
    <abstract-schema-name>AddressAPS</abstract-schema-name>
    <cmp-field>
        <field-name>name</field-name>
    </cmp-field>
    ...
    <cmp-field>
        <field-name>city</field-name>
    </cmp-field>
    ...
</entity>
...
```

The type of the return value is no longer a bean object, but the type of the attribute name of the abstract persistence schema AddressAPS. Since the query can return more than one result, the select method defines the return value to be of type Collection.

Searches over Relationships

In addition to attributes, the persistent relationships also belong to the abstract persistence schema of an entity bean. They can be used like attributes in search queries. On the one hand, the attributes of the participating entity beans can be used for limiting the result set, while on the other hand, the participating entity bean objects and values of their persistent attributes can be returned by the search query.

Let us assume that the person bean has defined the following select methods:

```
public abstract AddressLocal ejbSelectAddress()
    throws FinderException;
public abstract String ejbSelectCity()
    throws FinderException;
public abstract Collection ejbSelectPersonWithZip(Integer zip)
    throws FinderException;
```

The method ejbSelectAddress should return the address that is linked via the persistent one-to-one relationship with the associated person bean. The method ejbSelectCity should return only the persistent attribute city of the Address bean for all existing persons. The method ejbSelectPersonWithZip returns all persons whose address contains a particular zip code. Listing 5-40 shows the queries belonging to the methods.

Listing 5-40. EJB-QL and persistent relationships.

```
...
<entity>
    <ejb-name>PersonBean</ejb-name>
    ...
    <abstract-schema-name>PersonAPS</abstract-schema-name>
    ...
    <query>
        <query-method>
            <method-name>ejbSelectAddress</method-name>
        </query-method>
```

```
            <ejb-ql>
                SELECT p.address FROM PersonAPS AS p
            </ejb-ql>
        </query>
        <query>
            <query-method>
                <method-name>ejbSelectCity</method-name>
            </query-method>
            <ejb-ql>
                SELECT p.address.city FROM PersonAPS AS p
            </ejb-ql>
        </query>
        <query>
            <query-method>
                <method-name>ejbSelectPersonWithZip</method-name>
                <method-params>
                    <method-param>java.lang.Integer</method-param>
                </method-params>
            </query-method>
            <ejb-ql>
                SELECT OBJECT(p) FROM PersonAPS AS p
                WHERE p.address.zip = ?1
            </ejb-ql>
        </query>
    </entity>
    <entity>
        <ejb-name>AddressBean</ejb-name>
        ...
        <abstract-schema-name>AddressAPS</abstract-schema-name>
        ...
        <cmp-field>
            <field-name>zip</field-name>
        </cmp-field>
        <cmp-field>
            <field-name>city</field-name>
        </cmp-field>
        ...
    </entity>
    ...
    <ejb-relation>
```

```
<ejb-relation-name>Person-Address</ejb-relation-name>
<ejb-relationship-role>
    ...
    <multiplicity>One</multiplicity>
    <relationship-role-source>
        <ejb-name>PersonBean</ejb-name>
    </relationship-role-source>
    <cmr-field>
        <cmr-field-name>address</cmr-field-name>
    </cmr-field>
</ejb-relationship-role>
<ejb-relationship-role>
    ...
</ejb-relationship-role>
</ejb-relation>
...
```

The relationship to the address bean is handled in the case of cardinality one like a persistent attribute. For referencing the participating entity bean the dot operator (SELECT p.address) is used. The navigation can be extended using the dot operator to the persistent attributes of the participating entity bean (SELECT p.address.city).

If the relationship to the address bean were not of cardinality one but of cardinality n (that is, one person can have several domiciles), then the definition of the select methods as well as the queries shown in Listing 5-40 would no longer be valid. The signatures of the select methods would have to be changed as follows:

```
public abstract Collection ejbSelectAddress()
    throws FinderException;
public abstract Collection ejbSelectCity()
    throws FinderException;
public abstract Collection ejbSelectPersonWithZip(Integer zip)
    throws FinderException;
```

Since the relationship is of cardinality one-to-n, the person bean can stand in relationship to several address beans. Therefore, the return value of the methods ejbSelectAddress and ejbSelectCity are of type java.util.Collection (alternatively, java.util.Set is possible). If navigation over a relationship is to take place within a query with cardinality n, then instead of the dot operator, the IN operator is used. Listing 5-41 shows the use of the IN operator.

Listing 5-41. Use of the IN *operator.*

```
...
<entity>
    <ejb-name>PersonBean</ejb-name>
    ...
    <abstract-schema-name>PersonAPS</abstract-schema-name>
    ...
    <query>
        <query-method>
            <method-name>ejbSelectAddress</method-name>
        </query-method>
        <ejb-ql>
          SELECT OBJECT(a) FROM PersonAPS AS p, IN(p.address) AS a
        </ejb-ql>
    </query>
    <query>
        <query-method>
            <method-name>ejbSelectCity</method-name>
        </query-method>
        <ejb-ql>
          SELECT a.city FROM PersonAPS AS p, IN(p.address) AS a
        </ejb-ql>
    </query>
    <query>
        <query-method>
            <method-name>ejbSelectPersonWithZip</method-name>
            <method-params>
                <method-param>java.lang.Integer</method-param>
            </method-params>
        </query-method>
        <ejb-ql>
          SELECT OBJECT(p) FROM PersonAPS AS p,
                           IN(p.address) AS a
            WHERE a.zip = ?1
        </ejb-ql>
    </query>
</entity>
<entity>
    <ejb-name>AddressBean</ejb-name>
    ...
</entity>
...
<ejb-relation>
```

```
    <ejb-relation-name>Person-Address</ejb-relation-name>
    <ejb-relationship-role>
        ...
        <multiplicity>One</multiplicity>
        <relationship-role-source>
            <ejb-name>PersonBean</ejb-name>
        </relationship-role-source>
        <cmr-field>
            <cmr-field-name>address</cmr-field-name>
        </cmr-field>
    </ejb-relationship-role>
    <ejb-relationship-role>
        ...
        <multiplicity>Many</multiplicity>
        <relationship-role-source>
            <ejb-name>AddressBean</ejb-name>
        </relationship-role-source>
    </ejb-relationship-role>
</ejb-relation>
```

In the case of a relationship with cardinality *n* the navigation can no longer take place via the dot operator. The objects that are linked to the entity bean over the relationship must first be bound to a variable using the IN operator. With this variable the persistent attributes of the linked entity beans can be referenced in the further course of the query. The variable is also used when the bound objects themselves are to be returned.

Additional Operators and Expressions

Table 5-1 shows the data types that can be used for the constants in EJB-QL instructions.

Table 5-1. Data types for constants in EJB-QL queries.

Data Type	Syntax for Constants
Strings	Strings are enclosed in single quotes
Integers	Whole numbers
Floating-point numbers	Numbers with decimal point
Boolean values	TRUE or FALSE

Table 5-2 executes all operators. The order of appearance is that of increasing precedence of the operators.

Table 5-2. EJB-QL operators.

Operator	Description
NOT	Logical negation
AND	Logical and
OR	Logical or
=	Equal
>	Greater than
>=	Greater than or equal
<	Less than
<=	Less than or equal
<>	Not equal
+ (unary)	Increment a number by 1
- (unary)	Decrement a number by 1
*	Multiplication sign
+ (binary)	Addition sign
- (binary)	Subtraction sign
.	Navigation operator for attributes and references within the deployment descriptor

The greater-than and less-than signs, both of which can be used in EJB-QL queries, belong to the XML syntax and therefore may not be used within XML elements. To avoid such symbols from causing problems with the XML parser, the EJB-QL query must be linked to a so-called CDATA section:

```
<query>
      <query-method>
          <method-name>...</method-name>
      </query-method>
      <ejb-ql>
        <![CDATA[
          SELECT l.sum FROM calculation AS r WHERE r.sum > 1000
        ]]>
      </ejb-ql>
</query>
```

The XML parser does not interpret data found within a CDATA section. It transmits them uninterpreted to the next level of the application layer.

Table 5-3 shows expression that can be used in the WHERE part.

Table 5-3. Expressions for the WHERE *clause.*

Expression	Description
BETWEEN	Checks whether a number lies between two given values. *Syntax:* `<value> [NOT] BETWEEN <value> AND <value>` *Example:* `... WHERE p.address.zip BETWEEN 01060 AND 01096`
IN	Checks whether a string appears in a collection of strings (not to be confused with the IN operator in the FROM part of a query). *Syntax:* `<String-value> [NOT] IN ( <String-value>,` `<String-value>, ... )` *Example:* `... WHERE p.address.city IN ('New York', 'New Haven', 'Hartford')`
LIKE	Compares a string with a simple regular expression to detect similar strings. The syntax of the regular expression allows for two special characters: The underscore (_) stands for an arbitrary character, and the percent sign (%) for a sequence of zero or more arbitrary characters. All other characters stand for themselves. To use a percent or underscore character, prefix the sign with a backslash (\ ). *Syntax:* `<String-value> [NOT] LIKE <regular expression>` *Example:* `... WHERE p.name LIKE ('%M_er%')`
IS NULL	Checks whether an attribute is set for an instance as a one-to-one or *n*-to-one relationship. *Syntax:* `<cmp/cmr-Feld> IS [NOT] NULL` *Example:* `... WHERE p.address IS NOT NULL AND ...`
IS EMPTY	Checks whether a one-to-*n* or *n*-to-one relationship is set for an instance. If the relationship does not refer to any instance, then the result is TRUE. *Syntax:* `<cmr-Feld> IS [NOT] EMPTY` *Example:* `... WHERE p.address IS NOT EMPTY` (one-to-*n* case)
MEMBER OF	Checks whether an object is a component of a set of objects. *Syntax:* `<cmp/cmr-Feld/parameters> [NOT] MEMBER [OF]` *Example:* `... WHERE p.address MEMBER OF ...`

Table 5-4 shows functions that can be used in a query.

Finally, we note that EJB-QL provides an enormous contribution to the portability of entity beans with container-managed persistence. Unfortunately, EJB-QL does not yet offer the level of functionality to which one has become accustomed with SQL. For example, the ORDER BY operator is lacking, which allows one to sort search results. Moreover, the data type java.util.Date is not supported. It is difficult to imagine an application in which persistent data are not used in some form. The next versions of the EJB specification will certainly provide some assistance in this direction.

Table 5-4. Built-in EJB-QL functions.

Expression	Description
CONCAT	Concatenates two strings. *Syntax*: CONCAT(<String1>, <String2>) *Example*: CONCAT ('abc', 'defg') returns the string 'abcdefg'
SUBSTRING	Extracts a substring from a given string. *Syntax*: SUBSTRING(<String>, <Startposition>, <Length>) *Example*: SUBSTRING ('abcdefg', 2, 3) returns the string 'cde'
LOCATE	Searches for a substring in a given string. *Syntax*: LOCATE(<String>, <Substring>, [<start>]) *Example*: LOCATE('abcdefg', 'cde') returns the value 2 (integer)
LENGTH	Determines the length of a string. *Syntax*: LENGTH(<String>) *Example*: LENGTH('abcdefg') returns the value 7 (integer)
ABS	Determines the absolute value for the data types *int*, *float*, and *double* *Syntax*: ABS (<int>) or ABS (<float>) or ABS (<double>) *Example*: ABS(- 11.72) returns 11.72
SQRT	Determines the square root. *Syntax*: SQRT(<double>) *Example*: SQRT(16) returns the value 4.0 (double)
COUNT	(Introduced in EJB 2.1) Counts the size of the result set. *Syntax*: COUNT(<attribute>) *Example*: SELECT COUNT(p.address.city) ...
MAX	(Introduced in EJB 2.1) Determines the largest item in a collection. *Syntax*: SELECT MAX (<attribute>) *Example*: SELECT MAX (p.address.zip) ...
MIN	(Introduced in EJB 2.1) Determines the smallest item in a collection. *Syntax*: SELECT MIN (<attribute>) *Example*: SELECT MIN (p.address.zip) ...
AVG	(Introduced in EJB 2.1) Determines the average of the specified attribute in the collection. *Syntax*: SELECT AVG (<attribute>) *Example*: SELECT AVG (employee.age) ...
SUM	(Introduced in EJB 2.1) Determines the sum of the specified attribute in the collection. *Syntax*: SUM (<attribute>) *Example*: SELECT SUM (sales.value) ...
DISTINCT	(Introduced in EJB 2.1) Determines the distinct values of the specified attribute in the collection. *Syntax*: DISTINCT (<attribute>) *Example*: DISTINCT (p.address.state) ...

Example: Warehouse Management (EJB 2.0)

Our goal in this section is to demonstrate, by means of an example, how the techniques discussed in the previous sections (persistent attributes, persistent relationships in connection with the local client view, EJB-QL) can be combined. In comparison to the other examples in this book, this example is quite complex. To maintain clarity and save space we will not reproduce here the complete source code of this example. We will restrict our attention to those parts that highlight the points that we wish to stress.

The Problem

The accounting department of Amalgamated Intergalactic Enterprises requires access to the data showing the state of the company warehouses (which we will call "stores"). The management of the stores is partially automated. However, the store management system has no client application that meets the needs of the accounting department. Therefore, a client application is to be developed for the accounting department that offers read access to the database of the store management system.

Figure 5-12 shows the principal features of the data model of the store management system. The table STORES keeps track of all the stores. This includes, for example, a store for product parts, a store for half-finished products, a store for end products, a store for warranty return, and so on. Each store contains a system of racks, stored in the table RACKS. Information as to which racks are contained in which store is stored via a foreign key (STOREID) in the table RACKS.

Each rack has several positions in which items can be stored. The store management system assumes that at a given position on a given rack only a single type of article can be stored (though there may be more than one of them). A particular position on a rack is pinpointed by the shelf (PROW) and position on that shelf (PCOLUMN). The positions available on a given rack are stored in a foreign key (RACKID) in the table POSITIONS. In the positions of a rack are to be found the various articles (ITEMS). The items that exist are stored in the table ITEMS. Which type of article is stored at a given position is stored via the foreign key ITEMID in the table POSITIONS.

The client program was developed on the basis of a needs analysis, which was carried out with input from the employees of the accounting department. Figure 5-13 shows the client program (ejb.store.client.StoreManager). In the top part of the application window appears a select box labeled Store. Here one can select the store whose status is to be investigated. The default position is to show the first store in the list of all existing stores. In the left column all racks in the selected store are shown. In the store Products, for example, the names Monitors, Housings, and Miscellaneous appear.

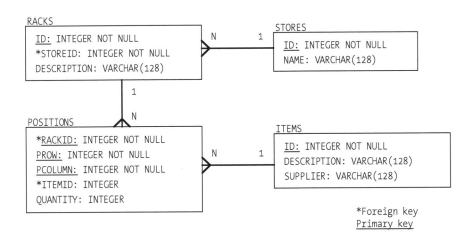

Figure 5-12. Database schema for the store management problem.

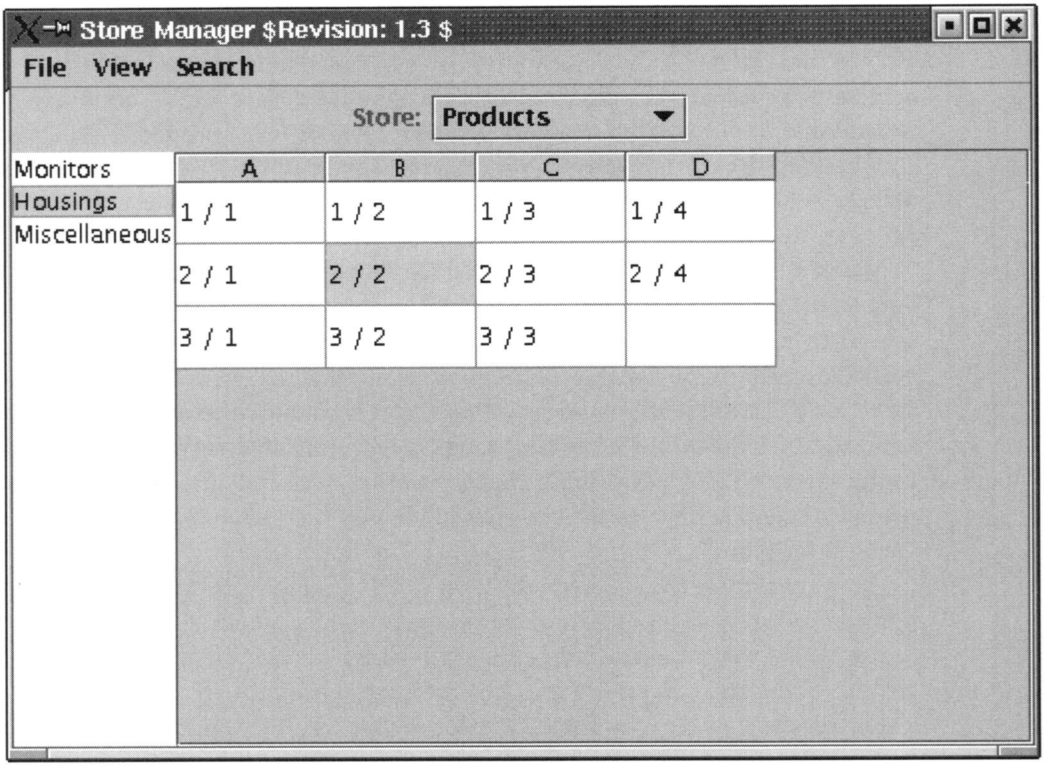

Figure 5-13. **StoreManager**.

When a rack is selected, a table appears in the middle of the application window that displays the available positions in the various racks. If a position is occupied, then the row and column of the position are displayed. If the position is unoccupied, then a blank field is displayed. In Figure 5-13 position 2/2 was displayed (location 2 on shelf 2). To see what articles are to be found at position 2/2 of the rack Housings, a dialog can be displayed by means of the menu selection View:Article, which displays the articles located at this position. One can see in Figure 5-14 that in position 2/2 of the rack Housings is stored the article Housings Big Tower produced by Plangate Inc.

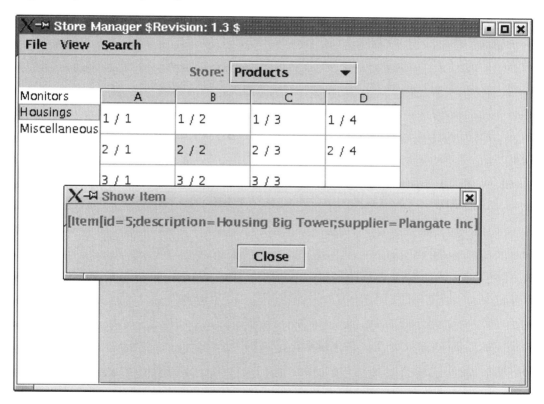

Figure 5-14. StoreManager: *article display.*

Instead of browsing through the different positions of a rack, one can search for the position of a particular article. For this the menu item Search:Article is used, as shown in the dialog box in Figure 5-15. In the upper part of the dialog box there appears a list of all articles available in the system. To see where the article TFT Monitor 15 inch is stored, that item is selected in the list and the button Search pressed. Then in the lower part of the dialog box a list appears with rack positions at which the article is stored. In the example of Figure 5-15 the article is stored in the rack Monitors at positions 1/1, 1/2, and 1/3.

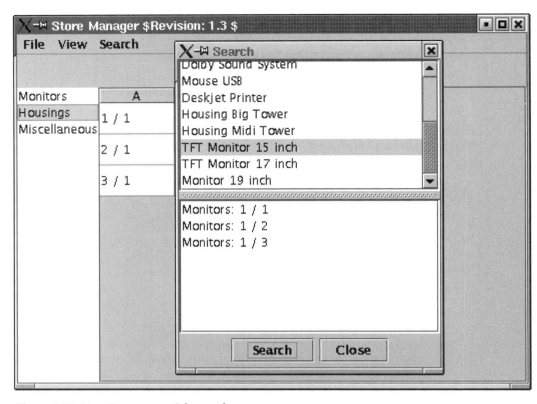

Figure 5-15. StoreManager: *article search.*

Now that we see what the client program and user interface need to look like, we can begin to solve our problem.

Solving the Problem

Each of the four database tables will be represented by an entity bean. The table columns are mapped to persistent attributes of the corresponding entity bean. The table's foreign key relations are relayed to the entity beans via persistent relationships. Figure 5-16 shows the entity beans and their interrelationships.

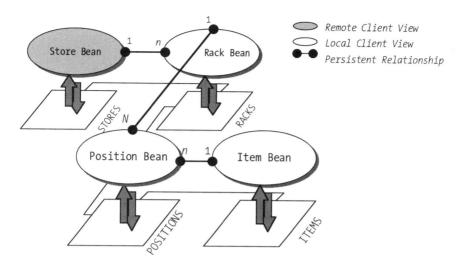

Figure 5-16. Modeling the data with entity beans.

The store bean is the only bean that supports the remote client view. All the other beans support the local client view. Because of the way they are related they must support the local client view; however, they can additionally offer a remote interface. The goal of this design strategy is to make only one bean, the store bean, accessible to the client. This offers the client an advantage, in that it does not have to know anything about the internal structure and dependencies on the server side. For the client there is only one location where communication takes place, namely, at the store (with the store bean), which alone provides the client the information that it needs. The result is that the use of the server interface is considerably simplified for the client. The internal relationships remain hidden. Thus there are no dependencies between the client and the internal workings of the server. As long as the store bean maintains its interface, the client is completely unaffected by changes on the server side.

The client sees Racks, Positions, and Items only in the form of simple Java classes (see Figure 5-17). These classes are container classes for the data of the rack, position, and item beans. The store bean supplies information to the client via these classes. It fills the instances of these container classes with data from the corresponding entity beans. The client knows nothing about the existence of rack, position, and item beans. The container classes are thus also components of the public interface of the store bean. Listing 5-42 shows the implementation of the class Rack. The classes Position and Item are developed along the exact same lines and are therefore not shown.

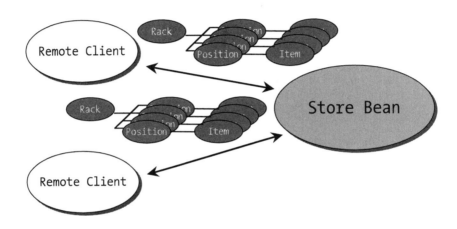

Figure 5-17. Communication with the remote client.

Listing 5-42. The container class Rack.

```
package ejb.store;
public class Rack implements java.io.Serializable {
    private Integer id;
    private String description;
    private Integer storeId;
    public Rack(Integer id, String desc, Integer storeId) {
        if(id == null || id.intValue() < 0)
            throw new IllegalArgumentException("id");
        if(desc == null)
            throw new IllegalArgumentException("desc == null!");
        if(storeId == null || storeId.intValue() < 0)
```

```
            throw new IllegalArgumentException("storeId");
        this.id = id;
        this.description = desc;
        this.storeId = storeId;
    }
    public Integer getId() {
        return this.id;
    }
    public String getDescription() {
        return this.description;
    }
    public Integer getStoreId() {
        return this.storeId;
    }
    public String toString() {
        return "[Rack[id=" + this.id +
                ";description=" + this.description + "]";
    }
}
```

Listing 5-43 shows the home interface, Listing 5-44 the remote interface, of the Store bean. The classes Rack, Position, and Item, as well as the two interfaces Store and StoreHome, together constitute the server interface for the client. Listing 5-45, which we shall discuss shortly, shows the deployment descriptor. It represents the most significant portion of the problem solution. All the information comes together in the deployment descriptor.

Listing 5-43. Home interface of the Store *bean.*

```
package ejb.store;
import javax.ejb.CreateException;
import javax.ejb.EJBHome;
import javax.ejb.FinderException;
import java.rmi.RemoteException;
import java.util.Collection;
public interface StoreHome extends EJBHome {
    public Store create(Integer id, String name)
        throws CreateException, RemoteException;
    public Store findByPrimaryKey(Integer key)
        throws FinderException, RemoteException;
    public Collection findAllStores()
        throws FinderException, RemoteException;
}
```

Listing 5-44. Remote interface of the store bean.

```
package ejb.store;

import javax.ejb.EJBObject;

import java.rmi.RemoteException;
import java.util.Collection;

public interface Store extends EJBObject {

    public Integer getStoreId()
        throws RemoteException;

    public String getStoreName()
        throws RemoteException;

    public Collection getStoreRacks()
        throws RemoteException;

    public Collection getStoreRackPositions(Rack rack)
        throws RemoteException;

    public Item getItemInPosition(Position pos)
        throws RemoteException;

    public Collection getAllStoreItems()
        throws RemoteException;

    public Collection getPositionsForItem(Item item)
        throws RemoteException;

}
```

The method findAllStores of the home interface is used to fill the select box labeled store with values (see Figure 5-13). If the user selects a particular store, the client application obtains access to the corresponding store using findByPrimaryKey.

In order to fill the list that shows the racks, the client application uses the method getStoreRacks of the remote interface. The store bean stands in a 1-to-n relationship to the rack bean (see Listing 5-45, the relation Store–Rack). Thus it is easy for the store bean to determine which racks are located in this store. It has only to navigate over the relation to obtain access to the relevant rack beans. The data of the rack beans are packaged in Rack objects and returned to the client application as the return value of the method call.

If the user selects a particular rack, then all the rack positions in the table must be displayed. For this the client application calls the method getStoreRackPositions and passes as parameter a Rack object for which the positions are desired. The store bean then obtains, by navigation over the relation, access to the corresponding rack bean. For its part, the rack bean is in a 1-to-n relation with the position bean (see Listing 5-45, relation Rack-Position).

The rack bean is instructed by the store bean to determine, via navigation over the relation, all of its position beans and to transform them into `Position` objects. These `Position` objects are returned by the store bean to the client as the result of the method call.

If the user selects a particular position, in order to display the articles contained therein (see Figure 5-14), then the client application calls the method `getItemInPosition`. It passes the `Position` object for which the article is to be displayed. The store bean obtains, by a call to `findByPrimaryKey` on the position bean's local home interface, access to the corresponding position bean. The position bean stands in an *n*-to-1 relation with the item bean (Listing 5-45, relation `Position-Item`). The position bean is instructed to determine, by navigation over the relation, the item bean belonging to it and to transform it into an `Item` object. This `Item` object is returned by the store bean to the client as the result of the method call and can be displayed by the client application. Alternatively, the store could have found the corresponding item bean with a select method linked to an EJB-QL query in the deployment descriptor.

To enable the user to undertake a search for positions of a particular article in the stores (see Figure 5-15), the search dialog must first be filled with the articles available in the system. To this end the client application calls the method `getAllStoreItems`. For this the store bean uses a select method that was linked to an EJB-QL query in the deployment descriptor (see Listing 5-45, method `ejbSelectAllItems`). The select method returns all item beans found in the system. The store bean transforms the local entity bean references into `Item` objects and returns them as result of the method call to the client program. The client program uses these `Item` objects to fill in the article list in the search dialog.

If the user selects a particular article and pushes the `Search` button, the client program calls the method `getPositionsForItem`. Here the store bean also uses a select method that was linked in the deployment descriptor with an EJB-QL query (see Listing 5-45, method `ejbSelectPositionsForItem`). The select method returns the position beans in which the article resides. The store bean transforms the local references into `Position` objects and returns them to the client program as result of the method call. The client program uses the `Position` objects to fill in the list of search results in the search dialog.

Listing 5-45. Deployment descriptor for warehouse management.

```xml
<?xml version="1.0" encoding="UTF-8"?>
<ejb-jar version="2.1" xmlns="http://java.sun.com/xml/ns/j2ee"
xmlns:xsi="http://www.w3.org/2001/XMLSchema-instance"
xsi:schemaLocation="http://java.sun.com/xml/ns/j2ee
http://java.sun.com/xml/ns/j2ee/ejb-jar_2_1.xsd">
    <enterprise-beans>
```

```
<entity>
    <ejb-name>Store</ejb-name>
    <home>ejb.store.StoreHome</home>
    <remote>ejb.store.Store</remote>
    <ejb-class>ejb.store.StoreBean</ejb-class>
    <persistence-type>Container</persistence-type>
    <prim-key-class>java.lang.Integer</prim-key-class>
    <reentrant>False</reentrant>
    <cmp-version>2.x</cmp-version>
    <abstract-schema-name>Store</abstract-schema-name>
    <cmp-field>
      <field-name>id</field-name>
    </cmp-field>
    <cmp-field>
      <field-name>name</field-name>
    </cmp-field>
    <primkey-field>id</primkey-field>
    <query>
      <query-method>
        <method-name>findAllStores</method-name>
        <method-params>
        </method-params>
      </query-method>
      <ejb-ql>
        SELECT OBJECT(s) FROM Store AS s
      </ejb-ql>
    </query>
    <query>
      <query-method>
        <method-name>ejbSelectAllItems</method-name>
        <method-params>
        </method-params>
      </query-method>
      <result-type-mapping>Local</result-type-mapping>
      <ejb-ql>
        SELECT DISTINCT p.item FROM Store AS s,
                                  IN (s.racks) AS r,
                                  IN(r.positions) AS p
      </ejb-ql>
    </query>
    <query>
      <query-method>
        <method-name>ejbSelectPositionsForItem
        </method-name>
```

```
        <method-params>
          <method-param>java.lang.Integer</method-param>
        </method-params>
      </query-method>
      <result-type-mapping>Local</result-type-mapping>
      <ejb-ql>
        SELECT OBJECT(p) FROM Store AS s,
                             IN (s.racks) AS r,
                             IN(r.positions) AS p
                        WHERE p.itemId = ?1
      </ejb-ql>
    </query>
  </entity>
  <entity>
    <ejb-name>RackLocal</ejb-name>
    <local-home>ejb.store.rack.RackLocalHome</local-home>
    <local>ejb.store.rack.RackLocal</local>
    <ejb-class>ejb.store.rack.RackBean</ejb-class>
    <persistence-type>Container</persistence-type>
    <prim-key-class>java.lang.Integer</prim-key-class>
    <reentrant>False</reentrant>
    <cmp-version>2.x</cmp-version>
    <abstract-schema-name>Rack</abstract-schema-name>
    <cmp-field>
      <field-name>id</field-name>
    </cmp-field>
    <cmp-field>
      <field-name>description</field-name>
    </cmp-field>
    <cmp-field>
      <field-name>storeId</field-name>
    </cmp-field>
    <primkey-field>id</primkey-field>
  </entity>
  <entity>
    <ejb-name>PositionLocal</ejb-name>
    <local-home>
        ejb.store.rack.position.PositionLocalHome
    </local-home>
    <local>ejb.store.rack.position.PositionLocal</local>
    <ejb-class>
        ejb.store.rack.position.PositionBean
    </ejb-class>
    <persistence-type>Container</persistence-type>
```

```
        <prim-key-class>
            ejb.store.rack.position.PositionPK
        </prim-key-class>
        <reentrant>False</reentrant>
        <cmp-version>2.x</cmp-version>
        <abstract-schema-name>Position</abstract-schema-name>
        <cmp-field>
          <field-name>rackId</field-name>
        </cmp-field>
        <cmp-field>
          <field-name>row</field-name>
        </cmp-field>
        <cmp-field>
          <field-name>column</field-name>
        </cmp-field>
        <cmp-field>
          <field-name>itemId</field-name>
        </cmp-field>
        <cmp-field>
          <field-name>quantity</field-name>
        </cmp-field>
    </entity>
    <entity>
        <ejb-name>ItemLocal</ejb-name>
        <local-home>ejb.store.item.ItemLocalHome</local-home>
        <local>ejb.store.item.ItemLocal</local>
        <ejb-class>ejb.store.item.ItemBean</ejb-class>
        <persistence-type>Container</persistence-type>
        <prim-key-class>java.lang.Integer</prim-key-class>
        <reentrant>False</reentrant>
        <cmp-version>2.x</cmp-version>
        <abstract-schema-name>Item</abstract-schema-name>
        <cmp-field>
          <field-name>id</field-name>
        </cmp-field>
        <cmp-field>
          <field-name>description</field-name>
        </cmp-field>
        <cmp-field>
          <field-name>supplier</field-name>
        </cmp-field>
        <primkey-field>id</primkey-field>
    </entity>
</enterprise-beans>
```

```
<relationships>
    <ejb-relation>
        <ejb-relation-name>Store-Rack</ejb-relation-name>
        <ejb-relationship-role>
            <ejb-relationship-role-name>
                store-has-racks
            </ejb-relationship-role-name>
            <multiplicity>One</multiplicity>
            <relationship-role-source>
                <ejb-name>Store</ejb-name>
            </relationship-role-source>
            <cmr-field>
                <cmr-field-name>racks</cmr-field-name>
                <cmr-field-type>
                    java.util.Collection
                </cmr-field-type>
            </cmr-field>
        </ejb-relationship-role>
        <ejb-relationship-role>
            <ejb-relationship-role-name>
                rack-belongs-to-store
            </ejb-relationship-role-name>
            <multiplicity>Many</multiplicity>
            <cascade-delete/>
            <relationship-role-source>
                <ejb-name>RackLocal</ejb-name>
            </relationship-role-source>
        </ejb-relationship-role>
    </ejb-relation>
    <ejb-relation>
        <ejb-relation-name>Rack-Position</ejb-relation-name>
        <ejb-relationship-role>
            <ejb-relationship-role-name>
                rack-has-positions
            </ejb-relationship-role-name>
            <multiplicity>One</multiplicity>
            <relationship-role-source>
                <ejb-name>RackLocal</ejb-name>
            </relationship-role-source>
            <cmr-field>
                <cmr-field-name>positions</cmr-field-name>
                <cmr-field-type>
                    java.util.Collection
                </cmr-field-type>
```

```
                    </cmr-field>
                </ejb-relationship-role>
                <ejb-relationship-role>
                    <ejb-relationship-role-name>
                        position-belongs-to-rack
                    </ejb-relationship-role-name>
                    <multiplicity>Many</multiplicity>
                    <cascade-delete/>
                    <relationship-role-source>
                        <ejb-name>PositionLocal</ejb-name>
                    </relationship-role-source>
                    <cmr-field>
                        <cmr-field-name>rack</cmr-field-name>
                    </cmr-field>
                </ejb-relationship-role>
            </ejb-relation>
            <ejb-relation>
                <ejb-relation-name>Position-Item</ejb-relation-name>
                <ejb-relationship-role>
                    <ejb-relationship-role-name>
                        position-has-item
                    </ejb-relationship-role-name>
                    <multiplicity>Many</multiplicity>
                    <relationship-role-source>
                        <ejb-name>PositionLocal</ejb-name>
                    </relationship-role-source>
                    <cmr-field>
                        <cmr-field-name>item</cmr-field-name>
                    </cmr-field>
                </ejb-relationship-role>
                <ejb-relationship-role>
                    <ejb-relationship-role-name>
                        item-is-in-position(s)
                    </ejb-relationship-role-name>
                    <multiplicity>One</multiplicity>
                    <relationship-role-source>
                        <ejb-name>ItemLocal</ejb-name>
                    </relationship-role-source>
                </ejb-relationship-role>
            </ejb-relation>
        </relationships>
    </ejb-jar>
```

Summary

Store, rack, position, and item beans can be understood as a sort of supercomponent that functions only in conjunction with all the Enterprise Bean components. The store bean is at once the controlling instance of this supercomponent and the interface for the client. The existence of the other entity beans is not apparent from the outside. The linking of Enterprise Beans into a supercomponent is accomplished by the EJB container by means of persistent relationships. It knows what instances of what Enterprise Beans belong together and looks after the resolution of relations at run time. It generates bean instances and equips them with data from the database whenever there is navigation over a relation. Communication between Enterprise Beans takes place via the local client view, which takes care of the requisite efficiency. The query language EJB-QL in connection with select or finder methods is a possibility for optionally accessing particular instances of bound Enterprise Beans within the supercomponent. This problem can be solved elegantly and with relatively little programming effort on the server side with the aid of persistent relationships (in connection with the local client view), select and finder methods, and the query language EJB-QL. Here the deployment descriptor plays a central role. It contains parts of the implementation (EJB-QL queries) and lays the foundation for the linking of Enterprise Bean instances over persistent relationships. Thus changes can be made in this part of the application without the code of the Enterprise Beans having to be altered. Moreover, the solution should be able to be ported without difficulty to other (EJB 2.0 conforming) application servers and other databases.

Container-Managed Persistence 1.1

The EJB specifications 2.0/2.1 have retained container-managed persistence from version 1.1 for the sake of backward compatibility. Existing entity bean applications can thus be migrated stepwise to version 2.0/2.1. The changes in version 2.0/2.1 in the area of container-managed persistence are rather extensive and have many advantages over version 1.1. Above all, this includes persistent relationships and the local client view. For the development of new applications and application modules in which persistence plays a role, CMP entity beans according to version 2.0 should certainly be used.

Overview

Figure 5-18 gives a complete overview of the classes and interfaces of entity beans with container-managed persistence of version 1.1. An EJB 1.1 entity bean is limited to the use of the remote client view. It can have neither a local home interface nor a local interface. Moreover, with EJB 1.1 entity beans there are no home methods and no select methods.

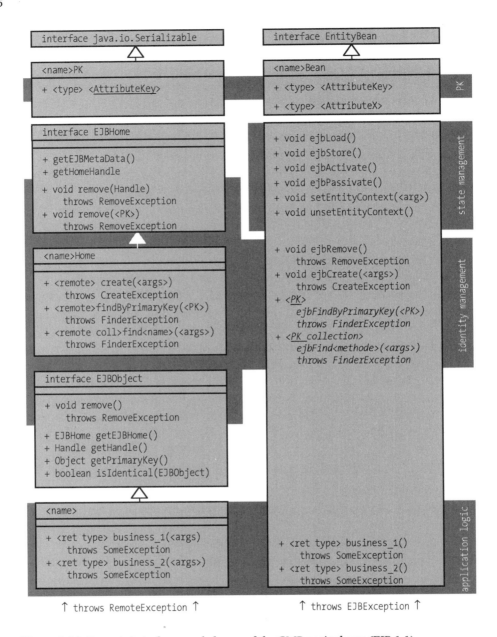

Figure 5-18. Remote interfaces and classes of the CMP entity bean (EJB 1.1).

On the right in Figure 5-18 can be found the entity bean classes. Instances of this class are managed at run time through the EJB container. On the left side can be seen the interfaces that are available to the client and are implemented by the home or remote object of the EJB container (see also Chapter 3).

Every entity bean class implements the interface `javax.ejb.EntityBean`. In contrast to EJB 2.0 entity beans, the bean class of an EJB 1.1 entity bean is a concrete class. All public attributes of the class are persistent by definition even though they are also defined in the deployment descriptor as persistent attributes. In the entity bean class the bean developer implements the actual functionality of the bean.

On the left in Figure 5-18 are the classes for the bean's primary key. Since objects of this class are transported across the network between server and client, the class must be serializable. It implements the interface `java.io.Serializable`. All persistent attributes of the entity bean class that belong to the primary key are brought over by the bean developer into the primary key class. The name and data type of these attributes are identical in both the entity bean class and the primary key.

The components of the entity bean class can be arranged in four groups:

- Attributes;

- State management;

- Identity management;

- Application logic.

In the rest of this section we will look at the individual components in detail.

Attributes

Every persistent attribute is defined in the (concrete) bean class as a member variable. The persistent attributes must be `public`, and may not be `final`, since otherwise, they cannot be modified by the EJB container. They may have the following data types:

- primitive data types of the programming language Java (`int`, `float`, `long`, etc.);

- serializable data types of the programming language Java (including, in particular, `java.lang.String`, `java.lang.Integer`);

- references to the remote or home interface of other Enterprise Beans.

Listing 5-46 shows an example of how an EJB 1.1 entity bean defines persistent attributes in the bean class.

Listing 5-46. Persistent attributes of an EJB 1.1 entity bean.

```
public class AddressBean implements EntityBean {

    public String name;
    public String firstName;
    public String street;
    public int postalCode;
    public String city;

    ...

}
```

Finally, the attributes become persistent only when they are declared thus in the deployment descriptor. Listing 5-47 shows how the persistent attributes from Listing 5-46 are declared in the deployment descriptor.

Listing 5-47. Deployment descriptor of an EJB 1.1 entity bean.

```
...
  <enterprise-beans>
    <entity>
      <ejb-name>Address</ejb-name>
      <home>AddressHome</home>
      <remote>Address</remote>
      <ejb-class>AddressBean</ejb-class>
      <persistence-type>Container</persistence-type>
      <prim-key-class>java.lang.String</prim-key-class>
      <reentrant>False</reentrant>
      <cmp-version>1.x</cmp-version>
      <cmp-field>
        <field-name>name</field-name>
      </cmp-field>
      <cmp-field>
        <field-name>firstName</field-name>
      </cmp-field>
      <cmp-field>
        <field-name>street</field-name>
      </cmp-field>
      <cmp-field>
        <field-name>postalCode</field-name>
      </cmp-field>
```

```
        <cmp-field>
          <field-name>city</field-name>
        </cmp-field>
        <primkey-field>name</primkey-field>
      </entity>
    </enterprise-beans>
...
```

With EJB 1.1 entity beans the value 1.x is entered in the element cmp-version. With EJB 1.1 entity beans there do not exist the elements abstract-schema-name and query. Otherwise, the instructions are largely identical to those for EJB 2.0/2.1 entity beans.

The EJB container is responsible for the initialization and synchronization of persistent attributes with the persistence medium. The attributes can be read and write accessed by the entity bean's application methods (those that are called by the client).

State Management

The methods of state management (see Figure 5-18) are the *callback methods*, which are called by the EJB container in order to inform the entity bean about a change of state. The individual states and state transitions are displayed in Figure 5-6. The methods have the same function as with EJB 2.0 entity beans, and so we shall go into them here only briefly.

void setEntityContext(EntityContext ctx)

The method setEntiyContext is called by the EJB container when a bean instance is generated and is transformed into the state Pooled. Its function is the initialization of the bean. The EJB container transfers to the entity bean its EntityContext. During this method the EntityContext object should be stored as a variable.

void unsetEntityContext()

This method is called by the EJB container when it no longer needs a bean instance and wants to remove it from the pool. The call informs the bean instance that its associated EntityContext is invalid.

void ejbActivate()

The EJB container calls this method to inform an entity bean instance that it has received a particular identity. In the entity context the primary key can now be queried. The bean instance is transformed into the state Ready-Async.

void ejbPassivate()

This method is the complement of ejbActivate. It is called by the EJB container when a bean instance changes from the state Ready to the state Pooled. The bean instance then no longer possesses a bean identity.

void ejbLoad()

With a call to this method the EJB container informs the bean instance that it has newly provided the bean with persistent attributes. This is necessary in the case in which the bean has not yet been initialized or if the database content has been changed through parallel access. The EJB container can synchronize the bean at any time in the state Ready. This often happens before a method of the application logic is called. The bean changes from the state Ready-Async into the state Ready-Sync.

For example, this method can be used by the entity bean to recalculate transient variables from persistent variables recently synchronized with the persistence medium.

void ejbStore()

Through a call to this method the EJB container informs a bean instance that it will write the bean's persistent attributes into the persistence system. The bean instance changes from the state Ready-Sync into the state Ready-Update.

Identity Management

The methods for identity management form the second group of methods displayed in Figure 5-18. They enable the generation, deletion, and searching of entity bean identities. These methods are also found in the home interface and are available to the client before it has a bean instance.

ejbFind<name>(<args>)

In this group there are one or more search methods. The methods are defined in the home interface. A search method can target either a single entity bean or a set of them. The search methods for entity beans begin with the prefix find. Each entity bean must define at least one method findByPrimaryKey with the primary key as sole parameter. The remaining finder methods can have arbitrary signatures. The finder methods are neither declared nor implemented in the bean class, but are generated by the EJB container (the various ejbFind methods in the bean classes of Figure 5-18 are indicated in a slant font). The findByPrimaryKey method for generation is not otherwise complex. For the remaining finder methods instructions must be given in the form of search queries. As mentioned already, EJB 1.1 knows nothing about EJB-QL. The formulation of such queries therefore depends on what is offered by the application server. This state of affairs limits the ease of portability of EJB 1.1 entity beans.

<primKeyClass> ejbCreate(<args>)

For the generation of beans there are one or more methods, all of which are called ejbCreate and define the bean's primary key class as return value. The methods are distinguished by their parameters, and can otherwise be defined according to the wishes of the developer. These methods are not part of the entity bean interface, since the parameter types and return value types differ for each bean class.

These methods are available to the client and are therefore also declared in the home interface. The signatures of the create methods in the home interface (create) and in the bean class (ejbCreate) are distinguished by their return values. The methods in the home interface have the bean's remote interface as return value. The methods of the bean class use the primary key. The EJB container manages the required conversion. The implementation of this method uses parameters to initialize the persistent attributes of the entity bean. As result, null is always returned.

void ejbPostCreate(<args>)

For every ejbCreate method the bean developer must define an ejbPostCreate method with the same parameter types. The ejbPostCreate method is always executed by the EJB container according to the corresponding ejbCreate method with the identical transaction context (see Chapter 7 for details).

Additional initialization steps can be executed in these methods. The bean identity is available to these methods, in contrast to the ejbCreate methods.

With the execution of `ejbCreate` and `ejbPostCreate` the bean instance changes from the state `Pooled` to the state `Ready-Update`. However, the new bean identity is frequently stored in the database only after the subsequent execution of the method `ejbStore`.

void ejbRemove()

For management of bean identities one also has methods for deleting beans. The client issues the command to delete an entity bean identity by a call to the method `remove` in the home or remote interface. The method `ejbRemove` of the bean instance is, however, called by the EJB container, which transmits the client's call.

The bean instance is simply informed of its impending state change. The EJB container takes care of deletion of data. Frequently, additional resources must be freed in a call to this method before the bean instance changes into the state `Pooled`.

Like `ejbPassivate`, this method is called when the state of a bean instance changes from `Ready` to `Pooled`. However, here the bean identity is deleted. After the call the bean instance no longer has an identity. Any reserved resources must be released before the bean instance changes into the state `Pooled`. The method `ejbPassivate` is not called in this state transition.

Application Logic

The fourth group of methods consists of those for the application logic, which are located in the remote interface. These methods are implemented by the bean developer in the bean class. The definition in the bean class has the same signature as in the definition in the remote interface. As a rule, with these methods read and write access will be made to the persistent attributes.

Bean-Managed Persistence

In contrast to the entity beans with container-managed persistence, entity beans with bean-managed persistence themselves take care of communication with the persistence medium (e.g., a database). All access to reading and writing of data is programmed in the bean class by the bean provider. The EJB container does not know which of the entity bean's data are persistent or in what persistence medium they have been stored.

For the bean developer, entity beans with bean-managed persistence definitely mean greater programming effort. They may further be portable only with restrictions, since the bean's code is often optimized for a particular storage medium. Nevertheless, there are cases in which one cannot or does not wish to use container-managed persistence, such as when an entity bean—for example, images in the form of GIF files—is to be stored in a database and must use the data type BLOB (binary large object). Precisely this data type often requires special handling that the EJB container or persistence manager does not support. Another example is that in which an entity bean stores data not in a database, but in an electronic archive. For such systems there is no support from the EJB container or persistence manager. If such a system must be used as a storage medium, then the persistence can be realized using entity beans with bean-managed persistence.

Overview

Figure 5-19 gives an overview of the classes and interfaces of an entity bean with bean-managed persistence that supports the remote client view. To the right are the entity bean classes whose instances are managed by the EJB container at run time. On the left are to be found the interfaces that are implemented through the home and remote objects of the EJB container (see Chapter 3). Through these interfaces the client obtains access to the entity bean.

Every entity bean class implements the interface `javax.ejb.EntityBean`. It is in this entity bean class that the bean developer implements the actual functionality. The bean developer has considerable freedom in the organization of the persistent data. He or she does not have to specify the persistent attributes in the deployment descriptor.

Even in the case of bean-managed persistence a primary key is defined that identifies the bean class uniquely. The primary key class appears at the top left of the figure. It implements the interface `java.io.Serializable`.

Figure 5-20 shows the classes and interfaces of an entity bean with bean-managed persistence that supports the local client view. To the right is the entity bean class, and to the left, the interfaces that are used by the local client and are implemented through the local home object and local object of the EJB container. The entity bean class of the local client view is identical to that of the remote client view. The differences between the two cases are handled by the EJB container through the implementation of the relevant interfaces. The bean class and bean instance remain untouched. The differences for the client of an entity bean between the local and remote client views are the same as for session beans. These differences were discussed in Chapter 4.

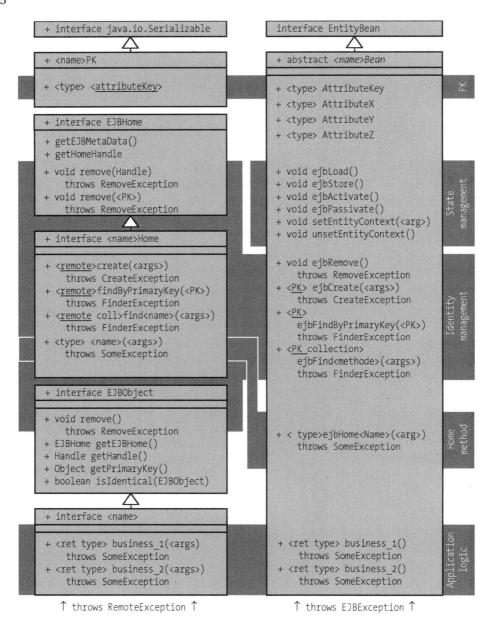

Figure 5-19. Remote interfaces and classes of the BMP entity bean.

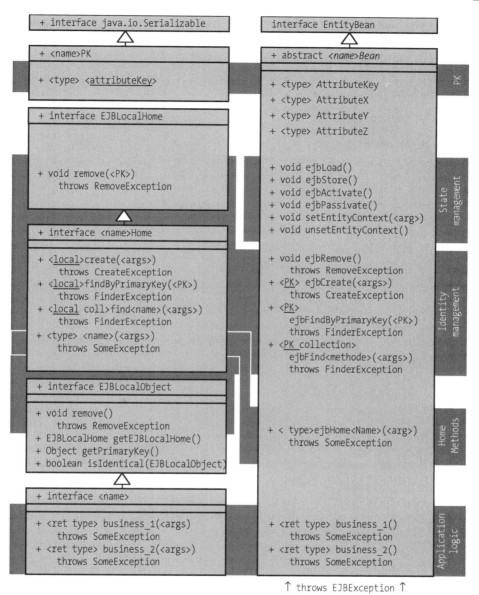

Figure 5-20. Local interfaces and classes of the BMP entity bean.

The components of an entity bean with bean-managed persistence can be divided into four groups:

- Attributes;

- State management;

- Identity management;

- Application logic.

The example at the end of this section offers a practical introduction to programming entity beans with bean-managed persistence. In that example we will discuss all components of the entity bean in detail.

Attributes

In contrast to the case of entity beans with container-managed persistence, here the bean provider is completely free to choose the definition of the attributes. The visibility and type of attributes can be chosen completely freely by the bean provider. In the end, he or she is responsible for synchronizing the attributes with the storage medium.

State Management

At the top of Figures 5-19 and 5-20 can be seen the methods for state management. The EJB container calls these methods to initiate a state transition and to inform the bean about a change in state (see Figure 5-6).

void setEntityContext(EntityContext ctx)

The method setEntityContext is called by the EJB container when a bean instance is generated and changes into the state Pooled. It serves to initialize the bean. The EJB container gives the bean its EntityContext. This method should only store the EntityContext and possess no additional business-related functionality.

void unsetEntityContext()

This method is called by the EJB container when it no longer has need of a bean instance and wishes to remove it from the pool. The call informs the bean instance that its associated EntityContext is no longer valid.

void ejbActivate()

The EJB container calls this method to inform an entity bean that it has received a particular entity bean identity. The bean instance changes into the state Ready-Async. In this state, in the EntityContext, the primary key can already by queried with getPrimaryKey and the remote interface with getEJBObject. The bean instance will not yet be synchronized with the database, and thus the values of the persistent attributes not yet set.

This method can be used to open database connections or to reserve other resources. One should note that no transactions are available to this method.

void ejbPassivate()

This method is the complement to ejbActivate. It is called by the EJB container when a bean instance changes state from Ready to Pooled. The bean instance then no longer possesses a bean identity. However, the bean identity can still be used in the method.

This method is used to release resources that were reserved with ejbActivate or later in the state Ready.

void ejbLoad()

The method ejbLoad is called by the EJB container to synchronize the state of a bean instance with the persistence medium. This is necessary if the bean instance has not yet been initialized or if, for example, the database content has been changed by a parallel access. The EJB container can synchronize the bean at any time in the state Ready. This frequently happens before a method of the application logic is called. The bean changes from the state Ready-Async to Ready-Sync.

With this method the bean provider programs the functionality for loading the attribute values from the persistence medium. Additionally, it can be necessary to recalculate transient attributes.

The transaction context for the method cannot be easily predicted. The method that causes the synchronization also determines the transaction context. If, for example, an EJB container synchronizes the bean before each method call of the application logic, then the transaction attribute of the following method determines the transaction context (for transactions, see Chapter 7).

void ejbStore()

When a client changes the state of a bean, the altered attribute values must be written to the persistence medium. In this way the bean instance changes from the state Ready-Update to the state Ready-Sync. This method implements the storage of the persistent attributes.

Normally, this method is called by the EJB container before it terminates a transaction. All data in temporary storage must be written to the database, since otherwise, they will not be persistent (see Chapter 7 on transactions).

Identity Management

The methods for identity management form the second group in Figure 5-19 and Figure 5-20. They enable the generation, deletion, and search of entity bean identities. These methods are again found in the home interface and are available to the client even before it has a bean instance.

ejbFind<name>(<args>)

There are one or more search methods. The number of targets of a search method can be either a single entity bean or a collection of several entity beans. The methods are defined in the home interface and there are available to the client. In contrast to container-managed persistence, the associated search methods must be implemented by the bean developer in the bean class. In the case of bean-managed persistence there is no possibility of implementing finder methods declaratively using EJB-QL.

As with container-managed persistence, there must be at least one method findByPrimaryKey in the bean's (local) home interface that is implemented in the bean class as ejbFindByPrimaryKey. The bean provided can, according to need, define additional finder methods, which are constructed with the same naming pattern.

One should note that the search methods of an entity bean return one or more instances of the primary key class, while the methods in the (local) home interface return one or more references to beans. The requisite conversion is managed by the EJB container. It ensures that a bean instance is activated with the corresponding bean identity and transmits its remote or local interface to the client.

Searches that can have only a single target directly use the class of the primary key or the remote or local interface as data type for the return value. If a search can have several targets, then java.util.Enumeration (Java 1.1) or java.util.Collection (Java 1.2) is used as data type for the return value.

All search methods can be executed by the EJB container in a transaction. The transaction attribute of the corresponding methods in the (local) home interface determines the behavior of the EJB container (again, see Chapter 7 for transactions).

In the case of bean-managed persistence there are no select methods.

`<primKeyClass> ejbCreate(<args>)`

There are one or more methods to create entity beans, all of which are called `ejbCreate` and define the primary key class of the bean as return value. These methods are distinguished one from the other by their parameters and can otherwise be defined by the developer at will. The methods are not a part of the entity bean interface, since the parameter and return value types are different for each bean class.

These methods are available to the client and are therefore also declared in the bean's (local) home interface. There the methods are called `create( ... )`, and are otherwise distinguished by the return value of their counterparts in the bean class. The methods in the (local) home interface have the bean's remote or local interface as return value. The corresponding `ejbCreate` methods in the bean class use instead the primary key. The EJB container provides the necessary conversion as well as the mapping of the `create` methods of the (local) home interfaces to the `ejbCreate` methods of the bean class.

Using the `ejbCreate` methods, the bean provider programs the placing of a corresponding data record in the persistence system. The transaction context of the `ejbCreate` methods depends on the transaction attributes of the methods in the deployment descriptor.

`void ejbPostCreate(<args>)`

For each `ejbCreate` method the bean developer defines an `ejbPostCreate` method with the same parameter types. The `ejbPostCreate` method is always executed by the EJB container after the corresponding `ejbCreate` method with the same transaction context.

In these methods further initialization steps can be executed. In contrast to the `ejbCreate` methods, the bean identity is available to these methods. With the execution of `ejbCreate` and `ejbPostCreate` the bean instance changes from the state `Pooled` to the state `Ready-Update`.

void ejbRemove()

To the class of methods for managing bean identities belong as well the methods for deleting beans. The client gives the order for the deletion of an entity bean identity by a call to the method remove in the (local) home, local, or remote interface. The call is delegated by the EJB container to the method ejbRemove of the bean instance.

In this method the bean provider programs the deletion of the data record in the persistence system. After the method has been executed, the bean identity is no longer allowed to exist in the persistence system. Additionally, reserved resources must be released in this method. The bean instance changes into the state Pooled and can be used for other bean identities. The method ejbPassivate is not called in this state transition.

The method ejbRemove can be called by the EJB container with a transaction. Here the associated transaction attribute in the deployment descriptor defines the behavior of the EJB container (see Chapter 7 on transactions).

Application Logic and Home Methods

The third group of bean methods is that of the methods for the application logic, which are defined in the local or remote interface and implemented in the bean class. The definition in the bean class has the same signature as the definition in the remote or local interface. The implementation is equivalent to that of entity beans with container-managed persistence.

Entity beans with bean-managed persistence can also define *home methods*. Here the same rules and behaviors hold as for entity beans with container-managed persistence.

In the case of an entity bean with bean-managed persistence as well, access to the database is generally not made in the application methods. This is reserved to the methods for state management and the management of identities.

Example: Counter

The best way to explain the differences between bean-managed persistence and container-managed persistence is by means of an example. To this end we return to the example Counter and implement it this time as an entity bean with bean-managed persistence. The counter bean will (as in the case of container-managed persistence) support the remote client view.

Listing 5-48 shows the remote interface of the counter bean. It is identical to the counter bean with container-managed persistence (compare Listing 5-8). The CounterOverflowException is also familiar, as is the database schema (compare Listing 5-14).

Listing 5-48. Remote interface of the counter bean (BMP).

```
package ejb.counterBmp;

import java.rmi.RemoteException;
import javax.ejb.EJBObject;

public interface Counter extends EJBObject {

    public void inc()
        throws RemoteException, CounterOverflowException;

    public void dec()
        throws RemoteException, CounterOverflowException;

    public int getValue()
        throws RemoteException;
}
```

Listing 5-49 shows the home interface of the counter bean. The only difference between this and the counter bean with container-managed persistence is that the method getAllCounterIds is lacking (compare Listing 5-10). Instead, we now have the method findAllCounters. The home method getAllCounterIds has used a select method in the implementation to find all counters. Since there are no select methods in the case of bean-managed persistence, this functionality was implemented this time, for the purpose of illustration, as a finder method. The implementation as a home method would have been possible as before. The home method would have to have implemented database access instead of relying on the select method.

Listing 5-49. Home interface of the counter bean (BMP).

```
package ejb.counterBmp;

import javax.ejb.CreateException;
import javax.ejb.EJBHome;
import javax.ejb.FinderException;
import java.rmi.RemoteException;
```

```
public interface CounterHome extends EJBHome {

    public Counter create(String counterId, int initCounterValue)
        throws CreateException, RemoteException;

    public Counter findByPrimaryKey(String primaryKey)
        throws FinderException, RemoteException;

    public java.util.Collection findAllCounters()
        throws FinderException, RemoteException;


}
```

For the client it makes no difference whether it is dealing with an entity bean with container-managed persistence or one with bean-managed persistence. This underscores the fact that the home and remote interfaces are left essentially unchanged.

On the other hand, the implementation of the bean class has changed considerably. Listing 5-50 shows the implementation. Already in the import statements it is clear that the bean itself accesses the database (java.sql.*).

In the method ejbCreate a new counter bean is placed in the database. It is called whenever the client wishes to generate a new counter and to this end calls the method create in the home interface. In addition to the initialization of the persistent attributes (which this time are declared private), the bean must see to it that the corresponding data record is placed in the database. This happens via the private auxiliary methods initDataSource and create. A further peculiarity of the ejbCreate method is that instead of null being returned (as with beans with container-managed persistence), what is returned is the bean's primary key instance. The implementation of the ejbPostCreate method remains empty, since no further intialization steps are necessary.

There follows the implementation of the two finder methods findByPrimaryKey (ejbFindByPrimaryKey) and findAllCounters (ejbFindAllCounters). In the case of container-managed persistence the finder methods are neither declared nor implemented in the bean class. They are defined with the help of EJB-QL in the deployment descriptor. The method ejbFindByPrimaryKey has the task of verifying whether a data record with the indicated primary key is to be found. If so, the relevant primary key is returned. The EJB container initializes a counter bean with this primary key instance in the state Pooled and returns the remote object of this bean to the client as return value for the findByPrimaryKey call. If such a data record is unavailable, then an exception is triggered. The same holds for the method ejbFindAllCounters, with the difference that an empty collection is returned if no data records are found. An important detail with these finder methods is the call to the auxiliary method initDataSource at the beginning of the method. Since the finder methods are called on the bean instance in the state Pooled, the data source for the database connection might be uninitialized.

Listing 5-50. Bean class of the counter bean (BMP).

```
package ejb.counterBmp;

import java.sql.Connection;
import java.sql.PreparedStatement;
import java.sql.ResultSet;
import java.sql.Statement;
import java.sql.SQLException;
import java.util.ArrayList;
import java.util.Collection;

import javax.naming.Context;
import javax.naming.InitialContext;
import javax.naming.NamingException;

import javax.sql.DataSource;

import javax.ejb.CreateException;
import javax.ejb.EJBException;
import javax.ejb.EntityBean;
import javax.ejb.EntityContext;
import javax.ejb.FinderException;
import javax.ejb.ObjectNotFoundException;

public class CounterBean implements EntityBean {
    public static final String dbRef =
        "java:comp/env/jdbc/CounterDB";

    public final static int VALUE_MAX = 100;
    public final static int VALUE_MIN = 0;

    private EntityContext ctx;
    private DataSource dataSource;

    private String counterId;
    private int counterValue;
     /*
      * the Create method of the home interface
      */
    public String ejbCreate(String counterId, int initCounterValue)
        throws CreateException
    {
        if(counterId == null) {
            throw new CreateException("id must not be null!");
```

```
        }
        if(initCounterValue < VALUE_MIN ||
           initCounterValue > VALUE_MAX)
        {
            throw new CreateException("initValue out of range!");
        }
        this.initDataSource();

        this.counterId = counterId;
        this.counterValue = initCounterValue;

        try {
            this.create();
        } catch(SQLException ex) {
            throw new CreateException(ex.getMessage());
        }

        return this.counterId;
    }
    public void ejbPostCreate(String accountId,
                              int initCounterValue)
    {}
     /*
      * Utility-Methods
      */
    private void initDataSource() {
        if(this.dataSource != null) {
            return;
        }
        try {
            Context c = new InitialContext();
            this.dataSource = (DataSource)c.lookup(dbRef);
        } catch(NamingException ex) {
            String msg = "Cannot get Resource-Factory:" + ex.getMessage();
            throw new EJBException(msg);
        }
    }
    private void create()
        throws SQLException
    {
        final String query =
            "INSERT INTO COUNTER(ID, VALUE) VALUES(?, ?)";
        Connection con = null;
        PreparedStatement st = null;
```

```
        try {
            con = this.dataSource.getConnection();
            st = con.prepareStatement(query);
            st.setString(1, this.counterId);
            st.setInt(2, this.counterValue);
            st.executeUpdate();
        } finally {
            try { st.close(); } catch(Exception ex) {}
            try { con.close(); } catch(Exception ex) {}
        }
    }

    /*
     * The finder methods of the home interface
     */
    public String ejbFindByPrimaryKey(String pk)
        throws FinderException
    {
        this.initDataSource();

        final String query =
            "SELECT ID FROM COUNTER WHERE ID=?";
        Connection con = null;
        PreparedStatement st = null;
        ResultSet rs = null;
        try {
            con = this.dataSource.getConnection();
            st = con.prepareStatement(query);
            st.setString(1, pk);
            rs = st.executeQuery();
            if(!rs.next()) {
                throw new ObjectNotFoundException(pk);
            }
        } catch(SQLException ex) {
            ex.printStackTrace();
            throw new FinderException(ex.getMessage());
        } finally {
            try { st.close(); } catch(Exception ex) {}
            try { rs.close(); } catch(Exception ex) {}
            try { con.close(); } catch(Exception ex) {}
        }
        return pk;
    }
```

```
public Collection ejbFindAllCounters()
    throws FinderException
{
    this.initDataSource();

    final String query =
        "SELECT ID FROM COUNTER";
    Connection con = null;
    Statement st = null;
    ResultSet rs = null;
    ArrayList ret = new ArrayList();
    try {
        con = this.dataSource.getConnection();
        st = con.createStatement();
        rs = st.executeQuery(query);
        while(rs.next()) {
            ret.add(rs.getString(1));
        }
    } catch(SQLException ex) {
        ex.printStackTrace();
        throw new FinderException(ex.getMessage());
    } finally {
        try { st.close(); } catch(Exception ex) {}
        try { rs.close(); } catch(Exception ex) {}
        try { con.close(); } catch(Exception ex) {}
    }
    return ret;
}

/*
 * The business methods of the remote interface
 */

public void inc() throws CounterOverflowException {
    if(this.counterValue < VALUE_MAX) {
        this.counterValue += 1;
    } else {
        String s = "Cannot increase above "+VALUE_MAX;
        throw new CounterOverflowException(s);
    }
}

public void dec() throws CounterOverflowException {
    if(this.counterValue > VALUE_MIN) {
        this.counterValue -= 1;
    } else {
        String s = "Cannot decrease below "+VALUE_MIN;
```

```
            throw new CounterOverflowException(s);
        }
    }
    public int getValue() {
        return this.counterValue;
    }
     /*
      * The methods of the entity bean interface
      */
    public void ejbActivate() {
        this.initDataSource();
    }
    public void ejbPassivate() {
        this.dataSource = null;
    }
    public void setEntityContext(EntityContext ctx) {
        this.ctx = ctx;
    }
    public void unsetEntityContext() {
        this.ctx = null;
    }
    public void ejbLoad() {
        this.counterId = (String)this.ctx.getPrimaryKey();
        final String query = "SELECT VALUE FROM COUNTER WHERE ID=?";
        Connection con = null;
        PreparedStatement st = null;
        ResultSet rs = null;
        try {
            con = this.dataSource.getConnection();
            st = con.prepareStatement(query);
            st.setString(1, this.counterId);
            rs = st.executeQuery();
            if(rs.next()) {
                this.counterValue = rs.getInt(1);
            } else {
                String s = this.counterId + " not found";
                throw new SQLException(s);
            }
        } catch(SQLException ex) {
            ex.printStackTrace();
            throw new EJBException(ex.getMessage());
        } finally {
```

```
                    try { st.close(); } catch(Exception ex) {}
                    try { rs.close(); } catch(Exception ex) {}
                    try { con.close(); } catch(Exception ex) {}
                }
            }
            public void ejbStore() {
                final String query =
                    "UPDATE COUNTER SET VALUE=? WHERE ID=?";
                Connection con = null;
                PreparedStatement st = null;
                try {
                    con = this.dataSource.getConnection();
                    st = con.prepareStatement(query);
                    st.setInt(1, this.counterValue);
                    st.setString(2, this.counterId);
                    st.executeUpdate();
                } catch(SQLException ex) {
                    ex.printStackTrace();
                    throw new EJBException(ex.getMessage());
                } finally {
                    try { st.close(); } catch(Exception ex) {}
                    try { con.close(); } catch(Exception ex) {}
                }
            }
            public void ejbRemove() {
                final String query =
                    "DELETE FROM COUNTER WHERE ID=?";
                Connection con = null;
                PreparedStatement st = null;
                try {
                    con = this.dataSource.getConnection();
                    st = con.prepareStatement(query);
                    st.setString(1, this.counterId);
                    st.executeUpdate();
                } catch(SQLException ex) {
                    ex.printStackTrace();
                    throw new EJBException(ex.getMessage());
                } finally {
                    try { st.close(); } catch(Exception ex) {}
                    try { con.close(); } catch(Exception ex) {}
                }
            }
        }
```

The implementation of the business methods inc, dec, and getValue remains unchanged. Instead of calling the abstract persistence methods (which do not exist in the case of bean-managed persistence), the methods rely on the member variables of the bean class.

The method ejbActivate initializes the bean instance with a state change from Pooled to Ready, using the auxiliary method initDataSource. The method ejbPassivate does exactly the opposite.

The method ejbLoad has the task of synchronizing the bean instance with the data from the database. The primary key is initialized via the EntityContext, while the remaining attributes are handled with the data from the database that go with this primary key. It is important to initialize the primary key attribute from the EntityContext, since the entity bean instance may have changed its identity since the last synchronization. A possible leftover value of the primary key attribute could be invalid.

The method ejbStore has the task of synchronizing the data in the database with the data from the bean instance. As a result, the data in the database are overridden with values of the persistent attributes.

The method ejbRemove has the task of deleting the data record that is represented by the given entity bean instance. The entity bean instance then changes into the state Pooled and must be prepared to be reused with another identity.

Listing 5-51 shows the deployment descriptor of the counter bean with bean-managed persistence. In the element persistence-type you will see that the value Bean has been specified instead of Container. An entity bean with bean-managed persistence has no abstract persistence schema that would have to be declared. Instead, a resource factory reference for access to the database is defined.

Listing 5-51. Deployment descriptor of the counter bean (BMP).

```
<?xml version="1.0" ?>
<ejb-jar version="2.1" xmlns="http://java.sun.com/xml/ns/j2ee"
xmlns:xsi="http://www.w3.org/2001/XMLSchema-instance"
xsi:schemaLocation="http://java.sun.com/xml/ns/j2ee
http://java.sun.com/xml/ns/j2ee/ejb-jar_2_1.xsd">
  <enterprise-beans>
    <entity>
      <ejb-name>CounterBmp</ejb-name>
      <home>ejb.counterBmp.CounterHome</home>
      <remote>ejb.counterBmp.Counter</remote>
      <ejb-class>ejb.counterBmp.CounterBean</ejb-class>
      <persistence-type>Bean</persistence-type>
```

```
      <prim-key-class>java.lang.String</prim-key-class>
      <reentrant>False</reentrant>
      <resource-ref>
        <description> Euro-Datenbank </description>
        <res-ref-name>jdbc/CounterDB</res-ref-name>
        <res-type>javax.sql.DataSource</res-type>
        <res-auth>Container</res-auth>
        <res-sharing-scope>Shareable</res-sharing-scope>
      </resource-ref>
    </entity>
  </enterprise-beans>

  <assembly-descriptor>
    <container-transaction>
      <method>
        <ejb-name>CounterBmp</ejb-name>
        <method-name>inc</method-name>
      </method>
      <method>
        <ejb-name>CounterBmp</ejb-name>
        <method-name>dec</method-name>
      </method>
      <trans-attribute>Required</trans-attribute>
    </container-transaction>
  </assembly-descriptor>
</ejb-jar>
```

A description of the appearance of the mapping of persistent attributes to the database is not necessary with bean-managed persistence.

Summary

Entity beans with container-managed persistence and bean-managed persistence have each of them their advantages and disadvantages. The big advantage of container-managed persistence is certainly its portability, since the important aspects of persistence are treated declaratively in a developer-independent manner. It is in this direction in particular that version 2.0 offers significant extensions of version 1.1. Additionally, persistent relationships, managed by the EJB container and a great help in the mapping of complex data structures, give container-managed persistence further advantages. Version 2.1 further enhances the standardized EJB-QL available functions. Finally, the programming effort is considerably less. Entity beans with container-managed persistence thus tend to be less subject to errors.

Bean-managed persistence offers greater flexibility. The bean developer has a free hand in data storage. He or she decides how and where data are to be stored and is not limited by the specification. With the use of bean-managed persistence, the potential for the developer in tuning database queries is a lot higher then when using container-managed persistence. That is because in the case of bean-managed persistence the bean developer writes all the data access code himself. When container-managed persistence is used, the data access code is generated by the EJB container tools and is hidden from the bean developer. Genericness has its price. If the entity bean has to deal with data types that the EJB container or persistence manager does not support or supports only minimally, then there is no avoiding bean-managed persistence.

#### CHAPTER 6

Message-Driven Beans

MESSAGE-DRIVEN BEANS WERE INTRODUCED WITH version 2.0 of the Enterprise JavaBeans specification and slightly enhanced with version 2.1 (Figure 6-1). With this component type, the Java Message Service (JMS) has become inseparably linked with Enterprise JavaBeans.

The significant difference between this and other bean types is that a client cannot directly access a message-driven bean. It can address it only indirectly, by sending a message over a particular channel of the message service. A message-driven bean of a particular type receives messages from a particular channel of the message service. It is also significant that the bean does not know which client or user has sent the message. The exchange of messages over a message service transpires anonymously. The application must itself take care of whatever identification may be required. To this end it could send an identifier with the message that enables the sender to be identified.

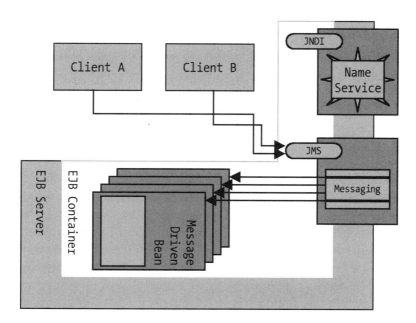

Figure 6-1. Overview of message-driven beans.

The component model of Enterprise JavaBeans is given two new aspects through message-driven beans:

- parallel processing;

- asynchronicity.

For example, if a client calls a method on the remote interface of an entity bean, then client execution will be blocked until the processing of the entity bean method on the server is complete. Thus we are dealing with a *synchronous* call. Sending a message via a message service is *asynchronous*. This means that the client can continue processing as soon as it has sent the message. The processing of the client will not be blocked until the message has been delivered or processed by the receiver. Message-driven beans thus work asynchronously, which distinguishes them in an important way from session and entity beans. Asynchronous processing can greatly reduce server response time. The client does not have to wait for the conclusion of processing-intensive actions, which can run in the background. On the other hand, the client does not automatically know when the processing of the asynchronous process has been completed or whether it was able to be completed successfully at all. The JMS specification takes a number of precautions to make the delivery of a message as secure as possible (with respect to data loss). However, there is no mechanism that provides for informing the client of the successful processing of a message, though such mechanisms can be implemented by means of JMS itself.

To process asynchronous events or to speed up processes in a program, one seeks, as a rule, to parallelize particular processing steps by means of threads. The specification forbids a bean from expressly beginning a new thread or from regulating threads (see also Chapter 3, the section "What an Enterprise Bean May Not Do"). One could attempt to parallelize processes on the client, in order to carry out several calls to Enterprise Beans simultaneously. Except for the case of stateless session beans, this is possible only with certain restrictions. Stateful session beans do not allow a client, for example, to execute several calls to an Enterprise Bean identity simultaneously. With an entity bean identity, simultaneously arriving calls (in different transactions) are serialized by the EJB container, that is, processed sequentially rather than in parallel (depending on the implementation of the EJB container). Such parallelism on the client side would increase the complexity of the client enormously. A reason for the introduction of Enterprise JavaBeans is not least in shifting complexity to the application server and simplifying and slimming down the client program. The application server is the place where one would like to use parallel processing for speeding up the application logic. With the help of the message service, message-driven beans make parallel processing possible.

For the proper implementation of message-driven beans a fundamental understanding of the Java Message Service is essential. The next section will therefore introduce the fundamentals of the Java Message Service. We shall restrict our attention to those aspects that are significant for an understanding of message-driven beans. A complete description of JMS can be found in [29]. It should be noted that as of the 2.1 specification, it is possible to use a non-JMS message service with message-driven beans via a resource adapter. This greatly expands and enhances the integration capabilities of message-driven beans. For the remainder of this chapter we will focus on the use of message-driven beans with the commonly used JMS standard.

Java Message Service (JMS)

Message systems also go under the name *message-oriented middleware* (MOM). They differ from the classical client–server architectures in a number of respects:

- Instead of being organized according to hierarchical structures, the clients of a message service are equal participants. Clients can be application programs, parts of application programs, application servers, or other processes.

- The clients are loosely coupled to the message service; that is, they can connect to or disconnect from the message service at any time and in any number.

- Message exchange proceeds asynchronously; that is, as soon as a client has transmitted a message to the message service, it can continue its processing without having to wait for the message to be received or processed.

- Message exchange proceeds anonymously; that is, a client that has received a message does not know what client has sent it. It knows only the channel of the message service over which it has received it.

JMS is an API (application programming interface) from Sun Microsystems. It is a vendor-independent interface for access to message systems from Java programs. If a Java program uses JMS for access to a message system, the message system used can be exchanged for another without the Java program having to be significantly changed. If the behaviors of the message systems are the same at run time (which is not ensured by API alone) and if they offer the same range of functionality, then as a rule, the client program will not have to be altered. Many message systems in addition to JMS are accessible by way of a vendor's proprietary API. Figure 6-2 clarifies these relationships.

Sun Microsystems has not provided a reference implementation for JMS. They simply offer a commercial implementation of JMS (Java Message Queue). Most producers of message systems have meanwhile begun to offer a JMS implementation. A producer of a JMS-compatible message service is called a *JMS provider*.

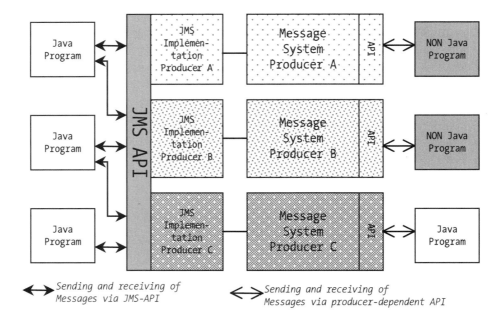

Sending and receiving of Messages via JMS-API

Sending and receiving of Messages via producer-dependent API

Figure 6-2. JMS and JMS providers.

Messaging Concepts

A message that is sent via a message service is not considered to be directed to a particular user, as in the case, for example, of e-mail. Messages in a message service are generally transmitted in a human-unreadable format. They serve primarily for communication between parts of a particular application or between different applications. Message services are frequently used for the purpose of triggering certain actions by the receiver of a message. They are also used to decouple lengthy processes. Such processes are shifted into the background to improve the response behavior of a system. Message services are well suited to execute collections of such actions. A message can, for example, be an instruction for the deletion of a data record in a database. Instead of opening a database connection upon receipt of such a message, these instructions can be collected. Once a sufficient number of instructions have accumulated, a connection to the database is opened and the actions executed as a block.

A message service is designed to provide *asynchronous* communication between *different processes*. Events, for example (as used in the Abstract Windowing Toolkit or with the JavaBeans component model), typically serve for communication internal to a process. A message service is thus primarily used for distributed processes in which parts of the application need to communicate with one another across process boundaries. Message services are also used for communication between different types of processes.

One distinguishes two principal types of communication message systems:

- point to point;

- publish and subscribe.

In the point-to-point model a message is sent from a sender to precisely *one* recipient. In the publish-and-subscribe model a message is sent from a sender to *many* recipients. The channel of the message service over which a message is sent in the point-to-point system is known as a queue. Under publish and subscribe the channel is called a *topic*. Conversely, one can say that a queue is a message channel of a message service by which a sent message is received by exactly one recipient. A topic is a message channel of a message service by which a sent message is received by several recipients (see Figure 6-3).

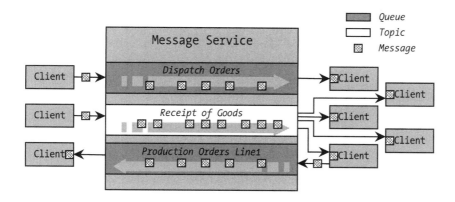

Figure 6-3. Messaging concepts (queue, topic).

Depending on the configuration, arbitrarily many queues and topics can be established within a message service. They are generally distinguished by having different names.

Queues and topics can be persistent. This means that the messages that are currently in a queue or topic are stored in, for example, a database or file system. As soon as they have been successfully received by the recipient client, they are deleted from the storage medium. In the case of a server crash, unreceived messages in persistent queues and topics are not lost. After a system restart the message service will attempt to deliver the messages that are in the persistent queue of a persistent topic.

Whether a queue or topic is persistent depends on its configuration. If a queue or topic is one over which important information is sent, then it is usually made persistent. In the case of less important messages one can do without persistence, where we note that each time a message is stored there is a negative effect on system performance.

Not all message systems support both forms of message delivery (publish and subscribe; point to point). Even when a message service makes only one of the two forms available, it is still possible to use it over JMS, which models both concepts in separate interfaces (see the next section).

JMS Interfaces

In this section we discuss how JMS maps the components of a message system, as described in the previous section, to interfaces. The use of interfaces will be detailed with examples in the course of this chapter.

javax.jms.ConnectionFactory

A connection factory is an object that enables a JMS client to establish a connection to a message service. It receives such an object via a naming service (JNDI lookup). Depending on whether a queue or a topic is to be used, this interface is further specialized to javax.jms.QueueConnectionFactory or javax.jms.TopicConnectionFactory. According to the JMS specification, it is the task of the administrator to configure connection factories. They are therefore called *administered objects*. The JMS implementation makes these available to the clients in the naming service at the startup of the message service.

javax.jms.Connection

A connection object represents a connection to a message service. It is generated over a ConnectionFactory object. According to whether a queue or topic is used, the object is of type javax.jms.QueueConnection or javax.jms.TopicConnection.

javax.jms.Session

A session is an object that is bound over a connection to JMS to a particular queue or a particular topic. A session is generated over a connection object, and messages are sent and received over a session. According to whether the session is linked to a queue or a topic, we are dealing with a javax.jms.QueueSession or a javax.jms.TopicSession.

`javax.jms.Destination`

Destination is the generic term for a topic or a queue. This interface is accordingly specialized further in `javax.jms.Queue` or `javax.jms.Topic`. An object of type queue or topic can be obtained over a JNDI lookup. Here, too, the JMS specification provides that they be set up by the administrator according to the configuration. Thus a queue or topic is called an *administered object*. The JMS implementation makes them available over JNDI to JMS clients at the startup of the message service. A connection or session to a queue or topic can be opened over a connection factory for sending or receiving messages.

`javax.jms.Message`

This interface represents a message that is sent over a queue or topic. A message has the following components:

- **Header**: In the header of a message, information is stored from the JMS client as well as the provider that serves for identification and delivery of a message. Message filters (see below) can be used in header fields.

- **Properties**: These provide an application that possesses a message service the ability to store additional application-related information in the message. Such information as a rule gives the recipient suggestions or instructions that affect the processing of the message. For example, information about the sender of the message can be transmitted in a property field, so that the recipient knows from whom the message was sent. Message filters (see below) can be used in property fields.

- **Body**: The body contains the actual content of the messge.

JMS defines five concrete forms of a message. They are derived from `javax.jms.Message` and represent various technical representations of useful data in a message (message body):

- `javax.jms.TextMessage`: A message that contains a string as the message body. With this message type it is possible, for example, to exchange messages in XML format. Many message systems offer extensive support for the XML format.

- `javax.jms.ObjectMessage`: A message that contains an arbitrary object as message body. The class of the object must implement the interface `java.io.Serializable`.

- `javax.jms.BytesMessage`: A message that contains a message body in the form of a byte stream. The individual bytes are not interpreted. It is up to the recipient of the message to interpret the message appropriately.

- javax.jms.StreamMessage: A message in which a stream of primitive Java data types and serializable objects can be sent. The primitives and the objects are written sequentially in the message and must be read by the recipient in the same order. The recipient must therefore know the order and type of the transmitted data. Thus the sending of a stream message requires a suitable serialization/deserialization protocol.

- javax.jms.MapMessage: A message in which name–value pairs can be sent as the message body. The names are transmitted in the form of strings, the values as primitive data types.

Every application should be capable of finding a suitable message type that fits its requirements. Such general types as javax.jms.ObjectMessage and java.jms.StreamMessage offer the developer wide scope.

javax.jms.MessageProducer

A message producer is an object that enables the sending and receiving of messages. Depending on the destination type, one here distinguishes the concrete forms javax.jms.QueueSender and javax.jms.TopicPublisher. A message producer is generated via a session object.

javax.jms.MessageConsumer

A message consumer is an object that enables messages to be received. Depending on the destination type, one here distinguishes the concrete forms javax.jms.QueueReceiver and java.jms.TopicSubscriber. A message consumer is generated via a session object.

Figure 6-4 represents once again the relationships among the central interfaces of JMS-API.

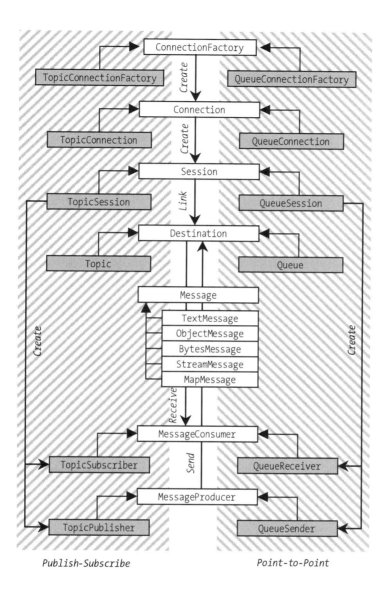

Figure 6-4. JMS interfaces.

JMS-Clients

A JMS client employs the interfaces of the Java message service for sending *and* receiving messages over a message service. A JMS client can send messages, receive messages, or do both. The implementation of the JMS interfaces is supplied by the provider of the message service. In addition to the interfaces of JMS, the client also uses the interfaces of JNDI (Java Naming and Directory Service). The use of JNDI has already been discussed in Chapter 4. With JNDI the JMS client can access JMS resources such as queues, topics, and connection factories (administered objects). These JMS resources are configured by the administrator of the message service (as we have already mentioned). The message system makes these resources available to the JMS clients at run time via a naming and directory service.

The following sections demonstrate the implementation of the individual aspects of a JMS client. All the examples use the auxiliary class Lookup, which has the method get. In order to limit the sample code to essentials, access to the naming service is encapsulated within this auxiliary class and the method get. The implementation of this auxiliary class is a part of the available sample source code to this book.

Sending a Message

Single-Threaded

Listing 6-1 shows the sending of a text message. The example demonstrates the use of a queue. The use of a topic is identical as regards the order of the steps. Instead of queue-specific interfaces one uses the topic-related interfaces (for example, TopicConnection instead of QueueConnection, and TopicSession instead of QueueSession).

Listing 6-1. Sending a text message.

```
...
    static final String FACTORY =
                    "SampleConnectionFactory";
    static final String QUEUE = "SampleQueue";
    QueueConnection qc     = null;
    QueueSession    qs     = null;
    QueueSender     qsend  = null;
    try {
        QueueConnectionFactory qcf = null;
```

```
        qcf = (QueueConnectionFactory)
                Lookup.get(FACTORY);
        qc = qcf.createQueueConnection();
        qs = qc.createQueueSession(false,
                            Session.AUTO_ACKNOWLEDGE);
        Queue queue = (Queue)Lookup.get(QUEUE);
        qsend = qs.createSender(queue);
        Message m = null;
        m = qs.createTextMessage("a text");
        qsend.send(m);
    } finally {
        try  { qsend.close(); } catch(Exception ex) {}
        try  { qs.close(); }    catch(Exception ex) {}
        try  { qc.close(); }    catch(Exception ex) {}
    }
```

In the first step the JMS client obtains, with the help of the class Lookup, a QueueConnectionFactory object from JNDI, which is provided by the administrator of the message service through the configuration. In the next step, the JMS client generates a QueueConnection via the queue connection factory with the help of which it then generates a QueueSession. The Queue over which it would like to send the message is taken (like the queue connection factory) from JNDI. The queue is also set up by the administrator of the message service by configuration. With the help of the QueueSession object, the JMS client generates a QueueSender for this queue. The Message object is also generated via the session. In our case we are dealing with an object of type TextMessage. In the last step the JMS client sends the message via the queue sender. Immediately after placing the message in the queue the method send returns and the JMS client can continue its processing.

Generally, a JMS connection and a JMS session require resources such as a network connection or a thread. It is thus to be recommended that these resources be released when no longer needed through a call to the various close methods. In our example the session and connection are immediately closed. If a client sends messages regularly, then it might be a good idea to keep the connection and session open and to close them only when the client program is terminated.

In sending a message the JMS client can give the message a priority (using the method Message.setJMSPriority). Messages with higher priority are sent before messages with lower priority. The priority can be transmitted with the send method (the send method possesses various signatures). If the priority is not specified, then the message is given a standard priority.

Multithreaded

A JMS session is not *thread-secure*. This means that a session cannot be used simultaneously by several threads. The JMS specification refers specifically to this situation (see [29]). One of the main reasons for this is that a session is the one unit in a message system that support transactions (to the extent that the message system supports transactions at all). It is difficult to implement transactions that are multithreaded. If a session is nonetheless used simultaneously by several threads, then the behavior of the JMS provider is uncertain, and it is quite likely that serious errors will arise.

The fact that a JMS session is not thread-secure is particularly critical in applications that use many threads. A typical example is that of Internet applications. They are simultaneously used by many users. Within the web container process there is thus at least one active thread for each parallel access. The type of message sending shown in Listing 6-1 is not very effective in web applications (assuming that messages are sent regularly). If many users and thus many threads are active simultaneously, then many JMS connections and JMS sessions will be constantly opened and then closed. To leave the JMS session open and close it only at program termination would lead to a JMS session using several threads simultaneously. Such problems are as a rule solved through the use of thread-secure pools. Listing 6-2 shows a simple example of how such a resource pool can be implemented.

Listing 6-2. Example of a session pool.

```
package jms.client;

import java.util.LinkedList;
import javax.jms.Session;
import javax.jms.JMSException;

public class SessionPool {

    private LinkedList sessions;
    private int        size;

    public SessionPool(int size) {
        sessions = new LinkedList();
        this.size = size;
    }
    public synchronized void addSession(Session s) {
        if(!sessions.contains(s)) {
            sessions.addLast(s);
        } else {
            throw new IllegalArgumentException ("session already in use!");
```

```
            }
        }
    public synchronized Session getSession() {
        Session ret = null;
        while(sessions.isEmpty()) {
            try {
                this.wait();
            } catch(InterruptedException ex) {}
        }
        ret = (Session)sessions.removeFirst();
        return ret;
    }
    public int getAvailable() {
        return sessions.size();
    }
    public synchronized void releaseSession(Session s) {
        if(sessions.size() >= size) {
            throw new IllegalStateException
                        ("pool is exceeding initial size");
        }

        if(sessions.contains(s)) {
            throw new IllegalArgumentException
                        ("session is available");
        }

        sessions.addLast(s);
        this.notify();
    }

    public synchronized void destroy() {
        for(int i = 0; i < sessions.size(); i++) {
            try {
                ((Session)sessions.get(i)).close();
            } catch(JMSException jmsex) {
                jmsex.printStackTrace();
            }
        }
        sessions.clear();
        sessions = null;
    }
}
```

Through the use of a session pool the continual generation and closing of sessions can be avoided. Moreover, use of the pool results in fewer JMS sessions being needed as active threads. Furthermore, the session pool prevents a JMS session from being used simultaneously by several threads. An available session is requested via the method getSession. If all available sessions are occupied by other threads, then the method puts a block on the threads via a call to the method wait. When a session object is no longer needed, it must be released via the method releaseSession. When a JMS session is terminated, a call to the method notify results in one of the threads blocked by the method wait being released. The thread can continue its processing and is now in possession of a JMS session object. If significantly more threads than there are available JMS sessions are continually active, the pool can develop a bottleneck, since threads will be constantly blocked. The problem can be solved by increasing the number of available JMS sessions in the pool. Listing 6-3 shows the use of a session pool in an arbitrary class.

Listing 6-3. Use of a session pool.

```
...
private QueueConnection queueCon = null;
private SessionPool     thePool  = null;
...
public void init() {
  ...
  //generation of the SessionPools, e.g., at the time of
  //initialization
  final int SIZE = 10;
  QueueConnectionFactory qcf;
  qcf = (QueueConnectionFactory)
           Lookup.get("ANY_FACTORY");
  Queue q = (Queue)Lookup.get("ANY_QUEUE");
  QueueConnection qc = qcf.createQueueConnection();
  SessionPool sp  = new SessionPool(SIZE);
  for(int i = 0; i < SIZE; i++) {
      sp.addSession(qc.createQueueSession
                      (false, Session.AUTO_ACKNOWLEDGE));
  }
  queueCon = qc;
  thePool  = sp;
  ...
}

public void send(String message)
```

```
        throws NamingException, JMSException
{
  QueueSession qs    = null;
  QueueSender  qsend = null;
  try {
    qs = (QueueSession)thePool.getSession();
    qsend = qs.createSender(theQueue);
    TextMessage tm = qs.createTextMessage();
    tm.setText(message);
    qsend.send(tm);
  } finally {
      try  { qsend.close(); } catch(Exception ex) {}
      thePool.releaseSession(qs);
  }
}
...
public void shutdown()
    throws JMSException
{
  ...
  //Termination of the Session Pool and closing of
  //the session when the process is ended
  thePool.destroy();
  queueCon.close();
  ...
}
...
```

If an application uses a session pool, as introduced in this section, it must make one such pool available per queue or per topic. In order to reduce the number of different kinds of pools that are used, it is suggested to use "generic" queues or topics. One then sends various types of messages via a queue or topic, which then trigger various actions from the recipient, rather than to set up a separate queue or topic for each type of action. In any case, it is important to release a session immediately after use. The longer a thread blocks a session object, the greater is the probability that for this reason another thread will be blocked and will have to wait for an available session. In our example the request for a session takes place in a try block, and the release of the session in an attached finally block. Without the use of the try–finally mechanism, the occurrence of unexpected exceptions could result in the session never being released. The result would be an unwanted reduction in the size of the pool of session instances. The session object would be lost, and the resources reserved by it could not be properly released.

Receiving a Message

In receiving messages the JMS client has several options as to how the reception is to occur. It can fetch the messages from the message service or, in a manner of speaking, have the messaging service deliver them. For the examples in this section we shall again illustrate the use of the point-to-point model. The use of the publish–subscribe model is identical as to the order of steps. Instead of queue-specific interfaces, the topic-related interfaces are brought into play. We shall call attention to the specific places where there is a difference in the behavior of the message service.

The Method receive

The method receive() on the interface QueueReceiver can be used to fetch messages from the message service. Listing 6-4 shows how the method is used.

Listing 6-4. Fetching a message.

```
...
    static final String FACTORY =
                    "SampleConnectionFactory";
    static final String QUEUE = "SampleQueue";
    QueueConnectionFactory qcf = null;
    QueueConnection       qc  = null;
    QueueSession          qs  = null;
    QueueReceiver         qr  = null;
    try {
        qcf = (QueueConnectionFactory)
                Lookup.get(FACTORY);
        qc = qcf.createQueueConnection();
        qs = qc.createQueueSession(false,
                            Session.AUTO_ACKNOWLEDGE);
        Queue queue = (Queue)Lookup.get(QUEUE);
        qr = qs.createReceiver(queue);
        qc.start();
        while(true) {
            Message m = qr.receive();
            //...
            //process the message
            //...
            m.acknowledge();
        }
```

```
    } finally {
        try { qr.close(); } catch(Exception ex) {}
        try { qs.close(); } catch(Exception ex) {}
        try { qc.close(); } catch(Exception ex) {}
    }
...
```

The first steps in receiving a message are identical to those in sending a message. Instead of a queue sender, the JMS client now generates a QueueReceiver object. A call to the start method on the QueueConnection object causes the JMS client to begin the message service at once with the sending of messages. A call to the receive method delivers the next queued message. If at the moment no message is available, then this method blocks the caller until the next message is available. We shall have more to say about the acknowledge method later. The method receive() is available in two forms: It can take a parameter timeout (a time interval in milliseconds). If no message is available for the JMS client, then this method is blocked until a message is available, but if no message is available within the time interval timeout, then the blockade is lifted. The method returns and delivers null instead of a message. The method receiveNoWait returns immediately to the caller in any case. If a message is available, then it is returned. If no message was available, then null is returned.

When receiving a message both the JMS connection and JMS session require certain resources. If the (receiving) JMS client releases these resources through a call to an appropriate close method, then the receipt of messages is terminated.

The Interface MessageListener

In contrast to the case of the receive method, in which the JMS client fetches the messages from the message service, here the client can have the messages delivered as soon as they become available. They are delivered asynchronously over the session's thread. For this to happen, the JMS client must register an object that implements the javax.jms.MessageListener interface with a QueueReceiver object. Listing 6-5 shows the use of this mechanism.

Listing 6-5. Receiving a message.

```
...
    static final String FACTORY =
                    "SampleConnectionFactory";
    static final String QUEUE = "SampleQueue";
    QueueConnectionFactory qcf = null;
    QueueConnection          qc  = null;
```

```
QueueSession          qs  = null;
QueueReceiver         qr  = null;
qcf = (QueueConnectionFactory)
          Lookup.get(FACTORY);
qc = qcf.createQueueConnection();
qs = qc.createQueueSession(false,
                     Session.AUTO_ACKNOWLEDGE);
Queue queue = (Queue)Lookup.get(QUEUE);
qr = qs.createReceiver(queue);
qr.setMessageListener(this);
qc.start();
...
```

To set the receipt of messages in motion, in this case as well the method start() on the QueueConnection object is called. A call to the setMessageListener method returns at once, and the JMS client continues its processing. With this method the JMS client registers the object that the javax.jms.MessageListener interface implements (in our example, this). This interface contains only the method onMessage (Message) (see Listing 6-6). If a message is to be delivered to the JMS client, this method will be called and the message delivered in the form of a Message object.

*Listing 6-6. Implementation of*MessageListener.onMessage().

```
...
  public void onMessage(javax.jms.Message m) {
     // ...
     // Process the message
     // ...
     try {
        m.acknowledge();
     } catch(javax.jms.JMSException jmsex) {
        jmsex.printStackTrace();
     }
  }
...
```

Within a session the sending of messages to a receiver is serialized, and a session always uses only one thread. The next message is sent only when the sending of a message to one or more recipients is closed. To run message sending in parallel the JMS client can either work with several threads within the onMessage method or use multiple sessions. In this way dealing with threads is left to the JMS implementation of the message service.

In the case of asynchronous receiving of messages the behavior of the message service depends on whether a queue or topic is used. If a JMS client receives messages from a queue and uses several sessions for this purpose, then which client receives the next message depends on the implementation of the JMS provider. What is certain, however, is that only one client receives the message. There are JMS providers that allow only one session and one recipient per queue. Under the publish–subscribe model each recipient receives every message for every session. Figure 6-5 shows this state of affairs.

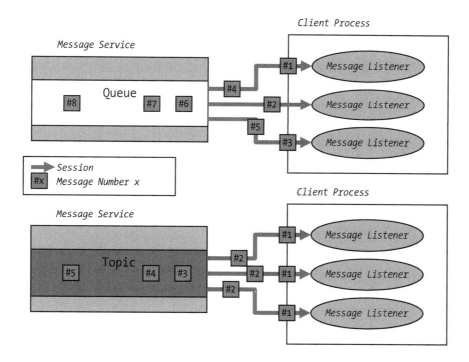

Figure 6-5. Receiving messages over several sessions.

If the JMS client uses more than one session for receiving messages in parallel and in each session registers the same MessageListener object, then the implementation of the MessageListener method must be thread-secure. Since each session uses a thread for sending, the onMessage method can be run simultaneously for multiple threads. If the JMS client registers a different MessageListener object for each session, then the implementation does not have to be thread-secure. However, in this case the JMS client must be concerned in some situations about the synchronization of parallel incoming messages.

The Server Session Pool

Another type of message reception is treated by the JMS specification in a section devoted explicitly to secondary themes that are not part of the range of standard functionality of a message service. The section *JMS Application Server Facilities* (see [29]) treats matters targeted at those who provide application servers. To this belongs the server session pool, which enables the parallel receipt of multiple messages.

Instead of opening and managing several sessions itself, the JMS client can leave this task to the application server, by using a server session pool. In the world of Java, by *application server* one understands typically a product that conforms to the specifications of Java 2, Enterprise Edition (that is, a server that in addition to a web and EJB container offers a message service and a JMS implementation). It is also possible that the JMS provider itself makes a server session pool implementation available. In the course of this section we will use the term *application server* for both cases.

A server session is an object that is made available by an application server. A server session joins a JMS session with a thread of the application server. The message service is responsible for delivering messages throughout a session. The application server manages the session and provides a thread for the JMS session. The JMS client merely provides the implementation of the MessageListener interface in a separate class, which is responsible for the processing of messages. Since a separate thread is provided to each MessageListener object, the implementation does not have to be thread-secure.

The processing of received messages does not take place in this case, as in both other cases, in the process of the JMS client, but in the process of the application server. If the JMS client wants to or has to for performance considerations process messages in parallel, then the use of a server session pool affords enormous simplification. It need not be concerned with managing multiple JMS sessions or with multiple threads, nor is the client process burdened at run time by the allocation of various resources such as network connections and threads. However, the resources of the application server are additionally burdened by a server session pool. Before a server session pool is used it should be considered whether the application server can bear the additional burden. Listing 6-7 shows an example of the use of a server session pool, while Listing 6-8 shows the implementation of the MessageListener interface, which is responsible for the processing of messages in the server session pool. An example of an application server that offers a message service and an implementation of a server session pool is the WebLogic application server from BEA Systems (see [35]). The example shown in Listing 6-7 was developed with WebLogic.

Listing 6-7. Generation of a server session pool.

```
...
    static final String FACTORY =
                    "SampleConnectionFactory";
    static final String QUEUE = "SampleQueue";
    static final String SSP_FACTORY =
                    "SampleSessionPoolFactory";
    static final String LISTENER = "jms.client.MQListener";
    QueueConnectionFactory qcf = null;
    QueueConnection         qc  = null;
    ConnectionConsumer      cc  = null;
    qcf = (QueueConnectionFactory)
            Lookup.get(FACTORY);
    qc = qcf.createQueueConnection();
    qc.start();
    Queue queue = (Queue)Lookup.get(QUEUE);
    ServerSessionPoolFactory factory =
        (ServerSessionPoolFactory)
            Lookup.get(SSP_FACTORY);



    ServerSessionPool sessionPool;
    sessionPool = factory.getServerSessionPool
                    (qc, 5, false,
                     Session.AUTO_ACKNOWLEDGE, LISTENER);
    cc = qc.createConnectionConsumer
            (queue, "TRUE", sessionPool, 10);
...
```

In order to generate a ServerSessionPool object the JMS client requires a ServerSessionPoolFactory. It acquires one, such as a connection factory, from JNDI. It is also made available from the administrator via the configuration. In generating the server session pool the following are specified: a Connection object, the size of the pool (the value 5 in the example), true or false (according to whether transactions are used), the type of acknowledgment, and the name of the class that implements the MessageListener interface and is responsible for the processing of messages (see Listing 6-8). The session pool is activated via the method createConnectionConsumer() on the QueueConnection object. The session pool opens the requisite number of server sessions, associates them with threads, and uses instances of the passed classes to process messages. The MessageListener class must be available to the application server, since it is responsible for the generation of instances.

Listing 6-8. Receiver class of the server session pool.

```
package jms.client;

import javax.jms.*;

public class MQListener implements MessageListener {

    public MQListener() {}

    public void onMessage(Message m) {
        // ...
        // process the message
        // ...
        try {
            m.acknowledge();
        } catch(JMSException jmsex) {
            jmsex.printStackTrace();
        }
    }
}
```

At this place we would like to reiterate that the instances of the MessageListener class are generated in the process of the application server and not in the process of the JMS client. Thus the processing of messages also takes place in the process of the application server and not in that of the JMS client.

Reception Behavior

A queue always delivers a message to a single recipient. If several recipients are registered with a single queue, then to which recipient the message is delivered depends on the implementation of the JMS provider. Queues have, as a rule, only a single recipient. The ability of a JMS implementation to permit multiple recipients is often used to achieve economy of scale. In using several sessions and several receivers for a queue, it can be a convenient option to process incoming messages in parallel.

Topics typically have multiple recipients. A message in a topic is delivered only to the currently active subscribers. Inactive subscribers do not receive the message. If a JMS client would like to ensure that it receives all the messages belonging to a particular topic, it can register as a *durable topic subscriber*. The messages of a topic are stored until they have been delivered to all *durable* registered recipients.

The situation of message distribution in a queue operates differently. If no recipient is currently registered with a queue, then the message remains in the queue until a recipient registers. It is thereby guaranteed that every message reaches precisely one client.

In the case of a server crash the above-mentioned guarantees remain in effect only if the queue or topic is persistent. The messages are then stored persistently by the message service, and they remain stored even in the case of a server crash or restart. The message service begins immediately after a restart with the delivery of any remaining messages.

Messages are normally delivered in the order in which they were added to the queue or topic. The order in which messages arrive at recipients depends on a number of factors. If the sender designates varying priorities for various messages, it thereby influences the order of delivery to the recipients. Messages with higher priority are delivered before messages with lower priority. If the recipient employs a message filter (see below), the order of delivery is again influenced.

Transactions and Acknowledgment

Simple Transactions

To automate the sending and delivery of messages, a JMS client can use a transactional session (assuming that the JMS provider supports this functionality). Listing 6-9 shows how a transactional session is generated.

Listing 6-9. Generation of a transactional session.

```
...
QueueConnectionFactory qcf = null;
qcf = (QueueConnectionFactory)Lookup.get(FACTORY);
QueueConnection qc = qcf.createQueueConnection();
qc.createQueueSession(true, Session.AUTO_ACKNOWLEDGE);
...
```

When the method `createQueueSession()` is called, the parameter `true` results in the session being transactional. The same holds for the method `createTopicSession`. Sent messages are transferred to a queue or topic only when `Session.commit()` is called. Received messages are considered to have been successfully received only when the recipient calls `Session.commit()`. The transaction bond encompasses the sending or receiving of a particular message. The sending *and* receiving of a particular message cannot be bound in a single transaction, since the receiving session is different from the sending session. Only the receiving and sending of different messages within a session is transactional.

When a sending JMS client uses a transactional session, it must call `commit` to finally transfer the message into the queue or topic. The same holds for a receiving JMS client when it uses a transactional session. A message that is sent via a transactional session can be received via a nontransactional session, and vice versa.

A call to `commit` not only closes the current transaction, but also opens simultaneously a new transaction. Transactions can therefore not be nested. If `Session.rollback()` is called, all messages sent since the last call to the method `commit` are discarded. None of these messages are transferred to the queue or topic. The same holds for the receipt of messages. Messages delivered after the last call to `commit` are considered to have been successfully delivered only when the method `commit` is again called. Only then are the delivered messages finally removed from the queue or topic. If `Session.rollback()` is called, the message service begins with a renewed delivery to the registered recipients of the messages left in the queue or topic since the last call to `commit`. Whether a session is transactional, that is, whether a JMS client must call the method `commit` for sending or receipt of messages, can be determined by a call to `Session.getTransacted()`. Whether a message was redelivered due to a call to the method `rollback` can be determined by the JMS client via the method `Message.getJMSRedelivered()`.

Distributed Transactions

The JMS provider can optionally support distributed transactions. (See Chapter 7 for details on transactions.) In contrast to simple transactions of a session, in the case of distributed transactions, actions of various services can be collected into a single action. These services can come into operation from various servers. A distributed transaction can, for example, comprise a method call to an Enterprise Bean and the placing of a message in a queue. If one of the two actions goes awry, then it is possible to cancel both actions. The context of a distributed transaction ends with the sending of a message. It is not extended to the receipt of the message. Thus the receipt and processing of a message cannot be components of a distributed transaction in which the message was sent. Here the same principle holds as with simple transactions.

The JMS supports distributed transactions via the JTA/XAResource API (details are discussed in Chapter 7). The support for distributed transactions in implemented by the JMS provider in the JMS sessions. The specification defines for this an interface `javax.jms.XASession`, which is derived from `javax.jms.Session`; XASession is specialized for the particular communication types (publish–subscribe, point to point). The transaction is steered by the transaction monitor via the XA interfaces. The JMS client does not come into direct contact with these interfaces. If it moves within a distributed transaction, it will obtain an XASession object, which, however, appears to it as a Session object. If the JMS clients attempts within a distributed transaction to call the method commit or rollback on the session object, then the method triggers an exception of type TransactionInProgressException. Support of distributed transactions in JMS is designed primarily for the integration of JMS into application servers.

Acknowledgment

When neither simple nor distributed transactions are used, the acknowledgment mechanism comes into play. It governs when delivered messages are finally removed from the queue or topic. The acknowledgment mechanism is of no importance in sending messages. At the time a session is created, the JMS client can specify the type of acknowledgment behavior that is desired. The mechanism is used by the JMS client via the methods Message.acknowledge() and Session.recover(). The method acknowledge is comparable to the commit method of a transaction, while the method recover is comparable to the rollback method. The JMS client can exhibit various acknowledgment behaviors when a JMS sessions is generated as follows:

- javax.jms.Session.AUTO_ACKNOWLEDGE: The JMS session automatically acknowleges a message after the receive method has been called successfully or after a call by the onMessage method to a message listener has returned. The delivered message is not sent again and is immediately removed from the queue or topic. In this way the sending of *one* message corresponds to an atomic action. Calls to the acknowledge method of the JMS client are ignored. A call to the recover method by the JMS client changes nothing in the behavior of the session.

- javax.jms.Session.CLIENT_ACKNOWLEDGE: The JMS client must call the acknowledge explicitly to confirm the receipt of one or several messages. As long as the acknowledge method is not called, already delivered messages are not removed from the queue or topic. If the JMS client calls the acknowledge method after each receipt of a message, the behavior is identical to that of AUTO_ACKNOWLEDGE. If the JMS client calls the method recover, the session halts the delivery of messages at once. The session returns to the message that was stopped after the last call to acknowledge and begins again with delivery. Messages that were redelivered due to a call to recover are recognized by the JMS client by a call to the method Message.getJMSRedelivered().

- javax.jms.Session.DUPS_OK_ACKNOWLEDGE: In this mode the JMS session confirms the receipt of a message automatically as in the mode

AUTO_ACKNOWLEDGE. However, it is up to the session to determine when the confirmation is made and the messages removed from the queue or topic. This means that in this mode, messages can be multiply delivered (the prefix DUPS stands for "duplicates"). In contrast to a call to the recover method in the mode CLIENT_ACKNOWLEDGE, there is nothing in the message to show whether it was delivered more than once. Thus this mode can be used only with JMS clients that can deal with doubly delivered messages. Calls to the methods acknowledge and recover have no effect. The advantage of this mode over AUTO_ACKNOWLEDGE is that the session can work more efficiently. For example, the removal of sent messages can take place in a separate thread, which runs in the background with lower priority.

AUTO_ACKNOWLEDGE is probably the mode best suited for most JMS clients. The increased cost of a JMS session at run time vis-à-vis the DUPS_OK_ACKNOWLEDGE mode is frequently made up for by its being less error-prone. The mode DUPS_OK_ACKNOWLEDGE is used with JMS clients to process incoming messages as a block to achieve greater run-time efficiency. This makes sense, for example, when in processing a message a database access is necessary. Instead of accessing the database for each incoming message, a collective query can be made to the database for several messages. In this way the cost of opening several connections is spared, and the database is burdened with fewer queries. If the action was successful, then the receipt of the other messages of the block to be processed can be confirmed with a call of the method acknowledge to the last-received message.

Filtering Messages

A JMS client has the ability of specifying a filter for receipt of messages. This filter results in only those messages being delivered to the client that satisfy the particular filter criteria. The JMS specification calls this filter mechanism the *message selector*. The filter can be specified when a recipient is created at the session interface in the form of a string object:

- QueueSession.createReceiver(Queue queue, java.lang.String messageSelector)

- TopicSession.createSubscriber(Topic topic, java.jang.String messageSelector, boolean noLocal)

The attribute noLocal, which can be specified only in relation to a topic, offers the possibility of excluding the delivery of messages that are sent over the same connection. This attribute is useful when a JMS client sends and receives messages over a particular topic (chat applications use this process, for example). With noLocal the client can determine whether messages that it sends itself are received.

The syntax of the message selector is based on the WHERE clause of the query language SQL92. For a description of the syntax see [29]. The message selector is applied only to the header fields and the properties of a message. It cannot be applied to the message body.

Example 1

```
...
QueueReceiver qr;
qr = queueSession.createReceiver(queue, "JMSPriority >= 5");
...
```

The receiver shown in this example will receive from the message service only the messages in the queue whose priority is greater than 5. JMSPriority is a header field defined by the JMS specification and is placed on every message. If the priority is not specified by the sender, the field JMSPriority is filled with a standard value. JMSPriority can assume the values 0 through 9, where 0 is the lowest priority and 9 the highest. The standard priority has the value 4.

Example 2

```
...
QueueReceiver qr;
String selector = "AppProp in ('aProp', 'bProp')";
qr = queueSession.createReceiver(queue, selector);
...
```

The receiver shown in this example will have only those messages from the queue delivered by the message service for which the property AppProp defined by the application has the value aProp or bProp. The sender of a message sets the property AppProp via the method setStringProperty on the interface javax.jms.Message.

The use of a message selector results in a particular recipient receiving only those messages that satisfy the selector criteria. In the case of a queue, the result is that the messages that do not meet the criteria remain in the queue until a recipient registers that meets one of the following criteria:

- Recipient uses no message selector;

- Recipient uses a message selector with the appropriate header and properties of this message.

With a topic, messages that are not delivered to any recipient as a result of the selector criteria are simply not delivered. For the recipient or recipients in question it is as if the message had never been sent.

Request-Reply

Message systems are designed for asynchronous communication. A JMS client sends a message and thereby sets off certain responses on the receiver side. It does not know exactly when the impact will occur (that is, when the message will be received), nor who will undertake the processing (that is, who receives the message). In a classical RPC (remote procedure call), for example, the client must wait until the processing of the procedure is complete. After the RPC has returned, the client receives the result of the processing as the return value. This return value can have various meanings for the RPC client. It can signal whether the processing was successful or whether it suffered errors. The return value can also influence the further actions of the client.

When a message service is used for communication between the components of a distributed application, the behavior just described is often desired. With the request–reply mechanism a behavior can be simulated over a message service that corresponds to a classical RPC. This means that synchronous communication can also occur over a message service. The only difference with respect to a classical RPC is that the caller cannot determine from whom the request is received.

The JMS specification provides auxiliary classes for achieving request–reply behavior. These classes are javax.jms.QueueRequestor for the point-to-point communication model and javax.jms.TopicRequestor for the publish–subscribe model. Listing 6-10 shows an example of how the class QueueRequestor is used (which corresponds to the use of the class TopicRequestor).

Listing 6-10. Request–reply with the class QueueRequestor.

```
...
    QueueConnection qc     = null;
    QueueSession    qs     = null;
    QueueSender     qsend  = null;
    QueueRequestor  qr     = null;
    try {
        QueueConnectionFactory qcf = null;
        qcf = (QueueConnectionFactory)
                    Lookup.get(FACTORY);
        qc = qcf.createQueueConnection();
        qc.start();
```

```
        qs = qc.createQueueSession(false,
                            Session.AUTO_ACKNOWLEDGE);
        Queue queue = (Queue)Lookup.get(qn);
        qsend = qs.createSender(queue);
        m = qs.createTextMessage("a message");
        qr = new QueueRequestor(qs, queue);
        Message ret = qr.request(m);
        //...
        //process the reply
        //...
    } finally {
        try { qr.close(); }    catch(Exception ex) {}
        try { qsend.close(); } catch(Exception ex) {}
        try { qs.close(); }    catch(Exception ex) {}
        try { qc.close(); }    catch(Exception ex) {}
    }
...
```

The code is largely identical to that for sending a message, as shown in the earlier section on sending a message. The significant difference consists in the use of the class QueueRequestor. Instead of generating a queue sender via a queue session, an instance of the class javax.jms.QueueRequestor is generated. To it are passed the queue session and the queue as parameters. For sending a message the JMS client calls the method request() and passes the message to be sent. The message is sent via the queue that was passed to the queue requestor in the constructor. Simultaneously, the queue requestor sets up a temporary queue, with which it awaits the answer. Temporary queues (and the same for temporary topics) are valid only as long as the connections over which they were created are active. Only the sessions that belong to the connection over which the temporary queue or topic was generated are allowed to generate a *receiver* for this temporary queue or topic. A call to the request() method blocks the call until an answer is received over the temporary queue. Listing 6-11 shows a receiver that has answered the sent message from Listing 6-10.

Listing 6-11. A JMS client's answer to a message.

```
...
    public void onMessage(Message m) {
        // ...
        // process Message
        // ...
        QueueSender qs = null;
        try {
```

```
            TextMessage tm =
                queueSession.createTextMessage();
            tm.setText("Reply:" +
                        ((TextMessage)m).getText());
            Queue reply = (Queue)m.getJMSReplyTo();
            qs = queueSession.createSender(reply);
            qs.send(tm);
            m.acknowledge();
        } catch(JMSException jmsex) {
            jmsex.printStackTrace();
        } finally {
            try { qs.close(); } catch(Exception ex) {}
        }
    }
}
...
```

To reply to a message the receiver evaluates the header field JMSReplyTo. It receives the (temporary) queue or topic over which the sender of the message is awaiting an answer. Under other circumstances it would have no access to the temporary queue. Due to the properties of temporary queues and topics (as described above) it is ensured that only the recipient of a message can send an answer. The field JMSReplyTo is set by the queue requestor via the method setJMSReplyTo() on the interface javax.jms.Message. The recipient generates a queue sender for the temporary queue and sends the answer over that queue to the sender of the original message. If the answer arrives at the sender, the call to the request() method returns, and the sender can evaluate the answer.

Since temporary queues and topics are employed in request–reply, no critical information should be contained in the answer. The sender of the message must take into consideration that the answer might, for example, become lost due to a server crash or loss of a connection. A temporary queue or topic exists, as already mentioned, only in the context of a particular JMS connection. Should this connection be broken, the temporary queue or topic is lost together with the messages it contains.

Concepts

The Client's Point of View Toward a Message-Driven Bean

From the point of view of the client, a message-driven bean is a message receiver (message consumer) in the sense of the Java Message Service. The client cannot address a message-driven bean directly, for it has no home, remote, local home, or local interface. The client can address a message-driven bean only indirectly, by sending a message over a particular channel (destination) of the JMS, from which it knows that the recipient is a particular message-driven bean. The client has no influence over the life cycle of a message-driven bean. This is governed completely by the EJB container. The client also has no influence over how many instances of a message-driven bean are used for the processing of messages of a particular channel. That is also controlled exclusively by the container. The instances of a message-driven bean are not exclusively available to the client, and they cannot store a state for it. They are stateless, like stateless session beans.

The client can localize a particular channel of the message service via JNDI (see the earlier section in this chapter on sending messages). A client that uses (indirectly) message-driven beans is not differentiated from a normal JMS client. If the client uses a session or entity bean, it is tightly coupled to it. If the client uses a message-driven bean over a channel of a message service, then it is loosely coupled to this Enterprise Bean. If the message-driven bean were to be exchanged at run time for another recipient (for example, another message-driven bean or a traditional Java class), this would have no effect on the client. The API of the Java Message Service stands between them as an indirection layer.

Life Cycle of a Message-Driven Bean

The life cycle of a message-driven bean is run exclusively by the EJB container. An instance of a message-driven bean can assume the following states:

- Nonexistent: The instance does not exist;

- Pooled ready: The instance exists and is available for method calls.

Figure 6-6 illustrates graphically the life cycle of a message-driven bean. It is clear from the figure that only the container can initiate a state change.

Instances of a message-driven bean are as a rule generated at the startup of the EJB container or when the EJB container increases the pool size for the purpose of ensuring relatively fast processing of incoming messages. The life cycle of a message-driven bean begins with a call to the constructor. Then the container calls the method setMessageDrivenContext and thereby gives the instance its context. A message-driven bean can communicate with the EJB container via the context. Then the container calls the method ejbCreate, which places the instance of the message-driven bean in the state Pooled Ready. From this time on, the bean can be used by the container for the processing of incoming messages that were sent by a client over a particular channel of the message service. The EJB container uses an arbitrary instance of a particular type of message-driven bean for the processing of an incoming message. It maintains a pool of instances for each type of message-driven bean.

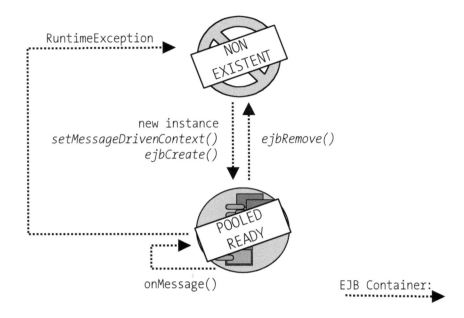

Figure 6-6. Life cycle of a message-driven bean.

When the EJB container no longer needs an instance of a message-driven bean, it calls the `ejbRemove` method. With the call to this method the life cycle of a message-driven bean comes to an end. That is the case when the EJB container is powered down or the EJB container decides to reduce the pool of instances of a particular bean type. The life cycle of a message-driven bean ends also when the message-driven bean instance throws an exception of type `RuntimeException` during the processing of a message.

Since the EJB container as a rule uses several instances of a message-driven bean, it can divide the processing of incoming messages arriving in sequence among several instances. Messages can be processed in parallel by instances of a single type of message-driven bean (see Figure 6-7). The container takes care of thread management and provides the message-driven bean the types of services that we have seen in regard to other bean types.

The concept that the EJB container implements for parallel processing of messages resembles closely the concept of the server session pool introduced earlier. One might give the following simplified formulation:

Server Session Pool + stateless session bean − Home/Remote or Local Home/Local Interface = **Message-Driven Bean**.

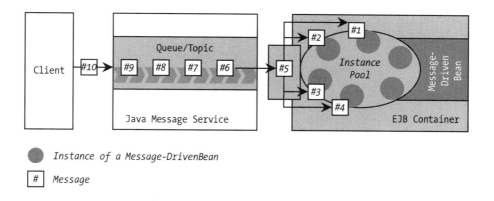

Instance of a Message-DrivenBean

Message

Figure 6-7. Parallel processing with message-driven beans.

Parallel processing means that a *particular* instance of a message-driven bean does not process messages in the order in which they are sent by the client.

The container must ensure that the calls to bean instances for processing messages are serialized. Thus the implementation of the bean class need not be thread-secure, which simplifies the development of message-driven beans.

Programming

Figure 6-8 provides an overview of the classes and interfaces of message-driven beans. The most conspicuous difference between session and entity beans is the lack of home and remote, and local home and local, interfaces.

Message-driven beans implement the interface javax.ejb.MessageDrivenBean and the interface java.jms.MessageListener (see the section in this chapter on receiving a message) either directly or indirectly. The class must be declared public. The class must have a parameterless constructor that is declared public. This is used by the EJB container to generate instances of a message-driven bean. The class is not permitted to implement the method finalize.

The methods of a message-driven bean can be divided into three categories:

- state management;

- identity management;

- application logic.

The following sections describe the individual methods in these groups. A study of the programming examples will provide a rapid introduction to programming of these methods.

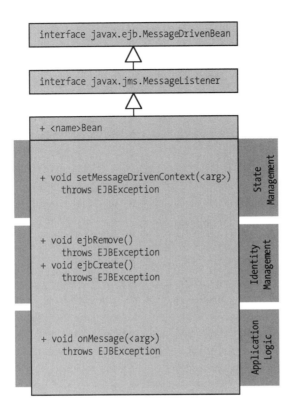

Figure 6-8. Interfaces of a message-driven bean.

State Management

With message-driven beans there is only one method that informs a bean instance of an imminent state change, namely, the method setMessageDrivenContext. In the case of message-driven beans a state change is initiated exclusively by the container. The implementation of the method setMessageDrivenContext stores the passed context. This can later be used to communicate with the container. (In the subsection on the message-driven context we will discuss context more fully.) In this method the specification allows access to the environment of the message-driven bean only over JNDI. How an Enterprise Bean accesses its environment is discussed fully in Chapter 4. Immediately after a call to the method setMessageDrivenContext there follows a transition into the state Pooled Ready.

Identity Management

The methods for identity management form the second group of methods of a message-driven bean. They make possible the generation and deletion of message-driven bean identities. In contrast to those of session and entity beans, these methods are used exclusively by the EJB container. The client has no way to influence the generation and deletion of message-driven bean identitites. An instance of a message-driven bean has no identity in relation to the client. The EJB container uses the identity internally for managing the instances of a particular type of message-driven bean.

ejbCreate

With a call to ejbCreate the EJB container places an instance of a message-driven bean in the state Pooled Ready and uses it immediately for processing incoming messages. A message-driven bean must define precisely one method ejbCreate without parameters. Within this method the message-driven bean is permitted access to its environment only over JNDI and possibly access to a user transaction object via the message-driven context. Access to the environment via JNDI is described in Chapter 4. Working with transactions and the use of the interface javax.transaction.UserTransaction are described in Chapter 7.

ejbRemove

When the EJB container no longer needs a bean instance, it deletes it by a call to the ejbRemove method. This destroys the identity of the instance. It can no longer be used for processing messages. If the bean has reserved resources, these must be released with the call to this method. As with the method ejbCreate, the bean is allowed acess to its environment only via JNDI and perhaps to a UserTransaction object via the message-driven context.

Application Logic

The application logic of a message-driven bean can be implemented only in a method, namely, onMessage. It cannot be called by a client. It is always called by the EJB container when a message arrives over the channel of the message service allotted to the message-driven bean. The EJB container must ensure that the calls to this method are serialized. The implementation of this method does not need to be thread-secure. The channel (destination) of the message service associated with the message-driven bean is set in the deployment descriptor.

The method onMessage provides access to the bean's environment via JNDI, to the services that the container offers (database, Java Message Service, etc.), and to other Enterprise Beans. Chapter 4 describes how an Enterprise Bean accesses its environment via JNDI. There it is also explained how an Enterprise Bean can access services and resources of the EJB container. If a message-driven bean uses another Enterprise Bean, it is then in this respect just an ordinary Enterprise Bean client. The viewpoint of a client toward a session or entity bean is described in Chapters 4 and 5.

In the case of transactions that are run by the container, the bean can use the methods getRollbackOnly and setRollbackOnly of the interface MessageDrivenContext. With transactions that are run by the bean itself, it can use a UserTransaction object to which it has access via the message-driven context. Transactions and the use of objects of type javax.transaction.UserTransaction are described in Chapter 7. The specification prescribes that a message-driven bean is *not* permitted to use the acknowledgment mechanism of the JMS. If the message-driven bean uses container-managed transactions, then the receipt of a message is automatically confirmed with the transaction's commit by the EJB container. If the message-driven bean manages its own transactions, then the receipt of a message is not a part of the transaction. In this case the specification recommends setting the acknowledge mode to AUTO_ACKNOWLEDGE. This setting is carried out in the deployment descriptor. If the setting of the acknowledgment mechanism is lacking in the deployment descriptor, then the EJB container automatically makes the setting AUTO_ACKNOWLEDGE.

The method onMessage declares no exceptions, and it should throw no exceptions as well (this holds also for javax.ejb.EJBException). A normal JMS client that receives messages has just as little possibility of throwing exceptions in this method. If the message-driven bean throws an exception of type RuntimeException, then it is placed in the state nonexistent by the EJB container. It assumes that this instance is no longer capable of processing messages correctly.

The Message-Driven Context

With the MessageDrivenContext an instance of a message-driven bean is able to communicate with the EJB container. With message-driven beans this is necessary above all for the control of transactions. The context of a message-driven bean can be changed by the EJB container during the lifetime of an Enterprise Bean. The context is transmitted via the method setMessageDrivenContext of the interface javax.ejb.MessageDrivenBean. We shall now present briefly the methods of the message-driven context.

setRollbackOnly

This method aids in control of transactions (see Chapter 7). It is used by a bean instance to make it possible to cancel all the actions of a transaction in case of error. This method can be used only by message-driven beans that use transactions controlled by the container.

getRollbackOnly

The method getRollbackOnly is the read counterpart of the method setRollbackOnly. With this method it can be checked whether the current method call can still be successfully completed. Like setRollbackOnly, this method can be used only by message-driven beans that use container-managed transactions.

getUserTransaction

This method can be called only by message-driven beans that manage their own transactions. The return value of this method is an object of type javax.transactionUserTransaction from the Java transaction API (see Chapter 7).

getCallerPrincipal

This method is inherited by the message-driven context from the interface EJBContext. A message-driven bean is not permitted to call this method. Normally, this method makes it possible to determine the user that makes this method call. Since a message-driven bean cannot be directly addressed by a client, a call to this method makes no sense in any case.

isCallerInRole

The same considerations hold for this method as for the method getCallerPrincipal. This method would make it possible to determine the role of the user that is making the current method call.

getEJBHome

This method, too, is forbidden to a message-driven bean. It, too, is inherited from the interface EJBContext. This method permits access to an instance of the implementation of the bean's (local) home interface. Since a message-driven bean has no need for a (local) home interface, a call to this method makes little sense.

An attempt by a message-driven bean to call a forbidden method on the message-driven context is acknowledged with

```
java.lang.IllegalStateException.
```

The Client

Programming the client corresponds exactly to the programming of a normal JMS client. The programming of JMS clients was dealt with in the first section of this chapter.

An Example

Let us consider an example in which an application system wishes to log entries in a stockroom. Since the logging data will be used later for auditing purposes, they should be maintained securely in a database. In order not to prolong a booking unnecessarily, a decision is made to carry out the logging asynchronously. Since the data must not be lost, the Java message service is used. With its support for distributed transactions and persistent queues and topics, it offers sufficient data security for this purpose. The message-driven bean LoggerBean is responsible for placing incoming data securely in a database table (see Listing 6-12).

Listing 6-12. Example of a message-driven bean.

```
package ejb.logger;
import javax.ejb.*;
import javax.jms.MessageListener;
import javax.jms.Message;
import javax.jms.TextMessage;
import javax.jms.JMSException;
import javax.naming.Context;
import javax.naming.InitialContext;
import javax.naming.NamingException;
import javax.sql.DataSource;
import java.sql.SQLException;
import java.sql.Connection;
import java.sql.PreparedStatement;
import java.sql.Date;
public class LoggerBean
```

```
implements MessageDrivenBean, MessageListener {
private static final String DS =
        "java:/comp/env/ds-name";
private static final String ST =
        "insert into logs(tst, msg) values(?, ?)";
private MessageDrivenContext mCtx      = null;
private transient DataSource dataSource = null;
public LoggerBean() {}
public void setMessageDrivenContext
                  (MessageDrivenContext ctx)
{
    mCtx = ctx;
}
public void ejbCreate() { }
public void ejbRemove() {
    dataSource = null;
}
public void onMessage(Message message) {
    try {
        initDataSource();
    } catch(NamingException nex) {
        //error reporting
        mCtx.setRollbackOnly();
        return;
    }
    String msg = null;
    try {
        msg = ((TextMessage)message).getText();
    } catch(ClassCastException ccex) {
        //error reporting
        mCtx.setRollbackOnly();
        return;
    } catch(JMSException jmsex) {
        //error reporting
        mCtx.setRollbackOnly();
        return;
    }
    try {
        logMessage(msg);
    } catch(SQLException sqlex) {
        //error reporting
        mCtx.setRollbackOnly();
        return;
    }
```

```
        }
    private void logMessage(String msg)
        throws SQLException
    {
        Connection          con = dataSource.getConnection();
        PreparedStatement pst = null;
        String              mm  = (msg == null) ? "" : msg;
        try {
            pst = con.prepareStatement(ST);
            Date dd = new Date(System.currentTimeMillis());
            pst.setDate(1, dd);
            pst.setString(2, mm);
            pst.execute();
        } finally {
            try { pst.close(); } catch(Exception ex) {}
            try { con.close(); } catch(Exception ex) {}
        }
    }
    private void initDataSource()
        throws NamingException
    {
        if(dataSource != null) {
            return;
        }
        Context ctx = new InitialContext();
        String dsname = (String)ctx.lookup(DS);
        dataSource = (DataSource)ctx.lookup(dsname);
    }
}
```

By way of its environment the LoggerBean obtains for itself the name of the data source that it uses for database access. Via JNDI it obtains access to this data source. When a message arrives the EJB container calls the onMessage method and sends the message to the Enterprise Bean. The LoggerBean awaits a message of type javax.jms.TextMessage. It takes the text message and stores it together with the date and time of receipt in a database table with the name logs. If an error occurs that the LoggerBean cannot overcome, it uses the method setRollbackOnly of the message-driven context. It thereby notifies the EJB container that the processing has gone awry. The LoggerBean uses the transactions managed by the EJB container (see the example deployment descriptor in Listing 6-13). If the transaction is not committed, then the unsuccessfully processed message is resent to the message service.

Listing 6-13 shows the deployment descriptor associated with the LoggerBean. For a complete description of the elements of the deployment descriptor for a message-driven bean, see [21].

Listing 6-13. Deployment descriptor of a message-driven bean.

```xml
<?xml version="1.0" ?>
<ejb-jar version="2.1" xmlns="http://java.sun.com/xml/ns/j2ee"
xmlns:xsi="http://www.w3.org/2001/XMLSchema-instance"
xsi:schemaLocation="http://java.sun.com/xml/ns/j2ee
http://java.sun.com/xml/ns/j2ee/ejb-jar_2_1.xsd">
  <enterprise-beans>
    <message-driven>
      <!-- name of the Enterprise Bean -->
      <ejb-name>loggerBean</ejb-name>
      <!-- class of the  Enterprise Bean -->
      <ejb-class>ejb.logger.LoggerBean</ejb-class>
      <!-- tells who should run the transactions -->
      <transaction-type>Container</transaction-type>
      <!-- tells for what queue or topic the
       Enterprise Bean is registered as recipient -->
      <message-driven-destination>
        <jms-destination-type>javax.jms.Queue
        </jms-destination-type>
      </message-driven-destination>
      <!-- environment entries -->
      <env-entry>
        <env-entry-name>ds-name</env-entry-name>
        <env-entry-type>java.lang.String</env-entry-type>
        <env-entry-value>wombatDS</env-entry-value>
      </env-entry>
      <!-- tells with what authorizations the,
       Enterprise Bean is equipped. -->
      <security-identity>
        <run-as-specified-identity>
          <role-name>guest</role-name>
        </run-as-specified-identity>
      </security-identity>
    </message-driven>
  </enterprise-beans>
</ejb-jar>
```

In order for an event to be logged, the message must be sent via the message service. For this each component of the system that carries out a booking can use an auxiliary class, as shown in Listing 6-14.

Listing 6-14. Example of a client of a message-driven bean.

```
package ejb.logger;
import javax.jms.JMSException;
import javax.jms.QueueConnectionFactory;
import javax.jms.QueueConnection;
import javax.jms.QueueSession;
import javax.jms.QueueSender;
import javax.jms.Queue;
import javax.jms.Session;
import javax.jms.Message;
import javax.jms.TextMessage;
import javax.naming.NamingException;
import ejb.util.*;
public class Logger {
    public static final String FACTORY   =
        "java:/env/jms/DefaultConnectionFactory";
    public static final String QUEUE_NAME =
        "java:/env/jms/LoggerQueue";

    private static QueueConnectionFactory queueCF  = null;
    private static Queue                  theQueue = null;
    static {
        try {
            queueCF  = (QueueConnectionFactory)
                        Lookup.get(FACTORY);
            theQueue = (Queue)
                        Lookup.get(QUEUE_NAME);
        } catch(NamingException nex) {
            nex.printStackTrace();
            throw new
                IllegalStateException(nex.getMessage());
        }
    }
    public static void log(String logMessage)
        throws NamingException, JMSException
    {
        QueueConnection qc   = null;
        QueueSession    qs   = null;
```

```
QueueSender      qsend = null;
try {
    qc = queueCF.createQueueConnection();
    qs = qc.createQueueSession
                (false, Session.AUTO_ACKNOWLEDGE);
    qsend = qs.createSender(theQueue);
    TextMessage tm = qs.createTextMessage();
    tm.setText(logMessage);
    qsend.send(tm);
} finally {
    try  { qsend.close(); } catch(Exception ex) {}
    try  { qs.close(); }    catch(Exception ex) {}
    try  { qc.close(); }    catch(Exception ex) {}
    }
  }
}
```

This example uses an auxiliary class called Lookup, which has the method get. Access to the naming service is contained within this auxiliary class and the method get in order to limit the example code to its essentials. The implementation of this auxiliary class is part of the example code for this book.

With the static method log a text message can be sent via the LoggerQueue. This message is received by an instance of the LoggerBean and stored in the database. The "client code" shown in Listing 6-14 for the use of a message-driven bean is no different from the code of a normal JMS client. The code shown could be optimized in two different ways. If messages are sent from only a single thread, then the JMS connections and the JMS session could be held open, to avoid continual opening and closing. If the class Logger is used in an application in which multiple threads send messages, then a session pool could be used, as described in the section on sending a message.

Summary

Message-driven beans are without doubt a positive addition to the component model of Enterprise JavaBeans. With message-driven beans both asynchronous and parallel processing of application logic are possible. This dual functionality is an important building block in the development of business applications. These functions help in system performance enhancement. Asynchronicity and parallel processing are very complex and difficult themes in information science. They bring many advantages and are indispensable for the use of many systems. However, they are difficult to implement. With message-driven beans the use of asynchronicity and parallel processing in the implementation of business logic are simplified for the bean provider.

A traditional JMS client can also enjoy the benefits of asynchronicity and parallel processing relatively easily and without too much programming effort, since a message service behaves ansynchronously by default, and parallel processing can be achieved by the JMS client through the use of several JMS sessions or the use of a server session pool. A JMS client is, however, in comparison to message-driven beans, not necessarily a component and is reusable only in rare cases. Furthermore, a message-driven bean enjoys services offered by the EJB container, in particular, distributed transactions.

A message-driven bean is not permitted to use the acknowledge mechanism (see the subsection on transactions and acknowledgment in the first section of this chapter). In many cases it would be very useful if the bean could, in fact, use this mechanism. The LoggerBean from the previous section could also profit from the acknowledge mechanism. It would then not have to log each incoming message, but could carry out the logging in blocks, without taking on the risk of losing information. A blockwise logging of data would reduce the burden on the database. Instead of the acknowledge mechanism, the LoggerBean could use simple transactions of the JMS session upon the receipt of messages in order to execute the logging in a secure manner. That is also impossible with message-driven beans. For that the message-driven bean must have access to the JMS session over which messages are delivered to it by the JMS provider. This JMS session is, however, under the control of the EJB container and for the message-driven bean inaccessible, since there is no way to synchronize the instances of the instance pool of a particular message-driven bean type. A particular instance is therefore incapable of deciding when an acknowledge or commit is reasonable, since it does not know which or how many messages have already been processed by the other instances in the pool.

The EJB container could, for example, offer the message-driven bean, via the message-driven context, a possibility to synchronize with the other instances in the pool and thereby use simple transactions of the JMS provider or the acknowledge mechanism. The message-driven context could contain a method acknowledge for this purpose and a method recover, which would have the same functionality as javax.jms.Message.acknowledge() or javax.jms.Session.recover(). However, by way of this indirection the EJB container would have the possibility of keeping track of the acknowledgment and commit functions and intervene as necessary.

On the other hand, in the case of the LoggerBean, parallel processing would not be absolutely necessary. *One* instance of this bean would suffice to process messages (assuming moderate message traffic). In any case, the queue would function as a secure buffer. There is no way of informing the EJB container that one instance of the message-driven bean suffices to reach the desired goal.

The resources of the EJB container would be less burdened at run time, since it does not have to manage a pool of LoggerBean instances. Moreover, the use of the acknowledge mechanism or simple transactions of the JMS session would be possible in this case, since there are no other instances of the message-driven bean with which synchronization would be required. The bean instance would in this case would be quite well able to decide when an acknowledge or commit made sense.

In the method onMessage the message-driven bean may throw neither self-defined nor system nor run-time exceptions. In the example of the LoggerBean, for example, a database access error results in the transaction being canceled. The message service would resend the message in such a case. If a problem that interferes with the correct processing of a message is of only a transitory nature, then the processing can perhaps be successfully continued after a resending of the message. Matters become difficult when the problem is of a fundamental nature or of lengthy duration. For example, say a LoggerBean is waiting for a message of type javax.jms.TextMessage. If a client were to place a message of type javax.jms.ObjectMessage in the LoggerQueue (for example, due to a programming error), that would lead to an exception of type ClassCastException in the method ClassCastException of the LoggerBean. The LoggerBean would break off the transaction and terminate processing. The breaking off of the transaction would lead to the message service resending the message. The LoggerBean has no way of informing the EJB container or the message service that it cannot process the message due to a fundamental problem. And furthermore, none of the other instances of the LoggerBean class will be able to process the message correctly after a resending. Thus the processing of the message is caught in an infinite loop. The LoggerQueue would then be blocked by this defective message and would grow continually. The handling of such a problem is solely the responsibility of the implementation of the message-driven bean. To solve such a problem one might do the following: In addition to the LoggerQueue there could be established an additional queue, the LoggerErrorQueue. The LoggerQueue could first place all messages that experience a fundamental problem that makes the correct processing of a message impossible in the LoggerErrorQueue (a sort of rerouting) and then continue as if the message had been processed correctly. Figure 6-9 depicts such a situation.

With this mechanism the LoggerQueue cannot be blocked by a defective message. The LoggerErrorQueue could have, for example, a normal JMS client as recipient that has messages delivered and then notifies the administrator (say, by e-mail). The administrator could inspect the contents of the LoggerErrorQueue with some tool (for example, with the help of a queue browser; see [29]) and analyze the problem. After the problem has been resolved, it could manually resend the message and remove it from the LoggerErrorQueue.

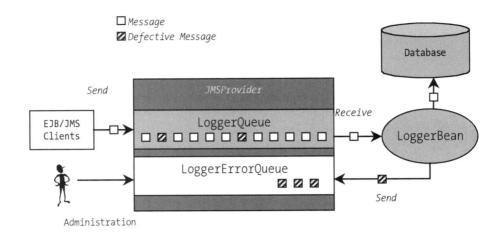

□ *Message*
▨ *Defective Message*

Figure 6-9. Error-handling with message-driven beans.

From the point of view of the bean provider it would, of course, be desirable for such a mechanism, or something similar, to be available to the EJB container. A message-driven bean could report, upon an exception of a particular type (e.g., javax.ejb.EJBException) being thrown, that the message cannot be processed correctly due to a fundamental problem and that the message-driven bean is incapable of resolving the problem. The EJB container could ensure that the message was removed from the queue or topic to avoid an infinite repetition of the message being sent via the message service. The EJB container could transform the message into another persistent state, for example, direct it into an "error" queue or topic or database or write it to a file. The EJB container provider could make tools available that support the administrator in analysis and repair of defective messages.

#### CHAPTER 7

Transactions

Fundamentals

Transactions represent a multifaceted and valuable mechanism and a decided strength of the EJB concept. They make possible the development of important business processes in a multiuser and multiresource environment.

Transactions bind several steps of a process into a single processing unit; a transaction provides a path from one consistent state in a database to another consistent state; and a successfully executed transaction leads to a persistent change in the data. A typical EJB application uses a transaction to change the contents of a database.

The path to the next consistent state often leads over several steps and inconsistent intermediate states. Therefore, a transaction has the task of uniting a number of individual processing steps into a single unit. If in the course of a transaction there arises a condition that prohibits the proper completion of the transaction, then all actions in the transaction taken up to that point are canceled. That is, a transaction is either executed completely, or else it leaves no effect on the state of the data. Thus a transaction is referred to as *atomic* or *inseparable*.

A typical example of a transaction is a bank transfer (see Figure 7-1). Here a certain amount of money is transferred from one account into another. If an error occurs during the withdrawal from one account or the deposit into the other, then the original state of the accounts, as the last consistent state, must be restored.

It is highly desirable that other users of the same data always see consistent states. Therefore, the transaction mechanism can ensure that inconsistent states remain hidden. This property is called *consistency of views* or *isolation of transactions*.

In the case of parallel access to the same data by several clients there are three categories of problems. That is, there are three different reasons that a client might see an inconsistent state:

1. *Dirty Reads (inconsistency):* At a particular moment there is an inconsistent state in the database (see Figure 7-1).

2. *Nonrepeatable Reads:* A client reads the data over time, reading the first part at time A and the second at time B. Another client's transaction, running in parallel, modifies the same data in the interval between time A

and time B. Even consistent states exist at times A and B, the reading client can nonetheless obtain a false view of reality.

In the example of Figure 7-1 an inconsistent view could arise as follows: A client reads from Account 1 before the represented transaction, and from Account 2 after the transaction. The client obtains the false view of Account 1 having a balance of 100 and Account 2 a balance of 70.

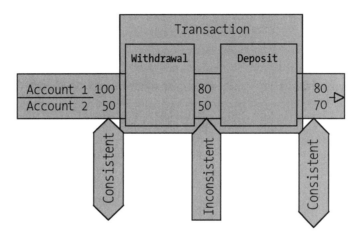

Figure 7-1. Bank transfer as example of a transaction.

3. *Phantom Reads:* This problem arises when new data elements are added to the database. At time A, a client reads all the data elements that satisfy certain criteria, and at time B executes a write operation that depends on the result obtained at time A. If between time A and time B a new data element is written to the database that satisfies the same criteria, then the write operation at time B should have taken it into account.

This problem can occur, for example, in storing articles. An article with a certain weight is to be stored. First it is determined whether the storage medium has the necessary capacity. The articles already in the store are determined, and their weights are totaled. If there is sufficient capacity remaining, the article is added to the list of articles in storage. If between the reading of the stored articles and the acceptance of the article into storage another article is taken into storage, the total capacity can be exceeded.

Present-day database systems are able to avoid these problems. Through the use of intermediate data storage for a running transaction (*caching*) and exclusive reservation of data elements (*locking*) for a transaction, each transaction can be guaranteed a consistent view. Each of these measures requires the expenditure of resources and thus diminishes the performance of the database.

Locking impairs the ability of transactions to run in parallel and in extreme cases can lead to the serialization of all transactions. To obtain complete consistency of views is thus expensive; that is, it has negative effects on the performance and parallelism of transactions. For this reason partial restrictions are accepted.

One distinguishes four levels of consistency (see [14] and the section on transaction isolation in this chapter). The quality of the consistency increases as the level rises from level 1 to level 4:

1. The problems of dirty and nonrepeatable reads are accepted for the sake of improved performance.

2. Only the problem of nonrepeatable reads is accepted. In contrast to level 1, here no inconsistency is permitted.

3. Consistent results are endangered by the phantom problem.

4. Complete consistency of views is always ensured.

The fundamental properties of transactions are frequently collected under the acronym ACID, which stands for *atomic, consistent, isolated*, and *durable*.

We distinguish between *transaction management* and *transaction control*. Transaction management (also called *transaction demarcation*) determines when a transaction begins and when it is ended or aborted. Transaction control is the technical implementation of the transaction mechanism. It consists of the communication mechanism for distributed transactions and the transaction monitor.

Compared to the theoretical knowledge that is necessary for an understanding of transactions, the programming of transaction management is very simple. Three commands form the basis for transaction management:

- The command begin starts a transaction.

- The command commit causes a transaction to end successfully.

- The command rollback causes a transaction to be aborted.

Concepts

The EJB architecture implements transactions with the assistance of a transaction service (see Figure 7-2). This service operates as a central instance that takes over the coordination of all participants in a transaction.

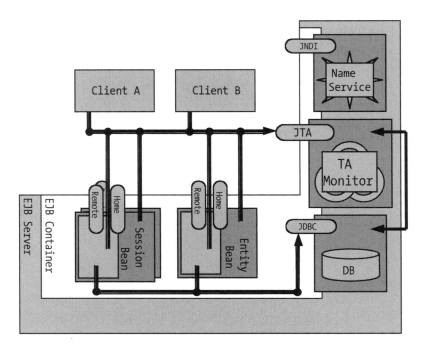

Figure 7-2. Communication paths in EJB transactions.

The participants in a transaction are a client, one or more transactional systems, one or more beans, and the EJB container. The client is the interface to the user and generally controls the execution of the processes. The transactional systems store the data that are changed in the course of the transaction. The most frequently used transactional system is a database. The beans are normally based on the data in the transactional systems, and the consistency of their states is ensured by the transaction. The EJB container works closely with the transaction service to provide an environment for the beans that in particular supports simple dealings with transactions.

Transaction management can be taken over by the client, the bean, or even the EJB container. In the last case one speaks of *declarative transactions*, since the transaction management is not programmed in the application logic, but is declared only at the time of deployment by the developer and handled at run time by the EJB container. This promotes the reuse of beans, since for a single bean various transactional behaviors can be declared. This allows beans to be more easily used and reused in a variety of applications.

For transaction management it is necessary that the Enterprise Bean support the remote or local client view, or both. The discussion in this chapter applies without restriction to both cases. Therefore, in this chapter we shall make no distinction between the remote and local client views. The implementations will relate to the standard case, the remote client view.

The distribution of roles in the EJB concept determines the principles for the management and control of transactions. Transaction control is handled completely by the creator of the EJB container, and thus the bean developer is completely relieved of such responsibility. This strategy has already long been used in database systems. However, in transaction management the EJB concept goes one step further. With declarative transactions the application developer can be freed from the problems of transaction management. This task is left to the experts who have an overview of how applications work together and can thus better determine the required transactional behavior and performance metrics for optimal performance.

EJB supports distributed transactions. One speaks of a distributed transaction when several transactional objects are involved in various services (such as JMS, database, EJB container) of a transaction (see Figure 7-3).

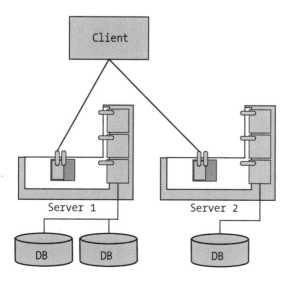

Figure 7-3. Example of a system involved in a distributed transaction.

The various services involved in the transaction can run on the same server or on different servers. For example, in a distributed transaction, data in a number of databases can be changed in a single transaction. A transaction can affect different databases of a single EJB container or those of different EJB containers.

View consistency (isolation of transactions) is only in part the responsibility of the EJB container. In most products the consistency level can be specified in the configuration of the application server for the database connection. The application server could also provide a nonstandard service to enable the setting of the consistency level in the application logic.

JTA and JTS

Java Transaction API (JTA) and *Java Transaction Service* (JTS) are specifications of Sun Microsystems. JTA defines the interfaces that the participating instances of a distributed transaction need for communication. The interfaces are located at a sufficiently high level of abstraction so that they are suitable for use by application programmers.

JTS is designed for those who offer transaction services. A transaction service controls the transaction. It coordinates the functioning of transaction in cooperation with various transactional systems. JTS contains the necessary definitions for developing a transaction service that supports JTA.

JTS is the link between Java and the *Object Transaction Service 1.1* (OTS). This is a standard of the OMG (Object Management Group), which defines transaction management and control with CORBA objects. JTS is a compatible subset of OTS.

The programming of the following example on transactions is based exclusively on a part of JTA. The complex mechanism of transaction management is invisible to the bean developer. Even though this quite simple interface hides the complexity, one must know the exact processes in order to write efficient programs.

In what follows we wish to give an overview of JTS. The concepts used here form the basis for the following representation of transactions by Enterprise JavaBeans. One should pay particular attention to the communication paths in the use of transactions. The complete specification of JTA and JTS can be found at the following Sun Microsystems web sites [23]:

- http://java.sun.com/products/jta

- http://java.sun.com/products/jts

Terminology and Concepts

JTS and OTS distinguish among types of objects according to their roles in transactions. The EJB concept is also reflected in the various object types:

- *Transactional clients* are programs that access objects on the server. They can take over the transaction management. They do not themselves store any transaction-secured data. Not all clients that work with Enterprise JavaBeans are transactional clients. With declarative transactions it is possible to decouple the client completely from the transaction management.

- *Transactional objects* are objects on a server that take part in transactions but do not store any of their own transaction-secured data. They do not actually take over transaction management, but can force a transaction to be aborted. All Enterprise JavaBeans are transactional objects.

- *Recoverable objects* are the objects that store the actual data. Access always proceeds in a transaction-secure manner. In the EJB model the database manages most of the recoverable objects. A recoverable object can then be a line in a database table. Moreover, other services, such as Java Messaging Service (JMS), can work with recoverable objects.

Furthermore, two fundamental types of transactions are distinguished:

- *Local transactions* deal only with data from a single database or from another single transactional system. The transactional object can manage the coordination with an independent transaction service.

- *Global transactions* can handle data from various databases and other transactional systems. The coordination is managed by an independent transaction service, which synchronizes the participating systems.

A method that is executed in a global transaction has a *transaction context*. The transaction context describes the unique identity of the transaction, its state, and possibly other attributes as well.

The *transaction service* coordinates all global transactions. It ensures that all operations on recoverable objects are transaction-secured. To make this possible, each object involved in a transaction must know its transaction context. The transaction service then associates the transaction context with the thread. In this way the transaction context is available to each object in the same thread.

In the case of a method call over a network or across a process boundary there is another concept that is necessary to consider. The *transactional context propagation* ensures that in such cases the transaction context is transmitted. The implementation is the responsibility of the application server and is usually based on an extension of the network protocol (RMI / IIOP).

The Architecture of JTS

Figure 7-4 shows schematically the interaction of objects involved in a transaction:

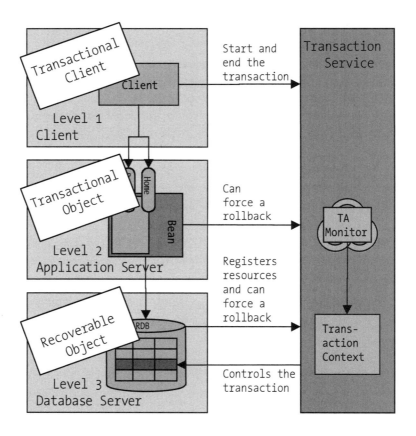

Figure 7-4. JTS and EJB.

- A central system, the transaction service, coordinates all transactions. It communicates directly with all objects that participate in a transaction (transactional clients, transactional objects, and recoverable objects).

- At the start of a transaction the transaction context is generated by the transactional client. This contains information about the transaction and the user. In Java, the transaction context is associated with a running thread. On the one hand, this means that all actions of this thread are executed in the transaction, and on the other hand, that there can always be only one transaction per thread.

- Every new transaction is registered with the transaction service. The transaction service knows the transaction context and the state of each running transaction.

- During a transaction the transactional client calls, once or several times, methods of transactional objects on the server. The methods of the transactional objects, in turn, call additional methods, either of additional transactional objects or recoverable objects.

- Every object that is involved in the transaction through some chain of calls must gain knowledge of the transaction context. As long as the calls remain in one system, this is no problem, since the transaction context is associated with a thread, and EJB forbids the initiation of new threads. However, if a network must be traversed, then there will be a necessary extension of the protocol, which relays, in addition to the data of the function call, the transaction context as well. This is called *transactional context propagation*.

- Every recoverable object that participates in a transaction through a chain of calls uses the transaction context to register its data with the transaction service. It informs the transaction service about local transactions that it uses for access. In this way, the transaction service knows all the data that are involved in a running transaction.

- At the end of the transaction the transactional client signals a successful conclusion (`commit`) or an aborting (`rollback`) of the transaction. If the transaction is to be successfully concluded, then all participating objects must give their consent. The transaction cannot be successfully concluded if a recoverable object experiences an error during access to its data or if a transactional system has previously set the status of the transaction to `rollback only`.

- The transaction service coordinates the conclusion of a transaction with the *two-phase-commit* (2PC) protocol. It ensures that all local transactions are either successfully concluded or aborted.

Programming JTA

The *Java Transaction API* (JTA) is the client API responsible for transaction management. With JTA we are dealing with a part of the interface of the Java Transaction Service (JTS) that is relevant for regular application developers. Since this concept is not taken into account with older application servers, access via JTS must be used to some extent.

- *import* instruction for JTA:

    ```
    import javax.transaction.*;
    ```

- *import* instruction for JTS:

    ```
    import javax.jts.*;
    ```

The following examples of transactions use exclusively the interface `javax.transaction.UserTransaction`.

Implicit Transaction Management

Implicit transaction management represents a very simple introduction to transactions. The developer of the application logic must be an expert in a particular application domain. Normally, he or she will not be an expert in transactions. Therefore, the complexity of transaction management and control should remain largely hidden.

Implicit transaction management is based on the separation of the actual application logic from the logic of the transaction management. The bean provider develops the application logic, while in creating the complete application, the application assembler defines the transaction management using transaction attributes.

With implicit transactions the EJB container takes over the transaction management. For every call to a bean method the EJB container ensures that a suitable transaction exists. In the deployment descriptor, a determination is made for each method as to whether a transaction is needed, and if so, of what type. If a call occurs with an unsuitable or missing transaction, the EJB container attempts to generate a suitable transaction. If this is impossible, this operation causes an error, and the EJB container triggers an exception.

Figure 7-5 presents an example of an implicit transaction. The client calls a bean method. Here the client assumes no responsibility for the transaction management. However, the execution of the called method requires a transaction. Since the EJB container has been notified of this with the deployment descriptor of the bean, the EJB container can launch the necessary transaction. After the successful execution of the method, the EJB container ends the transaction with a commit. In case of error, if an exception has occurred, then the EJB container terminates the transaction with a rollback.

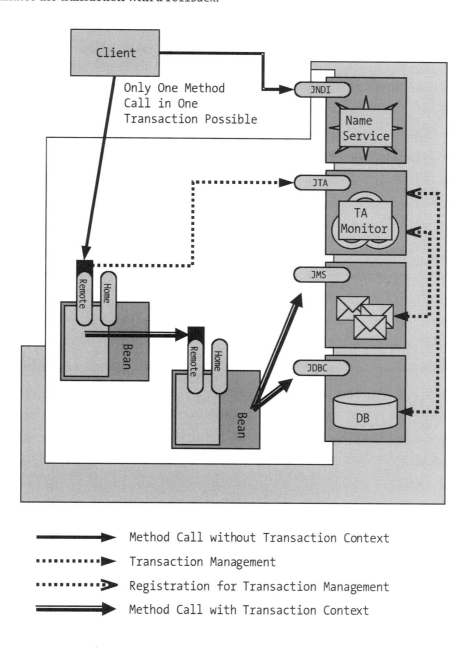

Figure 7-5. An example of data flow in an implicit transaction.

The called method can itself call additional methods. The transaction context is thereby further transmitted. The EJB container checks whether a suitable transaction exists for the called method. In the example the existing transaction can be used again.

A called method can also use a defined service of the EJB architecture. Examples are access to a database and to a messaging service. An entity bean may use the database implicitly through the storage of persistent data. These transactional systems manage the data affected by the transaction. For proper management of these data they use the transmitted transaction context and communicate directly with the transaction service over JTS.

Certain properties result from the particular objectives of implicit transactions, namely, the reduction of complexity for the application developer. The following list should provide an overview. The individual points are gone into in greater detail in the following sections with the help of concrete programming examples:

- Implicit transactions are declarative transactions. The transactional behavior is declared in the deployment descriptor.

- The transactional behavior of a bean is defined in the deployment descriptor. A transaction attribute can be given for each method (see the subsection on transaction attributes later in this chapter).

- An implicit transaction cannot extend over more than one client function call. As a rule, though, this suffices if on the server side the requisite interfaces are available.

- If an error situation arises in a bean, then the bean can compel the running transaction to be rolled back upon completion. However, the bean has no way to end the running transaction and in general, no mechanism to start a new one.

- A session bean can have itself informed by the EJB container about the state of a transaction and thereby has the ability of ensuring additional consistency conditions.

These particular properties of implicit transactions lead naturally to certain limitations. The EJB concept is nevertheless considerably shaped by the division of responsibility among the various players. Implicit transactions are an important step toward this goal, and were therefore deliberately chosen as a fundamental component of the EJB concept.

Whoever wishes to profit from the advantages of the EJB architecture should intensively promote the use of implicit transactions. The use of *explicit* transaction management, to be introduced in the next section, always indicates the partial surrender of the division of responsibility. The logic of transaction management is defined during the implementation and is not apparent in the deployment descriptor. The decision to use explicit transaction management is a far-reaching design decision that should remain the exception rather than the rule.

The following comparison of the advantages and limitations of implicit transactions should facilitate the choice of the correct mode for a particular application.

Advantages

- *Quality and maintenance:* The developer of the application logic is freed from the complexities of transaction management. This has a positive influence on both quality and maintainability. Each contributor to the development process does what he or she does best, and the complexity is reduced for each.

- *Reusability:* The reusability of a bean is much enhanced, since it is not until the time of deployment that the transactional behavior of this component must be determined.

Limitations

- *Limited flexibility:* The possibilities for development are limited purely on the side of the client. With declarative transactions the client cannot combine beans on the server to create new transactions. Furthermore, there are applications in which the application logic of the bean requires a particular transaction management, and thus this separation is disadvantageous. Due to these limitations the EJB concept provides for explicit transaction management.

- *Simple tasks become complex:* The division of responsibilities and the resulting action model make the development of simple prototypes unnecessarily complicated. The concept pays off only with larger projects.

Example Producer

The example Producer should provide a gentle introduction to programming transactions. This is a simple simulation of a supply chain. The session bean Producer is a producer that creates a product out of certain raw materials. The entity bean Stock simulates the storage of the raw materials and the end product.

Producer is a classic example of a transaction. The product can be produced only if the necessary raw materials are present and there is storage available for the end product. As long as there is only one client, this situation is trivial. Using transactions, the situation is also trivial for parallel access by several clients.

An important method for working with transactions is setSessionContext for session beans, setMessageDrivenContext for message-driven beans, and setEntityContext for entity beans. Here the bean is notified of its context, which contains information about the user and the transaction. Moreover, the context provides the bean limited influence over the transaction. The method setRollbackOnly forces a rollback. With getRollbackOnly it is possible to query as to whether the transaction can still be successfully completed.

We shall first consider the entity bean Stock. The constructor requires three parameters: a unique ID for each stock bean, the maximum capacity, and the current amount. Furthermore, the home interface (see Listing 7-1) defines the requisite findByPrimaryKey method.

Listing 7-1. StockHome: *the home interface of the entity bean* Stock.

```
package ejb.supplychain.stock;

import javax.ejb.CreateException;
import javax.ejb.EJBHome;
import javax.ejb.FinderException;
import java.rmi.RemoteException;

public interface StockHome extends EJBHome {

    public Stock create(String stockId,
                        int maxVolume,
                        int aktVolume)
        throws CreateException,
               RemoteException;

    public Stock findByPrimaryKey(String primaryKey)
        throws FinderException,
               RemoteException;

}
```

In the remote interface (see Listing 7-2) we see the functionality of the Stock bean. The method get allows material to be withdrawn from storage, and with the method put, material is stored. Both methods trigger a ProcessingErrorException if the action is impossible. The method getVolume allows one to query the current amount in storage.

Listing 7-2. Stock: *the remote interface of the entity bean* Stock.

```
package ejb.supplychain.stock;

import java.rmi.RemoteException;
import javax.ejb.EJBObject;

public interface Stock extends EJBObject {

    public void get(int amount)
        throws ProcessingErrorException, RemoteException;

    public void put(int amount)
        throws ProcessingErrorException, RemoteException;

    public int getVolume()
        throws RemoteException;
}
```

Once the functionality has been defined, we can determine the database design in Listing 7-3.

Listing 7-3. Database design for the entity bean Stock.

```
CREATE TABLE STOCK
  (STOCKID VARCHAR(10) NOT NULL,
   VOLUME INT,
   MAXVOLUME INT)
ALTER TABLE STOCK ADD
  CONSTRAINT PRIMKEY
  PRIMARY KEY (STOCKID)
```

We shall use the method get as a model for the implementation of the methods (see Listing 7-4). The method assumes that it will be executed in a transaction. First, the new count of what is in storage is computed, and then a check is made as to whether the amount is valid.

Listing 7-4. `StockBean.get`: *this method reduces the amount in storage.*

```
...
    public void get(int amount)
        throws ProcessingErrorException
    {
        int newStockVolume = this.getStockVolume() - amount;
        if(newStockVolume >= 0) {
            this.setStockVolume(newStockVolume);
        } else {
            throw new ProcessingErrorException("volume too small");
        }
    }
...
```

If it is a valid amount, the persistent variable stockVolume is updated. The EJB container ensures that this change is transaction-securely written to the database.

An invalid amount means an error for the method. The reaction to an error in a transaction can take one of two forms:

- *Exception:* The method triggers an exception and thus leaves the decision as to whether the transaction should be rolled back to the caller. If in a declarative transaction the exception is not caught by any bean in the calling hierarchy, the EJB container aborts the transaction and issues a rollback.

- *setRollbackOnly:* A call to this method of the bean context causes the transaction to be aborted with a rollback. This makes sense if data have already been changed in the database and thus an invalid intermediate state is present. The rollback is not immediately executed, but only after the transaction is ended. The decision for a rollback is final, and thus there is no sense in taking measures to recreate a valid state within this transaction. An exception can be triggered to shorten the further processing of the transaction.

In the Stock bean, errors are determined by checking the preconditions, before persistent data are changed. Therefore, a setRollbackOnly is pointless. An exception is triggered, and the caller can react to it.

The crucial question is now how one ensures that the methods are always executed in a transaction. For this one can specify in the deployment descriptor attributes for transactions for each method. The value Required always deals with a transaction. Either the running transaction is used, or a new transaction is launched by the EJB container. In the following subsection we provide a thorough description of the permitted values. Listing 7-5 shows the relevant portions of the deployment descriptor for the stock bean.

Listing 7-5. Portion of the deployment descriptor of the entity bean Stock.

```xml
<?xml version="1.0" ?>
<ejb-jar version="2.1" xmlns="http://java.sun.com/xml/ns/j2ee"
xmlns:xsi="http://www.w3.org/2001/XMLSchema-instance"
xsi:schemaLocation="http://java.sun.com/xml/ns/j2ee
http://java.sun.com/xml/ns/j2ee/ejb-jar_2_1.xsd">
  ...
  <enterprise-beans>
    <entity>
      <ejb-name>Stock</ejb-name>
      <home>ejb.supplychain.stock.StockHome</home>
      <remote>ejb.supplychain.stock.Stock</remote>
      <ejb-class>ejb.supplychain.stock.StockBean</ejb-class>
      <persistence-type>Container</persistence-type>
      <prim-key-class>java.lang.String</prim-key-class>
      <reentrant>False</reentrant>
      <cmp-version>2.x</cmp-version>
      <abstract-schema-name>StockBean</abstract-schema-name>
      <cmp-field>
        <field-name>stockId</field-name>
      </cmp-field>
      <cmp-field>
        <field-name>stockVolume</field-name>
      </cmp-field>
      <cmp-field>
        <field-name>maxStockVolume</field-name>
      </cmp-field>
      <primkey-field>stockId</primkey-field>
    </entity>
    ...
  </enterprise-beans>
  <assembly-descriptor>
    <container-transaction>
      <method>
        <ejb-name>Stock</ejb-name>
        <method-name>get</method-name>
      </method>
      <method>
        <ejb-name>Stock</ejb-name>
        <method-name>put</method-name>
      </method>
      ...
      <trans-attribute>Required</trans-attribute>
```

```
    </container-transaction>
  </assembly-descriptor>
</ejb-jar>
```

Instances of the stock bean are used by the producer bean, which is a stateful session bean. It takes a unit from storage S_1 and two units from S_2 and uses them to generate a product, which it places in storage T_1.

The home interface of the producer bean is shown in Listing 7-6; it offers only the standard create method.

Listing 7-6. ProducerHome*: home interface of the session bean* Producer.

```
package ejb.supplychain.producer;

import javax.ejb.CreateException;
import javax.ejb.EJBHome;
import java.rmi.RemoteException;

public interface ProducerHome extends EJBHome {

    public Producer create()
        throws CreateException, RemoteException;

}
```

The remote interface in Listing 7-7 defines only the method produce, which implements the production method described previously.

Listing 7-7. Producer*: remote interface of the session bean* Producer.

```
package ejb.supplychain.producer;

import java.rmi.RemoteException;
import javax.ejb.EJBObject;

public interface Producer extends EJBObject {

    public int produce(int amount)
        throws UnappropriateStockException, RemoteException;

}
```

The implementation of the bean itself consists mostly of familiar elements. Listing 7-8 shows the framework for the class definition.

Listing 7-8. ProducerBean: *class definition.*

```
package ejb.supplychain.producer;

import javax.ejb.CreateException;
import javax.ejb.EJBException;
import javax.ejb.FinderException;
import javax.ejb.SessionBean;
import javax.ejb.SessionContext;
import javax.ejb.SessionSynchronization;
import javax.naming.NamingException;

import ejb.supplychain.stock.ProcessingErrorException;
import ejb.supplychain.stock.Stock;
import ejb.supplychain.stock.StockHome;
import ejb.util.Lookup;

public class ProducerBean implements SessionBean, SessionSynchronization {
    public static final String STOCK_HOME =
        "java:comp/env/ejb/Stock";
    public static final String SOURCE_ID1 =
        "java:comp/env/idSource1";
    public static final String SOURCE_ID2 =
        "java:comp/env/idSource2";
    public static final String TARGET_ID =
        "java:comp/env/idTarget";

    private Stock source1;
    private Stock source2;
    private Stock target;

    private SessionContext sessionCtxt = null;

    ...
}
```

For the initialization an internal method, openResources(), is called in the ejbCreate method and in the ejbActivate method (see Listing 7-9). This ensures that all necessary resources are available. To this end it searches all stock beans in use and stores a reference in the variables source1 and source2 for the raw materials stores and in the variable target for the end product store. The stock bean that was used will later be marked as a reference in the deployment descriptor. The IDs of the stock beans are environment variables of the bean and are read using JNDI. These, too, will later be taken up in the deployment descriptor. Access to JNDI is encapsulated in the auxiliary class ejb.util.Lookup. The source code of this auxiliary class together with all the source code for this chapter is available with the code source for this book.

*Listing 7-9. Initialization of*ProducerBean.

```
...
    public void ejbCreate()
        throws CreateException
    {
        try {
            this.openResources();
        } catch(Exception ex) {
            throw new CreateException(ex.getMessage());
        }
    }
    public void ejbActivate() {
        try {
            this.openResources();
        } catch(Exception ex) {
            throw new EJBException(ex.getMessage());
        }
    }
    private void openResources()
        throws FinderException, NamingException
    {
        try {
            // get stock IDs
            String idSource1 =
                (String)Lookup.narrow(SOURCE_ID1, String.class);
            String idSource2 =
                (String)Lookup.narrow(SOURCE_ID2, String.class);
            String idTarget =
                (String)Lookup.narrow(TARGET_ID, String.class);
            // get home
            StockHome stockHome = (StockHome)
                Lookup.narrow(STOCK_HOME, StockHome.class);

            // get stocks
            this.source1 = stockHome.findByPrimaryKey(idSource1);
            this.source2 = stockHome.findByPrimaryKey(idSource2);
            this.target = stockHome.findByPrimaryKey(idTarget);
        } catch(java.rmi.RemoteException e) {
            throw new EJBException(e.getClass().getName()
                                    + ": " + e.getMessage());
        }
    }
...
```

The producer bean stores the session context, which is passed to it in the method setSessionContext (see Listing 7-10), in the variable sessionCtxt.

Listing 7-10. ProducerBean.setSessionContext: *setting the session context.*

```
...
    public void setSessionContext(SessionContext ctxt) {
        this.sessionCtxt = ctxt;
    }
...
```

With the method produce in Listing 7-11 things get interesting. This method assumes that it is executed in a transaction. It reduces the quantity of stored raw materials and increases that of stored end product. There is no prior check whether the execution of these actions is possible. If an error occurs, the entire transaction is simply rolled back. For this the method setRollbackOnly of the session context in the catch block is called. With this error not only is an exception triggered, but also setRollbackOnly is called, since a stock bean's value may have been changed, resulting in an invalid intermediate state in the database.

Listing 7-11. ProducerBean.produce: *Business logic of the session bean* Producer.

```
...
    public int produce(int amount)
        throws UnappropriateStockException
    {
        int ret;
        try {
            System.out.println("starting produce");
            this.source1.get(amount);
            this.source2.get(amount*2);
            this.target.put(amount);
            ret = amount;
        } catch(ProcessingErrorException e) {
            this.sessionCtxt.setRollbackOnly();
            throw new UnappropriateStockException();
        } catch (java.rmi.RemoteException re) {
            this.sessionCtxt.setRollbackOnly();
            throw new UnappropriateStockException();
        }
        return ret;
    }
...
```

The definitions of the producer bean and the stock bean are located in the same deployment descriptor. Listing 7-12 shows the relevant parts of the deployment descriptor for the producer bean (Listing 7-5 shows the relevant parts for the stock bean). For the method produce of the producer bean, Required is declared in the deployment descriptor as transaction attribute. Also, the environment variables for the producer bean are defined. Additionally, the deployment descriptor contains a reference to the stock bean.

Listing 7-12. Extract from the deployment descriptor of the session bean producer.

```
...
  <enterprise-beans>
    ...
    <session>
      <ejb-name>Producer</ejb-name>
      <home>ejb.supplychain.producer.ProducerHome</home>
      <remote>ejb.supplychain.producer.Producer</remote>
      <ejb-class>ejb.supplychain.producer.ProducerBean</ejb-class>
      <session-type>Stateful</session-type>
      <transaction-type>Container</transaction-type>
      <env-entry>
        <env-entry-name>idSource1</env-entry-name>
        <env-entry-type>java.lang.String</env-entry-type>
        <env-entry-value>stock1</env-entry-value>
      </env-entry>
      <env-entry>
        <env-entry-name>idSource2</env-entry-name>
        <env-entry-type>java.lang.String</env-entry-type>
        <env-entry-value>stock2</env-entry-value>
      </env-entry>
      <env-entry>
        <env-entry-name>idTarget</env-entry-name>
        <env-entry-type>java.lang.String</env-entry-type>
        <env-entry-value>stock3</env-entry-value>
      </env-entry>
      <ejb-ref>
        <ejb-ref-name>ejb/Stock</ejb-ref-name>
        <ejb-ref-type>Entity</ejb-ref-type>
        <home>ejb.supplychain.stock.StockHome</home>
        <remote>ejb.supplychain.stock.Stock</remote>
        <ejb-link>Stock</ejb-link>
      </ejb-ref>
    </session>
```

```
  </enterprise-beans>
  <assembly-descriptor>
    <container-transaction>
      ...
      <method>
        <ejb-name>Producer</ejb-name>
        <method-name>produce</method-name>
      </method>
      <trans-attribute>Required</trans-attribute>
    </container-transaction>
  </assembly-descriptor>
</ejb-jar>
```

We have created a test based on the test framework to be presented in Chapter 9 for the producer bean. The complete test, together with many other tests for the examples in this book, is contained within the source code for this book.

Listing 7-13 presents a section from this test for the producer bean, from which can be seen exactly the expected behavior of the producer bean for the method previously described.

Listing 7-13. A section of the test for the session bean Producer.

```
...
Stock stock1 = this.stockHome.create("stock1", 500, 200);
Stock stock2 = this.stockHome.create("stock2", 500, 500);
Stock stock3 = this.stockHome.create("stock3", 100, 0);
int step = 1;
Producer p = this.producerHome.create();
p.produce(10);
this.assertEquals(step+":volume stock1", 190, stock1.getVolume());
this.assertEquals(step+":volume stock2", 480, stock2.getVolume());
this.assertEquals(step+":volume stock3", 10, stock3.getVolume());
step++;
p.produce(40);
this.assertEquals(step+":volume stock1", 150, stock1.getVolume());
this.assertEquals(step+":volume stock2", 400, stock2.getVolume());
this.assertEquals(step+":volume stock3", 50, stock3.getVolume());
step++;
p.produce(50);
this.assertEquals(step+":volume stock1", 100, stock1.getVolume());
this.assertEquals(step+":volume stock2", 300, stock2.getVolume());
this.assertEquals(step+":volume stock3", 100, stock3.getVolume());
```

```
step++;
try {
    p.produce(10);
    this.fail("Expected UnappropriateStockException");
} catch(UnappropriateStockException ex) {
    //as expected
}
this.assertEquals("final:volume stock1", 100, stock1.getVolume());
this.assertEquals("final:volume stock2", 300, stock2.getVolume());
this.assertEquals("final:volume stock3", 100, stock3.getVolume());
...
```

First, the test generates three stock beans, stock1, stock2, and stock3. The beans stock1 and stock2 are the stores from which the producer bean takes material for constructing the end product. The finished product is then stored in the store stock3 (see again Listing 7-12, the deployment descriptor of the producer bean). After generation of the producer bean, ten units are produced. The test ensures, using the method assertEquals, that stock1 now contains 190 units (200 units were there at the beginning; one unit was taken for each unit of end product); that stock2 contains 480 units (500 units at the beginning, with two units taken for each unit of end product); and that stock3 contains ten units of end product (there were none at the start). Then, forty units are produced, and then 50, and the corresponding numbers checked. In the last step of the test an error is produced. Ten units are produced, which the store stock3 cannot take in, since its maximum capacity was specified to be one hundred units. The test ensures that the method produce triggers an exception on account of the full store stock3 and that after the invalid call to the method produce a consistent state in the stored quantities exists. If the method produce had not been executed in a transaction, then the values of stores stock1 and stock2 would have been reduced by the appropriate quantities, but the amount in stock3 would not have been raised accordingly, since it was full. The data would then have been in an inconsistent state.

Transaction Attributes

Transaction attributes are used to define the transactional behavior for the methods of Enterprise Beans. The attributes are registered in the deployment descriptor, and the EJB container uses them to provide a suitable transaction context for the execution of the methods. Moreover, the transaction attributes define the interplay of the Enterprise Beans among themselves and with the client with regard to transactions.

In the following all transaction attributes are described that are supported by EJB version 2.1 and EJB version 2.0.

NotSupported

A method with the transaction attribute NotSupported in the deployment descriptor does not support transactions. This means that the method will not be executed in a transaction controlled by the EJB container.

In developing such a method this must be taken into account to the extent that that there is no possibility for actions once executed to be undone with a rollback. For access to transactional systems—a database, for example—one works generally only with a local transaction.

A method with the transaction attribute NotSupported is normally addressed by the client (recall that the client can also be an Enterprise Bean) without a global transaction context. If the client should nevertheless use a transaction for the call, this will not be used in the method. The client's transaction is uninfluenced by it. The method's actions are not bound to this transaction. We note once more that the EJB concept does not support nested transactions.

This transaction attribute may not be used by beans that implement the SessionSynchronization interface (see the later subsection on synchronization).

The constant NotSupported can be used in the deployment descriptor in EJB versions 1.1 and beyond. For the serialized deployment descriptor of EJB version 1.0 the corresponding Java constant is TX_NOT_SUPPORTED.

Required

Methods that have the transaction attribute Required are always executed in a transaction.

If the method is called by the client with a global transaction, then this is used for the execution of the method. If the call takes place without a transaction, then the EJB container automatically launches a transaction. This guarantees that the method is always executed within a global transaction.

Access to other beans and transactional systems is thus also ensured, since the global transaction context is inherited.

In the use of the transaction attribute Required it should always be kept in mind that global transactions are expensive. There often is a way to increase performance through doing without global transactions to some extent.

For EJB version 1.0 the corresponding constant is TX_REQUIRED.

Supports

The transaction attribute Supports means that a method can be executed either with or without a transaction.

If there is already a transaction when a call is made, then this is available for use in the execution of the method. If the method is called without a transaction, then there is no transaction available.

Methods for which this transaction attribute is to be used must therefore be able to deal with both these cases. The implementation must be able to perform its tasks with and without a transaction context.

The EJB specification states specifically that the transaction attribute Supports can be used instead of Required to improve performance. If the precise implementation of the method is unknown, then at deployment, caution is advised in the use of the transaction attribute Supports.

This transaction attribute may not be used by beans that implement the SessionSynchronization interface (see also the subsection on synchronization later in this chapter), and it cannot be used by message-driven beans.

For EJB version 1.0 the corresponding constant is TX_SUPPORTS.

RequiresNew

A method with the transaction attribute RequiresNew possesses its own private transaction. Before the method is started the EJB container always launches a new global transaction. After leaving the method, the EJB container always attempts to end the transaction with a commit.

The transaction with which the client (which, as already mentioned, can be an Enterprise Bean) calls the method remains completely isolated. The actions of the method are not bound to this transaction. The new transaction will be inherited in the usual way with access to other beans or with the use of a transactional system.

This transaction attribute cannot be used by message-driven beans. For EJB version 1.0 the corresponding constant is TX_REQUIRES_NEW.

Mandatory

A method with the transaction attribute Mandatory must always be called by a client with a global transaction. If there is no transaction when the method is called, this leads to an error (TransactionRequiredException).

The client's transaction is used for the execution of the method and is also further transmitted. It is guaranteed that the method is always executed in a global transaction context. This transaction attribute cannot be used by message-driven beans. For EJB version 1.0 the corresponding constant is TX_MANDATORY.

Never

A method with the transaction attribute Never may never be called by a client in a transaction context. This would lead to an error (RemoteException).

The method is always executed without a transaction. For development the same restrictions are in force as with the transaction attribute NotSupported.

This transaction attribute may not be used by beans that implement the SessionSynchronization interface (see also the subsection on synchronization), and it cannot be used by message-driven beans.

The transaction attribute Never has been supported since EJB version 1.1.

Transaction Isolation

The isolation level of transactions was described at the beginning of this chapter. We would like to consider again the four isolation levels, only now a bit more deeply:

1. **Read Uncommitted:** This level is the weakest level with respect to data consistency and the strongest with respect to performance. If this isolation level is used for access to data (in a database, for example), then the problems of dirty reads, nonrepeatable reads, and phantom reads can occur.

2. **Read Committed:** This level is the next strongest after Read Uncommitted with respect to data consistency. In a transaction with this isolation level data that have been changed by other transactions but not yet committed cannot be read. All that can be read is the state that the data have had since the last successfully executed commit. Thus the problem of dirty reads can no longer occur. The problem of nonrepeatable reads and that of phantom reads can still occur.

3. **Repeatable Reads:** In comparison to the Read Committed isolation level, data that have just been read by another transaction cannot be changed in this transaction. Write access to the data is blocked until the reading transaction has terminated with commit or rollback. From this behavior it is clear that with increasing data consistency, performance suffers in parallel accesses, since write accesses can be blocked at this level. At this level of isolation only the phantom read problem can occur.

4. **Serializable:** On this isolation level none of the problems dirty reads, nonrepeatable reads, and phantom reads can occur. A transaction has exclusive read and write access to the data. Other transactions can neither read nor change the data. Read and write access by other transactions is blocked until the transaction is terminated with commit or rollback. This level is the strongest with respect to data consistency, the weakest with respect to performance.

The developer of a bean can determine the isolation level at which operations in the transaction are to occur. This is specified, as a rule, in the developer-dependent additions to the deployment descriptor. Many developers additionally offer the option of configuring the isolation level to that of the database driver. If a bean accesses a database directly, then it has the option of setting the isolation level for the current transaction via the method setTransactionIsolation of the interface java.sql.Connection.

Setting the isolation level holds great potential for optimization. One must find the proper balance between data consistency and performance. It all depends on the requirements of the application.

Synchronization

For the synchronization of beans with container transactions the bean can implement the interface javax.ejb.SessionSynchronization. Session beans that manage their own transactions do not require this mechanism, since they themselves have full control over the transactions. Nor do entity beans need this interface. It is reserved for stateful session beans that use transactions managed by the container.

The interface consists of three methods, which are called by the EJB container when a transaction is in certain states (see Listing 7-14). The implementation of this interface is optional and necessary only in rare cases.

In order to ensure that methods are correctly called by the EJB container there are restrictions with respect to the transaction attributes. Beans that implement the SessionSynchronization interface may use only the transaction attributes Required, RequiresNew, and Mandatory.

Listing 7-14. Definition of the interface java.ejb.SessionSynchronization.

```
public void afterBegin()
   throws javax.ejb.EJBException,
          java.rmi.RemoteException;
public void beforeCompletion()
   throws javax.ejb.EJBException,
          java.rmi.RemoteException;
public void afterCompletion(boolean committed)
   throws javax.ejb,EJBException,
          java.rmi.RemoteException;
```

The method afterBegin is called to notify a bean that the following method calls are to be executed in a new transaction. The method is not necessarily executed at the beginning of the transaction, but only when the EJB container is aware that a particular bean is to take part in a transaction. This method is used, for example, to enable the caching of database contents for increasing access performance.

The method beforeCompletion is called before a transaction is completed. At this time it is not yet known whether a rollback or a commit will be executed. In this method a rollback (method setRollbackOnly) can still be forced. This method is used to write temporarily stored database contents back to the database or to check additional consistency conditions.

The method afterCompletion is called after the end of a transaction to notify the bean as to whether the transaction was ended with rollback or commit. Warning: When this method is called the transaction is already over. The method is executed outside of all transactions. This method is used to release resources that were needed especially for the transaction. A Boolean parameter is also passed to this method to indicate whether the transaction was committed or rolled back. This parameter can be used to indicate to the developer to reset variables to the correct state for the session bean.

Explicit Transaction Management

Transaction Management in the Client

Explicit transaction management in the client means that the client itself takes over control of the transaction. Before a call to a bean it launches a global transaction. It then ends this transaction with a rollback or commit.

At a call to a bean the client's transaction is transmitted to the server and used by the EJB container. Depending on the bean's transaction attributes, the EJB container can react in various ways. One possibility is that it uses the client's transaction for executing the bean's methods. In another case one of the bean's own transactions is used, which is either started by the EJB container or is already in existence.

Explicit transaction management by the client thus does not stand in opposition to implicit transaction management. The concepts are interrelated, and each contributes to the other.

Figure 7-6 shows a schematic example of explicit transaction management by the client. Here is shown how the beans use the transaction context of the client and transmit it further. Possible transaction attributes for the beans that support the use of a transaction launched by the client are Required, Supports, and Mandatory.

The client is responsible for the transaction management. It access the transaction monitor directly over the *Java Transaction API* (JTA). To make this possible, JTA must be offered to the client as a service and be registered in the name service. Here, unfortunately, the various application services show differing behaviors, since the names in the name service differ. The relevant information must be taken from the documentation of the individual product.

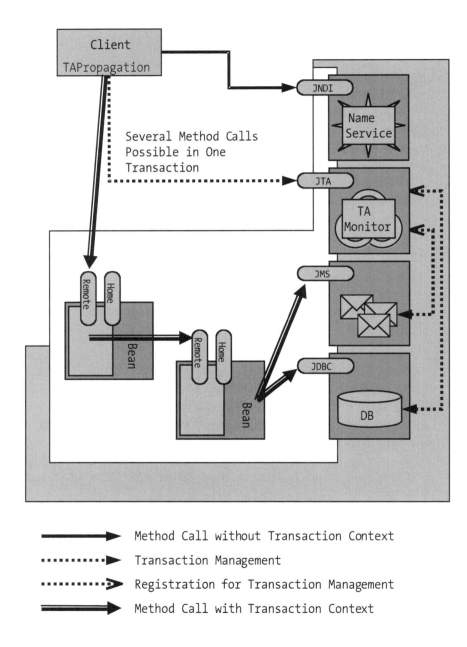

Figure 7-6. Example of data flow in a client's explicit transaction management.

After the client has obtained access to JTA, it can launch a global transaction. The transaction monitor will ensure the transmission of the transaction context via the *Java Transaction Service* (JTS).

The client can call any number of methods within the transaction, even from different beans. After all actions of the transaction have been executed, the client ends the transaction with a commit or rollback.

In the transaction, every method call to a bean on the server also transmits the transaction context. In our example the called bean uses the client's transaction for executing its methods.

When a method is called on further beans or when access is made to a transactional system, the transaction context is always inherited. Thus all actions are linked to the client's transaction and executed in common (commit) or rolled back together.

In the case of an error, each participating bean can determine that the transaction should be rolled back upon termination. The bean context offers the required interface. Therefore, the developer of a bean does not have to access JTA.

Explicit client transaction management allows a great deal of program logic to be implemented in the client. This must be viewed critically, since the architecture of an application and reusability can suffer as a result of explicit transaction management. One should always check whether the declarative transactions of the EJB concept perhaps offer a better solution.

The advantage of explicit transaction management by the client is that application development is possible by programming only the client. The existing beans on the server are simply used, without extending or changing them. In contrast to this, it is necessary with implicit transactions to develop a new bean when several method calls are to take place within a transaction.

Explicit client transaction management thus makes possible the more rapid development of prototypes. This path is also of interest when the greatest part of the application logic consists of purchased beans and one has not developed the beans oneself.

Example Producer

At this point we return to our Producer example, which we used in discussing implicit transactions.

The same logic is to be implemented, but this time with transaction management in the client. The reason for this might be that only the entity bean Stock exists, and we do not wish to develop any new beans. The client will have the same functionality as the session bean Producer and additionally, take over transaction management.

Listing 7-15 shows that the client obtains access to transactions in the constructor. From the name service it obtains a stub of the class UserTransaction, a lightweight object that offers the JTA interface to the client. The class UserTransaction is a central component of JTS (package javax.jts) and is also published in JTA (package javax.transaction) for ordinary application developers.

Listing 7-15. Client transactions: access to JTA.

```
package ejb.supplychain.client;

import ejb.supplychain.stock.Stock;
import ejb.supplychain.stock.StockHome;
import ejb.util.Lookup;

import javax.transaction.UserTransaction;

public class Client {

    private final static String STOCK_HOME =
        "Stock";
    private final static String USER_TA =
        "javax.transaction.UserTransaction";

    private UserTransaction userTx = null;

    private StockHome stockHome = null;

    private Stock stock1;
    private Stock stock2;
    private Stock stock3;

    public Client() {
        try {
            this.userTx = (UserTransaction)
                Lookup.narrow(USER_TA, UserTransaction.class);
            this.stockHome = (StockHome)
                Lookup.narrow(STOCK_HOME, StockHome.class);
        } catch(javax.naming.NamingException ex) {
            ex.printStackTrace();
            throw new IllegalStateException(ex.getMessage());
        }
    }
...
```

As with implicit transaction management, in Listing 7-16 the client initializes three instances of the entity bean Stock. Here we would like to point out that these actions are executed without a global transaction. The EJB container automatically launches a transaction via the transaction attribute Mandatory. This shows how simple it is to combine implicit and explicit transaction management.

Listing 7-16. Client transactions: initialization of three instances of the entity bean Stock.

```
...
    public void preconditions()
        throws java.rmi.RemoteException
    {
        this.stock1 = this.createStock("stock1", 100, 100);
        this.stock2 = this.createStock("stock2", 100, 100);
        this.stock3 = this.createStock("stock3", 100, 0);

        System.out.println("Stock1 created. Current Volume: + this.stock1.getVolume());
        System.out.println("Stock2 created. Current Volume: + this.stock2.getVolume());
        System.out.println("Stock3 created. Current Volume: + this.stock3.getVolume());
    }
    private Stock createStock(String name, int max, int cap)
        throws java.rmi.RemoteException
    {
        Stock stock = null;
        try {
            stock = this.stockHome.findByPrimaryKey(name);
            stock.remove();
        } catch(javax.ejb.FinderException ex) {
            //do nothing
        } catch(javax.ejb.RemoveException ex) {
            ex.printStackTrace();
            throw new IllegalStateException(ex.getMessage());
        }
        try {
            stock = this.stockHome.create(name, max, cap);
        } catch(javax.ejb.CreateException ex) {
            ex.printStackTrace();
            throw new IllegalStateException(ex.getMessage());
        }
        return stock;
    }
...
```

The actual functionality (see Listing 7-17) is executed by the client in a global transaction. For transaction management the interface UserTransaction is used. Three methods are used for transaction management: begin, commit, and rollback.

With begin the client launches a new transaction. Here we mention once more that nested transactions are not supported. Each transaction in a thread must be ended before the next one may be started.

However, this does not mean that a client with a transaction of its own is not permitted to call a bean method that itself uses its own transaction. The client program and the bean method are executed in two different threads. The EJB container propagates the transaction only if the relevant transaction attributes are defined for the method. Thus in this case as well nested transactions are not needed.

With commit the client signals that the transaction was successful from its point of view and should be ended. The transaction is ended with a commit only if no other beans involved in the transaction have previously called setRollbackOnly.

It is possible that errors will arise in a transaction. For example, a store can exceed its capacity. Since the entity bean Stock does not react to an error with setRollbackOnly, but simply triggers an exception, it would be possible to implement a procedure for removing the error. However, our example simply responds with a rollback.

Listing 7-17. Client transactions: program segment that executes production.

```
...
    public void doProduction(int volume)
        throws java.rmi.RemoteException
    {
        boolean rollback = true;
        try {
            this.userTx.begin();
            System.out.println("Producing " + volume + " units ...");
            this.stock1.get(volume);
            this.stock2.get(volume*2);
            this.stock3.put(volume);
            System.out.println("done.");
            rollback = false;
        } catch(Exception ex) {
            System.out.println("FAILED.");
            System.err.println(ex.toString());
        } finally {
            if(!rollback) {
                try {
                    this.userTx.commit();
                } catch(Exception ex) {}
            } else {
```

```
            try {
                this.userTx.rollback();
            } catch(Exception ex) {}
        }
    }
    System.out.println("Stock1 Volume: " + this.stock1.getVolume());
    System.out.println("Stock2 Volume: " + this.stock2.getVolume());
    System.out.println("Stock3 Volume: " + this.stock3.getVolume());
    }
    public static void main(String[] args)
        throws java.rmi.RemoteException
    {
        Client c = new Client();
        c.preconditions();
        c.doProduction(10);
        c.doProduction(20);
        c.doProduction(50);
    }
}
```

Now the functionality of the client is complete. Listing 7-18 shows the output that the client produces at run time.

Listing 7-18. Client transactions: client output at run time.

```
Stock1 created. Current Volume: 100
Stock2 created. Current Volume: 100
Stock3 created. Current Volume: 0
Producing 10 units ...
done.
Stock1 Volume: 90
Stock2 Volume: 80
Stock3 Volume: 10
Producing 20 units ...
done.
Stock1 Volume: 70
Stock2 Volume: 40
Stock3 Volume: 30
Producing 50 units ...
FAILED.
ejb.supplychain.stock.ProcessingErrorException: volume to small
Stock1 Volume: 70
Stock2 Volume: 40
Stock3 Volume: 30
```

In comparison to implicit transaction management, with explicit transaction management the client has considerably more functionality. Given the choice between these two solutions, implicit transaction management should be used where possible. The effort to implement the necessary functionality is better invested in a reusable server component.

Transaction Management in the Bean

Session beans can themselves take over complete control of a transaction (since the EJB 1.1 specification this is no longer possible for entity beans). The client's transaction context is not transmitted by the EJB container to the bean. The transaction context of the bean remains completely isolated from this.

Message-driven beans can also manage transactions. However, a bean can begin a transaction only within the onMessage method. The transaction must be terminated before the end of the onMessage method (either with commit or rollback). A transaction cannot extend over several onMessage calls. Moreover, the receipt of a message via the onMessage method cannot be a component of a transaction controlled by a message-driven bean. Only actions that the message-driven bean executes upon receipt of a message in the onMessage method can belong to the transaction.

An Enterprise Bean is able to work with both global and local transactions. With the use of global transactions there can be only one active transaction at a given time. This means that before the start of a global transaction all local transactions must be terminated as well as any previous global transactions.

Figure 7-7 shows a schematic example of the explicit transaction management by a bean that is working with a global transaction. The bean does not inherit the transaction context from the client, but launches its own global transaction via direct access to the transaction service over JTS. As we know, the global transaction is transmitted if the bean uses other beans or transactional systems.

The programming of such a scenario can be derived from the example of a client with explicit transaction management. In particular, access to JTA is identical.

The bean can also use the same transaction over several method calls by the client. The EJB container manages the transaction context for the bean. If the bean does not close a global transaction before the end of a method, then a subsequent method call will be automatically associated with the same transaction context.

However, transaction management in the bean does not have to work with global transactions. By restricting to local transactions the bean developer can go more freely into the peculiarities of the database or other transactional system in use. Figure 7-8 shows a schematic example for explicit transaction management of a bean that works with local transactions.

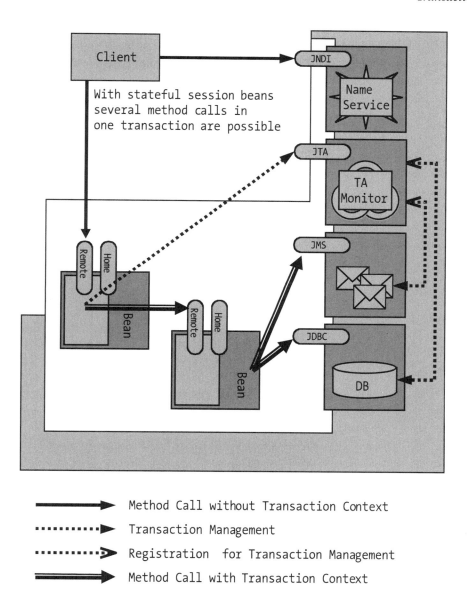

Method Call without Transaction Context

Transaction Management

Registration for Transaction Management

Method Call with Transaction Context

Figure 7-7. Data flow example for explicit transaction management by a bean with a global transaction.

Systems that participate in a global transaction must offer the JTS interfaces or be addressed specially by the EJB container. For example, it is only since JDBC 2.0 that JTS global transactions have been supported. Older database systems can be used only because EJB containers take the older interfaces into account. The exclusive use of local transactions in a bean makes it possible to use any transactional system. Here the bean uses the specific interfaces for the system in question for managing a local transaction.

In the following section the example `Migration` will be used to clarify the use of local transactions in a bean.

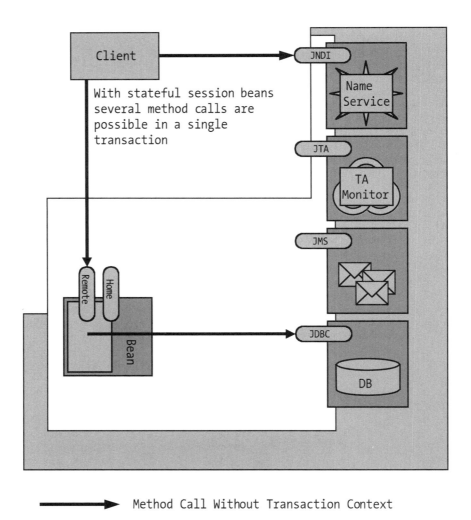

Figure 7-8. Example of data flow with explicit transaction management of a bean with a local transaction.

Example Migration

The following example shows how a bean explicitly manages the local transactions of a database. The program could also serve as an example of programming JDBC. Local database transactions are managed solely by beans over JDBC.

The example Migration shows how currency in a database is converted ("migrates") from German marks (DM) to euros. A session bean carries out this conversion in a local transaction.

Migration is only a simple example. However, the local transactions used here would offer the bean further opportunities. For similar scenarios it might be necessary to use long-term transactions or locks on tables or rows (to avoid data inconsistencies due to concurrent access to the data being converted).

First, we show the deployment descriptor in Listing 7-19. Note that in the segment *transaction-type* the keyword bean is specified. This indicates that the bean takes over the explicit transaction management. At the same time, this value prohibits the definition of transaction attributes in the assembly descriptor.

Listing 7-19. Deployment descriptor of the session bean Migration.

```xml
<?xml version="1.0"?>
<ejb-jar version="2.1" xmlns="http://java.sun.com/xml/ns/j2ee"
xmlns:xsi="http://www.w3.org/2001/XMLSchema-instance"
xsi:schemaLocation="http://java.sun.com/xml/ns/j2ee
http://java.sun.com/xml/ns/j2ee/ejb-jar_2_1.xsd">
  <enterprise-beans>
    <session>
      <ejb-name>Migration</ejb-name>
      <home>ejb.migration.MigrationHome</home>
      <remote>ejb.migration.Migration</remote>
      <ejb-class>ejb.migration.MigrationBean</ejb-class>
      <session-type>Stateless</session-type >
      <transaction-type>Bean</transaction-type>
      <resource-ref>
        <description>
          reference to the target database
        </description>
        <res-ref-name>jdbc/Migration</res-ref-name>
        <res-type>javax.sql.DataSource</res-type>
        <res-auth>Container</res-auth>
      </resource-ref>
    </session>
  </enterprise-beans>
  <assembly-descriptor>
  </assembly-descriptor>
</ejb-jar>
```

The home (see Listing 7-20) and the remote (Listing 7-21) interfaces show the simple interface. The conversion is initiated with a call to the method migrate. The exception MigrationErrorException signals an error in execution.

Listing 7-20. Home interface of the session bean Migration.

```
package ejb.migration;
import javax.ejb.CreateException;
import javax.ejb.EJBHome;
import java.rmi.RemoteException;
public interface MigrationHome extends EJBHome {
    public Migration create()
        throws CreateException, RemoteException;
}
```

Listing 7-21. Remote interface of the session bean Migration.

```
package ejb.migration;
import java.rmi.RemoteException;
import javax.ejb.EJBObject;

public interface Migration extends EJBObject {
    public void migrate()
        throws MigrationErrorException, RemoteException;
}
```

Listing 7-22 shows the implementation of the bean class. In the method ejbCreate the bean obtains a reference to a data source over which connections to the database can be established. In the method ejbRemove this reference is deleted. The entire functionality of the bean is implemented in the method migrate.

Listing 7-22. Bean class of the session bean Migration.

```
package ejb.migration;
import java.sql.Connection;
import java.sql.PreparedStatement;
import java.sql.Statement;
import java.sql.SQLException;
```

```
import javax.ejb.CreateException;
import javax.ejb.EJBException;
import javax.ejb.SessionBean;
import javax.ejb.SessionContext;
import javax.sql.DataSource;

import ejb.util.Lookup;

public class MigrationBean implements SessionBean {

    public static final float EXCHANGE_RATE = 1.98f;
    public static final String RESOURCE_REF =
        "java:comp/env/jdbc/Migration";

    private SessionContext sessionCtx;
    private DataSource dataSource;

    public MigrationBean() { }

    public void ejbCreate()
        throws CreateException
    {
        try {
            this.dataSource = (DataSource)
                Lookup.narrow(RESOURCE_REF, DataSource.class);
        } catch(Exception ex) {
            String msg = "Cannot get DataSource:" + ex.getMessage();
            throw new EJBException(msg);
        }
    }

    public void ejbRemove() {
        this.dataSource = null;
    }

    public void ejbActivate() { }

    public void ejbPassivate() { }

    public void setSessionContext(SessionContext ctx) {
        this.sessionCtx = ctx;
    }

    private static final String QUERY1 =
        "UPDATE INVOICE SET AMOUNT=AMOUNT/? " + "WHERE CURRENCY='DEM'";

    private static final String QUERY2 =
        "UPDATE INVOICE SET CURRENCY='EU' " + "WHERE CURRENCY='DEM'";

    public void migrate()
        throws MigrationErrorException
    {
        Connection con = null;
```

```
PreparedStatement st1 = null;
Statement st2 = null;
boolean success = false;
try {
    con = this.dataSource.getConnection();
    con.setAutoCommit(false);
    st1 = con.prepareStatement(QUERY1);
    st1.setFloat(1, EXCHANGE_RATE);
    st1.executeUpdate();
    st2 = con.createStatement();
    st2.executeUpdate(QUERY2);
    success = true;
} catch(SQLException ex) {
    String msg = "Failed migrating data:" + ex.getMessage();
    throw new MigrationErrorException(msg);
} finally {
    if(success) {
        try { con.commit(); } catch(Exception ex) {}
    } else {
        try { con.rollback(); } catch(Exception ex) {}
    }
    try { st1.close(); } catch(Exception ex) {}
    try { st2.close(); } catch(Exception ex) {}
    try { con.setAutoCommit(true); } catch(Exception ex) {}
    try { con.close(); } catch(Exception ex) {}
    }
  }
}
```

For readability we have split the conversion of German marks (DM) to euros into two separate statements. After a database connection has been established via the data source, the auto-commit mode is turned off. In auto-commit mode a commit would be carried out automatically in the active transaction after the execution of a statement. In our case we could then not guarantee that the data would be in a consistent state at the end of the method.

With the turning off of the auto-commit mode we are ensuring that both statements in the same (local) database transaction will be executed. If an error occurs in one or both statements, then the flag success is not set to true. This results in a rollback being executed for the transaction in the finally block. If both statements have been executed successfully, then a commit is executed. Before we close the database connection with Connection.close, we reset auto-commit to its default value before closing it and returning it to the connection pool. The bean could also be provided the possibility of setting a particular isolation level for the transaction using the method `Connection.setTransactionIsolation`.

In summary, we can say that a session bean with explicit transaction management is programmed like a normal database client if it works with local transactions. If global transactions are in play, then the programming is comparable to that of an EJB client with explicit transaction management (see the earlier section on the example `Producer`, with explicit client transactions).

Transactions in the Deployment Descriptor

The transactional properties of a bean are defined in three steps.

Step 1

In the first step the bean provider specifies whether transactions are to be managed by the EJB container or the bean. The bean provider gives these instructions exclusively in the bean's deployment descriptor.

In the case of explicit transaction management of the bean, the bean provider defines the transaction type Bean in the bean's deployment descriptor in the segment `enterprise-beans`:

```
<transaction-type>Bean</transaction-type>
```

In the case of declarative transaction management no specifications about the transactional properties are made in the bean's deployment descriptor. These are established only in the following steps, with the transaction attributes.

Step 2

In the second step the application assembler defines the transaction attributes. The application assembler makes specifications about the bean exclusively in the section `assembly-descriptor`.

A separate transaction attribute can be specified for each permitted method. This defines the transactional behavior of the bean with implicit transaction management by the EJB container.

The EJB specification gives precise instructions as to which methods from the home and remote interfaces can be assigned to a transaction attribute:

- for session beans, only for the defined business methods;

- for entity beans, for the defined business methods and also for the methods `find`, `create`, and `remove` from the home interface.

The EJB specification specifies three different forms for keeping the definition in the deployment descriptor simple and understandable:

1. The same transaction attribute is assigned to all methods of a bean:

```
<method>
  <ejb-name>Stock</ejb-name>
  <method-name>*</method-name>
</method>
```

2. One transaction attribute is assigned to one method name. If there are several methods with the same name but with differing parameters, then the transaction attribute is assigned to all these methods:

```
<method>
  <ejb-name>Stock</ejb-name>
  <method-name>get</method-name>
</method>
```

3. One transaction attribute is assigned to exactly one method. The method is completely specified by its name and parameter types:

```
<method>
  <ejb-name>Stock</ejb-name>
  <method-name>get</method-name>
  <method-param>int</method-param>
</method>
```

It is possible that methods will exist with identical signatures in the home and remote interfaces. With the additional attribute method-intf one can differentiate between Home and Remote:

```
<method>
  <ejb-name>Stock</ejb-name>
  <method-intf>Home</method-intf>
  <method-name>create</method-name>
  <method-param>
    java.lang.String
  </method-param>
  <method-param>int</method-param>
  <method-param>int</method-param>
</method>
```

These three systems can also be used simultaneously. In this case the more precise definition always takes precedence over the less precise.

Step 3

In the third step the deployer can change and extend the instructions in the application assembler. The deployer must ensure that for each bean with implicit transaction management a unique transaction attribute is defined for each method.

CHAPTER 8

Security

Introduction

This chapter is concerned with the protection of data against unauthorized access in an Enterprise JavaBeans application. The security of systems for implementation throughout an enterprise is a large and extensive topic. A strategy for addressing the following topics is necessary in the design of such systems:

- Identification of users (authentication);

- Access restriction (authorization);

- Secure data transfer (encryption);

- Management of user data, certification, etc.

The relevant security concepts are components of the Java 2 Enterprise Edition (J2EE) together with certain extensions. The most important extensions of the Java platform in the area of security are the Java Cryptography Extension (JCE; see the reference [30]), the Java Authentication and Authorization Service (JAAS; see [31]), and the Java Secure Socket Extension (JSSE; see [32]).

JCE might be considered a library for data encryption that allows seamless integration of the components of the Java run-time environment into the Java platform via the security API (package java.security.*). JSSE is a library for encrypted data transfer over network sockets (secure socket layer, or SSL), which allows integration into the Java platform as seamless as that of the JCE. Thanks to the flexible architecture of the Java run-time environment (see java.net.SocketImplFactory), normal network sockets can be replaced by secure network sockets of JSSE without the overlying layers being affected. JAAS is a service for the authentication and authorization of users that is provided to an application over a separate API.

A product that supports these security mechanisms enables the configuration and administration of the corresponding services and provides the developer the relevant Java interfaces. These security mechanisms are of a fundamental nature and affect Enterprise JavaBeans only indirectly. This chapter concentrates on the security concepts of the EJB architecture, which are specified for every EJB container by the EJB specification. Extensive information on these topics can be found in [11] and [16]. The EJB security management specification has a distinct focus on flexibility and portability.

In this chapter we consider the following topics:

- *Definition of roles:* Enterprise Beans work with defined roles, which are mapped to users or user groups. Users and user groups are defined externally to the EJB container.

- *Access to the identity of a user and its roles:* In the context of every Enterprise Bean (class `EJBContext`) there are methods available for access to the user. Furthermore, checking of role membership is possible.

- *Access protection for methods:* For methods of the home and remote home interfaces of an Enterprise Bean one can define the roles that users must possess in order for them to be allowed to call the methods.

- *Execution of Enterprise Beans with a defined user context:* It is possible to configure an Enterprise Bean in such a way that its methods are not executed in the context of the registered user, but in another user context.

The following sections are devoted to exploring these topics in detail. An overview is given in Figure 8-1.

In addition to the defined security concepts, the EJB container can offer additional services, such as certificate management or a key service. The EJB container offers such services via JNDI in the bean's environment. However, whoever uses such services risks limiting Enterprise Bean portability, since another EJB container may not offer those services, or offer them in a different form.

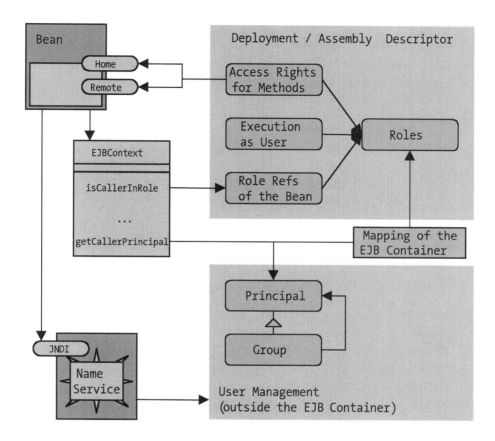

Figure 8-1. Schematic representation of EJB security.

Programming

Rights for Methods

One method for protecting application systems is to limit access to specific areas of functionality to certain users. The EJB architecture supports such limitations by enabling the definition of roles (which are mapped to existing users). Access to the methods of Enterprise Beans is then allowed only to users with certain defined roles.

In order to limit access to methods in this way, the following steps must be carried out:

1. Setting up the necessary users and groups via user management. This is external to the EJB container.

2. Definition of the roles in the assembly descriptor.

3. Definition of access rights for methods.

4. Associating the defined roles with the existing users and groups.

In the following we will describe the necessary steps for protecting the methods of the session bean EuroExchangeSL (see the example in Chapter 4, in the section on stateless session beans). Note here that no program lines need to be written for the definition of access rights for methods. This configuration cannot take place until the assembly of the application with the application assembler. Like the transaction context, the security context is implicitly propagated from client to component and between components without the need for the explicit definition of extra parameters in the interfaces of the EJBs.

An application server either has its own user management or uses the user management of another system. Thus an application server could employ the users of the operating system in order to avoid a double management burden. Correspondingly varied are the user interfaces that are employed for user administration. What is common to all of them is that they enable the definition of users and passwords, and structure the users into groups. The example definition in Listing 8-1 provides the users system, UserA, and UserB with passwords and defines a user group Administrators. They will be used again in the course of this chapter. The specific sample used below employs the following naming conventions:

```
user.<user name>=password and group.<group name>=<group members>.
```

Listing 8-1. Sample user definition for an application server.

```
user.system=systempassword
user.UserA=password1
user.UserB=password2
group.Administrators=system,
group.AllUsers=system,UserA,UserB,
...
```

The assembly descriptor describes the interplay of all Enterprise Beans in a Java archive (JAR). Here the various user roles are also defined. The roles are also used to restrict access to methods. The example in Listing 8-2 defines the roles everyone and admins.

Listing 8-2. Definition of user roles in the deployment descriptor.

```
<assembly-descriptor>
  ...
  <security-role>
    <description>
      all users of the euroExchangeBean
    </description>
    <role-name>everyone</role-name>
  </security-role>
  <security-role>
    <description>
      all Administrators
    </description>
    <role-name>admins</role-name>
  </security-role>
  ...
</assembly-descriptor>
```

Access to the Enterprise Bean is configured in such a way that only users with the role everyone can access the bean's methods. The methods for setting the exchange rate are more highly protected, and can be called only by users with the role admins (Listing 8-3).

Listing 8-3. Definition of access rights for methods in the deployment descriptor.

```
</assembly-descriptor>
  ...
  <method-permission>
    <role-name>everyone</role-name>
    <method>
      <ejb-name>EuroExchangeSL</ejb-name>
      <method-name>
        changeFromEuro
      </method-name>
    </method>
    <method>
      <ejb-name>EuroExchangeSL</ejb-name>
      <method-name>
        changeToEuro
      </method-name>
    </method>
  </method-permission>
  <method-permission>
    <role-name>admins</role-name>
    <method>
      <ejb-name>EuroExchangeSL</ejb-name>
      <method-name>
        setExchangeRate
      </method-name>
    </method>
  </method-permission>
  ...
</assembly-descriptor>
```

The definition of access rights uses the same syntax as the definition of transaction attributes (see Chapter 7). For an Enterprise Bean the rights can be defined for all methods, all methods with a particular name, or one method with a particular name and particular parameters. Moreover, the methods of the home and remote interfaces can be distinguished.

Now the users and groups of the application server will be assigned their roles. This takes place with the deployment tools of the EJB container. Our example (Listing 8-4) shows the assignment using an XML descriptor. Your EJB container's (application server's) administration guide contains precise instructions as to how this step is to be carried out.

Listing 8-4. Sample assignment of roles to users and groups.

```
<security-role-assignment>
  <role-name>everyone</role-name>
  <principal>UserA</principal>
  <principal>Administrators</principal>
</security-role-assignment>
<security-role-assignment>
  <role-name>admins</role-name>
  <principal>UserB</principal>
  <principal>Administrators</principal>
</security-role-assignment>
```

After all these definitions have been made and the deployment of the Enterprise Bean has again been carried out, the client program can be tested with various users. A prohibited access attempt triggers an exception (java.rmi.RemoteException).

It should be noted that the above mapping solution, although common, does not offer the most complete flexibility. Consider the scenario whereby a user's privilege is to be revoked (such as UserB in the above listing). According to the above configuration, the deployment descriptor would have to be modified and the bean redeployed. This is clearly unmanageable for a system that contains hundreds of users.

An alternative method would be to assign each role to a specific security group and manage this group directly from the underlying security system, such as an LDAP (Lightweight Directory Access Protocol) server. An assignment of roles for this strategy is given in Listing 8-5.

Listing 8-5. Sample alternative assignment of roles to groups.

```
<security-role-assignment>
  <role-name>everyone</role-name>
  <principal>AllUsers</principal>
</security-role-assignment>
<security-role-assignment>
  <role-name>admins</role-name>
  <principal>Administrators</principal>
</security-role-assignment>
```

If a method is to be executed explicitly without security checking, then it can be given the attribute unchecked in the assembly descriptor. Listing 8-6 shows an example in which the methods changeFromEuro and changeToEuro of the EuroExchangeSL bean can be called without security checking. Any user can call these methods. Only the method setExchangeRate remains limited to users with the role admin.

Listing 8-6. Use of the attribute unchecked *in the assembly descriptor.*

```
</assembly-descriptor>
  ...
  <method-permission>
    <unchecked/>
    <method>
      <ejb-name>EuroExchangeSL</ejb-name>
      <method-name>
        changeFromEuro
      </method-name>
    </method>
    <method>
      <ejb-name>EuroExchangeSL</ejb-name>
      <method-name>
        changeToEuro
      </method-name>
    </method>
  </method-permission>
  <method-permission>
    <role-name>admins</role-name>
    <method>
      <ejb-name>EuroExchangeSL</ejb-name>
      <method-name>
        setExchangeRate
      </method-name>
    </method>
  </method-permission>
  ...
</assembly-descriptor>
```

Manual Access Verification

Another way of protecting particular application functions against unauthorized access is to check the identity and roles of the user in the application logic. One can then include additional conditions at run time in checking access rights.

The following steps are necessary if the Enterprise Bean wishes to access the user's identity and roles.

1. Setting up the requisite users and groups via user management; this is external to the EJB container;

2. Definition of role references;

3. Definition of roles in the assembly descriptor;

4. Assigning of role references to roles;

5. Use of the methods `getCallerPrincipal` and `isCallerInRole` in the application logic of the Enterprise Bean.

The following example uses the same users and groups as the previous example. The final definition of the roles is carried out, as before, by the application assembler. The bean developer therefore does not yet know the names of these roles and must work with provisional names during programming. These provisional names are called role references (`security-role-ref`). Listing 8-7 defines the two role references `exchange` and `setCurrency` for our session bean.

Listing 8-7. Definition of role references in the deployment descriptor.

```
<enterprise-beans>
  <session>
    ...
    <security-role-ref>
      <description>
        role reference to exchange
      </description>
      <role-name>exchange</role-name>
    </security-role-ref>
    <security-role-ref>
      <description>
        role reference to
        setting the exchange rate
      </description>
      <role-name>setCurrency</role-name>
    </security-role-ref>
    ...
  <session>
</enterprise-beans>
```

Now the names of the defined role references can be used in programming. The `EJBContext` provides two methods for access to the user:

- java.security.Principal getCallerPrincipal(): This method returns the identity of the current user as an object of the class Principal. This object can also be used for *access control lists*.

- boolean isCallerInRole(java.lang.String name): This method determines whether the current user has a particular role. The name specified here corresponds to the name of the role reference.

The method checkSecureAccess will serve as an example of the use of these methods (see Listing 8-8), which for each access outputs the name of the user over the error output stream (stderr). Additionally, a check is made as to whether the user has the role reference setCurrency. In programming, the names of the role references are used exclusively, and not the roles.

Listing 8-8. Bean method for access protection.

```
...
public class EuroExchangeBean implements SessionBean {
...
    public void setExchangeRate(String currency, float euro, float foreignCurr)
    {
        if(currency == null) {
            throw new EJBException("illegal argument: currency");
        }
        if(!checkSecureAccess()) {
            throw new EJBException("Access denied");
        }
        ...
    }
    private boolean checkSecureAccess() {
        java.security.Principal principal;
        String name;
        boolean mayAccess;
        mayAccess = ctx.isCallerInRole("setCurrency");
        principal = ctx.getCallerPrincipal();
        name = principal.getName();
        if(mayAccess){
            System.err.println("Accessed granted to " + name);
        } else {
            System.err.println(name + ": Access denied!");
        }
        return mayAccess;
    }
    ...
}
```

It is only after the completion of the Enterprise Bean that the roles are defined and the users and groups assigned to them. Only then have the correct names for the roles used in the program been set. Of course, the program is not changed, but rather the relationship between the role references and the roles is defined. In the example in Listing 8-9 the role reference exchange is assigned to the role everyone, and the role reference setCurrency to the role admins. The deployment descriptor is adapted to this at deployment.

Listing 8-9. Assignment of role references to roles in the deployment descriptor.

```
<enterprise-beans>
  <session>
    ...
    <security-role-ref>
      <description>
        role for changing from euros
      </description>
      <role-name>exchange</role-name>
      <role-link>everyone</role-link>
    </security-role-ref>
    <security-role-ref>
      <description>
        role for setting the exchange rate
      </description>
      <role-name>setCurrency</role-name>
      <role-link>admins</role-link>
    </security-role-ref>
    ...
  <session>
</enterprise-beans>
```

Figure 8-2 shows once again the chain of mappings. The Enterprise Bean uses the names of the role references (deployment descriptor). These refer to the roles defined at deployment (assembly descriptor). The users (Principal) and groups (Group) of the application server are assigned the roles.

This chain of mappings is very helpful for the clear distribution of labor between the roles of the bean developer, application assembler, and deployer (see the section in Chapter 3 on EJB assignment of roles). However, for the developer this can mean an additional burden if in the test domain all roles are united in one person.

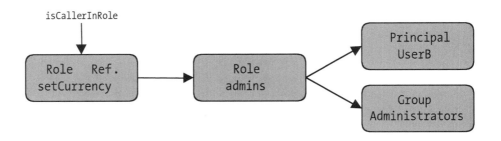

Figure 8-2. Chain of mappings for roles.

Enterprise Beans with Defined User Context

When one Enterprise Bean uses another Enterprise Bean, the user context is passed on. The method getCallerPrincipal always returns the user that has registered with the client. This makes an overall security plan possible (Figure 8-3).

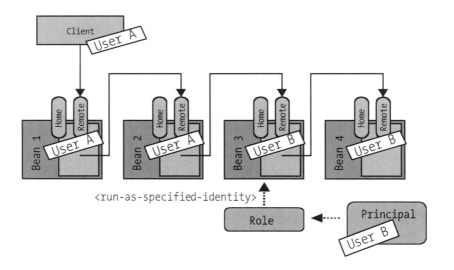

Figure 8-3. User context in a chain of calls.

With message-driven beans that are not called directly by a user, but through an asynchronous message, the definition of a user is always required.

The defined user is always valid for an entire Enterprise Bean. With session and entity beans the defined user context (Listing 8-10) is used for the execution of all methods of the home and remote interfaces. With message-driven beans the method onMessage is executed with the given user context. Moreover, all Enterprise Beans that are called by another Enterprise Bean with specified user context then work with this user. Such an action makes sense in many applications, for example, when the user works with extended access rights.

Listing 8-10. Definition of a user context for a bean.

```
<enterprise-beans>
  <session>
    <ejb-name>ejb/EuroExchangeSL</ejb-name>
    ...
    <security-identity>
      <run-as-specified-identity>
        <role-name>Special</role-name>
      </run-as-specified-identity>
    </security-identity>
    ...
  </session>
...
</enterprise-beans>
```

In the extract in Listing 8-11 from the deployment descriptor of the session bean EuroExchangeSL, it is defined that the bean should be executed with the rights of the role Special. These instructions are given by the application assembler. It must also define the associated roles. The following example shows the associated definition for the user Special.

Listing 8-11. Defining the user role Special.

```
<enterprise-beans>
  <session>
    ...
    <security-role-ref>
      <role-name>Special</role-name>
    </security-role-ref>
    ...
  <session>
<enterprise-beans>
```

Later, the deployer will assign this role to a single user. This user will then be used for execution, and will also be returned as result by the method `getCallerPrincipal`.

Summary

It would be a mistake to conclude much about the significance of the subject of security in the domain of EJB from the comparatively brief treatment in this chapter. The subject of security was considered very early in the development of Java, where notions of security became a fundamental part of the language. For example, Java contains a `security manager` that enables the execution of program segments with various access rights and thereby limits access to secure system functions. There are also the earlier-mentioned services and class libraries for *authentication, authorization, encryption,* and the management of associated objects. Language concepts and services together form a complete security concept.

A J2EE-conforming application server provides an infrastructure for making use of the security services. It implements a user management system or incorporates an existing one such as the operating system security or LDAP server. The application server can be so configured that only encrypted network connections will be accepted by the client. A variety of authentication methods can be supported, such as registration with user name and password or with the use of a certificate.

The application server is responsible for relaying the identity of the user through all levels of the application, for example, to the Enterprise Beans by registration at a web page via JSP, and on to the database or another system. Thus each layer can take over responsibility for security and allow the user more or fewer rights in accessing its functionality.

Even the Enterprise Beans in the EJB container take their share of responsibility for the security of the entire system. Through configuration, access rights for methods can be allocated. Through programming, the identity of the users can be used for decisions in the business logic. Furthermore, the automatic transmittal of the user's identity can be interrupted and a user determined for the execution of an Enterprise Bean. Many other aspects of security do not fall in the area of responsibility of Enterprise Beans, but are taken over by the application server or the persistence systems.

This process works as long as the matter of security is not the actual object of the application. If a management system for certificates is being written or even if only an access control list is to be defined, then the procedures described here are insufficient. In that case an Enterprise Bean will require an additional resource that offers specialized security services. For example, for servicing users, an Enterprise Bean might use a service for user management instead of a database as persistence system. The application server has the task of providing a suitable service that grants the Enterprise Bean access to the users. Through the use of the known resource references this service can be made known to the Enterprise Bean. For the Enterprise Bean to remain portable, one must see to it that the service used is standardized and usable on application servers of other providers.

In summary, one may say that a J2EE-conforming application server supports the development of secure applications from a technical viewpoint. The concepts are suitable for a variety of security strategies and designed to embed the application server in an existing environment. Since this does not go without saying with respect to application servers of other platforms, this fact gives EJB a significant advantage in the marketplace.

Practical Applications

IN THIS CHAPTER WE WOULD like to consider some topics that are dealt with only superficially or not at all in the EJB specification. Often, it is precisely these points that are particularly useful in the development of practical systems. That is not to say that we consider the specification incomplete or flawed. The goal of this chapter is to give suggestions and examples for implementations on selected topics and to discuss these suggestions.

Performance

As already mentioned in Chapter 2, the programming language Java suffers from a reputation for poor performance. Particularly in the domain of business applications, which is without doubt the main focus of Enterprise JavaBeans, this is a critical point. Applications that run too slowly represent costs to an enterprise, since it means that employees are able to work less efficiently. System-dependent wait times are not conducive to motivation in the workplace. Employee work flow is impaired, and employees are thereby less able to focus on their tasks. This diminishes users' acceptance of slowly running applications.

This section has set itself the task of introducing to the reader once again the peculiarities of the architecture of Enterprise JavaBeans, in order to make the reader more conscious in a performance-related way of how they are used. To this end we would like to consider more carefully than we did in Chapter 3 the processes that take place inside the EJB container.

An abstract example of a simple session bean and a simple entity bean should clarify the nature of the objects involved as well as the processes and the interrelationships among all of these things. We shall assume that both beans support the remote client view. The following implementations make no attempt to be applicable in detail to every server or container implementation, but the principle, which is what we are interested in here, is the same for all implementations.

Example: Currency Exchange

The entity bean (we are going to assume container-managed persistence) is to represent the exchange rate of a particular currency with respect to the euro. Given the exchange rate, the session bean should be able to convert an amount in euros to another currency. Both beans, which the bean provider develops, declare both a home and remote interface (ExchangerateHome, ExchangerateRemote, ConversionHome, and ConversionRemote) and provide a bean class with the actual implementation (ExchangerateBean and ConversionBean). Both beans use declarative transactions. The entity bean (ExchangerateBean) has two attributes: the currency as a String variable and the exchange rate with respect to the euro as a Float variable. The currency serves as the primary key (represented by the class ExchangeratePK). The bean offers the method exchangerateAsFloat(), to permit access to the exchange rate as a Float value for calculations. The session bean (ConversionBean) has the method convert() in its remote interface. This method expects as parameter the amount in euros and the exchange rate in the form of a Float value and returns as result the amount in the target currency.

During the installation of the two beans in an EJB container, the deployment tools of the container provider will be used to generate additional classes. Implementation classes are generated for the home and remote interfaces, based on the instructions in the deployment descriptor (which we name ExchangerateHomeImpl, ExchangerateRemoteImpl, ConversionHomeImpl, and ConversionRemoteImpl, and which we met as the EJBHome and EJBObject classes in Chapter 3). Since the implementation classes of the home and remote interfaces must be addressable at run time as remote objects via RMI, the corresponding RMI classes must be generated (for each implementation class a stub class and a skeleton class). Moreover, for the abstract bean class of the entity bean an implementation class is generated that extends the code of the bean with the code of the persistence manager for access to the database. In order to install these two primitive beans in a server, we thus need sixteen classes and four interfaces. The four interfaces, the two bean classes, and the primary key class are created by the bean provider, while the remaining classes are generated using tools of the container and the persistence manager provider (where the actual number of generated classes will ultimately depend on the implementation of the container and that of the persistence manager).

The client code for using both beans might in simplified form look like that in Listing 9-1 (a fixed amount of 100 euros is to be converted to US dollars).

Listing 9-1. Client code for currency conversion.

```
...
InitialContext ctx = new InitialContext();
///////////
//Step 1 : The client ascertains the current Exchangerate.
Object o = ctx.lookup("Exchangerate");
ExchangerateHome wh = (ExchangerateHome)
        PortableRemoteObject.narrow(o, ExchangerateHome.class);
```

```
//search for the Exchangerate
ExchangeratePK pk = new ExchangeratePK("US-Dollar");
ExchangerateRemote wr = (ExchangerateRemote)

wh.findByPrimaryKey(pk);
//read the Exchangerate
Float exchangerate = wr.exchangerateAsFloat();

//Step 2 : Convert the amount into the desired currency
Object o1 = ctx.lookup("Conversion");
ConversionHome uh = (ConversionHome)
        PortableRemoteObject.narrow(o1, ConversionHome.class);
//generate the session bean
ConversionRemote ur = (ConversionRemote)uh.create();
//convert 100 euros into the target currency
float result = ur.convert(100, exchangerate);
...
```

In the following we will look at the mechanisms that these few lines of code of the client program set in motion at run time on the server (or in the container) and which objects are involved.

When the server is started, the implementations of the home interfaces are instantiated for the installed beans, and the associated stub objects are made available in the naming service.

Step 1: The Client Ascertains the Appropriate Exchange Rate

Table 9-1 provides an explanation of the steps in Figure 9-1. The client uses a JNDI lookup to obtain a stub object of the home interface implementation in its process space. To find the desired exchange rate, the client instantiates and initializes a PrimaryKey object and passes it as parameter in the call to the findByPrimaryKey method. The PrimaryKey object is serialized in the stub object and sent with the RMI protocol over the network to the associated skeleton object. The skeleton object deserializes the data, evaluates it, and carries out an appropriate method call on the object of the home interface implementation.

The home interface implementation checks with the help of the persistence manager whether a data record with the appropriate primary key is to be found. This requires access to the persistence layer. Then it is checked whether an available instance of the bean class exists in the pool. If not, a new instance is generated. Then a skeleton object of the remote interface is instantiated. The bean instance is supplied with an EntityContext object. As result of the operation, the RemoteInterface instance is returned to the skeleton object of the exchange rate home interface implementation. There the associated stub object is serialized and is delivered as return value to the client with the RMI protocol over the network.

Table 9-1. Explanation of the steps in Figure 9-1.

Execution Step	Explanation
1	JNDI lookup on the home interface of the exchange rate bean (network access required).
2	Generation of a `PrimaryKey` object and call to the `findByPrimaryKey` method (network access required).
3	Call to the `findByPrimaryKey` method on the instance of the home interface implementation belonging to the skeleton.
4	Search the data via the persistence manager, generate the bean instance and the remote interface skeleton, or use pooled instance, initialization of instances.
5	Remote interface stub is returned to the client as result of `findByPrimaryKey` call.
6	Client calls the method `exchangerateAsFloat()` to ascertain the exchange rate (network access required).
7	Call to `exchangerateAsFloat()` on the remote interface skeleton.
8	The implementation of the remote interface skeleton opens a transaction. The persistence manager obtains persistent data and places the data on the bean instance.
9	Call to `ejbLoad()` and `ejbActivate()` on the bean instance.
10	Call to the method `exchangerateAsFloat()` on the bean instance and return of the result. In the implementation of the remote interface skeleton, after the end of the method call on the bean instance, the transaction is closed and the result is returned to the client.

To obtain the exchange rate in the form of a `Float` variable, the client calls a corresponding method, `exchangerateAsFloat()`, of the newly received remote interface stub of the exchange rate bean. This call goes over the network via the RMI protocol from the stub to the associated skeleton object on the server, which in turn transmits the call to the remote interface implementation. Before the call from the remote interface implementation can be further transmitted to a bean instance, it must be determined whether a bean instance with the correct bean identity has already been activated. If so, the EJB container simply uses this instance. If no bean instance with the proper identity is available in the state `Ready`, then an instance from the pool is used and initialized with the requisite bean identity.

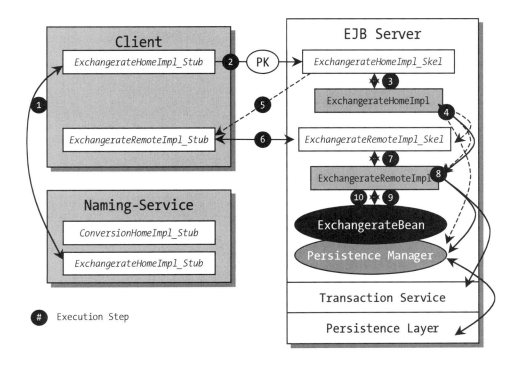

Figure 9-1. Example: ascertaining the exchange rate.

Then the EJB container instructs the persistence manager to fetch the persistent data from the persistence layer and to initialize the attributes of the bean instance. Then the EJB container calls the method `ejbActivate` of the bean instance in order to inform it of the change into the state `Ready`. If there is no free instance available in the pool, then an active bean instance must be passivated, or the EJB container must generate a new instance. Only when a bean instance with the correct bean identity is present in the state `Ready` can the EJB container relay the method call to the instance.

In considering aspects of performance we shall assume that the transaction attributes and transaction context of the client are such that the EJB container has to start a new transaction and must terminate it after running the method. Normally, the EJB container always uses global transactions. This means that a transaction service always coordinates the transactions. The EJB container accesses the transaction service over the interface `UserTransaction` and thereby manages the transaction. Communication between the EJB container and the transaction service can take a variety of forms. A typical constellation is that the transaction service is provided by the application server and runs on the same computer in a separate process. In the case of a large system, however, issues of scaling come to the fore. If several EJB containers access the same data, then they require a central transaction service. In this case, the transaction service usually runs on its own server. Each access by an EJB container to the transaction service then goes over a network path.

First, the EJB container launches a global transaction with a call to the method begin in the interface UserTransaction. The thread now possesses a transaction context. Each system that takes part in the transaction must be informed about this context so that it can register itself with the transaction service. The context will be automatically transmitted only for calls within the thread. If the transaction context is to be transmitted in the case of calls across the network, then a special stub must manage this task.

If, for example, a database is accessed from within a transaction, then the JDBC driver (also a type of stub) transmits the transaction context to the database service. The database service registers itself with the transaction service using the transaction ID from the context. Then a local transaction associated with the transaction context is begun in the database. If, for example, a global transaction is later terminated with commit, the database service is notified of this by the transaction service. The two-phase commit that is used requires at least two calls (see Chapter 7, on transactions).

This process is identical for all global transactions, independent of whether the bean or the persistence manager accesses the database. If we assume that application server, database, and transaction service run on their own machines, a transaction results in at least four additional calls (begin, registration, and two commits) over a network path.

In our example the actual method call is transmitted to the bean instance after the begin. After the execution of the method, the EJB ends the transaction with commit or rollback, depending on the occurrence of any errors in the method. Then the result of the method is passed in the form of the return value to the skeleton. There, as with findByPrimaryKey, the result is serialized for network transmission and sent back to the client stub, which deserializes the data and makes it available to the calling object in the form of the return value.

Step 2: Converting the Amount into the Desired Currency

Table 9-2 clarifies the steps in Figure 9-2. This step is essentially a repetition of what was shown in detail in the first step. Instead of a findByPrimaryKey call, now we have a create call (since we are dealing with a session bean). Moreover, the persistence-relation operations are lacking. It could happen, depending on the server implementation, that the handling of entity and session beans is different with regard to pooling.

Table 9-2. Explanation of the steps in Figure 9-2.

Execution Step	Explanation
11	JNDI lookup on the home interface of the conversion bean.
12	Call to the create method (RMI).
13	Call to the create method on the home interface skeleton of the conversion bean.
14	Generation of the bean instance and remote interface skeleton or use of instances in the pool, initialization of instances.
15	Remote interface stub returned to the client as result of create call.
16	Client calls the method convert() to convert the amount into the target currency (RMI).
17	Call to convert() on the remote interface skeleton.
18	Possible opening of transaction or use of bean instance in the pool.
19	Call to the method convert() on the bean instance and return of the result to the client, possible termination of transaction.

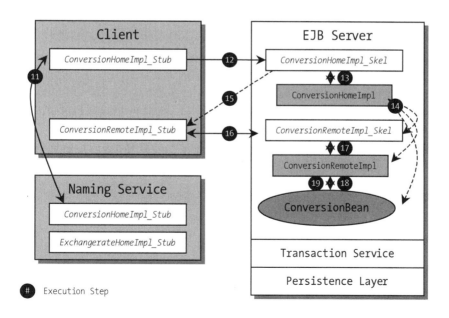

Figure 9-2. Example: conversion to the target currency.

The rather detailed description of the processes in the container classes in our example should have suggested that operations on Enterprise Beans are relatively expensive. With a component model like Enterprise JavaBeans a certain amount of overhead cannot be avoided.

Communication over RMI is, to be sure, simple and convenient for the developer, but this convenience results in a decrease in execution speed. The resulting container code for every bean type cannot—or at least only to a small extent—be divided among the various bean types, since the code is generated from the specific instructions of the deployment descriptor of an Enterprise JavaBean. At run time a skeleton object of the home interface is required for each bean type (this holds for entity and session beans). With entity beans a skeleton object of the remote interface is necessary for each bean in the state Ready. With session beans what is required is one object for each bean type and bound client.

The extent of the container overhead (that is, the scope of the container objects present at run time) is directly proportional to the number of installed and employed beans (with session beans the number of clients bound to the server plays a role as well). The size of the bean itself has relatively little to do with the generated container code. A bean with a small home or remote interface does not have significantly less container code and fewer run-time objects than a bean with a large home or remote interface.

Conclusions

An important consideration in the use of Enterprise JavaBeans with respect to good performance is the design of the network interface. By this we mean the bean's home and, most of all, remote interfaces. The goal is to offer as few methods as possible containing as much functionality as possible and allowing the exchange of the greatest possible quantities of data. As the implementations presented show, calls to bean methods are expensive operations. Thus for the sake of optimization it is a good idea to consider processing speed as early as the design phase. Fine-grained operations (such as ascertaining the exchange rate in our example) are marked by a certain disparity between the scope of the functionality and the container overhead. They have a negative effect on the performance of the application system.

No less important a role in the performance of EJB applications is played by the design of the data model. Entity beans are heavyweight conglomerates of run-time objects. Fine-grained entities, that is, data records with few data fields that appear in large quantity, are to be avoided if possible. A negative example is the entity Exchangerate as used in this section. As with the network interface, it is a good idea to define coarse-grained entities. The goal is to keep the number of entity-bean and container-class instances as small as possible. The definition of coarse-grained entities and the modeling of methods that offer a great deal of functionality and permit the transfer of large quantities of data also lowers the number of necessary network accesses.

The implementations that we have shown relativize themselves when an Enterprise Bean is addressed via the local client view. Since the client and the Enterprise Bean are deliberately located in the same process, there is no network communication overhead. With the lack of serialization of parameters and return values and the lack of network latency, the local client view has a significant performance advantage over the remote client view. Whether the interface of the Enterprise Bean is fine-grained or coarse-grained plays a secondary role in this case. What remains with the local client view are container overhead, overhead of global transactions, and in the case of entity beans, the transport of data to and from the database.

The local client view gives the design of EJB applications a new dimension. Through the optimal combination of Enterprise Beans with remote client view (coarse-grained interfaces for remote clients) and local client view (local interfaces that are primarily addressed by other Enterprise Beans) one can achieve a significant influence at the design stage on the performance of the future system.

The performance behavior is generally a function of the type of bean (independent of whether the remote or local client view comes into play). With session beans, from the point of view of performance one would favor stateless over stateful session beans. The EJB container can manage stateless session beans much more efficiently through pooling than it can stateful session beans. With the latter type, object serialization through the activation and passivation mechanisms has an additional negative effect on performance. In the case of entity beans the form of persistence mechanism chosen plays a role. With the use of container-managed persistence one is dependent on the implementation of the persistence manager, which affects the performance of data storage routines. The persistence manager provider must make available generic routines, which are always less efficient (in the case of bean-managed persistence) than algorithms designed especially for a particular data model. Thus in particular cases it can be necessary to do without the convenience of container-managed persistence for the sake of speed of execution.

Message-driven beans hold a special position to the extent that they have no public interface. They cannot be addressed directly by the client. Moreover, message-driven beans are not persistent. Thus for this bean type the overhead of the EJB container is significantly less than with entity and session beans. Message-driven beans can be managed by the EJB container with a similar efficiency as for stateless session beans.

On account of the possibility of parallel processing, message-driven beans have a tendency to increase the performance of a system. For parallel processing to be possible, several threads must be available. The EJB container takes over management of the threads and the assigning to instances of message-driven beans. The greater the number of different types of message-driven beans that are deployed, the greater the number of threads that are needed by the EJB container to guarantee the parallel processing of the various types of message-driven beans.

Threads are a valuable resource of the operating system, but they bring with them considerable management overhead. The use of message-driven beans to improve performance should therefore not be excessive, since the effect of increased performance by the increased effort of the operating system for the management of threads can be impaired. Moreover, not every type of message-driven bean can make use of its own pool of threads. Within an application server (the EJB container is, together with other containers, a component of such a server) there is generally a central thread pool available, which is divided among the various services and containers. The greater the number of different types of message-driven beans used, the more easily the resource Thread can become in short supply, leading to a bottleneck.

To parallelize a process through the use of several threads does not automatically mean that better performance can be attained. Whether the processing runs more quickly or more slowly depends on a number of factors. One of these factors is the hardware on which the system is run. A computer with one CPU can always have only one thread running while the other threads wait until they receive a share of CPU time. To parallelize a CPU-intensive process over several threads on a computer with a single CPU can result in worse performance overall. In addition to the time that the CPU needs for processing the instructions there is also the time necessary for managing the CPU time for several threads and the switching between threads. However, if the processing is of the form, say, where an e-mail message must be fetched, data read from a database, and a file fetched from an FTP server, then the division into several threads can be profitable even on a computer with a single CPU. While one thread is waiting for the answer to the e-mail (thus is using no CPU time), the other thread can already begin to take data from the database.

Transactions are also a burden on the performance of an application system. If one cannot do without transactions, then it is advisable to avoid the use of global transactions. Since global transactions use a great deal of communication over the network, local transactions show much better performance. Global transactions can be avoided by not including several entity beans in disparate locations in a single transaction. A global transaction is also necessary, for example, when an entity bean accesses several databases.

Finally, we note that the examples in this book do not always follow the principles stated in this section. The goal of the examples in the other sections and chapters is to foster an understanding of EJB-related matters, not to achieve optimal performance.

Processes, Enterprise Objects, and Services

The architecture of applications, no matter how complex they may be, continually presents software designers with new challenges. With each new step in the direction of more advanced technology and with each new challenge brought in from the application areas of business and information technology, the design aspect must grow in a new dimension. Enterprise JavaBeans spares the software developer some of the design decisions through the component model. For problems such as distribution, scaling, and persistence there are answers to be found in the specification, and a closer look will reveal many known design patterns (for example, the EJBObject represents a combination of proxy and decorator patterns, and the home interface corresponds to the factory pattern [5]). Frequently, however, the developer will be searching for answers to questions such as these:

- For what tasks should I use entity beans?

- For what tasks should I use session beans?

- For what tasks should I use message-driven beans?

- Should the client communicate with all components or only with particular components?

- How should components cooperate and communicate?

The goal of this section is to give some suggestions for the use of entity, session, and message-driven beans.

One models business processes on computer-supported systems in order to learn how to handle them better and more efficiently. As a rule, one attempts to relate these models to actual conditions. The reality of everyday business meets us in the form of processes, business objects, and services. The following implementations should help to clarify what we understand by processes, business objects, and services and how they are mapped to Enterprise JavaBeans.

Business Objects

By a *business object* we mean an actual object or item of a concrete application area. For example, in the area of marketing, a business object might be a customer, a supplier, or an invoice; in manufacturing, such an object might be a machine, a parts list, or a production list. The immediate connection of these objects to the business world is underscored through the name *business object*. Business objects are are represented and identified by their data. Thus a customer has a name, a shipping address, a billing address, and so on. In a data-processing system the customer will be assigned a unique customer number as means of identification.

The same holds for suppliers. Product parts, say, are represented by the data that describe their technical properties and are identified by a unique part number. All of these properties lead to the decision to model such business objects as entity beans (see Chapter 5). Entity beans are persistent objects, and they can be identified and located by a unique key. Business objects are not to be viewed each in isolation, but in relationships among one another. A production list refers generally to an order (vertical relation), while a parts list consists of several modules, which themselves are divided into individual segments (horizontal relation). Thus business objects reflect the *structural* aspects of an organization.

Processes

Processes represent the *dynamic* aspects of an organization. By a process we understand a defined sequence of individual operations. At a given time, a process is in one of a number of states, which makes it possible to guide and control the execution of the process. Furthermore, state transitions are defined. The individual operations of a process are carried out on the data of business objects (that is, they are used and/or altered). Table 9-3 shows the process of executing an incoming order.

Table 9-3. Steps in processing an order.

Process Step	State
Receipt of order documentation	Process is started
Checking of order data	Data being checked
Transmittal to the group of unprocessed orders	Order being processed
Completing order data	Order being processed
Release of order	Released

In this process one can include (according to the type of business) the business objects Customer (who places the order), Endproduct (the object being ordered), Rawmaterial (inventory control for meeting a promise of delivery), and Order.

Processes are ideally suited for modeling as session beans (see Chapter 4). Since processes have states, one should use stateful session beans. Stateful session beans are transient, and are available to a client exclusively for one session.

Services

By services we mean all operations that do not belong to a single business object or process. Such operations play a supporting role. They can be grouped into those that support objects and those that support processes. Services can be modeled as stateless session beans or message-driven beans. Stateless session beans model *synchronous* services, while message-driven beans model *asynchronous* services.

Synchronous services are used when further processing depends on the result of the deployment of the service. If the result plays no role or does not influence the further execution of a process (that is, the result can be accessed at a later time), then the service can be asynchronous. The use of asynchronous services can improve performance if the processing of the service can take place on another computer or processor while the original process continues running in parallel. Asynchronous services can also be used to launch processes asynchronously or to execute processes in parallel. In such a case a message-driven bean, as opposed to a (stateful) session bean, takes the role of the EJB client. The message-driven bean is provided all the relevant information, via a message, that is needed for the launching and execution of the process.

The following two examples should serve to clarify the mapping of business processes onto objects, processes, and services.

Example: Bookkeeping System

The (stateful) session bean Booking shown in Figure 9-3 contains the logic for implementing double-entry bookkeeping.

It can force the order of execution of the individual steps (for example, by triggering an exception in the case of a violation of the preset order) and thus ensure an orderly execution of the process. The method setDebitAccount() initializes a new accounting entry process and checks with a findByPrimaryKey call whether an account exists for the given account number. At the same time, the session bean obtains a reference to an entity bean to be able later to make the entry in this account. The same holds for setCreditAccount(). With a call to setAmount() the session bean can check various conditions, for example, whether an account has been overdrawn. A call to book() will open a transaction context, which includes the participating accounts, and will execute the entry using setBalance(). An account will be represented by an entity bean according to the above implementations, since an account is an object with a persistent state. The components offer an interface by which the state of the account can be modified.

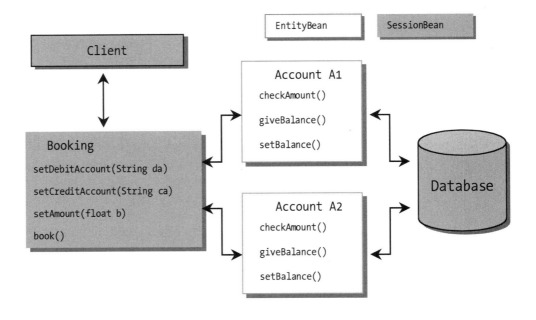

Figure 9-3. Example: accounting system.

The process for a double entry can be used by every client via a (stateful) session bean. The logic is available in a central location for the entire system. Furthermore, the client communicates exclusively via the session bean. To make the entry it is not necessary to communicate directly with entity beans. In this case the session bean would support the remote client view, while the entity bean supports the local client view.

A minimal requirement of such a primitive bookkeeping system is the keeping of an accounts journal, in which all entries are recorded and with whose help all accounting processes can be checked and reconstructed. The recording of the individual entries is of particular importance if entries must be able to be canceled at a later time. The accounting journal consists of individual entries. An entry consists at least of a unique entry number, the debit and credit accounts, the entry amount, entry date, time of the entry, and the user that made the entry. The addition of a journal entry and querying of information from the journal is not a process, but a stateless concatenation of individual operations. The accounting journal is not classifiable as a typical business object. Since the accounting journal can grow very large, the modeling as an entity is critical from the standpoint of performance. The accounting journal is in our sense to be seen as a classical example of a service, which offers the logging of accounting procedures and inquiry into the state of the data arising from such logging.

The message-driven bean JournalEntry and the (stateless) session bean JournalService (see Figure 9-4) represent the interface to the accounting journal. In our example the accounting journal is stored in a database. It would also be possible to store it in an archive system. Writing a journal entry is an asynchronous service that can be executed by sending a message to the JournalEntry bean. An asynchronous service has the advantage that the bean Booking does not have to wait until the data have been stored. During the writing of a journal entry the call returns to the client. The bean Booking does not expect a result from this procedure. The Java message service takes care of the requisite data security. To locate data in the accounting journal an asynchronous service is employed in the form of a JournalService bean. For locating data a limited number of methods with fixed functionality can be specified (as shown in Figure 9-4), although one might also consider developing a primitive query language. For extensive and lengthy data searches an asynchronous service could also be employed. After the client has started the search, it could continue with other actions. The result of the search would then be delivered later, for example, by the Java message service or by e-mail.

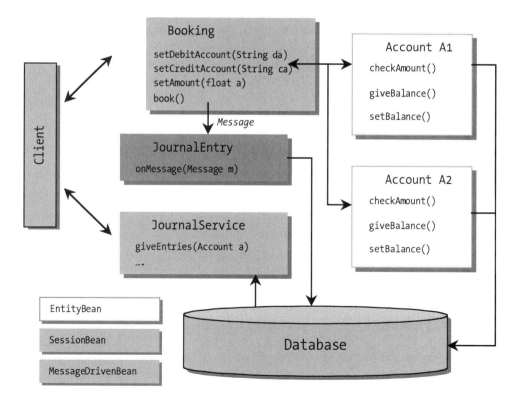

Figure 9-4. Example: accounting procedure with extensions.

Example: Production Monitor

The (stateful) session bean `Productionmonitor` depicted in Figure 9-5 contains the logic for monitoring a production process of a product that is produced by a single machine.

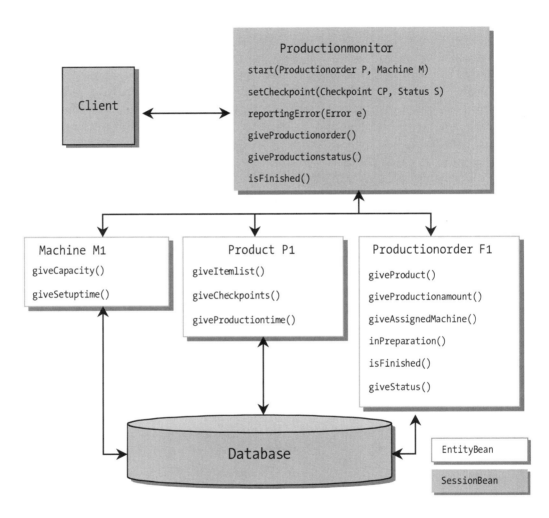

Figure 9-5. Example: production monitor.

In this example the client is an existing machine that can produce the product and that is directly linked into the system (for example, via a Java or CORBA interface). Into the process are brought the business objects `Machine` (the logical representation of the machine in the system), `Product` (which is produced by the machine, also in the form of a logical representation), and `Productionorder` (which relates to the product and specifies in detail the number of items to be produced, in what time period, and on what machine).

For example, through a service a (real) machine obtains all production orders, which were assigned by an optimization process. Thus the machine knows what product is to be produced and in what quantity. Each production order is processed by the (real) machine using the session bean `Productionmonitor`. The session bean can then check by calling the method `start()` whether in its production order the (real) machine corresponds to the associated (logical) machine. In the course of the production process checkpoints are set by the (real) machine via `setCheckpoint` (for example, a checkpoint can be set after each process step, after the completion of a piece, or after the completion of a particular job lot). The session bean compares the set checkpoint with the list of checkpoints required by the procuct P_1 (`Product.giveCheckpoints()`). The prescribed checkpoints arise from the technical specification of the product and are built into the system or the machine configuration by technicians. For the case in which the checkpoints fail to correspond or other irregularities arise (which can be reported by the real machine via `reportError()`), the session bean can set corresponding reporting mechanisms in motion (for example, a technician can be summoned by a pager). After the requisite number of pieces have been processed, the production order is reported as `complete`. Thus the progress of the entire production process can be monitored.

Not every situation of a given business domain can define processes (which can be modeled by stateful session beans), business objects (modeled by entity beans), or services (modeled by stateless session beans or message-driven beans). Nor is every entity bean automatically a business object, a stateful session bean a process, or a stateless session bean or message-driven bean a service. The mapping of a problem to the domain of Enterprise JavaBeans is nonetheless easier if in the analysis of the problem one always keeps in mind the semantics of these three entities.

Aggregation of Enterprise Beans

The topic that we wish to discuss in this section relates to the (sometimes run-time) aggregation of Enterprise Beans and the creation of a cooperative environment for Enterprise Bean components on the *server side*. We would like to mention briefly the various standard alternatives, so that we can present later in the section an application-oriented aggregation plan.

Alternative 1: Static Aggregation over the Client View

A (static) aggregation of components is possible, in that they operate over the view of a client (see the subsection on the client view in Chapter 4). Information is placed in the section ejb-ref of the deployment descriptor that describes the type of Enterprise Beans that will be used by beans to be installed over the client view. Through the field ejb-link the application assembler binds these references to concrete installed implementations of this bean type. Through the use of the local client view, communication among Enterprise Beans can be optimized when they are installed in the same application server.

Alternative 2: Dynamic Aggregation over the Metadata Interface

For the run-time dynamic aggregation, the specification of Enterprise JavaBeans offers the metadata interface (javax.ejb.EJBHome.getEJBMetaData). In combination with the Java reflection API it is possible to program dynamic method calls in Enterprise Beans. Such an aggregation is very generic and relatively expensive in programming effort. Data type checking during compilation is lost. Moreover, the use of the Java reflection API is always critical for execution speed. One often wishes to have a less generic but better-performing option for dynamic aggregation of Enterprise Beans at run time. Furthermore, this type of dynamic aggregation is limited to the remote client view. The method getEJBMetaData in javax.ejb.EJBLocalHome is not available.

Alternative 3: Dynamic Aggregation over Events

A common type of dynamic aggregation of components consists of events (see the section after next). An event model, similar to that for JavaBeans, by which Enterprise Beans trigger events via the EJB container and can receive events, would be ideal for the dynamic aggregation of Enterprise Bean components at run time. If the triggering and receiving of events is possible only via the EJB container, then there is no conflict with life cycle management or client calls. For example, the EJB container can block client calls or the passivation or deletion of an Enterprise Bean until the processing of a received event is complete, or suppress the assignment of events to passivated or deleted Enterprise Beans. The specification for Enterprise JavaBeans provides no event model for Enterprise Beans, and therefore an aggregation over events is not possible.

Alternative 4: Dynamic Aggregation over Messages

Another common type of dynamic aggregation is the exchange of messages over a message service such as the Java Message Service. However, the Java Message Service is designed for communication between processes over a network. For communication strictly within a process it is not very efficient. Furthermore, an entity bean or a session bean cannot use asynchronous message delivery over the javax.jms.MessageListener interface (see Chapter 6), since the specification explicitly forbids it. If it were to permit this mechanism for entity and session beans, the result could be conflicts between the life cycle management of the EJB container and message delivery through the JMS provider. Furthermore, the justification for the existence of message-driven beans would be called into question. Therefore, the Java Message Service is unsuitable for dynamic aggregation of Enterprise Beans.

Alternative 5: Static Aggregation over the Creation of an Enterprise Bean

The application assembler can enable an aggregation of Enterprise Beans using the specification by programming a new Enterprise Bean. The client would use the Enterprise Bean of the application assembler, which uses other beans for carrying out desired tasks and enables their cooperation.

Alternative 6: Aggregation of Entity Beans over Persistent Relationships

Persistent relationships (container-managed relationships) are in a certain sense also a means of collecting Enterprise Bean components into aggregates. This is, on the one hand, a static aggregation, since the relationships are set in the deployment descriptor and are thus limited to particular types of Enterprise Beans. However, the actual aggregation between the instances of the Enterprise Beans involved in the relationship is dynamic, since the connection between the instances (which are implemented, for example, in a database via a foreign key relation) can be created or deleted at run time. The example of warehouse management in Chapter 5 illustrates this situation. Communication among the Enterprise Beans aggregated in this manner takes place over the local client view and is therefore relatively efficient. The resolution of references among entity bean instances arising from the relationship is taken over by the EJB container. Persistent relationships are thus the only form of aggregation that is actively supported by the EJB container. This type of aggregation is, however, relevant to entity beans only.

In addition to alternative 6, alternatives 1, 2, and 5 are relevant for the aggregation of Enterprise Beans. In the remainder of this section we would like to show a further alternative for the aggregation of Enterprise Beans and the creation of a cooperative environment.

Through a server-side *application-oriented* framework a cooperative environment can be created that enables Enterprise Beans to link dynamically and replace each other as necessary without other beans being affected. To illustrate, we shall develop an application-oriented framework for a simple accounting application. This framework (which serves the subject-matter aspects) rests on a system-oriented framework (which covers the technical requirements) and offers loose and dynamic coupling of Enterprise Beans (without a new bean having to be programmed). For this we use the previously introduced example from this chapter of the bookkeeping system.

We first present a traditional form of implementation in order to point out the differences in using a framework (which will be discussed afterwards).

Figure 9-6 shows the session bean Booking, which provides the client with an interface for carrying out double-entry bookkeeping. It uses the entity bean Account and the session bean JournalService for booking the entry.

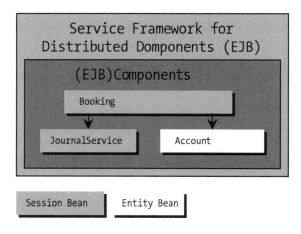

Figure 9-6. Example: Accounting application.

The code of a traditional client program might look something like that of Listing 9-2.

Listing 9-2. Example of a traditional client.

```
...
InitialContext ctx = new InitialContext();
//fetch the home interface of the session bean Booking
final String BOOKING = "java:comp/env/ejb/Booking";
Object o = ctx.lookup(BOOKING);
BookingHome bh = (BookingHome)
        PortableRemoteObject.narrow(o, BookingHome.class);
//generate the BookingBean and fetch the remote interface
Booking b = bh.create();
//execute the booking
b.setDebitAccount("0815");
b.setCreditAccount("0915");
b.setAmount(100);
b.book();
b.remove();
...
```

The implementation of the relevant methods of the remote interface in the BookingBean class would look something like that of Listing 9-3, using the traditional way of proceeding.

Listing 9-3. Example of a traditional session bean implementation.

```
...
private Account debitAccount;
private Account creditAccount;
private AccountHome accountHome;
private JournalServiceHome journalHome;
...
public void ejbCreate()
  throws RemoteException, CreateException
{
 final String ACCHOME = "java:comp/env/ejb/Account";
 final String JHOME = "java:comp/env/ejb/JournalService";
 ...
```

```
  try {
   //fetch the home interface of the entity bean Account and
   //the session bean JournalService
   Context ctx = new InitialContext();
   Object o = ctx.lookup(ACCHOME);
   accountHome = (AccountHome)
       PortableRemoteObject.narrow(o, AccountHome.class);
   o = ctx.lookup(JHOME);
   journalHome = (JournalServiceHome)
       PortableRemoteObject.narrow
                   (o,JournalServiceHome.class);
  }
  ...
}
...
public void setDebitAccount(String accno)
  throws RemoteException, BookingException
{
 ... //check routines
 //generate a PrimaryKey object
 AccountPK pk = new AccountPK(accno);
 try {
  //search the debit account
  debitAccount = accountHome.findByPrimaryKey(pk);
 }
 ... //error handling
}

public void setCreditAccount(String accno)
  throws RemoteException, BookingException
{
 ... //check routines
 //generate a PrimaryKey object
 AccountPK pk = new AccountPK(accno);
 try {
  //search the credit account
  creditAccount = accountHome.findByPrimaryKey(pk);
 }
 ... //error handling
}
...
public void setAmount(float amount)
  throws RemoteException, BookingException
{
```

```
... //check routines
try {
 //check whether the booking of the amount is permissible
 debitAccount.checkAmount(amount * (-1));
 creditAccount.checkAmount(amount);
}
... //error handling
}
...
public void book()
  throws RemoteException, BookingException
{
 ... //check routines
 //booking of the amount by changing the account states
 debitAccount.setBalance(debitAccount.getBalance()-
                            theAmount);
 creditAccount.setBalance(creditAccount.getBalance()+
                            theAmount);
 ... //error handling
 //logging of the process in the journal
 JournalService js = journalHome.create();
 js.record(debitAccount,
           creditAccount,
           theAmount,
           theContext.getCallerPrincipal());
 ... //error handling
}
...
```

The dependence of the session bean Booking on the entity bean Account and the session bean JournalService is documented in the deployment descriptor in Listing 9-4.

Listing 9-4. Example of a traditional deployment descriptor.

```
...
<ejb-jar>
  <description>
    This jar file contains all components
    needed for the bookkeeping application
  </description>

    <enterprise-beans>
      <session>
```

```
        <description>
          The session bean Booking provides
          an implementation for the execution
          of a double-entry bookkeeping system.
        </description>
        <ejb-name>Booking</ejb-name>
        ...
        <ejb-ref>
          <ejb-ref-name>ejb/JournalService</ejb-ref-name>
          <ejb-ref-type>Session</ejb-ref-type>
          <home>ejb.example.JournalServiceHome</home>
          <remote>ejb.example.JournalService</remote>
          <ejb-link>JournalService</ejb-link>
        </ejb-ref>
        <ejb-ref>
          <ejb-ref-name>ejb/Account</ejb-ref-name>
          <ejb-ref-type>Entity</ejb-ref-type>
          <home>ejb.example.AccountHome</home>
          <remote>ejb.example.Account</remote>
          <ejb-link>Account</ejb-link>
        </ejb-ref>
        ...
      </session>
      ...
    </enterprise-beans>
  ...
</ejb-jar>
```

As can be seen from these code fragments, the session bean Booking works directly with other beans. In the deployment descriptor the type of beans used is defined, and it must agree with the type used in the implementation. Should the need arise to replace, say, the Account bean with another type due to limited functionality or to use various types of accounts (which are also available as components), this would be possible only by changing the code of the session bean Booking. It would be possible using the ejb-link element of the deployment descriptor to bind the bean reference to another implementation of the same type. However, then a reinstallation of the session bean Booking would be necessary.

To eliminate the strict binding of the beans to each other they are embedded in an application-specific framework, allowing them to work together on a more abstract level (see Figure 9-7).

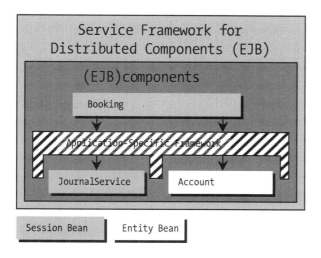

Figure 9-7. Booking with a framework.

The session bean Booking is the business process that the client wishes to work with, and this session bean still represents the server interface. The use of the JournalService and Account beans should take place over the abstract interfaces of a framework , which allows the inclusion of accounts and a journal service in the accounting process.

The framework represented in Figure 9-8 consists in our example simply of the three depicted interfaces. The framework becomes concretized and applicable through the implementation of these interfaces in Java classes. The functionality that we expect from an account and a journal service is contained in the Enterprise Beans. To bridge the gap between the framework implementation and the Enterprise Beans, we make use of the bridge pattern (see [5]). This allows the various abstractions (account, journal) to be decoupled from their implementations and thus remain flexible.

Figure 9-9 shows the classes JounalIF_Impl and AccountIF_Impl. They are generated on the initiative of the session bean Booking through the implementation of the interface AccountingFactory and used for the required operations. The implementation classes delegate the relevant method calls to other Enterprise Beans (in our case to the JournalService and Account beans). Thus the beans JournalService and Account are fully decoupled from the component Booking. Finally, it depends on the bridge classes as to which Enterprise Beans are actually used. Above all, this decision can be made at run time (with the proper implementation) based on conditions at the time.

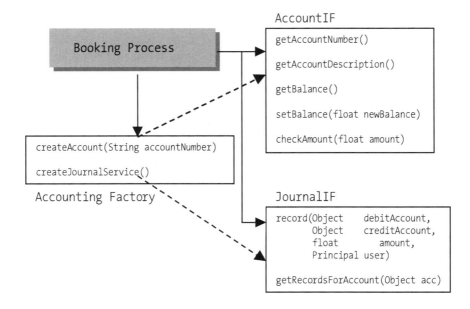

Figure 9-8. Application-oriented cooperation framework.

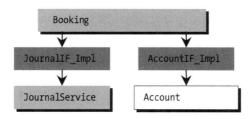

Figure 9-9. Example of cooperation in a framework.

The references to the Account and JournalService beans no longer need to be specified as bean references in the deployment descriptor of the session bean Booking. Access to both beans by the session bean Booking no longer takes place over JNDI, but over the framework. Nonetheless, it is worth noting that in the deployment descriptor the session bean uses the implementation class of the framework. The deployment descriptor should in any case be used in its capacity as central repository of installation instructions. The resulting documentation effect is very useful. Unfortunately, there is no place in the sections of the deployment descriptor in which one may register the factory class (which is the entry point into the framework). In view of the configuration options, an entry as resource factory reference is the most suitable [21]. Nonetheless, the implementation class of the AccountingFactory interface and our framework in no way corresponds to what the specification understands by a resource factory and a resource. We shall therefore limit ourselves to a note in the description field of the session bean Booking (see Listing 9-5).

Listing 9-5. Example: deployment descriptor with framework.

```
...
<ejb-jar>
  <description>
    This jar file contains all components
    necessary for the bookkeeping application.
  </description>

    <enterprise-beans>
      <session>
        <description>
          The session bean Booking provides
          an implementation for the execution
          of double-entry accounting.
          NOTE: This bean uses the
          Accounting framework !
        </description>
        <ejb-name>Booking </ejb-name>
        ...
      </session>
      ...
    </enterprise-beans>
</ejb-jar>
```

The implementation class of the AccountingFactory interface (FactoryImpl) is implemented as a singleton (see [5]; it will be treated following the modified implementation of the Booking class). This will avoid the generation of an instance via the bean class, and the management of the framework classes can be carried out at a central location in the process. The implementation in the bean class Booking would change as in Listing 9-6.

Listing 9-6. Example: session bean with framework.

```
...
  private AccountFactory theFactory;
  private AccountIF debitAccount;
  private AccountIF creditAccount;
  ...
  public void ejbCreate()
```

```
        throws RemoteException, CreateException
    {
      ...
      //fetch the factory implementation
      theFactory = FactoryImpl.getFactory();
      ...
    }
...
    public void setDebitAccount(String accno)
      throws RemoteException, Booking Exception
    {
     ... //check routines
     try {
      //search the debit account
         debitAccount = theFactory.createAccount(accno);
     }
         .. //error handling
    }

    public void setCreditAccount(String accno)
        throws RemoteException, Booking Exception
    {
     ... //check routines
     try {
      //search the credit account
      creditAccount = theFactory.createAccount(accno);
     }
     ... //error handling
    }
    ...
    public void setAmount(float amount)
      throws RemoteException, Booking Exception
    {
      //no changes
     ...
    }
    ...
    public void book()
      throws RemoteException, Booking Exception
    {
     ...
     //no changes
     ...
```

```
    //log the process in the journal
    JournalIF js = theFactory.createJournalService();
    js.record(debitAccount,
              creditAccount,
              theAmount,
              theContext.getCallerPrincipal());
  ...
 }
 ...
```

The implementation of the AccountingFactory interface is shown in Listing 9-7.

Listing 9-7. Example: factory interface implementation.

```
...
public class FactoryImpl implements AccountingFactory,
                                   java.io.Serializable
{
    private static AccountingFactory theFactory =
                                       new FactoryImpl();

    private FactoryImpl() {}

    public static AccountingFactory getFactory() {
        return theFactory;
    }

    public AccountIF createAccount(String accountNumber)
        throws AccountException
    {
        return new AccountIF_Impl(accountNumber);
    }

    public JournalIF createJournalService()
        throws JournalException
    {
        return new JournalIF_Impl();
    }
}
```

The implementation of the interface java.io.Serializable is necessary to avoid problems with the passivation of stateful session beans that store a reference to an object of this class in a member variable.

The classes AccountIF_Impl and JournalIF_Impl implement the relevant interfaces (including the interface java.io.Serializable) and delegate the calls to the respective beans. To clarify this we show in Listing 9-8 the constructor and a method of the class AccountIF_Impl.

Listing 9-8. Example: interface implementation.

```
...
public class AccountIF_Impl implements AccountIF,
                                    java.io.Serializable
{
    //the remote interface of the Account bean
    Account theAccount;

    public AccountIF_Impl(String accountNumber)
        throws AccountException
    {
        final String ACCHOME = "java:comp/env/ejb/Account";

        AccountPK pk = new AccountPK(accountNumber);
        //here a run-time decision can be made as to
        //which bean should be used
        try {
            AccountHome home;
            InitialContext ctx = new InitialContext();
            Object o = ctx.lookup(ACCHOME);
            home = (AccountHome)
                        PortableRemoteObject.narrow
                            (o, AccountHome.class);
            theAccount = home.findByPrimaryKey(pk);
        }
        catch(NamingException nex) {
            throw new AccountException(nex.getMessage());
        }
        catch(FinderException fex) {
            throw new AccountException(fex.getMessage());
        }
        catch(RemoteException rex) {
            throw new AccountException(rex.getMessage());
        }
    }
    ...
    public String getAccountNumber()
```

```
        throws AccountException
    {

        String ret;
        try {
            ret = theAccount.getAccountNumber();
        }
        catch(RemoteException rex) {
            throw new AccountException(rex.getMessage());
        }
        return ret;
    }


    public String getAccountDescription()
        throws AccountException
    {

        String ret;
        try {
            ret = theAccount.getAccountDescription();
        }
        catch(RemoteException rex) {
            throw new AccountException(rex.getMessage());
        }
        return ret;
    }
    ...
}
```

Summary

An application-oriented framework on the server side offers the possibility of
coupling Enterprise Beans loosely and run-time dynamically. One can create
an application-oriented cooperation framework. Moreover, the application
assembler can provide additional code necessary for the correct coupling of the
Enterprise Beans (*glue code*). This option also exists when custom Enterprise
Beans are developed for the purpose of the coupling. Thanks to the application-
oriented framework (even after deployment), the Enterprise Beans remain
exchangeable without a repetition of the deployment process or the Enterprise
Bean's code having to be altered. At run time a decision can be made as to which
components are to be used. This is useful, for example, when there is not a
single Account bean, but several, and a decision must be made, depending on
the account numbers, as to which bean type will be used (for example, securities
account or cash account). The handling of various account types is then also
hidden from the session bean.

In our case, the framework must be supplied by the provider of the session bean Booking (since the provider programs directly to its interfaces). The application assembler would analogously implement the interfaces of the framework and likewise install the beans used by the implementation classes in the server. It is advisable to note in the beans' description fields that they will be used by the framework classes in order to maintain the central documentation function of the deployment descriptor. The application assembler also decides through the implementation which Enterprise Beans will be used as accounts or journal service, and can provide the additional code necessary for the application.

Inheritance

Inheritance plays a large role in object-oriented programming. Its primary purpose is in the reuse of existing code and in the polymorphism of objects. Thus as with the component paradigm, in this topic we also meet the aspect of reuse. While the Enterprise JavaBeans specification 1.0 does not touch on the topic of inheritance at all, in version 1.1 there is a paragraph in the appendix devoted to it. There it is mentioned that the concept of inheritance is not defined for components. Nonetheless, the bean developer is allowed to use the standard mechanisms of the Java language, namely, the inheritance of interfaces and classes. The same holds for versions 2.0 and 2.1 of the EJB specification. However, there it is mentioned that component inheritance is a topic that will be dealt with in one of the next versions of the EJB specification (see [21]).

If one considers the significant aspects of a component (see Chapter 2), then the question presents itself as to what benefit inheritance of components might offer. Components are self-contained building blocks that offer a particular functionality and whose behavior should be externally configurable only within certain limits. Components hide their internal workings and present themselves to the outside world only through their interfaces (a *black box*). A framework, for example, is typically a *white box* approach; that is, one can examine it and see its architecture and participating classes, and it is necessary, in fact, to customize it to achieve a useful functionality from the framework. It is general practice in the implementation of a component to make use of the class and interface inheritance. However, what does inheritance look like when applied to the components themselves (or in our case, to Enterprise Beans)?

We shall discuss this issue using the bank account example. Say we have a checking account, savings account, and foreign currency account. All three types have the same properties (all possess an account number and account state), and they all have a certain functionality in common (one can query the current state, make deposits and withdrawals, etc.).

Figure 9-10 shows the class Bankaccount, which offers the basic functionality. The derived classes change the existing functionality as required (for example, one cannot exceed a certain limit in withdrawals from the checking account). The derived classes extend the basis class with additional properties (such as an interest credit in the savings account, a service charge in the checking account) and include additional functions (such as an interest calculation at the end of an interest period). Thus Bankaccount is a collective term for foreign currency, checking, and savings accounts. If Figure 9-10 where to show the fundamental structures of a framework for bank applications, then the class Bankaccount would surely be an abstract class. No bank offers only a generic bank account. A customer always has specialized accounts, such as a checking account. Thus an instance of type Bankaccount is useless, since the class Bankaccount simply offers the basic functionality, which taken by itself is of little practical interest. It is only when a bank account is specialized to an account such as a checking account that the code in the class Bankaccount can be usefully deployed.

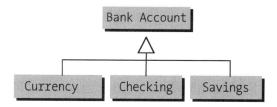

Figure 9-10. Inheritance in the bank account example.

Let us transpose this discussion to Enterprise JavaBeans and components. Does it make sense to model an Enterprise Bean (component) of type Bankaccount with the goal of modeling a basis for specialized derivations? A component that models a collective notion? Such a component would then have to be an abstract component, since there would be no sense in using it at run time. What would the deployment descriptor of an abstract component look like? A complicating factor is that the notion of component inheritance is not well defined. Nor, moreover, is there consensus about what component inheritance should look like.

Since in the specification of Enterprise JavaBeans component inheritance is expressly not supported, there cannot be a useful inheritance at the Enterprise Bean level. The reason for this is to be found in the create and find methods of the home interface of an Enterprise Bean. If there were an (abstract) Enterprise Bean Bankaccount, one could not use its create method to generate a Savingsaccount bean. In this case the bank account cannot serve as a factory to generate derived classes. But what purpose does a create method of an abstract component serve, if not for the generation of derived components?

The problem with the find methods is similar. Let us suppose that the home interface of the bank account bean possesses a find method that returns all accounts with a negative balance. If one calls this method, one can be certain that the set of results contains only checking and foreign currency accounts. Savings accounts cannot have a negative balance, and the bank does not offer any accounts of type *Bankaccount*. A list is to be created to notify the owners of the overdrawn accounts returned by this find method. With the checking accounts an overdraft charge is to be computed. The EJB container, which is responsible for the instantiation of Enterprise Beans and their remote interface implementations, would then generate instances of type Bankaccount, since the find method was called on the home interface of the bank account bean. No instances of type checking account or foreign currency account would be generated, since it knows nothing about inheritance relations. There is also no way to provide it with this knowledge. To call a method on an element of the set of results would be dangerous, since the specialized functionality of the derived Enterprise Bean types is unavailable. Particular methods like the calculation of the overdraft fee are completely unavailable. A type casting would lead to an exception, since the EJB container has actually generated nothing but Bankaccount instances. Polymorphism would be possible only if the EJB container knew about the inheritance relation. It would then generate the actual types of Enterprise Beans and their remote interface implementations, which then would appear to the client in the result set as all of type Bankaccount. The client would then be able to execute a type casting or to determine the actual type of the account with the help of the instanceof operator.

In a certain sense, an Enterprise Bean can be polymorphic. An interface Bankaccount could serve as the basis for the remote interface of special Enterprise Bean types. Then savings, checking, or foreign currency accounts could be treated together as bank accounts. For purposes of reusability an abstract class Bankaccount could be modeled from which the Enterprise Bean classes of the other account types inherit. Such a process is specifically approved by the specification. To model an Enterprise Bean Bankaccount from which the specialized Enterprise Beans inherit would be sensible only if actual accounts could be used polymorphically over their find and create methods. But as already mentioned, there is no support for this in the specification.

An alternative to inheritance with components is the development of configurable components. In the example that we have described, a (concrete) Enterprise Bean Bankaccount could be developed that contained, according to its configuration, a savings account, checking account, or foreign currency account. Through the development of configurable components a certain sort of polymorphism can be achieved. This polymorphism does not, however, refer to the type of the component, but to the configuration values of the particular instance. To implement such a component, a framework can be set up that is built on class inheritance. Figure 9-11 represents such an architecture schematically.

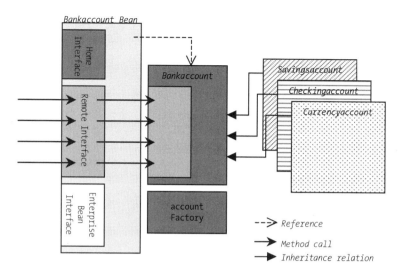

Figure 9-11. Architecture of a configurable component.

The class Bankaccount is an abstract base class that provides the methods of the remote interface of the Enterprise Bean Bankaccount. Derived from this are the concrete classes Savingsaccount, Checkingaccount, and Currencyaccount. When the bank account bean is initialized in one of the methods of the Enterprise Bean interface, it reads its configuration, for example, from the bean environment. It relays its configuration to an instance of the class AccountFactory, which selects a bank account implementation that is suitable for the configuration (savings, checking, or foreign currency). The AccountFactory class generates an instance and initializes it according to the configuration. This mechanism could also be provided with the necessary information using the persistent data of the particular account instead of the configuration data from the environment. The Enterprise Bean Bankaccount contains a reference to the instance of the particular account generated by the account factory. All calls to the methods of the remote interface are then delegated to this instance.

Through such an architecture the component remains clearly structured and easily extendible. It is assumed that a reasonable collection of methods of the remote interface can be defined for the various types. Through this process component inheritance can be gotten around quite elegantly. The component preserves its black-box character, while internally it uses a framework (white box) to achieve the requisite flexibility. The find and create methods of the home interface are fully usable. Polymorphism arises not through the type of the component, but through the values bound to a particular instance. The behavior of the component is determined corresponding to these instance-oriented values. The client could determine the actual type of a bank account through, say, a method getAccountType of the remote interface instead of with the instanceof operator. Particular methods of the remote interface could, moreover, be callable only for particular account types. The particular methods could demonstrate this, for example, through throwing an exception of type IllegalOperationException. However, from the documentation of the component it must be clear for which account types these methods may be called.

Configurable components that use class and interface inheritance internally in connection with a framework for necessary flexibility are an alternative to component inheritance that should be taken seriously. Complete support for inheritance in the component model of Enterprise JavaBeans would significantly increase their complexity. The container would have to be notified of the inheritance relation, in that the inheritance structure would have to be described declaratively in the deployment descriptor. In the case of entity beans, the persistence brings additional complexity. Component inheritance would also have an effect on the persistence manager. It, too, would have to know about the inheritance relation in order to be able to set the affected tables in proper relation to one another. Furthermore, it would have to enable the formulation of search requests for polymorphic components. The additional run-time overhead in the use of finder methods in the EJB container would detract from performance. For each element of the result set, the actual type would have to be determined. There remains the question of whether such additional complexity is justified by the increased usefulness.

Finally, we would like to point out the implementations of inheritance in the component model in [6] and [33], as well as the implementations of bean inheritance in [10].

Enterprise JavaBeans and Events

Events are occurrences that are understood as objects of particular event classes. Events can be used to inform about the arrival in particular states or the execution of particular actions. The Java AWT (Abstract Windowing Toolkit), for example, generates objects of type MouseEvent when a user executes an action with the mouse (mouse click, mouse movement) on the interface. In the JavaBeans model a PropertyChangeEvent object is generated by a bean whenever an attribute of the bean is changed. This event object is transmitted to other objects that are interested in such events. This type of event handling is called the delegation event model. An event pool offers interested parties (listeners) the opportunity to register for particular events. If such an event occurs, then an event object is generated from the event pool and transmitted to all registered listeners. The event pool thus does not deal with the event itself, but delegates the handling of the event to the listener objects.

As mentioned already in this chapter, an event model for the dynamic coupling of Enterprise Bean components would be desirable. What is frequently missed in the development of EJB-based applications is the ability to relay events from server to client. For example, a bookkeeping application that is used in parallel on a number of client computers wishes to be informed about the establishment or deletion of accounts in order to notify the user or to make its views current. For such cases one needs a particular event mechanism, namely, a distributed one. Since Enterprise Beans act in another process as the objects of the client application, the event (the event object) must be transported across process boundaries.

Versions 2.0 and 2.1 of the EJB specification allow for neither a local event mechanism for coupling of Enterprise Beans nor a distributed event mechanism for communication with other processes. What is does allow, however, is the integration of the Java Message Service.

In this section we wish to introduce a conception of distributed events in which objects of a remote client register themselves as interested parties (listeners) and over which Enterprise Beans can send event objects whenever a particular event occurs. Since the Java Message Service is specialized to asynchronous communication between processes over a network, it offers the ideal basis for such an implementation. A comparable mechanism can also support message-driven beans as event listeners. Session and entity beans cannot be used as event listeners.

In our implementation we will make the following assumptions:

- The solution should above all enable session and entity beans to transmit events across process boundaries. The beans will thus support the remote client view.

- An event should be relayed in the form of a lightweight Java object.

- An Enterprise Bean is not allowed to be capable of receiving events.

- The quality of message transmittal in this event mechanism should be low. That is, the sender of an event obtains no guarantee and no confirmation of an event object having reached the receivers.

- A sent message is relayed to all registered listeners, with the order of messages sent being random.

- The state of the event service (the registered listeners) should not be stored in the Enterprise Bean itself if possible, since that can result in conflicts with the life cycle management of the EJB container.

Figure 9-12 represents the implementation schematically. For each client process there is an EJBEventManager object available. The event manager offers listeners the possibility of registering over a particular interface for Enterprise Bean events. The event manager is in turn registered as recipient of the topic EJBEvents from the Java Message Service. If an Enterprise Bean wishes to trigger an event to inform one or more clients about a particular occurrence, it packages it into an EJBEvent object in an object of type javax.jms.ObjectMessage and sends it to the topic EJBEvents. The Enterprise Bean acts here like a normal (sending) JMS client. The JMS provider ensures that the message is transmitted to all recipients registered for this topic. The event manager receives the message, takes the EJBEvent object from the message, and distributes it to all registered parties (see Figure 9-13).

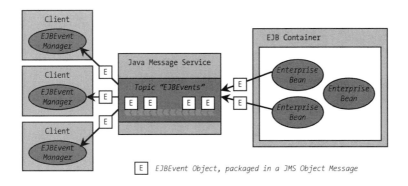

Figure 9-12. Distributed event service via Java Message Service.

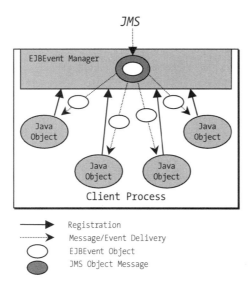

Figure 9-13. Process-internal communication with the event manager.

Various participants and implementations for the distributed event service for informing clients can be derived from this situation, and we shall discuss this more fully in the sequel.

The Event

Listing 9-9 defines the EJB event class.

Listing 9-9. Class EJBevent.

```
package ejb.event;

import javax.ejb.Handle;

public class EJBEvent implements java.io.Serializable {

    private int eventType;
    private Handle eventSource;

    public EJBEvent(int type) {
        this(type, null);
    }

    public EJBEvent(int type, Handle source) {
        eventSource = source;
        eventType = type;
    }

    public Handle getEventSource() {
        return eventSource;
    }

    public int getEventType() {
        return eventType;
    }

}
```

The class EJBEvent represents events that have occurred. The event can be identified via the attribute eventType. The attribute eventSource makes it possible to identify the trigger of the event. This attribute is of type javax.ejb.Handle. Via the handle the client is able to address the Enterprise Bean that triggered the event. Only message-driven beans possess no handle, since they cannot be directly addressed by a client. If message-driven beans should also be able to trigger EJB events, then the clients must be prepared for the fact that the attribute eventSource can assume the value null. An enterprise bean could also use a class derived from EJBEvent to send an event to the client. With derived classes the information content of an event is increased. Thus, for example, an event class NewAccountEvent (derived from NewAccountEvent) could provide information about the opening of a new account. Additionally, the NewAccountEvent class could possess an attribute accountNumber that informs the client of the account number of the newly opened account.

The Event Listener

Listing 9-10 defines the interface EJBEventListener.

Listing 9-10. The interface EJBEventListener.

```
package ejb.event;
public interface EJBEventListener {
    public void notify(EJBEvent event);

}
```

The class of an object that is interested in Enterprise Bean events must have implemented this interface to be able to register with the event manager as a listener. If an event occurs, the method notify() is called on a registered object, and the event object is passed as parameter.

The Trigger of Events

Events are triggered by Enterprise Beans. They trigger an event by generating an object of type EJBEvent or of a derived type. The Enterprise Bean passes its handle (or null if it is a message-driven bean) to the event object. Depending on the event class, the Enterprise Bean relays additional information to the event object. The event classes as well as the relevant values of an event object can be set arbitrarily by an application. If the application uses only the base class EJBEvent, then a central class or a central interface should be used in which values for the various event types are defined in the form of public constants.

To facilitate the triggering of EJBEvents for the Enterprise Bean, one could provide an auxiliary class, as shown in Listing 9-11.

Listing 9-11. The class EJBEventHelper.

```
package ejb.event;

import javax.jms.JMSException;
import javax.jms.ObjectMessage;
import javax.jms.Session;
import javax.jms.Topic;
import javax.jms.TopicConnection;
import javax.jms.TopicConnectionFactory;
import javax.jms.TopicPublisher;
import javax.jms.TopicSession;
import javax.naming.NamingException;
import ejb.util.Lookup;

public class EJBEventHelper {

    public static final String FACTORY =
        "java:/env/jms/DefaultConnectionFactory";
    public static final String TOPIC_NAME =
        "java:/env/jms/EJBEvents";

    private static TopicConnectionFactory topicCF = null;
    private static Topic ejbEvent = null;

    public EJBEventHelper()
        throws NamingException
    {
        topicCF = (TopicConnectionFactory)Lookup.get(FACTORY);
        ejbEvent = (Topic)Lookup.get(TOPIC_NAME);
    }

    public void fireEvent(EJBEvent event)
        throws JMSException
    {
        if(event == null) {
            throw new
              IllegalArgumentException("event must not be null!");
        }
        TopicConnection tc = null;
        TopicSession ts = null;
        TopicPublisher tpub = null;
```

```
        try {
            tc = topicCF.createTopicConnection();
            ts = tc.createTopicSession(false,
                                    Session.AUTO_ACKNOWLEDGE);
            tpub = ts.createPublisher(ejbEvent);
            ObjectMessage om = ts.createObjectMessage();
            om.setObject(event);
            tpub.publish(om);
        } finally {
            try { tpub.close(); } catch(Exception ex) {}
            try { ts.close(); } catch(Exception ex) {}
            try { tc.close(); } catch(Exception ex) {}
        }
    }
}
```

An Enterprise Bean BankAccount could inform the clients with the following code fragment dealing with the creation of a new bank account:

```
Handle h = theContext.getEJBObject().getHandle();
EJBEvent event = new EJBEvent(EventTypes.NEW_ACCOUNT, h);
EJBEventHelper helper = new EJBEventHelper();
helper.fireEvent(event);
```

Since the Java Message Service operates asynchronously, the Enterprise Bean will not be blocked for an unnecessarily long time by the triggering of an event. While the Enterprise Bean continues its processing, the JMS provider concerns itself with delivering the message, and the event manager is concerned with the distribution of the event to the listeners.

The Event Manager

Listing 9-12 defines the class EJBEventManager.

Listing 9-12. The class EJBEventManager.

```
package ejb.event;

import java.util.List;
import javax.ejb.EnterpriseBean;
import javax.jms.JMSException;
import javax.jms.Message;
```

```java
import javax.jms.MessageListener;
import javax.jms.ObjectMessage;
import javax.jms.Session;
import javax.jms.Topic;
import javax.jms.TopicConnection;
import javax.jms.TopicConnectionFactory;
import javax.jms.TopicSubscriber;
import javax.jms.TopicSession;
import javax.naming.NamingException;
import ejb.util.Lookup;

public class EJBEventManager implements MessageListener {

    public static final String FACTORY =
        "java:/env/jms/DefaultConnectionFactory";
    public static final String TOPIC_NAME =
        "java:/env/jms/EJBEvents";

    private static EJBEventManager theInstance = null;
    private static TopicConnectionFactory tcFactory = null;
    private static Topic ejbEvents = null;

    private TopicConnection tConnection = null;
    private TopicSession tSession = null;
    private TopicSubscriber tSub = null;
    private List tListeners = null;

    static {
        try {
            tcFactory = (TopicConnectionFactory) Lookup.get(FACTORY);
            ejbEvents = (Topic)Lookup.get(TOPIC_NAME);
            theInstance = new EJBEventManager();
        } catch(NamingException nex) {
            nex.printStackTrace();
            throw new IllegalStateException(nex.getMessage());
        }
    }

    private EJBEventManager() {
        tListeners = new java.util.ArrayList();
    }

    public synchronized void
            addEJBEventListener(EJBEventListener listener)
    {
        if(listener instanceof EnterpriseBean) {
            throw new
                IllegalArgumentException("beans are not allowed!");
        }
```

```
        if(tListeners.isEmpty()) {
            connect();
        }
        if(!tListeners.contains(listener)) {
            tListeners.add(listener);
        }
    }
    public synchronized void
            removeEJBEventListener(EJBEventListener listener)
    {
        tListeners.remove(listener);
        if(tListeners.isEmpty()) {
            disconnect();
        }
    }
    public static EJBEventManager getInstance() {
        return theInstance;
    }
    private void connect() {
        try {
            tConnection = tcFactory.createTopicConnection();
            tSession =
                tConnection.createTopicSession(
                    false,
                    Session.AUTO_ACKNOWLEDGE);
            tSub = tSession.createSubscriber(ejbEvents);
            tSub.setMessageListener(this);
            tConnection.start();
        } catch(JMSException jmsex) {
            jmsex.printStackTrace();
            throw new IllegalStateException(jmsex.getMessage());
        }
    }
    private void disconnect() {
        try {
            tConnection.stop();
            tSub.close();
            tSession.close();
            tConnection.close();
        } catch(JMSException jmsex) {
            jmsex.printStackTrace();
            throw new IllegalStateException(jmsex.getMessage());
        }
```

```
        }
        public void onMessage(Message msg) {
            EJBEvent event = null;
            try {
                event = (EJBEvent)((ObjectMessage)msg).getObject();
            } catch(ClassCastException ccex) {
                ccex.printStackTrace();
                System.err.println("expected ObjectMessage!");
                return;
            } catch(JMSException jmsex) {
                jmsex.printStackTrace();
                return;
            }
            EJBEventListener l = null;
            if(event == null) {
                return;
            }
            for(int i = 0; i < tListeners.size(); i++) {
                l = (EJBEventListener)tListeners.get(i);
                l.notify(event);
            }
        }
    }
}
```

The class EJBEventManager is implemented according to the singleton pattern (see [5]). The singleton pattern ensures that there can exist only one instance of this class in a Java process. In the case of the event manager this ensures that JMS resources are used sparingly. Since the constructor is given the attribute private, only the class itself can generate instances. The instance of the event manager is generated in the class's static initializer. This is executed once, after the class is loaded. There the event manager obtains a reference to the topic connection factory as well as to the topic over which events are to be distributed.

Clients obtain access to the instance of the event manager over the static method getInstance. They are able to register for events as listeners via the method addEJBEventListener. This method also ensures that no Enterprise Beans can register as listeners for events. If an Enterprise Bean were able to register as a listener, upon receipt of a message the event manager would call a method on the Enterprise Bean instance without the EJB container being able to monitor this. This situation would represent a significant strike against the specification. Event listeners can unregister via the method removeEJBEventListener. The event manager registers as recipient of a topic only when the first listener has registered. When the last listener has unregistered, the event manager automatically closes the connection to the topic. Thus the JMS provider does not deliver messages unnecessarily. As already mentioned in Chapter 6, messages distributed over a topic are delivered only to those recipients who at the time are registered as recipients.

If an Enterprise Bean triggers an event, the event manager instance is sent a message by the JMS provider by a call to the method onMessage. The event manager removes the event object from the message and distributes it to the listeners registered with it by calling the method notify on the interface EJBEventListener.

The Client

Listing 9-13 shows how a client would use the event manager to receive events triggered by Enterprise Beans.

Listing 9-13. Class EJBEventManager *client.*

```
package ejb.event;
public class Client implements EJBEventListener {
    ...
    public Client() {
        ...
    }
    public void init() {
        ...
        EJBEventManager em = EJBEventManager.getInstance();
        em.addEJBEventListener(this);
        ...
    }
    public void shutdown() {
        ...
        EJBEventManager em = EJBEventManager.getInstance();
        em.removeEJBEventListener(this);
        ...
    }
    public void notify(EJBEvent event) {
        switch(event.getEventType()) {
            case EventTypes.NEW_ACCOUNT: ...
            case EventTypes.REMOVE_ACCOUNT: ...
        }
    }
    ...
}
```

The client registers at initialization time (in our example, in the method `init`) as a listener for events. If an Enterprise Bean triggers an event, it is sent via the JMS provider to the event manager, which relays it to registered listeners by a call to the method `notify`. In the method `notify` the client evaluates the event object and triggers the appropriate actions. At termination of the client (in the example, in the method `shutdown`) it unregisters as an event listener.

To increase the information content of an event one could, as mentioned previously, create subclasses of the class `EJBEvent`. Furthermore, registration could be divided into categories. That is, listeners could register with the event manager for particular event types only. For this, the methods `addEJBEventListener` and `removeEJBEventListener` would have to be extended to include the attribute event class. Then a listener would no longer have to receive all events, but only those events in whose type it was truly interested.

Internet Connection

This section deals with the ins and outs of web-based EJB clients. We will look at two conceptually quite different approaches. Since we are dealing with a special form of the client view, which we have already considered in some detail, we shall not go further into the implementation details. It seems to us important, nevertheless, to discuss the need for a web client and its implications.

Originally, simple services were offered over the Internet (e-mail, FTP, HTML publishing), but today, complex transactions are carried out over this medium (for example, Internet banking). Security in a variety of forms (access security, consistency of data, etc.) plays an important role. The developer of web-based applications is confronted with a multiplicity of technical challenges.

As a basis for communication, HTTP (hypertext transfer protocol), which is primitive in comparison to other protocols, remains available for a browser's communication with an HTTP server. It is stateless and supports only a very limited number of operations. A (standard) HTTP server has no persistence interface, no application framework, and no transaction monitor, which is as it should be, since HTTP was developed not as a communications basis for transaction-oriented web-based application systems, but for the transfer of hypertext files (that is, files that contain HTML pages).

The technology for the implementation of applications runs from server-side C programs, Perl, Python, and Unix shell scripts (which are addressed over the CGI interface of an HTTP server) to proprietary HTTP server extensions (such as the NSAPI for the Netscape HTTP server and the ISAPI for Microsoft's Internet information server). And then there are servlets (CGI for Java) and technologies for server-side dynamic generation of HTML pages (active server pages from Microsoft and Java server pages from Sun). Many providers of databases offer HTTP interfaces for their products, where the database server can act directly as a web server and also web pages can be generated dynamically via proprietary APIs from the databases for the representation and modification of data. On the client side, pure HTML, dynamic HTML (Javascript), Java applets, and proprietary browser interfaces and libraries can be used.

Each of the above-named technologies has its purpose in particular application areas. Nevertheless, there is a serious problem in all this specialization. In the pioneer days of the Internet (which are not quite at an end even now), many web applications were originally planned as local solutions to small problems, but they soon developed into applications implemented throughout an entire enterprise. This development resulted in greatly changed demands on the application, and the technology chosen for the implementation did not always have the required flexibility. Today, many web applications possess a crucial importance for the success of an enterprise. The architecture of these applications should reflect their importance.

An application server is available as a platform that offers various services (persistence, user management, transactions, etc.), various communications protocols (HTTP, HTTPS, RMI, IIOP, etc.), and an EJB container. It offers all the capabilities that are expected today from a reliable application platform, which are nonetheless lacking in a (standard) HTTP server. Moreover, the technology portfolio is limited, which has a positive effect on maintainabilty and reusability. It is precisely the security mechanisms of the programming language Java (see also Chapter 2) that are at an advantage in the Internet arena. In Chapters 2 and 3 we mentioned that Sun Mircrosystems takes this into account through the Java 2 platform Enterprise Edition.

Frequently, native clients of an application system are extended (or even replaced) by web clients to make applications usable over the Internet (for example, so that one can use such enterprise applications as business expense calculation and recording of working hours). Likewise, applications are developed particularly with the Internet in mind (for example, e-commerce applications). One might also imagine applications based on web technologies operating in an intranet, such as for personnel without a fixed work place. Furthermore, this could reduce costs for installation and updating of client software. Often, however, limited, fast, and easy-to-implement alternative versions of applications are offered (for example, a simple working hours logging program for personnel who work on an hourly basis, or infoterminals for quick access to attendance lists, quality statistics in manufacturing, flextime balance, etc.).

We would like to discuss two approaches for the implementation of a web client for applications based on Enterprise JavaBeans that are quite different conceptually, but are both conceived for the Java 2 platform, Enterprise Edition. One of these involves an applet-based web client, the other, a purely HTML client that is supported by the servlet technology.

Java Applets

A client applet sent to the client embedded in an HTML page by the server using the HTTP protocol offers the user an interface of the type to which he or she is already accustomed from proprietary clients (see Figure 9-14). The look and feel and user prompting of an applet-based client reflect those of traditional applications. As soon as it is loaded, the applet generally communicates directly with the application server. The implementation of the applet is not much different from that of a normal client. With an applet, one must pay attention to the size of the generated code in order to minimize the download time. An applet and a normal client are able to share large parts of the implementation. In the extreme case, the applet and the native client can be identical (an applet can be relatively easily transformed into an application). What can be problematic in this scenario is the use of the Java 2 platform. Current browsers support only JDK 1.1, though they can be adapted to Java 2 with plug-ins. Because of this limitation, applets are most successfully used in controlled deployment environments such as corporate intranets.

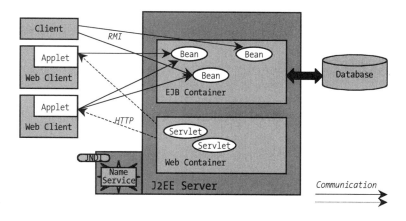

Figure 9-14. Internet connection with applets.

HTML and Servlets

As an alternative to an applet, one can use a pure HTML client (see Figure 9-15). On the server side a servlet (see [18]) is used to execute Enterprise Bean calls resulting from client requests and to generate HTML pages dynamically for the representation of results and the receipt of user input. This approach has the advantage over the applet solution of avoiding long download times for the applet code. Furthermore, the browser does not have to support Java. Thus the problem of users who have deactivated Java support on their browsers due to security concerns is also eliminated.

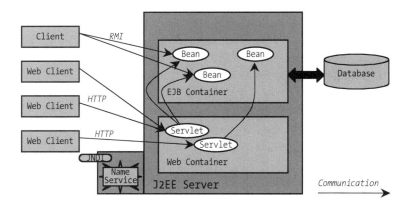

Figure 9-15. Internet connection with servlets.

HTML clients do not have the typical look and feel or the user prompting of a traditional application (determined by the server roundtrip, typical of HTML, in order to update the view after a user action). With the use of pictures the appearance can be greatly customized. A further significant difference between the two approaches is in the management of the state of an application. The applet, like the native client, can save the state until the next call of a server-side operation (for example, to collect user input data, manage undo lists, store references to Enterprise Beans) and in general communicate directly with the application server. A pure HTML client cannot store a state. It must rely on the support of the servlet. An HTML page in a browser contains only information about representation and no logic (ignoring here the use of client-side Java scripts). The servlet makes the logic available to arbitrarily many browsers. The servlet then has the following tasks:

- Manage the states of all clients that use it in parallel;

- Receive requests from the browser;

- Relate the requests to a session (that is, to a particular application state);

- Execute the requests of Enterprise Bean calls;

- Generate for the browser as reply a new HTML page (which represents the results of the bean call).

The issues discussed in this section apply equally well to the use of Java server pages (JSP) (see [18]). Java server pages are based on the servlet architecture and thus obey the same behavioral principles.

Summary

The two approaches are fundamentally different and to a certain extent represent opposite poles. Through the use of other technologies and combinations of them (for example, client or server-side JavaScript, proprietary browser interfaces) one can conceive of an infinite variety of approaches. What is important here is that an existing system based on Enterprise JavaBeans can be extended relatively easily through web-based clients. The implementation effort for the web client is then relatively little if during implementation of the application system one keeps in mind a consistent realization of the three-tier architecture (see Chapter 2). In this case, the entire functionality and application logic are available in the form of Enterprise Beans. Only the view scenarios of thin clients must be developed anew. For applications that are developed exclusively for Internet use (e-commerce applications) Enterprise JavaBeans is also a platform of interest. With Enterprise JavaBeans it is possible to achieve high quality, security, and maintainability in Internet applications relatively easily. Furthermore, developers do not have to be experts in Internet technologies (these are needed only for development of client scenarios).

Finally, one should not forget the fact that security considerations become significantly more important when an application is opened to an intranet or internet. Encrypted data transfer between web client and application server, a firewall concept, and various other security mechanisms should be considered as an extension of the security requirements described in the Enterprise JavaBeans specification.

Entity Beans and Details Objects

The fundamentals of entity beans were discussed in Chapter 5. In this section we consider a particular aspect of the use of entity beans.

Based on performance considerations, it is useful to change the data of an entity bean using interfaces that permit bulk data operations. To this end, the data of an entity bean are collected in a single class. Sun Microsystems recommends this technique in a publication of the J2EE blueprint (see [27]). Classes that collect the data of an entity bean are generally identified by adding the word "details" or "value" to their names. As an example, let us take the entity bean Part, which models a part in a production system and which supports the remote client view. Such a part has the attributes part number, part description, name of the supplier,

and price of the part. Listing 9-14 shows the home interface of the Enterprise
Bean Part.

Listing 9-14. Interface PartHome.

```
package ejb.part;

import java.rmi.RemoteException;
import javax.ejb.EJBHome;
import javax.ejb.CreateException;
import javax.ejb.FinderException;

public interface PartHome extends EJBHome {

    public Part create(String partNumber)
        throws CreateException, RemoteException;

    public Part findByPrimaryKey(String partNumber)
        throws FinderException, RemoteException;

}
```

A part is identified by its part number. This is assigned when a new entity
is generated. The part number serves as primary key, and it is possible to locate
particular parts with the part number. Listing 9-15 shows the remote interface of
the Part bean.

Listing 9-15. Interface Part.

```
package ejb.part;

import java.rmi.RemoteException;
import javax.ejb.EJBObject;

public interface Part extends EJBObject {

    public void setPartDetails(PartDetails pd)
        throws RemoteException;

    public PartDetails getPartDetails()
        throws RemoteException;

}
```

Instead of a large number of get/set methods for each attribute of the entity
bean, the remote interface exhibits precisely one get method and exactly one set
method. As parameter and return value there is an object of type PartDetails,
which contains all the attributes of the entity bean. All attributes of the Enterprise
Bean are transmitted bundled, which results in greater efficiency, since for the

transmission of attributes only one network access is required. Listing 9-16 shows the implementation of the class `PartDetails`.

Listing 9-16. Class PartDetails.

```
package ejb.part;
public class PartDetails implements java.io.Serializable {
    String partNumber;
    String partDescription;
    String supplierName;
    float price;
    public PartDetails() {
    }
    public String getPartNumber() {
        return partNumber;
    }
    public void setPartDescription(String desc) {
        partDescription = desc;
    }
    public String getPartDescription() {
        return partDescription;
    }
    public void setSupplierName(String name) {
        supplierName = name;
    }
    public String getSupplierName() {
        return supplierName;
    }
    public void setPrice(float p) {
        price = p;
    }
    public float getPrice() {
        return price;
    }
}
```

For the client, the attributes of the Enterprise Bean are transmitted in a `PartDetails` object into which they have been collected, and the client calls the associated getter/setter methods on the `PartDetails` object instead of on the Enterprise Bean. It can change the attributes and then transmit them bundled back to the Enterprise Bean to execute the changes. Usually, some simple plausibility checks are made in the get/set methods of a details object. For example, in many cases null is not permitted to be passed as a parameter, or integer values are required to fall within certain limits. This way of proceeding has the advantage that errors can be detected before data are transmitted to the Enterprise Bean. Often, it is difficult to determine the boundary between plausibility checks and business logic; that is, it is difficult to determine which implementations belong to the details object and which to the class of the Enterprise Bean.

Listing 9-17 shows the implementation of the Enterprise Bean class.

Listing 9-17. Class PartBean.

```
package ejb.part;
import javax.ejb.*;
public abstract class PartBean implements EntityBean {
    private EntityContext theContext;
    private PartDetails theDetails;
    /** Creates new PartBean */
    public PartBean() {}
    //The create method of the home interface
    public String ejbCreate(String partNumber)
        throws CreateException
    {
        setPartNumber(partNumber);
        theDetails = new PartDetails();
        theDetails.partNumber = partNumber;
        return null;
    }

    public void ejbPostCreate(String partNumber)
        throws CreateException
    {}
    //Abstract getter/setter methods
    public abstract void setPartNumber(String num);
    public abstract String getPartNumber();
    public abstract void setPartDescription(String desc);
    public abstract String getPartDescription();
    public abstract void setSupplierName(String name);
    public abstract String getSupplierName();
    public abstract void setPrice(float p);
    public abstract float getPrice();
```

```
    //The method of the remote interface
    public void setPartDetails(PartDetails pd) {
        setPartDescription(pd.getPartDescription());
        setSupplierName(pd.getSupplierName());
        setPrice(pd.getPrice());
        theDetails = pd;
    }

    public PartDetails getPartDetails() {
        return theDetails;
    }
    //The methods of the javax.ejb.EntityBean interface
    public void setEntityContext(EntityContext ctx) {
        theContext = ctx;
    }

    public void unsetEntityContext() {
        theContext = null;
    }

    public void ejbRemove()
        throws RemoveException
    {}
    public void ejbActivate() {
    }

    public void ejbPassivate() {
    }

    public void ejbLoad() {
        if(theDetails == null) {
            theDetails = new PartDetails();
        }
        theDetails.setPartNumber = this.getPartNumber();
        theDetails.setPartDescription =
                            this.getPartDescription();
        theDetails.setSupplierName = this.getSupplierName();
        theDetails.setPrice = this.getPrice();
    }
    public void ejbStore() {
    }
}
```

The Enterprise Bean contains a reference to a `PartDetails` object. This is returned when the client requests the attributes of the Enterprise Bean via the method `getPartDetails`. If the client wishes to change the attributes of the Enterprise Bean, the reference with the new details object is overwritten. When the Enterprise Bean is first generated, the details object contains only the part number. The client gradually provides the Enterprise Bean with the remaining data. Each time the client changes the attributes of the Enterprise Bean, the values are taken from the details object and relayed to the get/set methods, so that the persistence manager can see to the storage of the changed values. If an existing `Part` bean is loaded, then a new `PartDetails` object is generated and provided with the appropriate values.

The process just described is recommended by the J2EE blueprint. Here there is an important feature related to the remote client view that we would like to discuss in the remainder of this section.

Suppose that a database contains the product part indicated in Table 9-4.

Table 9-4. Original data of the `Part` *bean.*

Part Number	Description	Provider	Price
0815	housing	Provider A	$1.50

Let us further assume that there is an application for managing product parts. Two users wish to use this application to change part 0815. Figure 9-16 shows this situation.

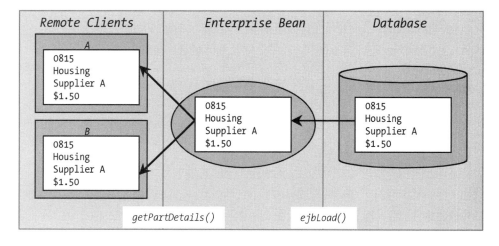

Figure 9-16. Use of a details object.

The Enterprise Bean contains a copy of the data from the database; the remote clients contain their own copies of the data in the form of a details object. Suppose that client A changes the supplier to "Supplier C" and stores the data. The altered details object is relayed to the Enterprise Bean, the attributes of the Enterprise Bean are adjusted, and the persistence manager stores the data in the database. Then client B changes the price from $1.50 to $1.60 and stores those data as well. In this case as well, the altered details object of client B is transmitted to the Enterprise Bean, which adjusts the attributes of the Enterprise Bean, which then are stored by the persistence manager in the database. The expected status of the database is shown in Table 9-5.

Table 9-5. Expected data of the `Part` *bean after change.*

Part Number	Description	Provider	Price
0815	housing	Provider C	$1.60

But in fact, the actual data are as shown in Table 9-6.

Table 9-6. Actual data of the `Part` *bean after change.*

Part Number	Description	Provider	Price
0815	housing	**Provider A**	$1.60

Client B has overwritten client A's changes, because both had their own copies of the details object, and client B knew nothing about the previous changes made by client A. Such a situation can arise when client A is a user from the purchasing department and is allowed to make changes only to suppliers. Client B could be an employee in the auditing department who is allowed to change only prices. If the Enterprise Bean had separate get/set methods, the state of the database would be as one had expected. Client A would have changed only the supplier, and client B would have changed only the price. However, because of the use of details objects, a client can only change all the attributes of an Enterprise Bean at once. For this reason, we get the behavior just described. Whether this behavior is acceptable depends on the situation. In this section we will show some alternatives that can keep this undesirable situation from arising.

The class `PartDetails` could be programmed to notice the changes made by the client. For this to happen, a flag would have to be defined for each attribute (for example, in the form of a Boolean variable or through a bit field where each bit represents the state of change of a particular attribute). If the attributes of the Enterprise Bean are reset, then only those attributes are overwritten that have actually been changed in the details object. With this solution one must be sure that the flags are reset after a successful change has been effected. This solution is relatively simple to implement. The integrity of the data is endangered, however, if the flags in the details object are not reset, or not reset at the correct time.

An alternative solution could involve the Enterprise Bean Part triggering an event via a mechanism like the one described in the previous section when data are changed. All currently active clients would receive the event and would know that their local copy of the PartDetails had become invalid. A change to the data without previous updating of the details object would mean that a previous change could be overwritten. This process would be easy to implement, but in an extreme case could lead to high network traffic between the server and the client. This holds especially when this mechanism is used generally with entity beans to avoid conflicts in data storage. This mechanism would be unworkable if the client ignored the event or for some reason had not yet received the event.

Another solution would be to add a time stamp to the class PartDetails. We will look at this alternative in detail and to this end employ a new class, TsPartDetails. Listing 9-18 shows the implementation of this class. The differences between this class and the class PartDetails are shown in boldface.

Listing 9-18. Class TsPartDetails.

```
package ejb.part;
public class TsPartDetails implements java.io.Serializable {
    String partNumber;
    String partDescription;
    String supplierName;
    float price;
    private long timestamp = 0;

    TsPartDetails() {
    }

    public boolean isOutDated(TsPartDetails details) {
        return details.timestamp < this.timestamp;
    }

    void updateTimestamp(javax.ejb.EntityContext ctx,
                         long tt)
    {
        if(ctx == null) {
            throw new IllegalStateException("ctx == null");
        }
        timestamp = tt;
    }
```

```
    public String getPartNumber() {
        return partNumber;
    }

    public void setPartDescription(String desc) {
        partDescription = desc;
    }

    public String getPartDescription() {
        return partDescription;
    }



    public void setSupplierName(String name) {
        supplierName = name;
    }

    public String getSupplierName() {
        return supplierName;
    }

    public void setPrice(float p) {
        price = p;
    }

    public float getPrice() {
        return price;
    }

    public String toString() {
      StringBuffer sb = new StringBuffer("[[TsPartDetails]");
      sb.append("partNumber=").append(partNumber)
        .append(";");
      sb.append("partDescription=").append(partDescription)
        .append(";");
      sb.append("supplierName=").append(supplierName)
        .append(";");
      sb.append("price=").append(price).append(";");
      sb.append("]");
      return sb.toString();
    }

}
```

The Method isOutdated makes it possible to compare two TsPartDetails objects and determine whether the passed object is older than the object to which it is being compared. This method is used later by the Enterprise Bean to determine whether the passed details object is obsolete in comparison with the given object. The method updateTimestamp will be used later by the Enterprise Bean to update the time stamp of the detail object after a change in attributes. An instance of the entity bean context must be passed to the method to ensure that only one entity bean can call this method. A client cannot legally access an object of type javax.ejb.EntityContext. The time stamp is passed as a variable of type long, which contains the time in milliseconds.

The implementation of the method toString, inherited from java.lang.Object, is introduced here, though it will become relevant only later.

Listing 9-19 shows the changed remote interface of the Enterprise Bean Part.

Listing 9-19. Changed interface Part.

```
package ejb.part;

import java.rmi.RemoteException;
import javax.ejb.EJBObject;

public interface Part extends EJBObject {

    public TsPartDetails setPartDetails(TsPartDetails pd)
        throws RemoteException, OutOfDateException;

    public TsPartDetails getPartDetails()
        throws RemoteException;

}
```

The return value of the method setPartDetails is no longer void, but of type TsPartDetails. This is necessary because for reasons of integrity only one entity bean can update the time stamp of the details object. When the setPartDetails method is called, the client passes a copy of the details object (with RMI, objects are generally passed as call by value). The time stamp of the details object referenced by the Enterprise Bean will indeed be updated, but not the time stamp of the detail object that the client references. So that the client will not have to call the method getPartDetails immediately after a successful call to the method setPartDetails in order to obtain possession of a current TsPartDetails object, the updated details object is returned immediately upon a call to the method setPartDetails. In this way a method call on the Enterprise Bean is avoided.

In order for this mechanism to function correctly, the time stamp of the last change must be stored with the data of the Enterprise Bean in the database. Many EJB containers use several instances of an entity bean identity to be able, for example, to execute incoming method calls in parallel running in their own transactions to a product part with, say, number 0815.

Listing 9-20 shows the new class PartBean. The changed parts of the code are shown in boldface.

Listing 9-20. Changed class PartBean.

```
package ejb.part;

import javax.ejb.*;

public abstract class PartBean implements EntityBean {

    private EntityContext theContext = null;
    private TsPartDetails theDetails = null;

    public PartBean() {}

    //The create method of the home interface

    public String ejbCreate(String partNumber)
        throws CreateException
    {
        this.setPartNumber(partNumber);
        theDetails = new TsPartDetails();
        theDetails.partNumber = partNumber;
        theDetails.partDescription = "";
        theDetails.supplierName = "";
        theDetails.price = 0;
        long tt = System.currentTimeMillis();
        this.setLastModified(tt);
        theDetails.updateTimestamp(theContext, tt);
        return null;
    }

    public void ejbPostCreate(String partNumber)
        throws CreateException
    {}

    //abstract getter/setter methods

    public abstract void setPartNumber(String num);
    public abstract String getPartNumber();
    public abstract void setPartDescription(String desc);
    public abstract String getPartDescription();
    public abstract void setSupplierName(String name);
    public abstract String getSupplierName();
    public abstract void setPrice(float p);
    public abstract float getPrice();
    public abstract long getLastModified();
    public abstract void setLastModified(long tt);

    //the method of the remote interface

    public TsPartDetails setPartDetails(TsPartDetails pd)
        throws OutOfDateException
```

399

```
    {
        if(theDetails.isOutDated(pd)) {
            throw new OutOfDateException();
        }
        this.setPartDescription(pd.getPartDescription());
        this.setSupplierName(pd.getSupplierName());
        this.setPrice(pd.getPrice());
        long tt = System.currentTimeMillis();
        this.setLastModified(tt);
        theDetails = pd;
        theDetails.updateTimestamp(theContext, tt);
        return theDetails;
    }
    public TsPartDetails getPartDetails() {
        return theDetails;
    }
    //the methods of the javax.ejb.EntityBean interface
    public void setEntityContext(EntityContext ctx) {
        theContext = ctx;
    }
    public void unsetEntityContext() {
        theContext = null;
    }
    public void ejbRemove()
        throws RemoveException
    { }
    public void ejbActivate() { }
    public void ejbPassivate() { }
    public void ejbLoad() {
        if(theDetails == null) {
            theDetails = new TsPartDetails();
        }
        theDetails.setPartNumber = this.getPartNumber();
        theDetails.setPartDescription = this.getPartDescription();
        theDetails.setSupplierName = this.getSupplierName();
        theDetails.setPrice = this.getPrice();
        long tt = this.getLastModified();
        theDetails.updateTimestamp(theContext, tt);
    }
    public void ejbStore() { }
}
```

In the method `setPartDetails` the Enterprise Bean first checks whether the passed details object is obsolete. If the passed object is obsolete, the Enterprise Bean triggers an exception of type `OutOfDateException`. Otherwise, the entity bean's data, the detail object's time stamp, and the time stamp of the `Part` bean will be updated. Then the updated details object will be returned to the client. The persistence manager ensures that after the method call the time stamp and other data of the Enterprise Bean are made persistent. The method `ejbCreate` initializes the time stamp, while the method `ejbLoad` sets the time stamp according to the persistent state.

The time stamp is not public data of the `Part` bean. Thus for reasons of efficiency a variable of type `long` is used instead of a data object. The `long` variable contains the time of the last change in milliseconds.

Listing 9-21 shows the deployment descriptor of the `Part` bean.

Listing 9-21. Deployment descriptor of the Part *bean.*

```
<?xml version="1.0" ?>
<ejb-jar version="2.1" xmlns="http://java.sun.com/xml/ns/j2ee"
xmlns:xsi="http://www.w3.org/2001/XMLSchema-instance"
xsi:schemaLocation="http://java.sun.com/xml/ns/j2ee
http://java.sun.com/xml/ns/j2ee/ejb-jar_2_1.xsd">
  <description>
    This deployment descriptor contains information
    about the entity bean Part.
  </description>
  <enterprise-beans>
    <entity>
      <ejb-name>Part</ejb-name>
      <home>ejb.part.PartHome</home>
      <remote>ejb.part.Part</remote>
      <ejb-class>ejb.part.PartBean</ejb-class>
      <persistence-type>Container</persistence-type>
      <prim-key-class>java.lang.String</prim-key-class>
      <reentrant>False</reentrant>
      <cmp-version>2.x</cmp-version>
      <abstract-schema-name>PartBean</abstract-schema-name>
      <cmp-field>
        <description>part number</description>
        <field-name>partNumber</field-name>
      </cmp-field>
```

```xml
          <cmp-field>
            <description>part description</description>
            <field-name>partDescription</field-name>
          </cmp-field>
          <cmp-field>
            <description>part supplier</description>
            <field-name>supplierName</field-name>
          </cmp-field>
          <cmp-field>
            <description>part price</description>
            <field-name>price</field-name>
          </cmp-field>
          <cmp-field>
            <description>time stamp of the last change</description>
            <field-name>lastModified</field-name>
          </cmp-field>
          <primkey-field>partNumber</primkey-field>
      </entity>
    </enterprise-beans>
    <assembly-descriptor>
      <container-transaction>
        <method>
          <ejb-name>Part</ejb-name>
          <method-name>setPartDetails</method-name>
        </method>
        <trans-attribute>Required</trans-attribute>
      </container-transaction>
    </assembly-descriptor>
</ejb-jar>
```

With this solution we have prevented clients from overwriting each other's changes. If the EJB container uses several instances of an Enterprise Bean identity for parallel processing of a method call in various transactions, it synchronizes the various instances through a call to the methods ejbLoad and ejbStore. Since the time stamp is persistent, this mechanism serves for this case as well.

The implementation shown in Listing 9-20 can lead to problems if several application servers are in use and their system clocks are not synchronized. This problem can be avoided if one delegates the allocation of the time stamp to the database, instead of placing it in the code of the Enterprise Bean. Since as a rule, only one database server comes into play, there will be no time conflicts. Another possibility is the use of a *time server*, which the application servers use to synchronize themselves. This ensures that the time is the same on all the server computers.

In certain situations the mechanism with the time stamp can result in a client being unable to store its changes because another client always gets in before it. Moreover, a client will have to implement a relatively complex error handling mechanism for the case of an exception of type OutOfDateException. It must obtain a current details object and attempt to combine the updated data with the user input. If that proves to be impossible, the user's changes will be lost, and the input will have to be repeated. To avoid this situation the mechanism with the time stamp can be extended to include a locking mechanism.

When a client locks an Enterprise Bean, the bean is closed to all other clients for write access. Even if a client is in possession of a current details object, it cannot update the data if another client has locked the Enterprise Bean. There are several ways that one might achieve the implementation of such a locking mechanism. The Enterprise Bean could manage the state of the lock itself, or one could provide a central service for the locking of Enterprise Beans. The lock can be persistent (the lock remains in force even with a restarting of the server) or transient (the lock is removed on restart). Implementing a transient locking mechanism in the code of an Enterprise Bean is certainly the simplest variant. In such a case, caution is advised if this Enterprise Bean is put into service in two different EJB container instances. This could happen if a *server cluster* is used to improve performance. Instead of one EJB container or application server, several identically configured EJB containers or application servers are used that divide up the collection of client requests. An application server or EJB container can process only a limited number of client requests simultaneously. In such a case a transient locking mechanism implemented in the code of an Enterprise Bean is unworkable. In the case of an entity bean the client will not want to lock the Enterprise Bean to itself. Rather, it will want exclusive access to the part number 0815. And in the case of a server cluster this can be available more than once. Even in the case in which the EJB container uses several instances of an entity bean identity to be able to process client requests in separate transactions, a transient locking mechanism implemented in the code of an Enterprise Bean is unworkable. In these cases a more complicated locking mechanism must be implemented.

We shall not go into more detail, on account of the complexity of the subject. However, it should be clear as to what can be achieved with a locking strategy and what issues must be dealt with.

If an Enterprise Bean uses the local instead of the remote client view, then a new problem arises. In the local client view, RMI will be completely ignored, since the (local) clients and the Enterprise Bean are located in the same process. The semantics of passing parameters and return values are no longer call by value, but call by reference. The scenario depicted in Figure 9-16 would look different with the employment of the local client view and unchanged code of the Part bean. There would no longer be three instances of the details object (one per remote client and one referenced by the Enterprise Bean), but only one instance. This one instance would be referenced by the (local) clients and by the Enterprise Bean. If a client changes the details object, then this change also affects the private data of the Enterprise Bean, without a call to the bean interface being implemented. The EJB container also knows nothing of the change. Above all, this has the consequence that the Enterprise Bean could transmit data that do not agree with the current persistent state. To avoid this situation, the Enterprise Bean would have to clone passed details objects before it stores them in an internal reference or outputs them as return value to the client (see Listing 9-22). Then the semantics of the method calls to setPartDetails and getPartDetails in the local client view would be the same as with the remote client view. In this case, the copying of details objects takes place not implicitly through the use of Java RMI, but explicitly via the Enterprise Bean.

Listing 9-22. Cloning in set/getPartDetails.

```
...
    public void setPartDetails(PartDetails pd)
    {
        this.setPartDescription(pd.getPartDescription());
        this.setSupplierName(pd.getSupplierName());
        this.setPrice(pd.getPrice());
        this.theDetails = pd.clone();
    }
    public PartDetails getPartDetails() {
        return this.theDetails.clone();
    }
...
```

To avoid the cloning of details objects, the details class could be conceived is such a way that it no longer has any set methods (see Listing 9-23). The local client would have to generate a new details object before it could change the data of an Enterprise Bean. It would then pass the newly generated details object to the Enterprise Bean in order to change the Enterprise Bean's data. In this way, the local client no longer has access to the private data of the Enterprise Bean. The problem of two clients (local or remote) being able to overwrite each other's changes is not solved by the read-only PartDetails class. It simply creates a new problem, arising from the call by reference semantics, in connection with the local client view.

Listing 9-23. PartDetails *read-only.*

```
package ejb.part;

public class PartDetails implements java.io.Serializable {
    String partNumber;
    String partDescription;
    String supplierName;
    float price;

    public PartDetails(String partNumber,
                       String partDescription,
                       String supplierName,
                       float price)
    {
        this.partNumber = partNumber;
        this.partDescription = partDescription;
        this.supplierName = supplierName;
        this.price = price;
    }

    public String getPartNumber() {
        return partNumber;
    }

    public String getPartDescription() {
        return partDescription;
    }

    public String getSupplierName() {
        return supplierName;
    }

    public float getPrice() {
        return price;
    }
}
```

If one decides to implement details objects in order to achieve optimized data transfer between client and Enterprise Bean, then one must be aware of the consequences. Whether the situation portrayed in this chapter is acceptable depends on the requirements of the application. If the situation is unacceptable, then there are several possibilities for improving things. How far one goes, that is, whether one provides the details object with a time stamp, how complex the error-handling algorithms are for an OutOfDateException exception, whether one introduces a locking strategy, whether one uses transient or persistent locks, whether a central locking service is employed, and so on, depends again on the requirements of the application. In deciding on a particular solution one should always weigh the tradeoffs between the complexity of the implementation and the benefits obtained.

Finally, we would like to refer the reader to Section 10.3 of [7], "Optimistic Locking Pattern."

Quality Assurance

A component should be reusable and be able to be employed in a variety of applications under a variety of conditions. In accomplishing this, the component makes only its interface available, hiding its internal workings. Furthermore, it should be able to be aggregated with other components to form supercomponents or partial applications. A component can meet all of these demands only if the implementation is of sufficiently high quality. A proven tool in quality assurance for software is the use of automated tests. Tests can help in discovering errors in the implementation. With each error removed, the quality of the software improves. Automated tests can also be used for the quality assurance of components.

There are several procedures for finding errors detected by tests. A common method is to use a debugger. A debugger enables the developer to focus on a single process and observe and scrutinize it. During execution one can query the state of variables, and with many debuggers even change them. Another, no less common, procedure is the use of *logging*. By logging is generally meant the output of reports to the computer monitor or to a file. The developer chooses what reports are output, since they are developer-implemented. Usually, information is output by which the sequence of steps executed and the states of variables can be reconstructed. With logging, the developer has essentially the same information available as with the use of debugging software. However, with logging, the developer is dependent on the quality of the logging output in the code of the application. Furthermore, in following the execution of the program using logging data the developer has no opportunity to influence the running of the program. Debugging software permits the developer to stop program execution, run the program step by step, or to jump to a particular point in the code.

The use of debuggers is made difficult with Enterprise JavaBeans because one is dealing with distributed applications. The debugger must be able to shift into an external process. In the execution environment of Enterprise Beans, the application server represents a heavyweight process in which many threads are active simultaneously. The analysis of program flow within such a heavyweight process takes a great expenditure of time, is very exacting, and demands great expertise.

In this section we would like first to develop a small framework for testing Enterprise Beans. For this we shall write some test cases for the entity bean

BankAccount from Chapter 3 and the entity bean Part from this chapter. What is special to the test framework is that for each test run, a result protocol is generated in HTML format. Thus the development history of an Enterprise Bean can be documented and the efficiency of the components put to the test. The test framework is small, easy to use, and easy to adapt to particular circumstances. We shall also show the use of logging in Enterprise Beans. With the aid of logging it is possible to localize errors that occur in tests or in later deployment. Logging and automated tests together form a significant part of the quality assurance of Enterprise Beans.

Tests

Software must undergo continual change. This applies to components as well. The requirements on software and thus on components grow with the experience gained in their use. Making changes to component software brings with it the danger of introducing errors. With the availability of tests one can check immediately after a change in the code has been implemented whether the component works as it did before the change (assuming, of course, that the tests are adequate).

In the development of applications one frequently uses third-party components. Developers have to rely on the correct behavior of the components employed. If a new version of a component suddenly exhibits altered behavior, this can endanger the functionality of the entire application. Thus it is sensible to institute tests for third-party components. These tests ensure that the components display the expected behavior over several versions. Before a new version of the component is put into use, one can check in advance whether the behavior of the component has changed. It can also simply be that components offered by a third party are defective, which would endanger the functionality of the system.

There are essentially two different types of test: black-box tests and white-box tests. Black-box tests test the correct functioning of a component by determining whether its interface functions according to its specifications. The internal states of the component are not tested. Moreover, no knowledge of the construction of the component is assumed in the selection of test cases. For Enterprise Beans this would mean that with a black-box test a component is tested only from the client viewpoint. White-box tests test the correct functioning of a component by testing the internal states of the component during execution, with test cases designed based on the implementation. As a rule, in testing software one uses a mixture of both elements. However, with Enterprise Beans white-box tests are difficult to execute. An Enterprise Bean always uses a run-time environment. For a white-box test one would have to simulate this run-time environment in order to observe the behavior and state of an Enterprise Bean, since it is otherwise completely shielded by the EJB container, which does not allow direct access to the instance of the Enterprise Bean. Such a process is very difficult to implement. In this chapter we restrict ourselves to black-box tests. Later, we will suggest a way in which one might institute white-box tests on Enterprise Beans with somewhat less effort than might otherwise be necessary.

The test framework for black-box tests of Enterprise Beans is made up, essentially, of two classes and three exceptions. One of the two classes forms the basis for the test cases. This class is called EJBTestCase and is shown in Listing 9-24.

Listing 9-24. The class EJBTestCase.

```
package ejb.test;
import java.util.Properties;
import javax.naming.Context;
import javax.naming.InitialContext;
import javax.naming.NamingException;
public abstract class EJBTestCase {
    private Properties theProps;
    private Context theContext;
    public EJBTestCase() {
    }
    void setProperties(Properties p)
        throws NamingException
    {
        if(p == null) {
            throw new
                IllegalArgumentException("null is not allowed!");
        }
        theProps = p;
        theContext = new InitialContext(theProps);
    }
    public Object lookup(String name)
        throws NamingException
    {
        this.assertNotNull("name", name);
        return theContext.lookup(name);
    }
    public Object narrow(String name, Class c)
        throws NamingException
    {
        this.assertNotNull("name", name);
```

```java
        this.assertNotNull("class", c);
        Object o = theContext.lookup(name);
        return javax.rmi.PortableRemoteObject.narrow(o, c);
    }
    public void fail(String msg) {
        throw new TestFailException(msg);
    }
    public void assertEquals(Object obj1, Object obj2) {
        assertEquals("values do not match", obj1, obj2);
    }
    public void assertEquals(float f1, float f2) {
        assertEquals("values do not match", f1, f2);
    }
    public void assertEquals(int i1, int i2) {
        assertEquals("values do not match", i1, i2);
    }
    public void assertEquals(String msg, Object o1, Object o2) {
        if(!o1.equals(o2)) {
            throw new
                AssertionException(msg + ": " +o1 + " != " + o2);
        }
    }
    public void assertEquals(String msg, float f1, float f2) {
        if(f1 != f2) {
            throw new
                AssertionException(msg + ": " +f1 + " != " + f2);
        }
    }
    public void assertEquals(String msg, int i1, int i2) {
        if(i1 != i2) {
            throw new
                AssertionException(msg + ": " +i1 + " != " + i2);
        }
    }
    public void assertNotNull(String name, Object obj) {
        if(obj == null) {
            throw new AssertionException(name + " is null");
        }
    }
    public Properties getProperties() {
        return theProps;
    }
```

```
        public abstract void prepareTest()
            throws Exception;
        public abstract void finalizeTest()
            throws Exception;
}
```

EJBTestCase is an abstract class and is the base class of all test cases. It is initialized with a Properties object, which is used primarily to generate a NamingContext. Derived classes can use this NamingContext indirectly via the methods lookup and narrow to obtain references to Enterprise Beans. The Properties object is generated from a configuration file. With this Properties object it would also be possible to parameterize a test case externally. The derived class must overwrite the methods prepareTest and finalizeTest. By convention, the actual tests must implement the derived class in methods whose names begin with test. These methods must be declared public and are not allowed to have parameters. The method prepareTest is called before the first test method is called, and it serves to initialize the test case. Then the individual test methods are called, and finally, the method finalizeTest, which carries out the housecleaning tasks. Readers familiar with the test framework Junit (see [12]) will recognize this process.

The class that takes care of executing the tests is called EJBTest and is shown in Listing 9-25. Because of its length we will show only the central methods of the class in all their gory detail, since it is these alone that are necessary for an understanding of the process. The full source code can be found at http://www.apress.com in the Downloads section.

Listing 9-25. The class EJBTest.

```
package ejb.test;
import java.io.*;
import java.util.*;
import java.text.DateFormat;
import java.lang.reflect.Method;
public final class EJBTest {
    ...
    //member variables
    private static final String TC = "test.class.";
    private Properties theProps;
    private Object[] theClasses;
    ...
    public EJBTest() {
        ...
```

```
        //initialization of the member variables
        ...
    }
    public void init(String propertyFile) {
        Properties p;
        ...
        //read in the property file,
        //store the values in the variable p, and
        //relay to init(Properties)
        ...
        init(p);
    }
    public void init(Properties p) {
        if(p == null) {
        throw new IllegalArgumentException("null ...");
        }
        theProps = p;
        ArrayList al = new ArrayList();
        Enumeration e = theProps.propertyNames();
        String name;
        String cname;
        Class c;
        while(e.hasMoreElements()) {
            name = (String)e.nextElement();
            if(name.startsWith(TC)) {
                cname = theProps.getProperty(name);
                try {
                    c = Class.forName(cname);
                    al.add(c);
                } catch(Exception ex) {
                    al.add(cname);
                }
            }
        }
        theClasses = al.toArray();
        initOutputBuffer();
    }
    private void initOutputBuffer() {
        ...
        //Initialization of the output buffer
        //for the test report, which is created
        //at the end of all test in HTML format.
        ...
    }
```

```
private void reportBeginSection (String name, Throwable t)
{
    ...
    //output of reports arising at the beginning
    //of the test in HTML format.
    ...
}
private void reportTestCase
                (String name, long time, Throwable t)
{
    ...
    //Output of reports that arise during a test
    //in HTML format
    ...
}
private void reportEndSection(String name) {
    ...
    //Output of reports that arise at the end of a test
    //in HTML format
    ...
}
private void closeOutputBuffer() {
    ...
    //Close the output buffer after execution
    //of all tests
    ...
}
private String formatThrowable(Throwable t) {
    ...
    //Format an exception for output
    //in HTML format
    ...
}
private String computeFileName(String path) {
    ...
    //Compute the file name for the test protocol
    ...
}
private String format(int num) {
    ...
    //Format integers for output
    //in HTML format
    ...
}
```

```
public void runTests() {
    Class cl;
    EJBTestCase tc;
    for(int i = 0; i < theClasses.length; i++) {
        if(theClasses[i] instanceof String) {
            try {
                cl = Class.forName
                            ((String)theClasses[i]);
            } catch(Exception ex) {
                reportBeginSection
                            ((String)theClasses[i], ex);
                continue;
            }
        } else {
            cl = (Class)theClasses[i];
        }
        try {
            tc = (EJBTestCase)cl.newInstance();
            tc.setProperties(theProps);
        } catch(Exception ex) {
            reportBeginSection(cl.getName(), ex);
            continue;
        }
        reportBeginSection(cl.getName(), null);
        runTest(tc);
        reportEndSection(cl.getName());
    }
    closeOutputBuffer();
}
private void runTest(EJBTestCase tc) {
    Class c = tc.getClass();
    Method[] ms = c.getMethods();
    String name;
    Class[] params;
    try {
        tc.prepareTest();
    } catch(Exception ex) {
        reportTestCase("prepareTest", 0, ex);
        return;
    }
    for(int i = 0; i < ms.length; i++) {
        name = ms[i].getName();
        params = ms[i].getParameterTypes();
        if(!(name.startsWith(MP) &&
```

```
                        params.length == 0))
            {
                continue;
            }

            try {
                long t1 = System.currentTimeMillis();
                ms[i].invoke(tc, params);
                long t2 = System.currentTimeMillis();
                reportTestCase(name, (t2 - t1), null);
            } catch(Exception ex) {
                reportTestCase(name, 0, ex);
            }
        }
        try {
            tc.finalizeTest();
        } catch(Exception ex) {
            reportTestCase("finalizeTest", 0, ex);
        }
    }
    public static void main(String[] args) {
        EJBTest et = new EJBTest();
        if(args.length == 1) {
            et.init(args[0]);
        } else {
            et.init(new Properties());
        }
        et.runTests();
    }
}
```

The class EJBTest is initialized with a configuration file, which is shown in Listing 9-26. It is available from the code source for this book.

Listing 9-26. Properties for the class EJBTest.

```
#
# JNDI settings
#
# The JNDI factory class
java.naming.factory.initial=weblogic.jndi.WLInitialContextFactory
# the JNDI URL
java.naming.provider.url=t3://localhost:7001
```

```
#
# database settings for test cases
# that access the database directly
#
# The class of the database driver
jdbc.driver=org.postgresql.Driver
# the database URL
jdbc.url=jdbc:postgresql://localhost/postgres
# the user name for the databse login
jdbc.user=postgres
# the associated password
jdbc.pwd=postgres

#
# the classes that contain the tests
#
test.class.0=ejb.testcases.TestPartBean
test.class.1=ejb.testcases.TestBankAccount
test.class.2=ejb.testcases.TestLogger
test.class.3=ejb.testcases.TestCounterBean
test.class.4=ejb.testcases.TestExchangeSLBean
test.class.5=ejb.testcases.TestExchangeSFBean
test.class.6=ejb.testcases.TestMigrationBean
test.class.7=ejb.testcases.TestSupplychain

#
# the directory into which the reports
# are to be written
#
test.output.dir=./
```

The method init is called via the main method of the class EJBTest. There the configuration file is loaded and read. The name of the classes that implement a test (they are entered in the configuration file with the name test.class.*) are stored separately. In the example these are, among others, the classes ejb.test.TestPartBean, and ejb.test.TestBankAccount (the implementation of the classes appears subsequently). After the initialization the tests are executed via the method runTests. For each test class an instance is generated. The instance is initialized via a call to the method setProperties. Tests are run in the method runTest. First, the test case is prepared with a call to the method prepareTest. Using the introspection mechanism of the programming language Java, all methods on this object are called that are declared public, whose names begin with test, and that expect no parameters. By convention, these methods implement the tests for the respective Enterprise Beans. After all test methods have been called, the test is finalized with a call to the method finalizeTest.

All information about the test (name, execution time, errors, etc.), are written to the logging file. For each test run a new logging file is created. The name of the file includes the date and time. An example of such a logging file appears later in this section.

Now that the foundation has been laid, we can write the tests for the Enterprise Beans. Listing 9-27 shows the test for the Enterprise Bean Part from earlier in this chapter.

Listing 9-27. The class TestPartBean.

```
package ejb.testcases;
import ejb.part.*;
import ejb.test.*;
import javax.ejb.*;
public class TestPartBean extends EJBTestCase {
    PartHome partHome;
    Part p1;
    Part p2;
    Part p3;
    public TestPartBean() {
        super();
    }
    public void prepareTest()
        throws Exception
    {
        partHome = (PartHome)narrow("Part", PartHome.class);
    }
    public void testCreate()
        throws Exception
    {
        final String one = "11111";
        p1 = partHome.create(one);
        assertNotNull("Part", p1);
    }
    public void testDelete()
        throws Exception
    {
        final String two = "22222";
        p2 = partHome.create(two);
        assertNotNull("Part", p2);
        p2.remove();
        try {
```

```
            p2 = partHome.findByPrimaryKey(two);
            fail("expected FinderException, part "
                + two + " should not exist");
        } catch(FinderException fex) {
            //expected
        }
    }
    public void testUpdate()
        throws Exception
    {
        final String three = "33333";
        p3 = partHome.create(three);
        assertNotNull("Part", p3);
        TsPartDetails pd = p3.getPartDetails();
        pd.setPartDescription("Test Part");
        pd.setSupplierName("Test Supplier");
        pd.setPrice(120);
        TsPartDetails pd1 = p3.setPartDetails(pd);
        assertEquals(pd.getPartNumber(),
                    pd1.getPartNumber());
        assertEquals(pd.getPartDescription(),
                    pd1.getPartDescription());
        assertEquals(pd.getSupplierName(),
                    pd1.getSupplierName());
        assertEquals(pd.getPrice(),
                    pd1.getPrice());
        try {
            p3.setPartDetails(pd);
            fail("expected OutOfDateException");
        } catch(OutOfDateException ex) {
            //expected
        }
    }
    public void finalizeTest()
        throws Exception
    {
        p1.remove();
        p3.remove();
    }

}
```

The test case checks the three main functions of the Enterprise Bean Part. These are the generation, alteration, and deletion of a product part. During the course of the test, first the method prepareTest is called via the class EJBTest. There the test obtains a reference to the home interface of the Part bean. Then through the introspection mechanism of the class EJBTest the three test methods testCreate, testDelete, and testUpdate of the class TestPartBean are called. The order of calls is random. To finalize the test, the method finalizeTest is called.

In the method testCreate, the method create of the home interface is tested. The method assertNotNull of the base class checks whether the passed object has the value null. If so, an exception of type AssertionException is triggered, and the test is terminated. The exception is trapped by EJBTest and logged in the output file.

In the method testDelete a newly generated Part bean is again deleted. After the deletion, an attempt is made to find precisely this Enterprise Bean via the method findByPrimaryKey. To be correct, the findByPrimaryKey method should trigger an exception of type FinderException, since this Enterprise Bean no longer exists. If it does not do this, the test has failed. The method fail of the base class triggers an exception of type TestFailException. This exception is also trapped by EJBTest and logged in the output file.

The method testUpdate generates a Part bean and changes its value. Then it ensures that the bean actually returns the changed values. The method assertEquals compares two objects or two values. If they are not equal, this method triggers an exception of type AssertionException, and the test is terminated. In this case, too, the exception is trapped by EJBTest and logged in the output file. Moreover, the method testUpdate tests the time-stamp mechanism that was introduced in the previous section of this chapter by way of the Part bean. If the method setPartDetails is called with an obsolete details object, then this method triggers an exception of type OutOfDateException. If it doesn't do this, then the test case is broken off with a call to the method fail (and the implicit throwing of an exception of type TestFailException).

As already mentioned, this is a black-box test. The only methods that are tested are those that are accessible via the public interface of the Enterprise Bean. The test does not go into the Enterprise Bean's internal states. In this example the tests are very simple, merely ensuring that the basic functions of the component are usable. Such tests can be made as extensive and complex as desired.

The test for the Enterprise Bean BankAccount is built on exactly the same plan and tests exactly the same aspects of the Enterprise Bean. Therefore, we shall omit a listing of this test. However, the source code can be found at http://www.apress.com in the Downloads section.

To execute a test run, both Enterprise Beans must be installed in an EJB container. The EJB container or application server must be started, since the Enterprise Bean requires a run-time environment. Then the test run can be carried out by a call to the method `main` in the class `EJBTest`. As argument the name of the configuration file is passed (Listing 9-26 shows an example). The result of the test run is a logging file in HTML format. Figure 9-17 shows the result of a test run for the test cases of the `Part` and `BankAccount` beans.

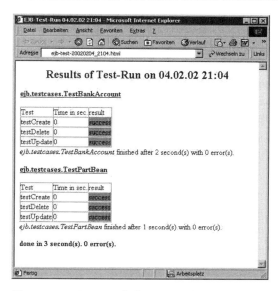

Figure 9-17. Test result for `TestBankAccount` *and* `TestPartBean`.

It is seen from the test protocol that all the tests were successful. Failed tests appear in red instead of green in the fields of the table. Instead of the word `success`, the exception that the aborted test caused is output.

After each change in one of the two components, tests should be run to ensure that the contract that binds the interface to the components is still being fulfilled.

Logging

Logging is a relatively easy method of detecting errors in software. Logging is used to limit errors and when no suitable debugger software is available (such as a production environment). If a customer reports an error in the software, it can usually be reconstructed with the help of the logging file. Even when one has suitable debugging software, it is often impossible to install it at a customer's site.

Logging is often criticized with the argument that it inflates the code and hampers the readability of the code. Another argument frequently voiced against logging relates to the effect on performance. The supporters of logging argue that logging code improves the readability of the remaining code, since the logging statements act as a form of documentation.

Moreover, the application of logging is often easier and less time-consuming than the use of complicated debugging software. The impact on performance is very small, and particularly with distributed applications it is easy to justify, since in such a segment logging is often the only way of finding and analyzing errors.

Many application servers offer logging services that can use an Enterprise Bean. These logging services can be more or less flexibly implemented, but in any case, they have the drawback that their interfaces are proprietary. If an Enterprise Bean uses such a proprietary logging service of an application server, then it cannot be deployed in any other application server without changing the code of the Enterprise Bean.

The reusability of an Enterprise Bean is thereby greatly reduced. In any case, Sun Microsystems has integrated a logging service into the run-time environment of Java 1.4. However, until this has been widely adopted in the application servers, the use of third-party logging tools remains a viable alternative. Should the Enterprise Bean be deployed in another application server, the logging tool of this third party must be made available to it. This dependency can be noted in the deployment descriptor of the Enterprise Bean. Such a logging tool should be freely available.

Such a tool exists in the form of the *Logging for Java* (log4j) library of the Apache project. This project (see [1]) is a development project, organized and coordinated over the Internet, for creating and maintaining software that is available free of charge. This type of software is called *open-source software*, since the source code is also freely available. Logging for Java offers a logging tool for the programming language Java. The flexibility of log4j is considerable, and the use of it relatively easy. Among other attributes, it possesses the capability of directing the logging output to various media (writing to file, output to the screen or to other servers). Log4j supports a variety of logging levels and hierarchical logging categories. An extensive description of the capabilities of log4j can be found at [2].

The output of reports via log4j, whether to the screen or a file, permits one to observe the behavior of an Enterprise Bean. For developers who are working with the component model of Enterprise JavaBeans for the first time, the use of logging offers an opportunity to learn about the behavior of the EJB container through the logging output of Enterprise Beans. Nonetheless, the primary purpose of logging is to detect errors.

To demonstrate the use of log4j we will equip the Enterprise Bean Part from the previous section with logging output. With the aid of the black-box test that we have implemented we will then generate a logging file. Listing 9-28 shows the altered class PartBean. The parts that are relevant to logging are shown in boldface. The method toString in the class TsPartDetails has been implemented to enable us to note the internal state of the Enterprise Bean (see Listing 9-18).

Listing 9-28. Class PartBean *with logging output.*

```
package ejb.part;

import javax.ejb.*;
import org.apache.log4j.Category;
import org.apache.log4j.BasicConfigurator;
import org.apache.log4j.FileAppender;
import org.apache.log4j.Layout;
import org.apache.log4j.PatternLayout;
import org.apache.log4j.Priority;
public abstract class PartBean implements EntityBean {
    private EntityContext theContext = null;
    private TsPartDetails theDetails = null;
    private Category log = null;
    public PartBean() {
        final String name = "PartBean";
        BasicConfigurator.configure();
        Category.getRoot().removeAllAppenders();
        if((log = Category.exists(name)) == null) {
            log = Category.getInstance(name);
            log.setPriority(Priority.DEBUG);
            Layout l = new PatternLayout(
                         PatternLayout.TTCC_CONVERSION_PATTERN);
            try {
              log.addAppender(new FileAppender(l, name + ".log"));
            } catch(java.io.IOException ioex) {
                throw new IllegalStateException(ioex.getMessage());
            }
        }
        log.info("initialized instance successfully");
    }
    //the create method of the home interface
    public String ejbCreate(String partNumber)
        throws CreateException
    {
        log.info("entering ejbCreate (" + partNumber + ")");
        this.setPartNumber(partNumber);
        theDetails = new TsPartDetails();
        theDetails.partNumber = partNumber;
        theDetails.partDescription = "";
        theDetails.supplierName = "";
        theDetails.price = 0;
        long tt = System.currentTimeMillis();
        this.setLastModified(tt);
```

```
        theDetails.updateTimestamp(theContext, tt);
        log.debug("Created new part with part-no:" + partNumber);
        log.info("leaving ejbCreate");
        return null;
    }
    public void ejbPostCreate(String partNumber)
        throws CreateException
    {
        log.debug("ejbPostCreate (" + partNumber + ")");
    }
    //abstract getter/setter methods
    public abstract void setPartNumber(String num);
    public abstract String getPartNumber();
    public abstract void setPartDescription(String desc);
    public abstract String getPartDescription();
    public abstract void setSupplierName(String name);
    public abstract String getSupplierName();
    public abstract void setPrice(float p);
    public abstract float getPrice();
    public abstract long getLastModified();
    public abstract void setLastModified(long tt);
    //the method of the remote interface
    public TsPartDetails setPartDetails(TsPartDetails pd)
        throws OutOfDateException
    {
        log.info("entering setPartDetails " + pd);
        if(theDetails.isOutDated(pd)) {
            log.warn("out of date part-details-object");
            log.info("leaving setPartDetails");
            throw new OutOfDateException();
        }
        this.setPartDescription(pd.getPartDescription());
        this.setSupplierName(pd.getSupplierName());
        this.setPrice(pd.getPrice());
        long tt = System.currentTimeMillis();
        this.setLastModified(tt);
        theDetails = pd;
        theDetails.updateTimestamp(theContext, tt);
        log.debug("part-data updated " + theDetails);
        log.info("leaving setPartDetails");
        return theDetails;
    }
    //public PartDetails getPartDetails() {
    public TsPartDetails getPartDetails() {
```

```
        log.debug("getPartDetails :" + theDetails);
        return theDetails;
    }

    //the methods of the javax.ejb.EntityBean interface
    public void setEntityContext(EntityContext ctx) {
        log.debug("setEntityContext " + ctx);
        theContext = ctx;
    }

    public void unsetEntityContext() {
        log.debug("unsetEntityContext");
        theContext = null;
    }

    public void ejbRemove()
        throws RemoveException
    {
        log.debug("ejbRemove");
    }

    public void ejbActivate() {
        log.debug("ejbActivate");
    }

    public void ejbPassivate() {
        log.debug("ejbPassivate");
    }

    public void ejbLoad() {
        log.info("entering ejbLoad");
        if(theDetails == null) {
            theDetails = new TsPartDetails();
        }
        theDetails.partNumber = this.getPartNumber();
        theDetails.partDescription = this.getPartDescription();
        theDetails.supplierName = this.getSupplierName();
        theDetails.price = this.getPrice();
        long tt = this.getLastModified();
        theDetails.updateTimestamp(theContext, tt);
        log.debug("data successfully loaded:" + theDetails);
        log.info("leaving ejbLoad");
    }

    public void ejbStore() {
        log.debug("ejbStore");
    }
}
```

The log4j classes are initialized in the constructor of the Enterprise Bean with a call to the method configure of the class BasicConfigurator. This method can be called repeatedly. Then, if it does not already exist, a separate logging category for the Enterprise Bean Part is set up with the name of the class (another instance of this bean class could already have generated this category). The interface Category is the central interface of the log4j library. All logging output takes place over this interface.

The logging level of the category for the Part bean is set via the method setPriority to DEBUG. Log4j defines the logging levels DEBUG, INFO, WARN, ERROR, and FATAL, where DEBUG has the lowest priority, and FATAL the highest. For each category, the interface Category offers a separate method (debug,info, warn, error, and fatal). To create logging output with the priority WARN, the method warn on the interface Category must be called. If at run time the logging level is set to ERROR, then a call to the method warn generates no output. In our case, each of the logging methods will generate output, since the logging level is set to the lowest priority. In our example, the setting is hard coded to keep things simple. As a rule, the setting of the logging level is read from the configuration. One could even offer a method on the remote interface of the Enterprise Bean that allowed the logging level to be raised or lowered from the client side. The raising or lowering of the logging level can be used to change the amount of logging output at run time. The Enterprise Bean could also be equipped with a logic that would raise or lower the logging level automatically at the occurrence of particular events.

To write logging output to a file, an object of type FileAppender is added to the category. Appenders are objects that represent the various output channels. A category can have several appenders. Appenders can be added to or deleted from a category dynamically. The file appender is initialized with the file name of the output file and with an object that defines the layout of the output. In our example, a standard layout is used, which will be explained later when we see an example of a logging file. The logging output of all instances of the class PartBean are written into a single output file with the name PartBean.log.

One could certainly question the use of FileAppender here. Namely, an Enterprise Bean is forbidden from accessing the file system (see Chapter 3). However, the Enterprise Bean does not access the file system directly, but indirectly via the log4j library. If an error should occur in writing to the file, this would not be passed to the Enterprise Bean. Log4j traps the error and handles it internally. The probability that the Enterprise Bean would be blocked during writing a logging entry (for example, on account of synchronization problems with the file system) is in any case very small, since the output into the file system is buffered by log4j. Proprietary logging services of an application server generally also use the file system as the location for logging output. However, if one were opposed to the use of FileAppender, then as an alternative, the SocketAppender could be used, which sends the logging output over a network connection to another server, where it is then stored. Another option is the development of a custom appender, which, for example, could write to a database. The necessary details for alternative appenders can be found in the log4j documentation (see [2]).

As a final action, in the constructor of the PartBean there is logging output with the priority INFO upon the successful initialization of an instance. In the remaining methods, the category generated in the constructor is used to create logging output with various priorities about program execution and the internal state of the components.

Since there is no place in the deployment descriptor in which one can refer to the use of third-party libraries, it is recommended to make this reference to the use of log4j in the description of the Enterprise Bean. Since the deployment descriptor is the central documentation instance of the component, this information should be placed there in any case. It is also a good idea to name the source where the deployer (being answerable for the Enterprise Bean) can obtain the library. Tips for installing the library would also be helpful. In the case of log4j, it is necessary only that the archive file log4j.jar be located in the Classpath of the EJB container. Alternatively, log4j.jar can be packed into the appropriate ejb.jar.

We used the black-box test for the Part bean from earlier in this chapter to generate a logging file. Listing 9-29 shows the content of this file. The comments describe the relation of the logging output to the methods and actions of the test case.

Listing 9-29. Logging output of the class PartBean.

```
//TestPartBean.testCreate
//generate Part 11111
631 [ExecuteThread-14] INFO PartBean -
    initialized instance successfully
631 [ExecuteThread-14] DEBUG PartBean -
    setEntityContext EntityEJBContextImpl@795cce
631 [ExecuteThread-14] INFO PartBean -
    entering ejbCreate (11111)
631 [ExecuteThread-14] DEBUG PartBean -
    Created new part with part-no:11111
641 [ExecuteThread-14] INFO PartBean - leaving ejbCreate
671 [ExecuteThread-14] DEBUG PartBean -
    ejbPostCreate (11111)
671 [ExecuteThread-14] DEBUG PartBean - ejbStore
//TestPartBean.testDelete
//generate Part 22222
```

```
731 [ExecuteThread-10] INFO PartBean -
    initialized instance successfully
731 [ExecuteThread-10] DEBUG PartBean -
    setEntityContext EntityEJBContextImpl@5507d3
731 [ExecuteThread-10] INFO PartBean -
    entering ejbCreate (22222)
731 [ExecuteThread-10] DEBUG PartBean -
    Created new part with part-no:22222
731 [ExecuteThread-10] INFO PartBean - leaving ejbCreate
761 [ExecuteThread-10] DEBUG PartBean -
    ejbPostCreate (22222)
761 [ExecuteThread-10] DEBUG PartBean - ejbStore
//delete Part 22222
781 [ExecuteThread-14] INFO PartBean - entering ejbLoad
811 [ExecuteThread-14] DEBUG PartBean -
    data successfully loaded:
    [[TsPartDetails]partNumber=22222;partDescription
    =null;supplierName=null;price=0.0;]
811 [ExecuteThread-14] INFO PartBean - leaving ejbLoad
811 [ExecuteThread-14] DEBUG PartBean - ejbRemove
//TestPartBean.testUpdate
//generate Part 33333
901 [ExecuteThread-14] INFO PartBean -
    initialized instance successfully
901 [ExecuteThread-14] DEBUG PartBean -
    setEntityContext EntityEJBContextImpl@79781
901 [ExecuteThread-14] INFO PartBean -
    entering ejbCreate (33333)
901 [ExecuteThread-14] DEBUG PartBean -
    Created new part with part-no:33333
901 [ExecuteThread-14] INFO PartBean - leaving ejbCreate
911 [ExecuteThread-14] DEBUG PartBean -
    ejbPostCreate (33333)
911 [ExecuteThread-14] DEBUG PartBean - ejbStore
//call to PartBean.getPartDetails
921 [ExecuteThread-10] INFO PartBean - entering ejbLoad
921 [ExecuteThread-10] DEBUG PartBean -
    data successfully loaded:
    [[TsPartDetails]partNumber=33333;partDescription=
    null;supplierName=null;price=0.0;]
921 [ExecuteThread-10] INFO PartBean - leaving ejbLoad
921 [ExecuteThread-10] DEBUG PartBean - getPartDetails :
    [[TsPartDetails]partNumber=33333;partDescription=
    null;supplierName=null;price=0.0;]
```

```
921 [ExecuteThread-10] DEBUG PartBean - ejbStore
//call to PartBean.setPartDetails
941 [ExecuteThread-14] INFO PartBean - entering ejbLoad
941 [ExecuteThread-14] DEBUG PartBean -
    data successfully loaded:
    [[TsPartDetails]partNumber=33333;partDescription=
    null;supplierName=null;price=0.0;]
941 [ExecuteThread-14] INFO PartBean - leaving ejbLoad
941 [ExecuteThread-14] INFO PartBean -
    entering setPartDetails
941 [ExecuteThread-14] DEBUG PartBean - part-data updated
    [[TsPartDetails]partNumber=33333;partDescription=
    Test Part;supplierName=Test Supplier;price=120.0;]
941 [ExecuteThread-14] INFO PartBean -
    leaving setPartDetails
941 [ExecuteThread-14] DEBUG PartBean - ejbStore
//call to PartBean.setPartDetails with obsolete
//TsPartDetails object
1001 [ExecuteThread-10] INFO PartBean - entering ejbLoad
1001 [ExecuteThread-10] DEBUG PartBean -
    data successfully loaded:
    [[TsPartDetails]partNumber=33333;partDescription=
    Test Part;supplierName=Test Supplier;price=120.0;]
1001 [ExecuteThread-10] INFO PartBean - leaving ejbLoad
1001 [ExecuteThread-10] INFO PartBean -
     entering setPartDetails
1001 [ExecuteThread-10] WARN PartBean -
     out of date part-details-object
1001 [ExecuteThread-10] INFO PartBean -
     leaving setPartDetails
1001 [ExecuteThread-10] DEBUG PartBean - ejbStore
//TestPartBean.finalizeTest
//delete Part 11111
1011 [ExecuteThread-10] INFO PartBean - entering ejbLoad
1011 [ExecuteThread-10] DEBUG PartBean -
    data successfully loaded:
    [[TsPartDetails]partNumber=11111;partDescription=
    null;supplierName=null;price=0.0;]
1011 [ExecuteThread-10] INFO PartBean - leaving ejbLoad
1011 [ExecuteThread-10] DEBUG PartBean - ejbRemove
//delete Part 33333
1021 [ExecuteThread-14] INFO PartBean - entering ejbLoad
1031 [ExecuteThread-14] DEBUG PartBean -
    data successfully loaded:
```

```
[[TsPartDetails]partNumber=33333;partDescription=
Test Part;supplierName=Test Supplier;price=120.0;]
1031 [ExecuteThread-14] INFO PartBean - leaving ejbLoad
1031 [ExecuteThread-14] DEBUG PartBean - ejbRemove
```

The format of the logging output can be customized. The Part bean uses a predefined format. In the first column, the time elapsed since the start of the application is given in milliseconds. The second column displays the name of the thread that has processed the client request. The third column contains the logging level (INFO, DEBUG, WARN, ERROR, or FATAL), and in the fourth column, the name of the logging category (in the case of the Part bean, it is the name PartBean). Finally, the text created in the various logging methods is output.

It can be seen from the example in Listing 9-29 that the processes taking place within an Enterprise Bean can be followed from the logging output. If an error occurs, it can be immediately localized. Errors can be logged either through the logging levels WARN, ERROR, and FATAL, or discovered by a logged exception in the logging file. If the internal state of the component and the program execution are logged together in advance of the occurrence of an error, the source of the error can be found relatively quickly. In our example, one can see at once from the WARN entry that a client has attempted to update the data of the Enterprise Bean with an invalid details object. It is assumed that the developer of the component has programmed the relevant informative logging output. For example, if an exception occurs that is trapped in the code but not written to the logging output, the error cannot be found through logging.

With logging, the behavior of the EJB container can be studied as well. From the knowledge obtained one can institute measures for optimization of the components. However, one should not do anything that causes a dependency on a particular EJB container.

White-box tests could be carried out with Enterprise Beans by analyzing logging files generated by black-box tests. The analysis of logging files requires a relatively large programming effort. Moreover, a protocol for logging output should be defined and adhered to. Since the programming effort occurs only once and can significantly improve the quality of the tests, it can be a worthwhile enterprise. For example, the entries in the logging file in Listing 9-29 are very homogeneous and would be suitable for a lexical analysis. For example, the directory in which the log files of the Enterprise Bean are located and which log file belongs to which test case could be made available to the class EJBTest via the configuration file. Furthermore, the class EJBTestCase could be extended to include the capability of analyzing (parsing) these log files according to a particular protocol. One could even go so far as to reconstruct objects from the entries in the logging file and analyze the derived classes. For example, the information [[TsPartDetails] partNumber = 33333; partDescription = Test Part; supplierName = Test Supplier; price = 120.0;] from the logging file immediately allows us reconstruct the object of type `TsPartDetails`. The derived class could then carry out the evaluation for the current test case and determine whether the internal state recorded in the logging file during the black-box test was correct.

It would also be interesting to investigate, using black-box and white-box tests, whether a component behaves the same way in different containers or whether the behavior of the EJB container corresponds to that described in the specification. This provides an indirect way of testing the EJB container.

Automated tests and logging are mechanisms that tend to improve the quality of a component. If the tests themselves are error-ridden or carelessly programmed, or if the logging output is incomplete or lacking in explanatory power, then it becomes questionable whether there is any real contribution to improved quality. To make testing and logging into a useful instrument, the developers of components and tests must exercise great care and discipline.

#### CHAPTER 10

Web Services
and Scheduling

Introduction

This chapter is concerned with two additional services and technologies that are offered as part of the EJB 2.1 specification: web services and timers. Web services, the major new feature in the EJB 2.1 specification, are a technology that allows for integration and interoperability between heterogeneous systems using standard protocols and XML documents. Web services allow integration between EJB and non-EJB systems (including non-Java systems such as Microsoft .NET). In this chapter we convert one of our existing EJB components into a web service and utilize a web service located outside of our local EJB system. Since EJB 1.0 there have been available numerous products to schedule and trigger notifications within the EJB system. With EJB 2.1, the timer service is now standardized, and in the future it will be the common approach for the scheduling of EJB invocations and batch jobs at specified regular or irregular intervals within the EJB system.

Web Services

There is a common misconception that web services are a competitive alternative to writing Enterprise JavaBeans components and that they should be used in lieu of Enterprise JavaBeans components to develop enterprise systems. This can, in fact, be an incorrect judgment, and in this section we will walk through one of the main motivations for the creation of web services, how they evolved, what problems they solve, and more importantly, how they complement Enterprise JavaBeans components to provide integration and interoperability between systems.

The Standardized World of J2EE

The Java 2 Enterprise Edition is a successful attempt at defining a standard enterprise platform for the development of distributed component-based applications. The benefits and architecture of J2EE applications have been covered in the earlier chapters of this book. In this section we will be review the architecture from a slightly different, and much higher, perspective.

Consider Figure 10-1. It illustrates a high-level view of the main components of the J2EE architecture. Components form the building blocks of J2EE applications and consist primarily of Enterprise JavaBeans. If you consider the J2EE architecture of the components/container philosophy closely, you will find that an EJB is entirely encapsulated from the outside world. The component lives inside the "standardized world" of J2EE. By "standardized world" we mean that every interaction and invocation that the EJB component wishes to make (or has made upon it) is within a totally defined environment, namely, that of the EJB container and J2EE application server. There are also components that allow web interfacing and interaction with the J2EE platform: servlets/JSPs and web applications; and these components also live within the defined environment of the web container and J2EE application server.

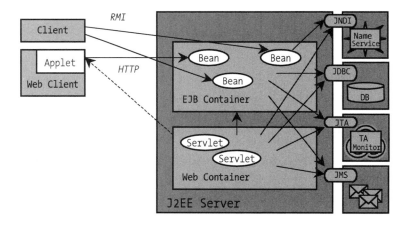

Figure 10-1. The "Standardized World" of J2EE.

If either of these components wishes to utilize the functionality of an existing enterprise service such as message-oriented middleware (MOM), an enterprise relational database management system (RDBMS), enterprise directory server (such as LDAP), or e-mail via an SMTP server, there are defined J2EE standards for the interfacing with these services: message-driven beans and JMS, databases via JDBC, e-mail via JavaMail, and naming and directory services via JNDI. Hence the world for the J2EE-based component is "standardized" in that all the required interfaces are defined.

Let us now identify the main tasks of distributed component software in today's enterprise. We aim to identify the required standardized features and functionalities, which are summarized in Table 10-1.

Table 10-1. Requirements for distributed component software.

Requirement	Standardized	J2EE Offering
Connectivity to other standardized vendor-provided products/services such as databases, message queues, and directory services.	Yes	Handled via the many J2EE specifications such as JDBC, JMS, JNDI.
Development of custom, reusable components containing business logic.	Yes	Handled via the EJB component model.
Interface between the system and the Internet via HTTP and markup languages such as HTML.	Yes	Handled via the J2EE servlets, JSP, and web application technologies.
Connectivity to proprietary transactional enterprise resource planning systems (ERPs).	Yes	Handled via the J2EE connectors architecture, which allows for the connectivity and security/transaction context propagation between J2EE and ERP systems.
Connectivity to other heterogeneous systems both internally, within an enterprise, and external to the enterprise.	No	Could be handled via custom message system, including CORBA ORBs and servlets. Legacy formats such as EDI also in use.

The Enterprise platform, that is, J2EE, is standardized and offers an excellent architecture for the first four items in the table. However, the final item can become a difficult task. We can break this item into two distinct problems: integration across/within an enterprise (also known as internal integration) and integration across multiple enterprises (external integration). We will now look at both of these items in more detail.

Internal Integration

Internal integration (see Figure 10-2) can be defined as the process of connecting multiple systems that belong to a single company or department. Both systems are well known and controlled and can usually be easily customized and extended to allow for integration. Integrating such systems poses a few challenges, including dealing with differences in platform, programming language, and the protocols used.

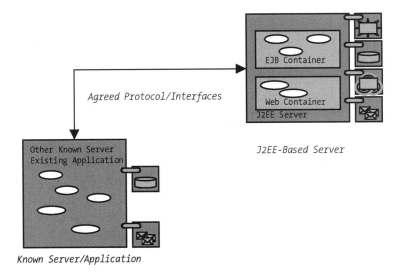

Figure 10-2. Internal integration.

External Integration

External integration (Figure 10-3) can be defined as the process of connecting multiple disparate systems that belong to differing companies (in a business-to-business, or B2B, scenario) or between two departments of a global company. The systems are relatively closed and isolated from one another, and interfaces between them are required to be explicitly defined; furthermore, technologies used between the systems may be incompatible and difficult to alter. Suppose, for example, that a merger takes place between two companies—Intergalactic Enterprises and Stellar Transport, say—that have disparate systems,. Intergalactic Enterprises has deployed an enterprise-wide infrastructure based on Microsoft technologies, while Stellar Transport has invested similar amounts of time and resources in a J2EE-based architecture. If the two companies merge and wish to integrate their systems, neither company expects to have to migrate its system to a different architecture. The same scenario can also be derived from a B2B scenario in which two trading partners wish to automate invoicing and delivery information between their systems.

With internal integratiom, because the same company owns and controls all systems they run, they have control over both systems. With external integration, because integration involves another third-party system, the company has control of only one system. Moreover, with external integration there is the added issue that transactions may have to run over the Internet.

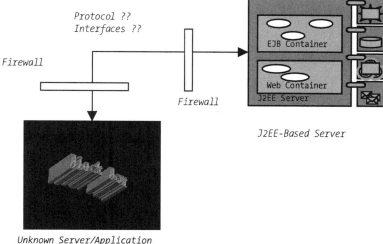

Figure 10-3. External integration.

Solving the Integration Problem

The challenge of achieving smooth integration (both internal and external) is a continually evolving task. As new technology evolves, there are more and more technologies that require integration. There have been many technologies that have attempted to provide solutions to integration challenges. Most of these technologies have evolved from the idea of determining a common denominator between all the systems that require integration. We will take a brief tour of some of these integration technologies.

Remote Procedure Calls (RPC)

Remote procedure calls have been used for many years for communicating between programs in different address spaces that are executing on separate machines. RPC utilizes an architecture based on stubs and skeletons, which work in tandem to marshal and unmarshal invocation packets to and from remote services. Common technologies that utilize RPC are the Distributed Computing Environment (DCE) and Tuxedo. Standard interfaces are developed using a pseudolanguage, which is in turn mapped to various supported languages that can either invoke or be invoked remotely. With RPC-based technologies we can begin to integrate our systems, although sometimes proprietary and expensive products have been a requirement, and the developed code and architecture have been largely procedural.

Common Object Request Broker Architecture (CORBA)

The Common Object Request Broker Architecture (CORBA) is a distributed object standard that has essentially brought popular object-oriented methodologies and designs to the RPC architecture. It is also a relatively standardized technology. CORBA was authored by the Object Management Group (OMG). The OMG is a consortium of hundreds of companies, including Sun Microsystems, IBM, Oracle, Borland, and BEA Systems. The OMG has also delivered the specification for the Unified Modeling language (UML), which is used for modeling object-oriented systems.

CORBA defines an object bus, commonly known as an ORB (Object Request Broker), and object services that "plug" into the orb to provide distributed services to applications. Common Object Services (COS) includes naming, transactions, events/notifications, and security. With CORBA, interface contracts are written in a standard pseudolanguage called IDL (Interface Definition Language). IDL is part of the CORBA standard and is a subset of C++.

A further portion of the CORBA specification is mappings of IDL into various different languages, including C++, Java, Smalltalk, and COBOL. IDL is related closely to a standard protocol called IIOP (Internet, Inter-ORB Protocol), which is a protocol that layers on TCP/IP and is used for inter-ORB and CORBA application communication.

It is IDL and IIOP that give CORBA its language independence. Language independence in CORBA allows distributed objects to be written in a wide variety of languages that have mappings, including Java, C++, and COBOL. Objects written in these different languages are able to communicate with each other. Objects can be written to encapsulate some existing functionality of a legacy system. This functionality is now brought into the new object world, and the object is now reusable. Other applications that use this object do not know or care what language the component is written in.

An example scenario is an IDL interface that is implemented by a COBOL application, which "wrappers" some existing mainframe code. A Java Client application could use the CORBA interface and call the COBOL code. CORBA assisted greatly in the development of distributed components and internal integration. Because CORBA is an open standard, it was implemented by many vendors, and it provided some interoperability, although there existed (and still do exist) many incompatibilities among various CORBA products.

Another item to consider when one is creating transactions that are to run over the Internet is security. With today's vast array of network-based viruses, most network administrators have strict network firewall policies that restrict a great deal of traffic that flows through a corporate firewall into an enterprise. IIOP is a protocol that is not accepted by most firewalls.

CORBA gave us integration between languages but introduced some product-related protocol compatibility problems. It also required that everyone adopt and potentially pay for a potentially expensive CORBA ORB, and the required manipulation of the corporate firewall could also be a significant factor to consider.

Web Services

The adoption of XML in the enterprise has seen an explosion of new trends and technologies that apply the XML standards to existing problems. The integration problem is no different. Because XML parsers are available on all platforms, XML can be used as an intermediate format to transfer messages between software components. Messages can be written, transferred, and read between many heterogeneous platforms. This solves the first problem of interoperability between platforms. The second problem to solve is the transferring of the XML data between systems, and the logical choice for this protocol is HTTP, which offers the distinct advantage of being the most common protocol to be allowed through firewalls.

XML-RPC was one of the first technologies to take advantage of XML. XML-RPC utilizes the standard HTTP POST mechanism to transfer content of type "text/xml" from client to server. It is a relatively simple model, yet is extraordinarily powerful. Listing 10-1 is a simple example of XML for a method invocation using XML-RPC. In this example, we will add two numbers.

Listing 10-1. XML-RPC representation of a method call.

```
<?xml version="1.0"?>
<methodCall>
  <methodName>calc.AddNumbers</methodName>
    <params>
      <param>
        <value>
          <int>10</int>
        </value>
      </param>
      <param>
        <value>
          <int>12</int>
        </value>
      </param>
    </params>
</methodCall>
```

The corresponding result of the XML-RPC call is shown Listing 10-2.

Listing 10-2. XML-RPC representation of a method call result.

```xml
<?xml version="1.0"?>
<methodResponse>
    <params>
        <param>
            <value>
            <int>22</int>
            </value>
        </param>
    </params>
</methodResponse>
```

The Simple Object Access Protocol, also known as SOAP, further builds on the pioneering work of XML-RPC and adds further definition of message envelopes, encoding, and RPC mechanisms. SOAP is implemented and supported on various platforms. The Apache development group, IBM, and Microsoft also show strong support for SOAP. SOAP is the underlying protocol of web services, and its lightweight design is proving to be a valuable asset. As an example of lightweight design, complex issues such as distributed garbage collection and the creation and destruction of distributed objects are left out of the standard. These issues are already dealt with in underlying implementations such as Enterprise JavaBeans, so there is no need to repeatedly reinvent and redefine the same architectures.

Where CORBA uses IDL for defining interfaces, web services use the Web Services Definition Language (WSDL) to define the interfaces of components and their location. It uses the HTTP protocol to send messages between components. WSDL can be used in conjunction with the Universal Description, Discovery and Integration Initiative (UDDI), which is a repository of available web services.

Using web services, compatibility among legacy systems, J2EE applications, and even Microsoft .NET applications is possible. These require a relatively small investment, since there is no run-time code that must be purchased (as with CORBA), and the required specifications are relatively simple to implement. Web services can be seen as the glue between the various technologies and legacy systems available in today's networked enterprise and business-to-business communication infrastructures.

Web Services and EJB

Web services allow components to connect to other components written in different technologies and located on different networks. So where do web services fit into J2EE? Web services are another connectivity interface to our EJB. We already have a local and a remote set of interfaces, and we simply introduce another interface that is known as a web service endpoint. This allows web-service connectivity into the J2EE environment.

The web service endpoint interface (Figure 10-4 is defined according to the JAX-RPC specification. JAX-RPC stands for Java API for XML-based RPC and is an API for developing web services using XML remote procedure calls. JAX-RPC supports the standard Java data types, JavaBeans, and collections. We will take the EuroExchange stateless session bean example from Chapter 4 and develop a web service endpoint for it. To achieve this, we define a service interface that extends the java.rmi.Remote interface. Each method signature must be defined to throw a java.rmi.RemoteException and follow the JAX-RPC rules for data types. The EuroExchange web service endpoint is defined in Listing 10-3. This interface looks very similar to the EJB remote interface, although as you will notice, it does not import or use any classes or interfaces from the javax.ejb package.

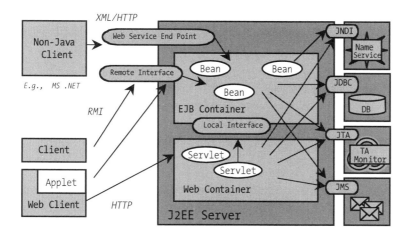

Figure 10-4. Web Service Endpoints in J2EE.

Listing 10-3. Web service interface for the EuroExchange *EJB.*

```
package ejb.exchangeSL;
import java.rmi.RemoteException;
import java.rmi.Remote;

public interface EuroExchangeService extends Remote {
  public float changeFromEuro(String currency, float amount) throws RemoteException;
  public float changeToEuro(String currency, float amount) throws RemoteException;
  public void setExchangeRate(String currency, float euro,float foreignCurr)
    throws RemoteException;
}
```

The reader may question why a new, separate interface is needed for a web service endpoint. It should be noted that the JAX-RPC web services packages are separate from the EJB packages, and it is possible to implement a web service endpoint without the use of EJB. For clarity, we have separated the interfaces. Many commercially available products have the ability to automatically generate the web service endpoint from an existing EJB remote interface. The generated web service endpoint will expose only those methods that adhere to the JAX-RPC specification and data types. Another approach to avoid the defining methods in multiple interfaces is to use interface inheritance (Listing 10-4) and create your EJB remote interface from the web service endpoint.

Listing 10-4. Using interface inheritance to create web service and EJB endpoints.

```
package ejb.exchangeSL;
import javax.ejb.EJBObject

public interface EuroExchangeEJB extends EJBObject, EuroExchangeService

{
}
```

Data Types Supported by JAX-RPC

JAX-RPC supports the data types and primitives shown in Table 10-2. Single and multidimensional arrays of supported types are also allowed. Your own developed classes and JavaBeans may also be used in the web service endpoint interface. They must, however, also adhere to the JAX-RPC rules.

Table 10-2. Supported Data Types in JAX-RPC.

boolean and `java.lang.Boolean`
byte and `java.lang.Byte`
double and `java.lang.Double`
float and `java.lang.Float`
int and `java.lang.Integer`
long and `java.lang.Long`
short and `java.lang.Short`
`java.lang.String`
`java.math.BigDecimal`
`java.math.BigInteger`
`java.util.Calendar`
`java.util.Date`
`java.util.ArrayList`
`java.util.LinkedList`
`java.util.Stack`
`java.util.Vector`
`java.util.HashMap`
`java.util.Hashtable`
`java.util.Properties`
`java.util.TreeMap`
`java.util. HashSet`
`java.util.TreeSet`

All JavaBeans, and classes and fields, should also have a public default constructor and must not implement the `java.rmi.Remote` interface.

In order to deploy our web service endpoint with our Enterprise JavaBean, we must also modify the `ejb-jar.xml` deployment descriptor file to allow for the additional service endpoint element. The updated deployment descriptor is shown in Listing 10-5.

Listing 10-5. Deployment descriptor for a web service endpoint.

```xml
<?xml version="1.0" encoding="UTF-8"?>
<ejb-jar version="2.1"
xmlns="http://java.sun.com/xml/ns/j2ee"
xmlns:xsi="http://www.w3.org/2001/XMLSchema-instance"
xsi:schemaLocation="http://java.sun.com/xml/ns/j2ee
http://java.sun.com/xml/ns/j2ee/ejb-jar_2_1.xsd">
  <display-name>sl3</display-name>
  <enterprise-beans>
    <session>
      <ejb-name>EuroExchangeBean</ejb-name>
      <home>ejb.exchangeSL.EuroExchangeHome</home>
      <remote>ejb.exchangeSL.EuroExchange</remote>
      <ejb-class>ejb.exchangeSL.EuroExchangeBean</ejb-class>
      <service-endpoint>ejb.exchangeSL.EuroExchangeService</service-endpoint>
      <session-type>Stateless</session-type>
      <transaction-type>Bean</transaction-type>
      <security-identity>
        <use-caller-identity/>
      </security-identity>
    </session>
  </enterprise-beans>
</ejb-jar>
```

The ejb-jar file is then run through a deployment tool. The J2EE Reference Implementation from Sun Microsystems contains a tool called wscompile, which is used for web service endpoint deployment. This tool generates the WSDL file from the service interface and deployment descriptor settings. The generated WSDL file is shown in Listing 10-6.

Listing 10-6. The WSDL file for the EuroExchange Service.

```xml
<?xml version="1.0" encoding="UTF-8"?>

<definitions name="EuroExchangeService"
targetNamespace="urn:Euro" xmlns:tns="urn:Euro"
xmlns="http://schemas.xmlsoap.org/wsdl/"
xmlns:soap="http://schemas.xmlsoap.org/wsdl/soap/"
xmlns:xsd="http://www.w3.org/2001/XMLSchema">
  <types/>
  <message name="EuroExchangeService_changeFromEuro">
    <part name="String_1" type="xsd:string"/>
    <part name="float_2" type="xsd:float"/></message>
```

```
<message name="EuroExchangeService_changeFromEuroResponse">
  <part name="result" type="xsd:float"/></message>
<message name="EuroExchangeService_changeToEuro">
  <part name="String_1" type="xsd:string"/>
  <part name="float_2" type="xsd:float"/></message>
<message name="EuroExchangeService_changeToEuroResponse">
  <part name="result" type="xsd:float"/></message>
<message name="EuroExchangeService_setExchangeRate">
  <part name="String_1" type="xsd:string"/>
  <part name="float_2" type="xsd:float"/>
  <part name="float_3" type="xsd:float"/></message>
<message name="EuroExchangeService_setExchangeRateResponse"/>
<portType name="EuroExchangeService">
  <operation name="changeFromEuro" parameterOrder="String_1 float_2">
    <input message="tns:EuroExchangeService_changeFromEuro"/>
    <output message="tns:EuroExchangeService_changeFromEuroResponse"/>
        </operation>
  <operation name="changeToEuro" parameterOrder="String_1 float_2">
    <input message="tns:EuroExchangeService_changeToEuro"/>
    <output message="tns:EuroExchangeService_changeToEuroResponse"/>
        </operation>
  <operation name="setExchangeRate" parameterOrder="String_1 float_2 float_3">
    <input message="tns:EuroExchangeService_setExchangeRate"/>
    <output message="tns:EuroExchangeService_setExchangeRateResponse"/>
        </operation></portType>
<binding name="EuroExchangeServiceBinding" type="tns:EuroExchangeService">
  <operation name="changeFromEuro">
    <input>
      <soap:body encodingStyle="http://schemas.xmlsoap.org/soap/encoding/"
          use="encoded" namespace="urn:Euro"/></input>
    <output>
      <soap:body encodingStyle="http://schemas.xmlsoap.org/soap/encoding/"
          use="encoded" namespace="urn:Euro"/></output>
    <soap:operation soapAction=""/></operation>
  <operation name="changeToEuro">
    <input>
      <soap:body encodingStyle="http://schemas.xmlsoap.org/soap/encoding/"
          use="encoded" namespace="urn:Euro"/></input>
    <output>
      <soap:body encodingStyle="http://schemas.xmlsoap.org/soap/encoding/"
          use="encoded" namespace="urn:Euro"/></output>
    <soap:operation soapAction=""/></operation>
  <operation name="setExchangeRate">
```

```
        <input>
          <soap:body encodingStyle="http://schemas.xmlsoap.org/soap/encoding/"
               use="encoded" namespace="urn:Euro"/></input>
        <output>
          <soap:body encodingStyle="http://schemas.xmlsoap.org/soap/encoding/"
               use="encoded" namespace="urn:Euro"/></output>
        <soap:operation soapAction=""/></operation>
      <soap:binding transport="http://schemas.xmlsoap.org/soap/http" style="rpc"/>
            </binding>
  <service name="EuroExchangeService">
    <port name="EuroExchangeServicePort"
          binding="tns:EuroExchangeServiceBinding">
          <soap:address location="REPLACE_WITH_ACTUAL_URL"/>
    </port>
  </service>
</definitions>
```

The compiler-generated WSDL file should then be modified with location information. This is simple and involves modification of the soap:address location value from REPLACE_WITH_ACTUAL_URL to the actual URL of the service. The value can be set to a URL such as http://www.apress.com/EuroExchangeService. After the EJB is deployed it can then be accessed via SOAP and the web service endpoint from both Java and non-Java clients. Of course, Java clients can still access the EJB via RMI-IIOP using the existing remote interface (firewalls permitting).

Web service endpoints utilize XML and HTTP, which by nature exhibit much inferior performance to that of pure Java RMI interfaces and the IIOP protocol used in many of the J2EE containers on the market. This is because of the verbose nature of XML, which results in rather large data packets being transported. The listing of the WSDL file above should serve as a sufficient example as to how verbose an XML document can become. As such, web service endpoints should be used as endpoints or integration points into the J2EE system.

An EJB Calling a Web Service

For an EJB to invoke a web service, the JAX-RPC client API can be used. The EJB 2.1 specification adds a new element to the deployment descriptor called the service reference. It is specified using the <service-ref> tag and allows a web service to be described in the deployment descriptor and used from inside an EJB. Web services that are defined using the <service-ref> tags do not have to be implemented in EJB or even Java. They may, in fact, be developed on the Microsoft platform.

Let us now use an EJB to call a web service. The first step is to define the service references in the deployment descriptor, which we show in Listing 10-7.

Listing 10-7. EJB deployment descriptor with service reference.

```
<session>
...
<ejb-name>WebServiceCallingBean</ejb-name>
<ejb-class>ejb.WebServiceCallingBean</ejb-class>
...
<service-ref>
    <description>
This is a reference to the EuroExchange Web Service used from Another EJB.
    </description>
    <service-ref-name>service/EuroExchangeService</service- ref-name>
<service-interface> ejb.exchangeSL.EuroExchangeService
</service-interface>
</service-ref>
...
</session>
```

The service reference tags are used to define a remote web service and are used in a similar manner to resource references. The `<service-ref-name>` value should follow the standard of `service/<service name>`, and the `java` interface for the web service is also specified. The calling EJB that utilizes the web service reference uses the local JNDI context to retrieve the reference in the name space `java:comp/env/service`. See Listing 10-8.

Listing 10-8. EJB as a client to a web service.

```
import javax.naming.*
...
Context ctx = new InitialContext();
javax.xml.rpc.Service service = ctx.lookup("java:comp/env/service/
            EuroExchangeService");

EuroExchangeService euroService = service.getPort(EuroExchangeService.class);

float value = euroService.changeToEuro ("USD", 100);
...
```

Web services offer interoperability between heterogeneous systems using standard protocols and XML documents. Web services are integrated into EJB 2.1 and allow integration between EJB and non-EJB systems (including non-Java systems such as Microsoft .NET). To convert an existing Enterprise JavaBean into an available web service, one must create a web service endpoint either manually or using a container-provided tool. The web service endpoint must adhere to the JAX-RPC specification. A Web Services Definition Language (WSDL) file is generated that must be accessible or supplied to clients. Clients of a web service endpoint can be non-Java or Java and can be EJB components. EJB components wishing to call web services should use the `<service-ref>` tags and the local JNDI context to access the web service.

Timers

The progression of Enterprise JavaBeans and J2EE standards into a robust platform has been further improved in version 2.1 with the introduction of a standard timer service. The timer service, somewhat analogous to the UNIX cron mechanism, allows notifications and services to be invoked based upon a timer that is configured within the J2EE environment.

The timer service is a new container-provided service that is used for a reliable and transactional notification mechanism for the EJB component model. The timer service can be used with stateless session, message-driven, and entity beans.

The timer architecture follows a publish-and-subscribe design. At a high level, the bean instance that wishes to be called back at a particular time implements the TimedObject interface, which provides a single ejbTimeout() method. The bean accesses the timer service via the EJBContext. A timer is then created and registered via the service. It is the responsibility of the container to manage the timer and at the expected time invoke the callback method ejbTimeout() of the bean instance.

Timers can be created using two categories of parameters, namely, expiration and interval, and can use a combination of both. The expiration parameter configures the callback invocation to occur at a specified time. For example, next Thursday, June 30, at 5:00 p.m.

The interval parameter configures the callback invocations to occur at specific intervals, for example, to execute every fifteen minutes. A timer can use a combination of these parameters to run at specified intervals, beginning at a particular expiration time. For example, execute next Thursday, June 30, at 5:00 p.m., and every fifteen minutes thereafter.

Timers are very useful for workflow applications, data maintenance, and for monitoring applications and batch jobs. Some examples of using the timer service are the following:

- A Payroll EJB component is notified and run every fifteenth day of the month to process the payroll of the company.

- An AccountsReceivable EJB component is invoked at the end of each business day to e-mail all customers whose accounts are overdue.

- An `OrderProcessing` EJB component is invoked after a sleep interval of an hour between each processing run. This component queries an incoming order table of a database and processes each order.

- A `SystemsManagement` EJB component is invoked every fifteen minutes to check the availability and performance of a database and external web service.

- A `Customer` EJB component is invoked at the end of each business day to archive customer records that have not been used for the past twelve months.

The timer service is integrated into the EJB component model architecture and makes use of the security, persistence, and transaction standards used with the container as follows:

- **Security:** Timed callbacks are invoked by the container and not directly by a calling client; the security model for timers uses the `<run-as>` setting in the deployment descriptor to set security information. Use of this tag was previously described in Chapter 8, "Security," and the example later in this section shows the use of the setting for timed objects.

- **Persistence:** The container provider implements the timer service and must provide persistence of timers as part of the service. This involves ensuring that any timers that are registered before a server crash or restart are reregistered, and any timers that should have been invoked while the server was unavailable will be invoked. This contract holds true for timers with expiration or interval parameters.

- **Transactions:** The timer service is transactional; this means that the registration and cancellation of timers, as well as the invocation of the timer callbacks, can be affected by transactions. If timers are registered or canceled within the scope of a transaction and the transaction is rolled back, then the timer operation is also rolled back. In this case, the timer will not be registered, and the cancellation will be undone. The EJB specification recommends setting the transaction attribute (described in Chapter 7, "Transactions") to `RequiresNew` for `ejbTimeOut` methods. If the transaction attribute is set to `RequiresNew`, upon timer invocation, if the container's invocation receives a transactional rollback, then it will retry the timeout callback.

The reader should note that the EJB specification specifically mentions that the timer service is not for real-time event processing, and the specification makes specific note that if multiple timers are registered to a particular bean at almost the same time, the invocations may occur out of order.

As mentioned earlier, only stateless session, message-driven, and entity beans can respond to timer events by implementing the TimedObject interface. Stateful session beans are prohibited from implementing the TimedObject interface. Timers are both persistent and transactional, and they can be canceled after their creation. The timer service consists of the interfaces shown in Figure 10-5.

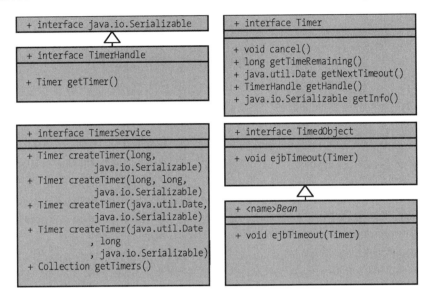

Figure 10-5. The interfaces of the timer service.

javax.ejb.TimedObject

To configure an existing EJB to be able to receive timer service callbacks, the EJB must implement the javax.ejb.TimedObject interface. This interface provides a single method, ejbTimeOut(), which is invoked by the timer service. The interface is implemented in the EJB implementation class and is not exposed in the home, remote, local home, local, and web service endpoint interfaces. The javax.ejb.TimedObject interface is shown in Listing 10-9.

Listing 10-9. The javax.ejb.TimedObject *interface.*

```
javax.ejb.TimedObject
public interface javax.ejb.TimedObject {
    public void ejbTimeout(javax.ejb.Timer timer);
}
```

This interface is implemented by bean instances that wish to listen for timer events. The single method ejbTimeout is invoked by the container and is passed a timer object. The timer object will be covered in detail below.

The EJB container treats timers for entity, stateless session, and message-driven beans differently. For stateless session and message-driven beans, timers can be set on any bean instance. At the time of callback invocation, the container will invoke the ejbTimeOut() callback method on any available component from the method-ready pool. In this case, the timer is registered with the stateless session or message-driven bean type, as opposed to a physical or logical instance.

For entity beans, timers are registered to a specific primary key. Upon invocation of the timer, the container will load an entity bean with the specific primary key and invoke the ejbTimeout() callback method on that specific entity bean. If the entity bean is removed, then any registered timers associated with the respective primary key are also removed by the container.

javax.ejb.TimerService

The javax.ejb.TimerService is the factory interface that represents the TimerService available in the EJB 2.1 specification. The container provider is responsible for the implementation of the TimerService interface. Access to the TimerService is via the EJBContext object. Depending on the type of EJB being implemented, this will be via the javax.ejb.SessionContext, javax.ejb.EntityContext, or javax.ejb.MessageDrivenContext object. To obtain the timer service, the getTimerService() method is invoked on the EJBContext to return a handle to the TimerService. Timers can then be registered, canceled, and queried by the EJB component.

Timer createTimer()

The overloaded createTimer() methods allow the creation of a timer. The choice of which method to use will be dependent on the behavior of the timer that is required. At the time of creation and registration, extra parameters can be supplied to the timer, which are in turn accessible by the bean instance upon the callback invocation. A timer can be created to execute after a particular interval, after a particular interval with a recurring interval, at a particular time, and at a particular time with a recurring interval.

Collection getTimers()

This method returns a collection of timers currently registered with the timer service. The collection can be enumerated for the management of timer registrations.

javax.ejb.TimerHandle

The TimerHandle provides a serializable handle to a specific timer. There is a restriction that states that the TimerHandle cannot be exposed though a remote interface (including a web service endpoint). The container provider is responsible for implementing this interface.

Timer getTimer()

This method gives the bean instance access to a timer object from the TimerHandle, which may have been serialized. The timer object can then be queried according to the APIs in the timer interface described below.

javax.ejb.Timer

The timer interface represents the registration of a timer notification in the system. It provides the ability to query the timer as well as to cancel an upcoming notification. The container provider is responsible for implementing this interface.

void cancel()

This method cancels the timer if it is called before the expiration time, which means that the container will not invoke the ejbTimeout() method of the associated bean implementing the TimedObject interface. If the cancel invocation is made within a transaction, and the transaction fails to commit, then the timer is not canceled. Further invocations on a timer that has already been canceled yield a javax.ejb.NoSuchObjectLocalException.

long getTimeRemaining()

This method returns the time remaining in milliseconds before the timer will invoke the associated bean implementing the TimedObject interface. This method is used with interval-based timers.

java.util.Date getNextTimeout()

For expiration-based timers, this method is used to determine when the next timeout period is scheduled to occur for the timer.

javax.ejb.TimerHandle getHandle()

This method returns a serializable handle to a timer. The interface of the TimerHandle is described above.

java.io.Serializable getInfo()

This method can be used to return information about the timer. The parameter can be any serializable object that was used in the aforementioned createTimer() method. The bean can use the getInfo() method of the passed timer object to recognize any of these domain-specific parameters and conditionally execute timer logic according to the value of the getInfo() method.

Example Payroll

To illustrate the fundamental concepts of the timer service capabilities, we will now look at a practical example of how the timer service can be employed to tackle a common timer-based application. Payroll within an enterprise is a commonly executed business operation. In this example, we will look at conducting our payroll every month and use the EJB 2.1 timer service for this purpose.

The code in this example will focus on the implementation and registration of timers, rather than on the intricacies of the federal tax laws. We will define a simple stateless session bean with a single exposed business method, processPayroll(). First, we define the remote interface of the EJB component in Listing 10-10.

Listing 10-10. Remote interface of the Payroll *EJB.*

```
package ejb.payroll;

import java.rmi.RemoteException;
import javax.ejb.EJBObject;
public interface Payroll extends EJBObject {
    public void processPayroll() throws RemoteException;
}
```

The home interface for the Payroll EJB is also very simple. Being a stateless session bean means that we have only a single create() method with no parameters (Listing 10-11).

Listing 10-11. Home interface of the Payroll *EJB.*

```
package ejb.payroll;

import java.rmi.RemoteException;
import javax.ejb.CreateException;
import javax.ejb.EJBHome;
public interface PayrollHome extends EJBHome {
    public Payroll create()
        throws RemoteException, CreateException;

}
```

Many examples that you will see create the timers in the ejbCreate method of an EJB. This is perhaps a bad practice. For example, with stateless session beans, the developer has no standard way to control how many instances of the bean are created in the method-ready pool. If the code to create the timer is in the ejbCreate method of that specific bean, then it may be executed multiple times, resulting in multiple timers being registered and later notified. Listing 10-12 shows the bean implementation of the Payroll EJB.

Listing 10-12. Bean implementation of the Payroll *EJB.*

```
package ejb.payroll;

import javax.ejb.CreateException;
import javax.ejb.EJBException;
import javax.ejb.SessionBean;
import javax.ejb.SessionContext;
import javax.ejb.TimedObject;
import javax.ejb.Timer;
```

```java
import javax.ejb.TimerService;
import javax.naming.Context;
import javax.naming.InitialContext;
import javax.naming.NamingException;
import javax.sql.DataSource;

public class PayrollBean implements SessionBean, TimedObject {
    private SessionContext beanCtx = null;

    public void ejbCreate()
        throws CreateException
    {
    }
    public void ejbRemove() {
    }

    public void processPayroll() {
        System.out.println("PayrollBean-processPayroll");
      //process the payroll
      //...

      //...

      //reregister payroll for next month
      registerPayroll();
    }

    private void registerPayroll() {
        System.out.println("PayrollBean-registerPayroll");
        TimerService timerService = beanCtx.getTimerService();
//Create a new Calendar and increment one month and reregister the invocation
        java.util.Calendar calendar = new java.util.GregorianCalendar();
        calendar.setTime(new java.util.Date(System.currentTimeMillis()));
        calendar.add(calendar.MONTH, 1);
        Timer timer = timerService.createTimer(calendar.getTime(),
                "Monthly Payroll");
    }

  public void ejbTimeout(Timer timer) {
      processPayroll();
    }

    public void ejbPassivate() { }
    public void ejbActivate() { }
    public void setSessionContext(SessionContext ctx) {
        this.beanCtx = ctx;
    }
}
```

The Payroll EJB component has a single private method that can create a new timer. Each time that the method processPayroll is invoked, a new timer registration is created using the private registerPayroll. It should be noted that the transactional attributes defined on the processPayroll method will affect the behavior of the timer service. If the transaction is rolled back, then the timer registration is revoked.

For our deployment descriptor settings, we have set the transactional attributes of the Payroll EJB to be required and the ejbTimeout method to be RequiresNew (Listing 10-13), so that any failed ejbTimeout invocations are automatically tried again by the container.

Listing 10-13. Deployment descriptor of the Payroll *EJB.*

```
<?xml version="1.0" ?>
<ejb-jar version="2.1"
xmlns="http://java.sun.com/xml/ns/j2ee"
xmlns:xsi="http://www.w3.org/2001/XMLSchema-instance"
xsi:schemaLocation="http://java.sun.com/xml/ns/j2ee
http://java.sun.com/xml/ns/j2ee/ejb-jar_2_1.xsd">
  <description>
    Deployment Descriptor for Session-Bean Payroll.
  </description>

  <enterprise-beans>
    <session>
      <ejb-name>Payroll</ejb-name>
      <home>ejb.payroll.PayrollHome</home>
      <remote>ejb.payroll.Payroll</remote>
      <ejb-class>ejb.payroll.PayrollBean</ejb-class>
      <session-type>Stateless</session-type>
      <transaction-type>Container</transaction-type>
      <security-identity>
      <run-as>
        <role-name>accounts</role-name>
       </run-as>
      </security-identity>
    </session>
  </enterprise-beans>
  <assembly-descriptor>
    <security-role>
       <role-name>accounts</role-name>
    </security-role>
```

```
  <container-transaction>
    <method>
      <ejb-name>Payroll</ejb-name>
      <method-name>*</method-name>
    </method>
    <trans-attribute>Required</trans-attribute>
  </container-transaction>
  <container-transaction>
    <method>
      <ejb-name>Payroll</ejb-name>
      <method-name>ejbTimeout</method-name>
      <method-params>
        <method-param>javax.ejb.Timer</method-param>
      </method-params>
    </method>
    <trans-attribute>RequiresNew</trans-attribute>
  </container-transaction>
  </assembly-descriptor>
</ejb-jar>
```

The deployment descriptor also shows the setting of the security role that the container will use for timer invocations. A future version of the specification may add the ability to configure timers directly in the deployment descriptor.

Summary

The timer service provides a standardized mechanism for the delayed notification of EJB components. An EJB component implements the `TimedObject` interface, which contains a single `ejbTimeout()` callback method that is invoked by the timer service. Timers are created via the timer service, which is accessed via the `EJBContext`. Extra information is supplied with the creation of the timer in the form of a serializable object that can be used to conditionally execute business logic. A timer can be created with interval and expiration-based parameters.

References

[1] Apache, http://www.apache.org.

[2] Apache, http://www.apache.org/projects/log4j.

[3] Behme, Henning, and Mintert, Stefan, *XML in der Praxis*. Addison-Wesley Longman, 1998.

[4] Eckel, Bruce, *Thinking in Java*. Prentice-Hall PTR, 1998.

[5] Gamma, Erich, Helm, Richard, Johnson, Ralph, and Vlisides John, *Designpatterns*, Addison-Wesley Longman, 1996.

[6] Griffel, Frank, *Componentware: Konzepte und Techniken eines Softwareparadigmas*, dpunkt-Verlag, 1998.

[7] International Technical Support Organisation (ITSO): Design and Implement Servlets, JSPs, and EJBs for IBM WebSphere Application Server, IBM Corporation, August 2000.

[8] I-Kinetics, ComponentWare: Component Software for the Enterprise, April 1997. www.i-kinetics.com/wp/cwvision/CWVision.html.

[9] International Technical Support Organisation (ITSO), Factoring Java Beans in the Enterprise, IBM Corporation, December 1997.

[10] International Technical Support Organisation (ITSO), Developing Enterprise Java Beans with Visual Age for Java, IBM Corporation, March 1999.

[11] Jaworski, Jamie, and Perrone, Paul, *Java Security Handbook*, Sams, 2000.

[12] JUnit Testing Resources for Extreme Programming, http://www.junit.org.

[13] Kredel, Heinz, and Yoshida, Akitoshi, *Thread- und Netzwerkprogrammierung mit Java*, dpunkt-Verlag, 1999.

[14] Lang, Lockemann, *Datenbankeinsatz*. Springer-Verlag 1995.

[15] Monson-Haefel, Richard, *Enterprise JavaBeans*. O'Reilly & Associates, 1999.

[16] Oaks, Scott, *Java Security*, O'Reilly & Associates, 1998, 2nd edition 2001.

[17] Orfali, R., and Harkey, D., *Client / Server Programming with Java and CORBA*. John Wiley & Sons, 1996.

[18] Roßbach, Peter, Schreiber, and Hendrik, *Java Server und Servlets*. Addison-Wesley Longman, 1999.

[19] Sun Microsystems, Java Beans Version 1.01, 1997. http://www.javasoft.com/beans/spec.html.

[20] Sun Microsystems, Enterprise JavaBeans Version 1.1 Public Release, 1999. http://www.javasoft.com/ejb/spec.html.

[21] Sun Microsystems, Enterprise JavaBeans Version 2.0 Public Release, 2001. http://www.javasoft.com/ejb/spec.html.

[22] Sun Microsystems, , JDBC 2.0 API, 1998 http://www.javasoft.com/products/jdbc.

[23] Sun Microsystems, Java Transaction API (JTA), 1999.

[24] Sun Microsystems, Java Transaction Service (JTS), 1999.

[25] Sun Microsystems, *Enterprise Java Beans Developers Guide*, beta version, September 1999.

[26] Sun Microsystems, The Java 2 Platform, Enterprise Edition (J2EE), http://java.sun.com/j2ee.

[27] Sun Microsystems, http://java.sun.com/blueprints/enterprise/index.html.

[28] Sun Microsystems, The J2EE Application Programming Model, Version 1.0, September 1999.

[29] Sun Microsystems, Java Messaging Service, Version 1.0.2, November 1999.

[30] Sun Microsystems, Java Cryptography Extension, http://www.java.sun.com/products/jce/index.html.

[31] Sun Microsystems, Java Authentication and Authorization Service, http://java.sun.com/products/jaas/.

[32] Sun Microsystems, Java Secure Socket Extension, http://developer.java.sun.com/developer/earlyAccess/jsse/index.html.

[33] Szyperski, Clemens, *Component Software*, Addison-Wesley Longman, 1998.

[34] Valesky, Tomas, *Enterprise JavaBeans*, Addison-Wesley Longman, 1999.

[35] Weblogic, http://www.weblogic.com.

Index

About Apress

Apress, located in Berkeley, CA, is a fast-growing, innovative publishing company devoted to meeting the needs of existing and potential programming professionals. Simply put, the "A" in Apress stands for *The Author's Press™*. Apress' unique approach to publishing grew out of conversations between its founders, Gary Cornell and Dan Appleman, authors of numerous best-selling, highly regarded books for programming professionals. In 1998 they set out to create a publishing company that emphasized quality above all else. Gary and Dan's vision has resulted in the publication of over 70 titles by leading software professionals, all of which have *The Expert's Voice™*.

Do You Have What It Takes to Write for Apress?

Apress is rapidly expanding its publishing program. If you can write and you refuse to compromise on the quality of your work, if you believe in doing more than rehashing existing documentation, and if you're looking for opportunities and rewards that go far beyond those offered by traditional publishing houses, we want to hear from you!

Consider these innovations that we offer all of our authors:

- **Top royalties with *no* hidden switch statements**
  Authors typically receive only half of their normal royalty rate on foreign sales. In contrast, Apress' royalty rate remains the same for both foreign and domestic sales.

- **Sharing the wealth**
  Most publishers keep authors on the same pay scale even after costs have been met. At Apress author royalties dramatically increase the more books are sold.

- **Serious treatment of the technical review process**
  Each Apress book is reviewed by a technical expert(s) whose remuneration depends in part on the success of the book since he or she too receives royalties.

Moreover, through a partnership with Springer-Verlag, New York, Inc., one of the world's major publishing houses, Apress has significant venture capital and distribution power behind it. Thus, we have the resources to produce the highest quality books *and* market them aggressively.

If you fit the model of the Apress author who can write a book that provides *What The Professional Needs To Know™*, then please contact us for more information:

editorial@apress.com